The Solution of Social Problems

FIVE PERSPECTIVES

MARTIN S. WEINBERG AND

EARL RUBINGTON

New York

OXFORD UNIVERSITY PRESS

London   1973   Toronto

PREFACE

Our previous book *The Study of Social Problems* describes five perspectives sociologists have used in seeking to conceptualize and understand social problems.[1] It seems logical to ask next what the implications of these perspectives are with regard to solving social problems, and our experience has been that once students come to grips with the various perspectives, they do go on to raise this question. The purpose of the present book is to deal with this subject.

The plan of the book follows its predecessor rather closely. One, we reiterate the various perspectives with an emphasis on the direction they provide with regard to solutions. Two, readings are presented that interpret a social problem from one of the perspectives and then, in accordance with that perspective, discuss a solution—be it a proposal or an established program. The last chapter considers how one can interrelate the perspectives in their applications.

We have tried to cover as many significant social problems as possible in a volume specifically designed to be small, primarily illustrative of its sociological point, and thus supplementary in its use. The book is meant to serve either as a companion for *The Study of Social Problems* or as a supplement to other books.[2]

1. Earl Rubington and Martin S. Weinberg, *The Study of Social Problems: Five Perspectives,* New York: Oxford University Press, 1971.
2. For suggestions and criticisms of an early draft of this book, we are grateful to La Rue Davis, Dean Jones, Tim Maher, Helen Matthews, Efrosini Gavaki, Joe Scott, and Debbie Wanous. We also wish to thank Marianne Siegmund and Shirley Leyva for their secretarial assistance, and Harriet Serenkin for her excellent house-editing. Finally, we are especially grateful to Robert Hunner for his assistance in the combing of the voluminous social problems literature, and to Sue Kiefer Hammersmith for her careful consideration of the reworked version of the manuscript.

iii

CONTENTS

GENERAL INTRODUCTION

Social problems in one form or another confront us everywhere. As a result, doubts about the quality of life, its meaning and purpose, and society's fundamental values have arisen in numerous quarters. What follows is a sample list of the problems and diagnoses that sustain and fortify this mood.

Some critics see doom in almost every aspect of our society. Modern mass society is seen by them as producing people who are emotionally barren, who are unable to relate intimately to those close to them or to empathize with those not so close—not enough, for example, to intervene to prevent a stranger's misfortune or even to phone the police when witnessing a crime. Other critics indict the economic system for promoting environmental pollution as well as greed, exploitation, and artificial consumption needs. Still others cry out that many groups are being denied equal opportunities; and the protests of such groups and reactions to them generate an atmosphere charged with hostility.

In the organization of towns and cities, critics see still more problems. Uncoordinated governmental units often provide inadequate or inefficient services. Crime is diagnosed as on the increase. And diverse cultural standards create problems when immigrants and migrants move into new locales.

As if this were not enough, a host of new varieties of drug use have been added to the traditional drug of use, alcohol. There has also been a resurgence of the kind of delinquent gang warfare that marked the '50's. Meanwhile, high, if not rising, rates of recidivism attest to the failure of correctional institutions to resocialize youthful offenders.

Even established interpretations of diverse behaviors are themselves becoming recognized as social problems. Many laws and traditional conceptions of morality are seen as harmful and in need of revision. For example, the criminal definition and penalties associated with marihuana use affect a large segment of the population who are engaging in this activity.

The above recitation lists some current varieties of dissatisfaction. These and other social problems, treated in considerable detail in the pages that follow, give the impression that modern society has succeeded in producing more pain than pleasure and more distress than relief. Implied is the notion that more social problems exist in the world now than ever before. Similarly, some critics imply that unless effective solutions are quickly developed, the destruction of the world is practically in sight. Even less pessimistic people agree that Freud was right when he said that as civilization increases, so does discontent.[1]

Freud's generalization parallels the sociological axiom that social problems are related to culture and social organization. Thus, as Kingsley Davis has pointed out, romantic love as interpreted in America is the cause of divorce as well as of marriage. In a traditional, familistic society, where persons are assigned mates at birth, romantic love is not the source of the conjugal bond, and divorce is not a social problem. China, in the early decades of this century, exemplified such a society. Custom forbade severing the marital bond by divorce, and divorce rates were low. Suicide still remained a possible escape, however, and studies show that the low divorce rates associated with traditional Chinese family customs were accompanied by high rates of suicide.

If social problems are related to culture and social organization, might the solutions apparent in the society not also be related to these factors? A closer examination of modern society suggests that this may very well be the case. One common-sense view suggests that like the Malthusian formula describing the relationship between food supply and population size, solutions grow only arithmetically while social problems grow geometrically. This "law" would seem to arm all street-corner prophets of doom and give weight to testimonies of the advancing Last Judgment.

There are several grounds, however, for concluding that this common-sense view is mistaken. Indeed, the opposite is possibly closer to the truth. That is, the source of many modern difficulties may be the proliferation of proposed solutions to the problems we face. If so, then a very real problem is not so much the growth and magnitude of contemporary social problems as it is the inability to choose from and to put into operation the available proposals for solving social problems. A spate of books, articles, institutes, and agencies have sprung up dedicating themselves to the solution of social problems, and if the overproduction of suggestions is not already a social fact, it may be in only a short while.

The student of social problems today could become a consumer of solutions tomorrow. If he is to rationally consider alternative proposals, perform the duties and exercise the rights of citizenship, he needs to have a set of values, a body of information, and some notion of contin-

---

1. Sigmund Freud, *Civilization and its Discontents,* translated from the German by James Strachey, New York: W. W. Norton, 1961.

gencies. One purpose of this book is to provide a framework for order-ing values, information, and contingencies with regard to the solution of social problems. For if one is to face an abundance of suggested solu-tions in the foreseeable future without a system that makes it possible to evaluate them, one will either choose solutions without sound judg-ment or give up choosing entirely.

PERSPECTIVES AND THEIR USES

Sociologists have typically studied social problems from five perspec-tives.[2] Defined simply, a perspective on social problems is an orienting idea about social problems which implies definition, conception, and action. The sociologist defines a problem in a certain way, develops a working conception of the problem which includes causes, conditions, consequences, and possible remedies. Then he seeks data fitting to his conception. The five sociological perspectives examined in this book are "social pathology," "social disorganization," "value conflict," "de-viant behavior," and "labeling."

Each of these perspectives provides an intellectual framework for devising, executing, and evaluating solutions. In learning about the per-spective, the student becomes familiar with its assumptions, its justi-fications, and its implications, and thus is in a better position to estimate its strengths, weaknesses, and probable consequences.

Before examining the different perspectives, the student should, how-ever, have some grasp of the complexity of social problems and their definition, of the relationships between problems and solutions, and of the complexity involved in the conditions under which solutions become viable. To help in this task, the student can organize his thinking around the several elements that comprise the framework of sociological per-spectives. Chapter 1 deals with these issues.

2. Earl Rubington and Martin S. Weinberg (eds.), *The Study of Social Problems,* New York: Oxford University Press, 1971.

THE PROBLEM

1 SOCIAL PROBLEMS AND THEIR SOLUTIONS

What is a social problem? Its definition would seem to be a relatively straightforward matter and follow from the words themselves. Thus, a problem is something that causes difficulty, and the adjective "social" indicates that the difficulty is being experienced by more than one person. Social problems, however, are not such straightforward matters. As a result, the problem of definition becomes important.

It would seem that defining social problems as the suffering experienced by a number of persons ought to suffice, but this definition may simply attest to numerous *individual* experiences. A million people could all be suffering from the common cold. However, insofar as their colds do not reflect what is considered a group condition and are not recognized as having appreciable consequences for them as a group, the common cold is not designated a *social* problem.

Also, extreme personal unhappiness need not by itself be considered either a social problem or a sign of one even when it is recognized as a group condition. For instance, the mentality of the Western activist causes him to recoil in horror at the quality of life in India, where poverty and starvation are the common lot of suffering millions. Yet most Indians, extremely fatalistic by reason of their passive Eastern mentality, see little cause for alarm. To them it is not a social problem at all, but simply a part of life.

In comparing Eastern and Western attitudes, it is possible to discern an important aspect of social problems. If some or even all people in a society suffer because of certain conditions and can conceive of no way out of their troubles, then regardless of the degree of hardship and suffering, that situation is generally not called a social problem, primarily because it does not become a "public issue." On the other hand, if some people experience suffering and discomfort in a situation which is not accepted as a part of life and for which a way out is also conceived, then, under conditions yet to be specified, that situation may come to be a public issue and so defined as a social problem. For example, if enough people in the society say "There is no reason in the world that people have to live this way," and if they know of an alternative that exists in their society which could alter the situation but is not being used, then that situation is designated a social problem.

Thus, a perception of unnecessary suffering forms the core of a social problem. If this suffering comes to be experienced by enough members of the society as something that should not and need not be an expected feature of social life, then the unnecessary aspects of the situation are communicated to others. Consequently, other persons may come to feel the same way and dedicate time, money, and knowledge in an effort to change the painful situation. It should be made clear that because of the numerous contingencies involved, all situations of unnecessary suffering do not achieve the status of a social problem.

Richard Fuller, an outstanding student of social problems, said, "A social problem arises when there is an awareness among a given people that a particular social situation is a threat to certain group values which they cherish and that this situation can be removed or corrected only by collective action."[1] His working definition of a social problem contains most of the features that sociologists before and since have included in their definitions.

The principal elements in the above definition are situation, values, people, and action. Clearly then, if a situation recurs frequently enough or sustains itself long enough, threatens important values, and disturbs enough people, they will call for corrective action. Fuller's working definition of social problems supports the common, relativistic notion that some problems get attention while others do not, and points to the necessary and sufficient conditions required for the situation to be considered a social problem.

PHASES IN THE SOCIAL-PROBLEM-SOLVING PROCESS

Problem and solution are paired concepts. Each implies the other, and it is doubtful that anyone can really talk about one without talking about the other. A problem is something that requires a solution, and a solution is the attempt to meet that requirement.

There is still another sense in which each concept implies the other. This implication is dialectical in that a solution to a given problem very frequently produces a new problem. For example, Thorstein Veblen observed that science, the most rational technique for solving problems, is also the greatest begetter of social problems. Science, according to Veblen, solves one problem only to produce three or four new ones in its place.[2]

1. Richard C. Fuller and Richard R. Myers, "The Natural History of a Social Problem," *American Sociological Review* 6 (June 1941), p. 327.
2. Thorstein Veblen, *The Place of Science in Modern Civilization, and Other Essays,* New York: Russell, 1919.

For the most part, Veblen was referring to the intimate relationship between science and technology. Saul Alinsky, whose activities have created social problems for some and solved them for others, made a very similar point concerning human relations. Alinsky said the relationship between problem and solution is dialectical, that men solve one problem only to find themselves caught up in a new one, and that this is a never-ending process from which there is no escape.[3]

These ideas raise the question of how to know when a problem stops and when a solution begins. Left unanswered, this question breeds pessimism and nihilism, and not only suggests that problems multiply faster than solutions but also raises the very question of whether problems ever really do get solved. It is here that Fuller's processual view is useful, for if we regard the phenomenon of a social problem as an instance in a problem-solving process replete with its own phases, then we may find it possible to avoid an either-or view of social problems and their solutions.[4]

To illustrate the social-problem-solving process as a set of phases divided into defining acts and solving acts, we delineate the elements of a social problem to examine first the defining and then the solving phases. If we bear in mind that defining and solving each has its own constituent, related, necessary, and sequential properties, we shall appreciate the enormous complexity involved in what may at first appear to be a simple phenomenon.

The act of defining.   It is not easy to distinguish a clear sequence of steps when defining a social problem or to draw a line between the awareness of the problem and the formulation of a collective line of action for meeting the problem. Consequently, here we discuss situation, values, people, and action as they combine to produce the problem definition. We then discuss how these elements combine to produce an orientation toward solving the problem.

a. Situation.   Three properties of any emergent situation that ultimately becomes classified as a social problem are violation, expectation, and reaction. Violation refers to the act, event, or process as a purported fact of social reality. Expectation refers to the tacit or explicit rule shared by many which charges such violation with social meaning. And reaction refers to the specific form of collective behavior elicited. These properties of the situation encompass natural and social disasters in addition to the usual kinds of problems (e.g. poverty, drug addiction) dealt with in textbooks on social problems. When one or more of the following—persons, events, activities, an increased frequency of acts,

3. Saul Alinsky, *Rules for Radicals,* New York: Random House, 1971.
4. Richard C. Fuller and Richard R. Myers, *op. cit.,* pp. 320–28.

and collective definition—bring the situation to public attention, then frequently violation, expectation, and reaction blend together. This blending points up the difficulty of knowing when the primary problem has ceased and solution has begun and when the incipient effort at solution has actually changed the shape, distribution, and, on occasion, the actual definition of the problem.

The drinking of alcoholic beverages affords an example of how violation, expectation, and reaction merge, blend, and complicate analysis of the situation. In the case of social drinking many have tacit expectations that men will drink in moderation, will drink without getting drunk, will drive cars only when sober, will go to work sober, and will support their wives and family. In the case of alcoholism in which uncontrolled drinking and frequent intoxication lead to absenteeism, hazardous driving, and nonsupport, these tacit expectations are breached, and a wide variety of reactions and attempts to control these forms of disturbing social behavior ensues. Examples of social control reactions include law enforcement (for public intoxication, drunken driving, and nonsupport), treatment (detoxification center, hospital, out-patient alcoholism clinic, private psychiatrist, half-way house, Alcoholics Anonymous), employer's responses (alcoholism programs in industry, warning or firing the problem drinker), and primary group pressures (kidding, gossip, persuasion, withdrawal of love, physical violence).

b. Values.   All instances of violated expectations are not necessarily seen as threats to values. For example, people often go to parties, movies, and plays expecting to enjoy themselves, only to be disappointed. It is only under some very special circumstances that personal troubles go on to become public issues. As noted earlier, if these personal troubles can be included in the category of unnecessary suffering, defining them as a social problem becomes possible. If a situation is incompatible with the core values of a culture, its chances of being certified as a social problem are certainly very good. For example, the obvious unacceptability of force and fraud as means of obtaining important cultural goals has led many sociologists to speculate that these actions are universally depicted as social problems. It seems reasonable to suggest that the higher a given value stands in a cultural hierarchy of values, the more likely it is that a threatening situation will be seen as incompatible with that value.

c. People.   What value seems threatened may be somewhat less important in making the situation a social problem than how many people share the value and voice objection to the situation. And even more important than numbers may be the social significance of the people voicing objection. Thus the transformation from a private matter to a public dispute may depend on whose values were offended and what persons took offense.

Intensity and extensity of suffering by themselves, then, do not produce public definition of the situation as a social problem. When, however, a person of high social rank protests, the issue becomes more salient. For example, during pre-Civil War days, the famous American social reformer, Dorothea Dix, inspected numerous county jails and publicized the fact that mentally and physically ill persons were being treated as prisoners rather than as patients. Dix's efforts brought considerable reform, at least to the extent of getting patients out of jail and into hospitals.[5] Similarly, Clifford W. Beers wrote a book about his experiences as a patient in a Connecticut state mental hospital.[6] In his book he spoke of numerous instances of staff brutality toward patients. After he publicized his experiences, changes took place in hospital ward administration. And Beers himself then established the National Association of Mental Health, one of the first organizations to be concerned with the rights of "problem persons." In each of these cases, a person of high social rank had launched a campaign to dramatize the social problem of mental illness and to propose new ways of handling persons designated mentally ill. Yet the unnecessary suffering that both Dix and Beers called attention to had existed for some time. Hence, it is hard to escape the conclusion that unless persons of high rank or power complain, many such situations receive little notice and are not defined as social problems. (By a singular social irony it seems that in a way the effectiveness of protests is inversely proportional to their frequency. High-ranking people protest seldom but are influential when they do. Low-ranking people protest with greater frequency only to often receive low credibility and sometimes increased punishment for their protests. In time, it is made to seem as if they deserve their punishment. When that occurs, the possibility of making their situation a recognized social problem decreases even further.)

Thus, poverty began to qualify as a social problem early in American colonial history when persons of rank called attention to the growing numbers of urban poor. In New York, for example, the profession of social work found its beginnings when upper-class women visited the homes of the poor. These women passed out Bibles, taught the poor how to budget their meager resources, and lectured on the evils of drink. The reactions of these upper-class women indicate that their expecta-

5. Albert Deutsch, *The Mentally Ill in America,* New York: Columbia University Press, 1949.
6. Clifford W. Beers, *A Mind that Found Itself: An Autobiography,* rev. ed., New York: Doubleday, 1948.

tions of piety, frugality, and temperance all were being violated by the poor.

The number of people involved in a situation of suffering has not then been the standard for defining it a social problem. For instance, in order to be designated poor today, a person's annual income must fall below the "poverty line." Current statistics indicate that there are probably now around 30 million poor people in the United States. Yet in earlier years as well as in different societies, a larger percentage of the population could actually have been living in considerably more abject poverty without being considered a social problem constituency. Thus, when members of a given society expect many of their fellow members to be poor as a matter of course and when no alternatives are imagined, discussed, or available, then poverty is unlikely to become a social issue and qualify as a social problem in that society.

d. Action.   In the "natural history of social problems," the last phase is action. Prior to this, the situation consisted of continued violations of moral expectations. Similarly, this final phase can affect both a large number of people and a body of significant, influential, and/or powerful people. If, however, no one bands together in order to redefine the situation and make other people see it as the social problem, as they have come to see it, it is most unlikely that a true social problem awareness will emerge.

The general field of public health provides excellent examples of instances in which only three of the four necessary conditions were fulfilled. That is, the violation existed, the threat to values was an accepted fact, and a significant number of people were affected. Nonetheless, the fourth and sufficient condition, that of action, was absent because the populace so affected was either apathetic, fatalistic, or actually antagonistic to known and existing remedies. Thus, the introduction of vaccination into the public school system as a means of coping with smallpox was fought by the working classes for years. Numerous campaigns to publicize illnesses, reduce their stigmata, and arouse the public continue to fall on deaf ears. The campaigns against tuberculosis, in the past, and alcoholism and venereal disease, in the present, afford several examples.

On the other hand, persons who conquer a public health threat such as smoking or alcoholism can take media action which both broadens and deepens the problem awareness. Thus, Gene Kelly speaks on television against smoking, reporting that seven years ago he smoked three packs a day and he has given it up. Mercedes McCambridge, having solved her drinking problem in Alcoholics Anonymous, reports her experiences at public meetings. Many movie stars have a favorite charity for which they labor hard to generate awareness and action vis-à-vis contributions for research or treatment. Franklin Delano Roosevelt is an outstanding example of how a victim can center awareness, then generate mass collective action. President Roosevelt became a living symbol of how far a person might go in the world in spite of having suffered from polio. It is impossible to calculate the number of people who, inspired by his image, became staunch supporters of the March of Dimes, perhaps one of the most successful fund-raising health campaigns in the history of the country.

Sometimes a dramatic event suffices not only to produce a sense of problem awareness and to define the situation as a social problem but also to lead into the phase of solving the problem. An example of how a dramatic event can produce a collective redefinition of a situation is the revolt in the correctional facility in Attica, New York, in the summer of 1971. For a short period of time, the story of this revolt dominated newspapers and television news coverage. Despite the tragic aftermath, it is unlikely that American prisons will ever be completely the same. The nation's underground press, editorial writers, and congressional committees have focused attention on a new problem constituency, the convict. Dramatic proof of the change in public awareness, aside from the spread of the spirit of prison revolt to other states, is the fact that Senator McGovern took his campaign for President right into Massachusetts correctional institutions.

A dramatic event, an untoward happening involving a person of high rank, or the efforts of a prestigious person can develop and sustain a heightened and continued sense of problem awareness. Such an awareness is essential to the formation of a consensus for mustering together a group and a spirit bent on solving the problem. To know what is required for the development and maintenance of the sense of problem awareness, however, is also to know that of many situations which call for designation as social problems, only a few have actually been so defined and acted upon. Fund raisers, muckrakers, and reformers would all probably say that the public is fickle and unlikely to be moved into action unless someone close becomes involved in a problem situation. Revolutionaries, for their part, would probably argue that only extreme and dramatic personal experience can generate a new consciousness of a situation formerly taken for granted. An illustration of their argument would be that many middle-class moderate college students became "radicalized at the end of a billy club" during the campus disorders of the '60's. But if drastic and extreme experience is the requirement for problem awareness in some instances, the simple "straw that broke the camel's back" or slow, incremental buildups, may be necessary for problem awareness in yet other kinds of social situations.

The act of solving. It should be clear how difficult it is for a situation to achieve the status of a social problem. A recurrent situation that violates moral expectations begins to gnaw away at the sensitivities of a number of people. They become aware that precious values now face a serious threat. The media may depict the enormity of their situation and the fact that some alternatives exist for rectifying it. When some consensus has been established and there is a new collective definition of the situation as a social problem, then the solving phase can, but does not always, begin. Like the defining phase, the solving phase also involves a number of steps that must be completed before collective action can become a reality.

a. Situation.   As Emile Durkheim, George Herbert Mead, and others have pointed out, the infraction of an important moral rule mobilizes sentiments of moral indignation sufficient to move the community against the offender and also to draw it together as a moral community that is now more certain than before about its own boundaries and the norms it has sworn to uphold.

Frequently, the new expectation that there will be a sustained reaction against persistent violation generates a campaign to seek out the source of troubles that have been plaguing the community. The Spanish Inquisition, the Salem witchcraft trials, the Palmer raids, Carrie Nation's onslaught on drinking places, Senator Joseph R. McCarthy's crusade against Communists in government, and police "rousting" hippies from public places are some examples of sustained reactions that mobilize a community and move it from the phase of definition to the phase of problem solving.

b. Values.   If the phase of problem defining is closer to the emotional, then the phase of problem solving is often closer to the rationally calculated. Repeated violations, when they threaten important values, can produce strong, emotional reactions. Incipient leaders in such volatile situations may be quite concerned about preventing followers from going off "half-cocked." For then the situation can really get out of hand—the group acts without a plan, squanders resources in the heat of passions, and finds when tempers cool that it has lost more than it has gained. A leader has to channel insecurity and orchestrate passions, or he will not develop and sustain a course of action.

This calls attention once again to how tenuous the processes of problem definition and problem solution are. Indeed, some of those who were hottest during the phase of problem definition may become the coolest during the solving phase, where the question of values looms most important. For even in the face of a consensus that a threat to values has taken place and the group does face a social problem, the fact that all values exist in a network sometimes reduces the chances of action. It is here that Willard Waller's observations are so trenchant.[7] To rephrase the matter in his terms, it is likely that during the phase of problem definition, humanitarian mores sway group sentiment. During the phase of forging a solution, however, organizational (viz., practical) mores assume primacy. When this happens, persons come to see that other values are more important. With this view, the new collective definition may recede quickly into the background and, with that, the status quo ante may return. In such cases we have a problem but no solution.

c. People.   It is much easier to muster sentiments than soldiers in the battle against a social problem. Perhaps this is why former victims of the problem, particularly when normative deviation is concerned, become the most effective allies in the campaign for corrective action. Thus, reformed alcoholics and drug addicts and exconvicts perform yeoman service in the cause of solving the respective social problems. They are dedicated because they are both committed and involved.

In a highly segmented society there are two kinds of consequences for eliciting the allegiance of persons on behalf of a campaign to take corrective action and change a problem situation of long standing. The first is that an issue of local concern can capture the imagination of a locality, neighborhood, or section of a city, while an issue of greater relevance for the larger society has less effect on and less drawing power in that community. The second kind of consequence is that social problem concerns can be turned over to professionals or a bureaucracy that specializes in the reform of specific problems. Here one is a passive member of a particular social problems public.

Periodically, these processes of professional and bureaucratic reform are upset when a charismatic leader appears. Paradoxically, Ralph Nader is a man of charisma who seeks social change and problem solution through institutional or legal channels. He is a most important middle-class reformer and no doubt there are thousands of citizens happy to be only segmentally involved as dues payers in his social problems constituency. However, the young lawyers who work for him are like the reformed alcoholics, more holistically committed and involved in the problems they tackle.

d. Action.   If it is to be successful, action on social problems must be organized. All students of corrective action look very closely for the signs and symbols of organization. Saul Alinsky says the appearance of size and organization is necessary when bargaining with the powerful

---

7. Willard Waller, "Social Problems and the Mores," *American Sociological Review* (December 1936), pp. 922–33.

on behalf of the powerless.[8] Without organization, no one listens to demands for change. Confronted with organized groups, those who understand power grant a hearing.

The appearance of organization, if not the reality, is essential for potential sanction. Once negotiation is underway, each side calculates rather coldly what the other side will do if it fails to live up to its end of the bargain. Consequently, the appearance of the ability to bring pressure is deemed by many to be the essential element in any realistic campaign to alter a painful situation.

These remarks on how situations, values, people, and actions combine in the phases of defining and solving social problems reveal a variety of possibilities and contingencies in the realm of social problems. This being the case, it is of course impossible to predict with absolute accuracy what the outcome will be in each of the phases and, within the phases, in each of the sequences. What reduces the variety of contingencies and possibilities is the particular perspective that gives form to the operations of problem definition and problem solution. Social problems, in part a species of collective behavior, must necessarily leave wide room for that emergent quality of social interaction to which several theorists have called attention. Nonetheless, a working knowledge of perspectives and how they outline the form of a solution is indispensable for increasing the student's understanding of social problems and their solution. Thus, we turn now to a consideration of perspectives and what they entail for the definition and solution of social problems.

PERSPECTIVES AND THEIR CHARACTERISTICS

Perspectives have certain general features in common. In turn, each gives rise to a type of formula to be followed in the solution of social problems. Perspectives and their formulas alike are collective products and, as such, have their own history. That is, they come into being, develop, change, fall into disuse, and under some conditions reappear.

There are at least three sources of perspectives on social problems in American society at present. First, there are lay perspectives, or the common-sense viewpoints of everyday life. Second, there are agent perspectives, the occupational or professional standpoints of those whose task it is to control society's recognized social poblems. Finally, there are sociological perspectives, the special points of view of the sociological student of social problems. All of these perspectives understandably have much in common. The difference between the sociological perspectives and the other two is, however, that in addition to taking a somewhat more abstract and detached attitude toward social

8. Saul Alinsky, *op. cit.*

problems (the very attitude implied by the social scientist's position) and seeking to construct its own special character, the sociological perspectives seek also to include both lay and professional perspectives within its own border formulations.

A perspective is, in effect, a viewpoint on the social world. It consists of a place (i.e. social location) from which one looks at something and the attitude with which he looks at it. People who look at the world from the same social location day in and day out tend to develop similar attitudes about that world. Thus, student culture contains perspectives on problems students face. Faculty share a somewhat different view of university life because they look at it from a different location and with a different attitude. Each group abstracts the problematic features of the situation as it appears to them from their particular vantage point. In doing so, each group develops its own perspective, with its particular content. Thus, students search for the common factors in those problems the faculty poses for them. Once they have succeeded in conceiving what these factors are and in giving names to them, they have fashioned the concepts and definitions that make up their perspective.

Conception and definition answer the question: "What is the problem?" People then construct formulas, the next step in the development of a perspective, in order to answer the question: "What should we do?" The formula includes a vocabulary, a statement of group beliefs and doctrines, and a recipe of prescription for action. Thus, students in medical school talk about "what the faculty wants us to know," share the belief that they must get along with the faculty if they are to get through medical school, and devise and share techniques of finding out what will be asked on examinations.[9]

All groups form perspectives and formulas on social problems in much the same way as students do with regard to school problems. The essential steps in the process of devising a perspective and then constructing a formula for solving the social problem—abstracting the key features of the situation as they appear from the vantage point of observation, classifying them, and then deriving the appropriate formula for coping with the situation—are generally the same.

Analytically, then, the characteristics of a perspective can be said to include a place, an attitude, and a content. Once the perspective moves from orientation (a concern with problem definition) to organization for action (the act of solving), it becomes involved with a formula. And the formula includes a set vocabulary, group beliefs and doctrines, and a recipe. A brief discussion of each of these characteristics follows.

The place.   One's social location, or the place, affects the stance one

9. Howard S. Becker, Blanche Geer, Everett C. Hughes, and Anselm L. Strauss, *Boys in White: Student Culture in Medical School,* Chicago: University of Chicago Press, 1961.

takes with regard to social problems. In so doing, it affects the vantage point from which thinking, feeling, and action come forth. Similarly, place defines the position that participants will take in the whole social problem process. Whatever interests and values may be at stake for participants can usually be traced to their social location.

The attitude.   The attitude refers to how a person in a given place looks at social problems. Place determines this to a large extent, though of course not completely. Sociologists, for instance, according to traditional standards, are supposed to look at social problems in a detached, objective, value-neutral fashion. This attitude, considered as a norm, is lived up to in varying degrees. Citizens are generally assumed to be emotionally involved and biased in their perceptions. Yet the average citizen is capable of a good deal of detachment and objectivity under appropriate conditions.

The content.   Content combines a set of alleged facts with some key ideas. For the social scientist, it can well mean a conceptual scheme or, at times, a well-articulated theory. Regardless of its complexity or simplicity, the specific content includes the major ideas the person uses in organizing a view of the problem situation.

Once the phase of problem defining has evolved into the phase of problem solving, the term "formula" is applicable. The formula, as previously noted, consists of a vocabulary, beliefs and doctrines, and a recipe.

The vocabulary.   Once a problem situation has been defined and a solution is in process, a vocabulary largely, though not exclusively, derived from the specific content forms the basis for talking and thinking about the immediate problem situation. This vocabulary is an important characteristic since the terms one uses exert powerful influences on the way one thinks, feels, and acts. Perhaps more important, the vocabulary provides a link between content and the statement of beliefs and doctrines.

Beliefs and doctrines.   The beliefs and doctrines constitute the fairly specific ideas behind the plan for dealing with the problem. In the case of the sociologist, the beliefs and doctrines frequently assume the form of a series of hypotheses derived from a broader theory contained in what we have called content. In the case of other perspectives, the statement outlines why a given line of action probably ought to be taken. This line of action also can be derived from the content.

The recipe.   Finally, theorizing produces a more or less specific plan of action designed to resolve the situation. The recipe designates roles that people will play and instructs them in how to carry out these roles. While the beliefs and doctrines afford the logical rationale, the recipe sets forth the practical program of action to be followed. Thus, the recipe is the end product, the logical consequence of the complex process of defining and constructing a solution. It is intended, when it becomes operational, to embody the values of the group which has devised the solution, as well as to test or support the generalized perspective. As the culmination of the previously discussed processes, it represents an organized reaction to a given social problem.

Taken together, these six characteristics comprise the basic features of a perspective on social problems. While some perspectives are relatively simple in these features, others are decidedly complex. Most of those that we deal with in this book have evolved with the growth and development of sociology; still others have come out of considerable experience with troublesome situations in daily life. In the respective chapters, we provide a synopsis of the history of each perspective in considering its features. Regardless of differences in origin, development, growth, and complexity, however, all perspectives outline the form that a proposed solution to a social problem is to take. In that sense they are much like a set of blueprints for rebuilding a social structure.[10]

To understand social action, a person has to know the grounds for that action. As we shall come to see, understanding the perspective from which the actions are formulated helps one to understand those grounds.

SUMMARY AND CONCLUSION

Social problems cannot be understood apart from the perspectives that groups construct about them. These perspectives, as conceptual and action schemes, not only define a situation as a social problem according to the perspective's own peculiar viewpoint, but also go on to specify guidelines for dealing in some collective fashion with the problematic situation. Consequently, to fully understand any given social problem

---

10. Whether the solution actually works, however, cannot be assumed in advance. This becomes a matter to be established in subsequent inquiry. Solutions can have differing combinations of intended and unintended effects. Unintended effects can be positive as well as negative. The outcome of policy solutions to social problems is the subject for another book. The developing fields of policy studies, applied social sciences, and evaluation research are all giving increased attention to the conditions under which policies based on scientific knowledge solve problems.

one must first come to grips with the means by which members of that society endow that situation with meaning, understand it as a social problem, and having so defined it, construct a line of action in response to their definition. Members of the society do all of this when they devise and adopt a perspective on social problems. We turn now to an examination of five popular sociological perspectives, the form of their solutions, and (in the final chapter) how they can be interrelated in their application.

SELECTED REFERENCES

Blumer, Herbert, "Social Problems as Collective Behavior," *Social Problems,* 18 (Winter 1971), pp. 298–306.

Acts of defining and acts of solving social problems have been oversimplified by writers on social problems. Blumer argues that defining and taking action are very complex, emergent processes, best understood as instances of collective behavior.

Lemert, Edwin M., *Human Deviance, Social Problems, and Social Control,* Englewood Cliffs, N.J.: Prentice-Hall, 1972 (2nd ed.).

A basic theme runs through this collection of theoretical articles and case studies on social problems. Lemert shows how the acts of solving a problem produce the public definition of a social problem situation. And, in certain circumstances, social controls succeed in perpetuating the very conditions they were designed to ameliorate.

Mannheim, Karl, *Ideology and Utopia,* New York: Harcourt, Brace and Co., 1946.

The most complete and extended discussion of perspectives in the sociological literature. Mannheim goes to considerable lengths to support his thesis that social position determines thought.

Rubington, Earl and Martin S. Weinberg (eds.), *The Study of Social Problems,* New York: Oxford University Press, 1971.

A codification of perspectives sociologists employ in their researches on social problems.

Smigel, Erwin O., *Handbook of the Study of Social Problems,* Chicago: Rand McNally, 1971.

An important collection of articles on the sociology of social problems. Tallman and McGee in their paper "Definition of a Social Problem," pp. 19–58, argue that social problems can be defined empirically rather than normatively.

THE PERSPECTIVES

2 SOCIAL PATHOLOGY

Dichotomization, or the division of things into two parts, has had a strong and natural appeal to mankind for a long time. To the extent that man's reason is based on his social and natural world, a dual-valued logic has come into being as a basis for human thought. For instance, in the social world, there are the rich and the poor, the strong and the weak, the well known and the unknown, the winners and the losers. In the world of nature, there are left and right, day and night, male and female, life and death.

Dichotomization also provides a basis for deciding if a situation is a social problem. At the outset, it is used to class those kinds of situations that most human beings do not like or want, as opposed to those situations that they do like or want. The reason that a situation constitutes a social problem, however, is more fundamental, more rooted in some very basic assumptions about man, nature, society, and culture. Thus, perhaps the most traditional and long-standing perspective on social problems centers on the dichotomies of good and bad, right and wrong, sick and well.

Other terms simply help to complete these moral classifications. Normal and abnormal, natural and unnatural are other dichotomies which are evaluations of the units so classified. The use of these either-or modes of categorization becomes but another facet of the taken-for-granted, or those vast portions of culture called common sense. In addition to the explicit or implicit moral evaluation, there is also a sense of tension and opposition. This sense of tension and opposition, in turn, is firmly grounded in the experience of violated expectations, the very heart of the social problem conception. The experience of violation is the basis for the thought and feeling that something is immoral and for triggering the actions appropriate to such strong feelings.

This sense of tension and opposition is seen clearly in the sick-well dichotomy. The state of health stands directly opposed to its opposite member, sickness. When this ancient dichotomy is added to still another old pairing, the individual versus society, the character of the social pathology perspective stands out quite clearly. The combining of these

19

categories produces two very old yet still powerful ways of viewing social problems. Social problems are either caused by sick individuals or by a sick society.

CENTRAL FEATURES OF THE SOCIAL PATHOLOGY PERSPECTIVE

Pathology refers to the study of the causes and nature of diseases and to unhealthy conditions and processes caused by disease. Social pathology, by extension, refers to unhealthy social conditions and processes caused by, and productive of, social disease. Phenomena that qualify according to this definition are seen as social problems. Thus, alcoholism, crime, delinquency, drug addiction, and mental illness can all be viewed as social diseases of mind, body, and spirit. They can be seen to "spread" through society in much the same way as cancer, heart disease, poliomyelitis, and syphilis "spread" through individuals causing pain, suffering, and ultimately death to millions.

Similarly destructive processes, somewhat more complex in their course, are seen in the realm of society. Ultimately, then, it is possible to think of certain institutions as being sick—those not functioning according to moral expectation. For example, pathological tendencies appear when economic institutions produce people who are greedy, when political institutions generate persons who lust for power, and when institutions emphasizing prestige evoke urges and strivings for fame. Analysts can and have diagnosed whole societies as "sick." Thus, after the close of World War II, a psychiatrist wrote a book which asked the question: "Are the Germans paranoid?" In answering the question "yes," he went on to supply copious material supporting his diagnosis of a whole people as mentally ill.[1]

The place.   Since the concept of illness is universal, it is understandable that a medical or biological model can be used by anyone to diagnose a disturbing social situation as "unhealthy" and therefore a problem. For instance, parents assess innumerable situations as possible risks to their children's health. Thus, it is only second nature to use this particular point of view in deciding whether or not a given social situation constitutes a social problem. As a result, no word seems to enjoy more currency in the course of everyday life when it comes to assessing social problems than the term "sick." Decisions to assassinate a presidential candidate or to continue waging an unpopular war are simultaneously attributed to either "sick" persons, on the one hand, or to a "sick" society on the other.

1. Robert M. Brickner, *Is Germany Incurable?*, Philadelphia, Pa.: J. B. Lippincott Co., 1943.

Similarly, after campus disturbances, civil disorders, and prison revolts, persons in government speak of a "sick" society. By this they mean that the use of force and violence, either to protest or to quell protest, are symptoms of pathology in both those who use force and in the conditions that breed such responses.

In university circles, the metaphor of the "sick" society has made its appearance in the very influential writings of Erich Fromm, Herbert Marcuse, Charles Reich, and Philip Slater (excerpts from books by the last two authors are reprinted in this section).[2] These writers center their attention on the entire society, rather than individuals, as they diagnose most of the social problems of the day as being ultimately attributable to a very "sick" society.

Finally, Martin Luther King and other civil rights leaders have diagnosed the traditional patterns of race relations in the United States as the obvious symptoms of a "sick" society. Unlike Gunnar Myrdal, who titled black-white relations "the American dilemma," many civil rights leaders prefer to call it "the American disease."

The attitude.   Essentially, the social pathology perspective is a philosophy of social problems. The perspective sets forth a very broad explanation for the whole universe of the phenomena classified by its proponents as social problems. In this perspective, there are four principal orientations: *critical, reformist, holistic,* and *apocalyptic.*

To diagnose sickness, doctors have a systematic body of knowledge on how organ systems work and what constitutes pathological functioning. No one, however, can claim that kind of expertise for how persons, institutions, or whole societies work. On the other hand, a person can and does rightfully claim to have a set of values about himself and the social world in which he lives. In describing others or the society as "sick," he makes a clear-cut moral judgment about the situation, albeit in quasi-medical language. In making this folk diagnosis, he clearly opposes himself to the person, situation, or society so described by him as "sick." As far as he is concerned, that person, situation, or society is "not working right" according to his own scheme of values. It is because of this orientation that the attitude is critical.

Insofar as the person, situation, or society is unhealthy, there exists a clear and present danger. The diagnosis of "sick" calls for corrective, moral action to rectify the situation, to ease the pain and suffering of all those affected by the pathological process underway. For if it goes unchecked, this unhealthy condition can spread and only do more harm

2. Erich Fromm, *The Revolution of Hope,* New York: Harper & Row, 1968; Herbert Marcuse, *Eros and Civilization,* Boston: Beacon Press, 1955; *One-Dimensional Man,* Boston: Beacon Press, 1964; *An Essay on Liberation,* Boston: Beacon Press, 1969; Charles Reich, *The Greening of America,* New York: Random House, 1970; Philip Slater, *The Pursuit of Loneliness,* Boston: Beacon Press, 1970.

and injury. Writ large, a broad campaign for moral and social reform may result.

Another attitudinal aspect of the philosophy of social pathology is the fact that it is holistic. Persons who view social problems from this point of view seek to find the underlying essence, the heart of the pathological matter, as it were. In so doing, they address themselves to "character" in the broadest sense. The view typically leads one to find that the problem is rooted in the essence, being, or total character of the person, situation, or society. As a result, corrective efforts must deal with the whole person, the whole situation, or the whole society, and not with just one ailing part of it.

Finally, the attitude is also apocalyptic. There is a sense in which the clinical judgment of pathology leads to a final judgment of death and destruction, and social pathologists may sound like prophets of doom. The diagnosis is frequently global and irreversible. Almost as frequently, however, it is millennial. That is, there is the notion that if the diseased person, situation, or society cleanses and heals itself of the unhealthy condition, then an unparalleled state of human happiness will follow.

These attitudes fit together rather neatly. A problem exists and is seen as a symptom of sickness because it offends the viewer's moral sensibilities. He especially wishes to treat the symptom because he sees it as standing for a larger, more dangerous whole, which, if unchecked, can only bring more and more problems which result, according to prediction, in catastrophe.

The content.   The perspective of social pathology draws on a very old tradition of thought in which biological analogies and organic analogies are fused with naturalistic observations on the cycle of life and death. Interference with or interruptions of those processes which are considered to be life-giving and life-sustaining are considered harmful, undesirable, and, therefore, pathological. This view rests on an ancient yet powerful assumption that many still cling to, viz., that there is and always will be a fundamental opposition between the individual and his society. Other ideas follow from this key assumption.

a. Life in society is a struggle (e.g. life against death, health against sickness, the strong against the weak).

b. The inner struggle is against the way society controls and misdirects human impulses.

c. The outer struggle is against those persons who cannot or will not regulate their impulses in accordance with morality.

d. When there is a *modus vivendi* worked out between these contending forces, outward harmony or social peace is the case.

e. When, however, either the individual or the society manifests abnormal growth in some important area affecting the lives of many others, the pathological condition emerges to threaten life in society and thereby comes to be designated a social problem.

Thus, a normative model rooted in folk biology, in the study of nature, and in medical terminology, provides a framework for making observations on social problems. Regardless of whether problems concern individuals, institutions, or the whole society, they are all rooted in pathology. This means that either individuals, institutions, or the society violates expectations and is not working right. There is something abnormal about the anatomy, physiology, and psychology of the individual, or about the structure and functioning of the institutions or the society. In all cases, an unhealthy process is underway.

THE FORMULA

Because of the implacable struggle that goes on between the individual and society, social problems arise and vary with the fortunes of either side. Certainly a good part of the time there is an equilibrium of forces, such that the society may be said, from the viewpoint of social pathologists, to be in a steady state of health. From time to time, however, there have been outbreaks of ill health. In some instances, individuals have gotten completely out of hand. This means that society has failed to check and regulate their impulses, with the result that their sick behavior now manifests itself in a number of places. In other instances, the society has succeeded so well in regulating man's impulses that his basic human needs go unmet. This kind of situation is diagnosed by pathologists as a social problem indicative of a "sick" society. The remedy in both instances, however, is to treat the individual, not the society.

The vocabulary.   The basic terms of social pathology come from biology and medicine. There are, however, some holdovers from philosophy and religion, and some very important newcomers from the lexicon of humanistic psychology. A few of the more common words are: *abnormal, alienation, anomalies, anxiety, breaking point, consciousness, dehumanization, depersonalization, feelings, growth, humanism, health, hypertrophy, illness, love, needs, paranoid, pathology, social consciousness,* and *symptom.*

The beliefs and doctrines.   The health of individuals, of institutions, and of the whole society is a cardinal value. Thus, for example, a whole society may ultimately decay when it orients too many activities around one value such as greed, lust, or warfare, or ignores a cardinal value such as humanism, thus destroying rather than enhancing human life. Such processes are frequently seen as almost irreversible; hence they require massive intervention and change.

The social pathology perspective not only diagnoses the problem but also outlines the general form that a solution must take. The outline of that solution is itself contained in the statement of beliefs and doctrines, which joins the conception and definition of the problem with the kind of collective action that points the way to a remedy. A summary of the beliefs and doctrines underlying the social pathology formula follows.

a. The ultimate source of all social problems lies in the individual, not in the society.

b. There are constructive as well as destructive impulses in men.

c. The task is to simultaneously quell or restrain the destructive urges and release the constructive impulses.

d. The only way that this is possible is for men to attain their more human potentials.

e. This task can only be accomplished through an individualized conception of social problems.

f. Thus, to solve social problems, change individuals; in time, changed individuals will produce a changed society.

By viewing all social problems as problems of the individual, the social pathology perspective maintains that the solution of all social problems is to be found in the basic changes that individuals make in their consciousness of themselves and of their world.

The recipe.   Health, whether mental or physical, is a property of individuals. If persons can be restored to health before it is too late, their cumulative contribution to the problem as it manifests itself and as it affects other people can be reduced, if not completely eliminated. Piecemeal reform will not achieve these goals; therefore, some very drastic changes are necessary. Members of society acquire their human and moral characteristics in the course of socialization, and, ultimately, to solve social problems, these must be changed. The totalistic remedy to social problems, according to the social pathology perspective, must thus be found in moral education. The social pathologist may call for conversion, a change in consciousness or in values, or more often, a return to and a revitalization of those thoughts, feelings, and actions in which people can achieve their common humanity. In any case, it is the persons involved in the social problems who must change.

THE HISTORY OF THE SOCIAL PATHOLOGY PERSPECTIVE

The pathology perspective on social problems is quite simple in nature, especially when compared with its successors. Nonetheless, it has had traditional sources, extended influence, and a paradoxical renaissance. The perspective, as codified by early American sociologists, drew on liberal social philosophy, middle-class rural norms, and Darwinian evolution. It harnessed reformist efforts within sociology on behalf of the solution of social problems. Its renaissance is paradoxical because though the focus has shifted, the remedy remains the same. More nonsociologists than sociologists now make use of the perspective, and when they do they stress the problems of the Unhealthy Society more than the problems of Unhealthy Individuals.

Social pathology as a perspective ascended within sociology during the first decade of the twentieth century. Crises within sociology and society during the middle thirties caused the viewpoint to decrease in popularity though textbooks with the title *Social Pathology* continued to appear. In its peak period, the works of Charles Henderson and Samuel Smith exemplified the perspective.[3] Their writings epitomized concern for social progress and the necessity for retaining small-town virtues in growing cities. They stressed the notions that the heredity of some groups was less defective than that of others and that evolution along Darwinian lines would speed up rather than impede progress. Caught in the middle of the nature-nurture controversy, the principal writers in this tradition sought to give both heredity and environment their due. Ultimately, for them, however, the explanation of problems in society lay in the biological abnormalities of individuals.

Pathology's paradoxical renaissance lies in the fact that more and more nonsociologists (and some sociologists as well) ascribe most social problems to a latter-day version of this perspective. In its present and revised form, the new pathologists lay most of today's social troubles at the doorstep of unresponsive and expanded social institutions. Institutional hypertrophy is the basic abnormality which, if unchecked, threatens not only the pursuit of happiness but the actual physical survival of humanity. Institutions and their by-products, such as modern technology, control men today. As a result men have become increasingly dehumanized. They have lost touch and contact with other men, no longer know their own feelings, have become alienated from themselves and others, and have become passive objects, rather than active subjects, of a social reality they do not understand.

Early social pathologists sought the mantle of science and set forth their discussions in textbooks on social problems. Contemporary social pathologists eschew the descriptive norms of scientific writing for evaluative and prescriptive rhetoric. They are openly critical of society as it is now constituted and working. For them, society as it is now represents a "pathology of normalcy." Consequently, contemporary social pathologists indict society and issue a prescription for ameliorating problems before it is too late.

3. Charles Henderson, *Introduction to the Study of the Dependent, Defective, and Delinquent Classes and of Their Social Treatment,* Boston: D. C. Heath, 1909; Samuel Smith, *Social Pathology,* New York: Macmillan, 1911.

When their prescription is examined, however, one sees that while they focus on society, the remedy continues to remain with the individual. Health, harmony, creativity, and feeling can all be restored through self-resocialization.

A moral community cannot exist unless it has men of moral character. Although society has caused their moral education to be sadly neglected, individuals can restore this moral character by developing more humanistic qualities.

SUMMARY AND CONCLUSION

Social pathology is an old and revived perspective on social problems. From this viewpoint, it is primarily the tensions between the individual and society which underlie social problems. In its early version, most frequently seen and heard from sociologists within the university, solutions to social problems would come from the reconstitution of the moral status and character of the individual. In the latter-day version, new pathologists inside, but more often outside, the university locate social problems in the abnormal qualities of institutions and society. However, their remedy for these problems remains true to the original formula: to heal a sick society, treat the sick individuals who constitute it.

DEHUMANIZATION AND NUCLEAR WAR

Viola W. Bernard, Perry Ottenberg, and Fritz Redl

In the first reading, Bernard et al. *argue that the conditions of modern life may very well be increasing the probability of nuclear holocaust. For example, automation, bureaucracy, urban living, and the mass media provide conditions creating almost daily exposure to frustration and tragedy; and if man allowed himself to fully experience every frustration or empathize with every suffering, the emotional burden would be unbearable. Thus, in order to cope, modern man dehumanizes himself and others, becoming emotionally barren and subsequently*

From Viola W. Bernard, Perry Ottenberg, and Fritz Redl, "Dehumanization: A Composite Psychological Defense in Relation to Modern War," in *Behavioral Sciences and Human Survival,* edited by Milton Schwebel, Palo Alto, Calif.: Science and Behavior Books, Inc., 1965, pp. 64, 65–66, 67, 68–69, 70–71, 72, 73–76, 76–81, 81–82. Reprinted by permission of the editor and the publisher.

experiencing neither his own individuality nor kinship with his fellow man. The danger of this adaptation, according to the authors of the following article, is that such dehumanization renders the destruction of mankind by nuclear warfare no longer unthinkable. The steps necessary for revitalizing our sense of humanity and the interdependence of all mankind are indicated.

We conceive of dehumanization as a particular type of psychic defense mechanism and consider its increasing prevalence to be a social consequence of the nuclear age. By this growth it contributes, we believe, to heightening the risks of nuclear extermination.

Dehumanization as a defense against painful or overwhelming emotions entails a decrease in a person's sense of his own individuality and in his perception of the humanness of other people. The misperceiving of others ranges from viewing them *en bloc* as "subhuman" or "bad human" (a long-familiar component of group prejudice) to viewing them as "nonhuman," as though they were inanimate items or "dispensable supplies." As such their maltreatment or even their destruction may be carried out or acquiesced in with relative freedom from the restraints of conscience or feelings of brotherhood.

• • •

It seems to us that the extensive increase of dehumanization today is causally linked to aspects of institutional changes in contemporary society and to the transformed nature of modern war. The mushrooming importance in today's world of technology, automation, urbanization, specialization, various forms of bureaucracy, mass media and the increased influences of nationalistic, totalitarian, and other ideologies have all been widely discussed by many scholars. The net long-term implications of these processes, whether constructive or destructive, are beyond the scope of this paper, and we do not regard ourselves qualified to evaluate them.

We are concerned here, however, with certain of their more immediate effects on people. It would seem that, for a vast portion of the world's population, elements of these broad social changes contribute to feelings of anonymity, impersonality, separation from the decision-making processes, and a fragmented sense of one's integrated social roles, and also to pressure on the individual to constrict his affective range to some machine-like task at hand. Similarly, the average citizen feels powerless indeed with respect to control over fateful decisions about nuclear attack or its aftermath.

The consequent sense of personal unimportance and relative helplessness, socially and politically, on the part of so many people specifically inclines them to adopt dehumanization as a preferred defense against many kinds of painful, unacceptable, and unbearable feelings referable to their experiences, inclinations, and behavior. *Self-directed dehumanization* empties the individual of human emotions and passions. It is paradoxical that one of its major dynamic purposes is protection against feeling the anxieties, frustrations and conflicts associated with the "cog-in-a-big-machine" self-image into which people feel themselves pushed by socially induced pressures. Thus, it tends to fulfill the very threat that it seeks to prevent.

These pervasive reactions predispose one even more to regard other people or groups as less than human, or even nonhuman. We distinguish among several different types and gradations of *object-directed dehumanization.* Thus, the failure to recognize in others their full complement of human qualities may be either partial or relatively complete. Partial dehumanization includes the misperceiving of members of "out-groups," *en masse,* as subhuman, bad human, or superhuman; as such, it is related to the psychodynamics of group prejudice. It protects the individual from the guilt and shame he would otherwise feel from primitive or antisocial attitudes, impulses, and actions that he directs—or allows others to direct—toward those he manages to perceive in these categories: if they are subhumans they have not yet reached full human status on the evolutionary ladder and, therefore, do not merit being treated as human; if they are bad humans, their maltreatment is justified, since their defects in human qualities are their own fault. . . .

In its more complete form, however, object-directed dehumanization entails a perception of other people as nonhumans—as statistics, commodities, or interchangeable pieces in a vast "numbers game." Its predominant emotional tone is that of indifference, in contrast to the (sometimes strong) feelings of partial dehumanization, together with a sense of *noninvolvement in the actual or foreseeable vicissitudes* of others. Such apathy has crucial psychosocial implications. Among these —perhaps the most important today—is its bearing on how people tolerate the risks of mass destruction by nuclear war.

• • •

The only occasions to date on which nuclear bombs have been used in warfare took place when the "baby bombs" were dropped on the civilian populations of Hiroshima and Nagasaki. Lifton (1) has reported on reactions among the Hiroshima survivors, as well as his own, as investigator. His observations are particularly valuable to us since, as a research psychiatrist, he was especially qualified both to elicit and to evaluate psychodynamic data. According to the survivors whom he interviewed, at first one experienced utter horror at the sudden, strange scene of mass deaths, devastation, dreadful burns, and skin stripped from bodies. They could find no words to convey fully these initial feelings. But then each described how, before long, the horror would almost disappear. One would see terrible sights of human beings in extreme agony and yet feel nothing. The load of feeling from empathic responsiveness had become too much to endure; all one could do was to try to survive.

Lifton reports that during the first few such accounts he felt profoundly shocked, shaken, and emotionally spent. These effects gradually lessened, however, so that he became able to experience the interviews as scientific work rather than as repeated occasions of vicarious agony. For both the survivors and the investigator, the "task" provided a focus of concentration and of circumscribed activity as a means of quelling disturbing emotions.

In these instances, the immediate adaptive value of dehumanization as a defense is obvious. It remains open to question, however, whether a further, somewhat related, finding of Lifton's will in the long run prove to be adaptive or maladaptive. He learned that many people in Japan and elsewhere cannot bear to look at pictures of Hiroshima, and even avoid the museum in which they are displayed. There is avoidance and denial of the whole issue which not infrequently leads to hostility toward the A-bomb victims themselves, or toward anyone who expresses concern for these or future victims. May not *this* kind of defense reaction deflect the determination to seek ways of preventing nuclear war?

We believe that the complex mechanism of dehumanization urgently needs to be recognized and studied because its use as a defense has been stepped up so tremendously in recent times, and because of the grave risks it entails as the price for short-term relief. This paper represents only a preliminary delineation, with main attention to its bearing on the nuclear threat.[1]

Many people, by mobilizing this form of ego defense, manage to avoid or to lessen the emotional significance for themselves of today's kind of war. Only a very widespread and deeply rooted defense could ward off the full import of the new reality with which we live: that warfare has been transformed by modern weaponry into something mankind has never experienced before, and that in all-out nuclear war there can be no "victory" for anyone.

• • •

1. Because of this primary emphasis, we shall refrain from exploring many important facets of dehumanization which seem less directly relevant to the threat of nuclear warfare. Yet, it permeates so many aspects of modern life that, for clarity in describing it, our discussion must ramify, to some extent, beyond its war-connected context. Still we have purposely neglected areas of great interest to us, especially with regard to psychopathology, psychotherapy, and community psychiatry, which we think warrant fuller discussion elsewhere.

No one, of course, could possibly retain his mental health and carry on the business of life if he remained constantly aware of, and emphatically sensitive to, all the misery and injustice that there is in the world. But this very essentiality of dehumanization, as with other defenses, makes for its greatest danger: *that the constructive self-protection it achieves will cross the ever-shifting boundaries of adaptiveness and become destructive to others as well as to the self.** In combination with other social factors already mentioned, the perfection of modern techniques for automated killing on a global scale engenders a marked increase in the incidence of dehumanization. Correspondingly, there is intensified risk that this collective reaction will break through the fragile and elusive dividing line that separates healthy ego-supportive dehumanization from the maladaptive callousness and apathy that prevent people from taking those realistic actions which are within their powers to protect human rights and human lives.

A "vicious cycle" relationship would thus seem to obtain between dehumanization as a subjective phenomenon and its objective consequences. Conscience and empathy, as sources of guilt and compassion, pertain to human beings; they can be evaded if the human element in the victims of aggression is first sufficiently obscured. The aggressor is thereby freed from conscience-linked restraints, with injurious objective effects on other individuals, groups, or nations. The victims in turn respond, subjectively, by resorting even more to self-protective dehumanization, as did the Hiroshima survivors whom Lifton interviewed.

One might argue, and with some cogency, that similar conversion of enemies into pins on a military map has been part of war psychology throughout history, so are we not therefore belaboring the obvious? The answer lies in the fundamental changes, both quantitative and qualitative, that nuclear weapons have made in the meaning of war. In fact, the very term "war," with its pre-atomic connotations, has become something of an outmoded misnomer for the nuclear threat which now confronts us. "Modern war"—before Hiroshima—reflected, as a social institution, many of the social and technological developments which we have already noted as conducive to increased dehumanization. But with the possibility of instantaneously wiping out the world's population— or a very large section of it—the extent of dehumanization as well as its significance for human survival have both been abruptly and tremendously accelerated.

In part, this seems to be due to the overtaxing of our capacity really to comprehend the sudden changes in amplitudes that have become so salient. In addition to the changed factors of *distance, time,* and *magnitude* in modern technology, there is the push-button nature of today's

---

* Our italics, M. S. W. and E. R.

weaponry and the *indirectness* of releasing a rocket barrage upon sites halfway around the world, all of which lie far outside our range of previous experience. When we look out of an airplane window, the earth below becomes a toy, the hills and valleys reduced to abstractions in our mental canvas; but we do not conceive of ourselves as a minute part of some moving speck in the sky—which is how we appear to people on the ground. Yet it is precisely such reciprocal awareness that is required if we are to maintain a balanced view of our actual size and vulnerability. Otherwise, perceptual confusion introduces a mechanistic and impersonal quality into our reactions.

The thinking and feeling of most people have been unable as yet to come to grips with the sheer expansion of numbers and the frightening shrinkage of space which present means of transportation and communication entail. The news of an animal run over by a car, a child stuck in a well, or the preventable death of one individual evokes an outpouring of sympathetic response and upsets the emotional equanimity of many; yet reports of six million Jews killed in Nazi death camps, or of a hundred thousand Japanese killed in Hiroshima and Nagasaki, may cause but moderate uneasiness. Arthur Koestler has put it poignantly, "Statistics don't bleed; it is the detail which counts. We are unable to embrace the total process with our awareness; we can only focus on little lumps of reality." (2)

It is this unique combination of psychosocial and situational factors that seems particularly to favor the adoption of the composite defense we have called "dehumanization"—and this in turn acts to generate more and more of the same. The new aspects of time, space, magnitude, speed, automation, distance, and irreversibility are not yet "hooked up" in the psychology of man's relationships to his fellow man or to the world he inhabits. . . .

We are confronted with a *lag in our perceptual and intellectual development* so that the enormity of the new reality, with its potential for both destructive and constructive human consequences, becomes blurred in our thinking and feeling. The less elastic our capacity to comprehend meaningfully new significances, the more we cling to dehumanization, unable to challenge its fallacies through knowledge and reason. Correspondingly, the greater our reliance on dehumanization as a mechanism for coping with life, the less readily can the new facts of our existence be integrated into our full psychic functioning, since so many of its vital components, such as empathy, have been shunted aside, stifled, or obscured.

Together, in the writers' opinion, these differently caused but mutually reinforcing cognitive and emotional deficiencies seriously intensify the nuclear risk; latent psychological barriers against the destruction of millions of people remain unmobilized, and hence ineffective, for those who feel detached from the flesh and blood implications of nuclear war. . . .

Whether it be adaptive or maladaptive, dehumanization brings with it, as we have noted, a temporary feeling of relief, an illusion of problems solved, or at least postponed or evaded. Whatever the ultimate effects of this psychic maneuver on our destiny, however, it would seem to be a wise precaution to try to assess some of its dangerous possibilities.

Several overlapping aspects of maladaptive dehumanization may be outlined briefly and in oversimplified form, as follows:

1. *Increased emotional distance from other human beings.* Under the impact of this defense, one stops identifying with others or seeing them as essentially similar to oneself in basic human qualities. Relationships to others become stereotyped, rigid, and above all, unexpressive of mutuality. People in "out-groups" are apt to be reacted to *en bloc;* feelings of concern for them have become anesthetized.

● ● ●

2. *Diminished sense of personal responsibility for the consequences of one's actions.* Ordinarily, for most people, the advocacy of or participation in the wholesale slaughter and maiming of their fellow human beings is checked by opposing feelings of guilt, shame, or horror. Immunity from these feelings may be gained, however, by a self-automatizing detachment from a sense of *personal* responsibility for the outcome of such actions, thereby making them easier to carry out. (A dramatic version of the excuse, "I was only carrying out orders," was offered by Eichmann at his trial.)

One "safe" way of dealing with such painful feelings is to focus only on one's fragmented job and ignore its many ramifications. By blocking out the ultimately destructive purpose of a military bombing action, for instance, one's component task therein may become a source of ego-acceptable gratification, as from any successful fulfillment of duty, mastery of a hard problem, or achievement of a dangerous feat. The B-29 airplane that dropped the atomic bomb on Hiroshima was named Enola Gay, after the mother of one of its crew members. This could represent the psychological defense of displacing human qualities from the population to be bombed to the machine.

One of the crew members is reported to have exlaimed: "If people knew what we were doing we could have sold tickets for $100,000!" and another is said to have commented, "Colonel, that was worth the 25¢ ride on the 'Cyclone' at Coney Island." (3) Such reactions, which may on the surface appear to be shockingly cynical, not only illustrate how cynicism may be used to conceal strong emotions (as seems quite likely in this instance); they also suggest how one may try to use cynicism to bolster one's dehumanization when that defense is not itself strong enough, even with its displacement of responsibility and its focusing on one's fragmented job, to overcome the intensity of one's inner "humanized" emotional protest against carrying out an act of such vast destructiveness.

3. *Increasing involvement with procedural problems to the detriment of human needs.* There is an overconcern with details of procedure, with impersonal deindividualized regulations, and with the formal structure of a practice, all of which result in shrinking the ability or willingness to personalize one's actions in the interests of individual human needs or special differences. This is, of course, the particular danger implicit in the trend toward bureaucracy that accompanies organizational units when they grow larger and larger. The task at hand is then apt to take precedence over the human cost: the individual is seen more as a means to an end than as an end in himself. Society, the Corporation, the Five-Year-Plan—these become overriding goals in themselves, and the dehumanized man is turned into a cost item, tool, or energy-factor serving the mass-machine.

Even "scientific" studies of human behavior and development, as well as professional practices based on them, sometimes become dehumanized to a maladaptive extent. (4) Such words as "communicate," "adjust," "identify," "relate," "feel," and even "love" can lose their personal meaningfulness when they are used as mere technical devices instead of being applied to specific human beings in specific life situations.[2] In response to the new hugeness of global problems, patterns of speech have emerged that additionally reflect dehumanized thinking. Segmented-fragmented concepts, such as "fallout problem," "shelter problem," "civil defense," "deterrence," "first strike," "pre-emptive attack," "overkill," and some aspects of game theory, represent a "move-countermove" type of thinking which tends to treat the potential human victim as a statistic, and to screen out the total catastrophic effect of the contemplated actions upon human lives. The content of strategy takes on an importance that is without any relation to its inevitable *results,* the defense of dehumanization having operated to block out recognition of those awesome consequences that, if they could be seen, would make

2. Within our own discipline this is all too likely to occur when thousands of sick individuals are converted into "cases" in some of our understaffed and oversized mental hospitals. Bureaucratic hospital structure favors impersonal experience. In an enlightening study (6), Merton J. Kahne points up how this accentuation of automatic and formalized milieu propensities thwarts the specific therapeutic need of psychiatric patients for opportunities to improve their sense of involvement with people.

On another occasion we hope to enlarge on how and why maladaptive uses of dehumanization on the part of professionals, officials, and the general public hamper our collective effort as a community to instill more sensitivity to individual need into patterns of congregate care, not only in mental hospitals but also in general hospitals, children's institutions, welfare and correctional facilities, etc.

the strategy unacceptable. The defense, when successful, narcotizes deeper feelings so that nuclear war, as "inevitable," may be more dispassionately contemplated and its tactical permutations assayed. In the course of this, however, almost automatic counteractions of anxiety are frequently expressed through such remarks as: "People have always lived on the brink of disaster," "You can't change human nature; there will have to be wars," and "We all have to die some day."

4. *Inability to oppose dominant group attitudes or pressures.* As the individual comes to feel more and more alienated and lonely in mass society, he finds it more and more difficult to place himself in opposition to the huge pressures of the "Organization." Fears of losing occupational security or of attacks on one's integrity, loyalty, or family are more than most people can bear. Self-directed dehumanization is resorted to as a defense against such fears and conflicts: by joining the party, organization, or club, and thus feeling himself to be an inconspicuous particle in some large structure, he may find relief from the difficult decisions, uncertainties, and pressures of nonconformity. He may also thereby ward off those feelings of guilt that would arise out of participating in, or failing to protest against, the injustices and cruelties perpetrated by those in power. Thus, during the Nazi regime, many usually kindhearted Germans appear to have silenced their consciences by emphasizing their own insignificance and identifying with the dehumanized values of the dictatorship. This stance permitted the detached, even dutiful, disregard of their fellow citizens, which in turn gave even freer rein to the systematic official conducting of genocide.

5. *Feelings of personal helplessness and estrangement.* The realization of ones relatively impotent position in a large organization engenders anxiety[3] which dehumanization helps to cover over. The internalized perception of the self as small, helpless, and insignificant, coupled with an externalized view of "Society" as huge, powerful, and unopposable, is expressed in such frequently heard comments as: "The government has secret information that we don't have"; or, "They know what's right, who am I to question what they are doing?"; or "What's the use? No one will listen to me. . . ."

The belief that the government or the military is either infallible or impregnable provides a tempting refuge because of its renunciation of one's own critical faculties in the name of those of the powerful and all-knowing leader. Such self-directed dehumanization has a strong appeal to the isolated and alienated citizen as a protective cloak to hide from himself his feelings of weakness, ignorance and estrangement. This is particularly relevant to the psychological attraction of certain dangerous social movements. The more inwardly frightened, lonely, helpless,

---

3. This has been particularly well described in novels by Kafka and Camus.

and humiliated people become, the greater the susceptibility of many of them to the seductive, prejudiced promises of demagoguery: the award of spurious superiority and privilege achieved by devaluating the full humanness of some other group—racial, religious, ethnic, or political. Furthermore, as an added advantage of the dehumanization "package," self-enhancing acts of discrimination and persecution against such victim groups can be carried out without tormenting or deterrent feelings of guilt, since these are absorbed by the "rightness" of the demagogic leader.

In recent decades and in many countries, including our own, we have seen what human toll can be taken by this psychosocial configuration. It has entered into Hitlerism, Stalinism, U.S.A. "lynch-mobism." If it is extended to the international arena, against a "dehumanized" enemy instead of an oppressed national minority, atomic weapons will now empower it to inflict immeasurably more human destruction and suffering.

The indifference resulting from that form of dehumanization which causes one to view others as inanimate objects enables one, without conscious malice or selfishness, to write off their misery, injustices, and death as something that "just couldn't be helped." As nonhumans, they are not identified with as beings essentially similar to oneself; "their" annihilation by nuclear warfare is thus not "our" concern, despite the reality that distinctions between "they" and "we" have been rendered all the more meaningless by the mutually suicidal nature of total war.

• • •

A case history of community apathy . . . was recently provided by A. M. Rosenthal, an editor of *The New York Times*. (5) At first glance, perhaps, his account of dehumanization, involving but one individual and in peacetime, may not seem germane to our discussion about nuclear war. But the macrocosm is reflected in the microcosm. We agree with Mr. Rosenthal that the implications of this episode are linked with certain psychological factors that have helped pave the way for such broad social calamities as Fascism abroad and racial crises in this country, both in the North and South. It does not seem too farfetched, therefore, to relate them to the nuclear threat as well.

For more than half an hour, one night in March, 1964, thirty-eight respectable, law-abiding citizens in a quiet middle-class neighborhood in New York City watched a killer stalk and stab a young woman in three separate attacks, close to her home. She was no stranger to these onlookers, her neighbors, who knew her as "Kitty." According to Rosenthal, "Twice the sound of their voices and the sudden glow of their bedroom lights interrupted him and frightened him off. Each time he returned, sought her out and stabbed her again. Not one person telephoned the police during the assault; one witness called after the woman was dead." Later, when these thirty-eight neighbors were asked about their baffling failure to phone for help, even though they were safe in their own homes, "the underlying attitude or explanation seemed to be fear of involvement—any kind of involvement." Their fatal apathy gains in significance precisely because, by ordinary standards, these were decent, moral people—husbands and wives attached to each other and good to their children. This is one of the forms of dehumanization that we have described, in which a reaction of massive indifference—not hostility—leads to grievous cruelty, yet all the while, in another compartment of the self, the same individual's capacity for active caring continues, at least for those within his immediate orbit.

Rosenthal describes his own reaction to this episode as a "peculiar paradoxical feeling that there is in the tale of Catherine Genovese a revelation about the human condition so appalling to contemplate that only good can come from forcing oneself to confront the truth . . . the terrible reality that only under certain situations, and only in response to certain reflexes or certain beliefs, will a man step out of his shell toward his brother. In the back of my mind . . . was the feeling that there was, that there must be some connection between [this story and] the story of the witnesses silent in the face of greater crimes—the degradation of a race, children hungering. . . . It happens from time to time in New York that the life of the city is frozen by an instant of shock. In that instant the people of the city are seized by the paralyzing realization that they are one, that each man is in some way a mirror of every other man. . . . In that instant of shock, the mirror showed quite clearly what was wrong, that the face of mankind was spotted with the disease of apathy—all mankind. But this was too frightening a thought to live with, and soon the beholders began to set boundaries for the illness, to search frantically for causes that were external and to look for the carrier."

As we strive to distinguish more clearly among the complex determinants of adaptive-maladaptive, humanized-dehumanized polarities of behavior, we recognize that stubborn impulses toward individuation are intertwined with the dehumanizing trends on which we have focused. Both humanization and dehumanization are heightened by interpenetrating social and psychological effects of current technological and institutional changes. The progress of the past hundred years has markedly furthered humanization: it has relieved much of human drudgery and strain, and helped to bring about increased leisure and a richer life for a larger part of the world's population. Despite the blurring of personal distinctiveness by excessive bureaucracy, there are now exceptional opportunities, made possible by the same technology that fosters uniformity, for the individual to make rapid contact with, and meaningful contribution to, an almost limitless number of the earth's inhabitants. The same budgets, communication networks, transportation delivery systems, and human organizations that can be used to destroy can also be turned toward the creative fulfillment of great world purposes.

Our situation today favors contradictory attitudes toward how much any individual matters in the scheme of things, both subjectively and from the standpoint of social reality. At one extreme a few individuals in key positions feel—and are generally felt to have—a hugely expanded potential for social impact. Among the vast majority there is, by contrast, an intensified sense of voiceless insignificance in the shaping of events. Objectively, too, there is now among individuals a far greater disparity in their actual power to influence crucial outcomes. More than ever before, the fate of the world depends on the judgment of a handful of heads of state and their advisers, who must make rapid decisions about actions for which there are no precedents. Ideas and events, for better or worse, can have immediate global impact.[4] A push-button can set a holocaust in motion; a transatlantic phone call can prevent one.

In spite of humanizing ingredients in modern life, and the fact that men of good will everywhere are striving ceaselessly toward goals of peace, freedom, and human dignity, we nevertheless place primary emphasis, in this paper, on dehumanization because we feel that the dangers inherent in this phenomenon are particularly pervasive, insidious, and relevant to the risk of nuclear war.

From a broad biological perspective, war may be viewed as a form of aggression between members of the same species, Homo sapiens. The distinguished naturalist, Lorenz, has recently pointed out a difference, of great relevance to the relationship between dehumanization and nuclear warfare, in the intraspecies behavior of animals who live in two kinds of groups. (6) In the one, the members live together as a crowd of strangers: there are no expressions of mutual aggression, but neither is there any evidence of mutual ties, of relationships of affection, between individuals in the group. On the other hand, some of the fiercest beasts of prey—animals whose bodily weapons are capable of killing their own kind—live in groups in which intense relationships, both *aggressive and affectionate,* exist. Among such animals, says Lorenz, the greater the intraspecies aggression, the stronger the positive mutual attachments as well. These latter develop, through evolution, out of those occasions, such as breeding, when cooperation among these aggressive animals becomes essential to their survival as a species.

---

4. The news of President Kennedy's assassination circled the earth with unparalleled speed, and evoked a profound worldwide emotional response.

Furthermore—and this is of the utmost importance for survival—the greater the capacity for mutual relationships, the stronger and more reliable are the *innate inhibitions* which prevent them from using the species-specific weapons of predatory aggression, fangs, claws or whatever, to maim or kill a member of thier own species, no matter how strong the hostile urge of one against another. For example, when two wolves fight, according to Lorenz, the potential victor's fangs are powerfully inhibited at what would be the moment of kill, in response to the other's ritualized signal of immobile exposure to his opponent of his vulnerable jugular.

Man's weapons, by contrast, are not part of his body. They are thus not controllable by reflexes fused into his nervous system; control must depend, instead, in psychological inhibitions (which may also function through social controls of his own devising). These psychic barriers to intraspecies aggression—which can lead to our becoming extinct—are rooted in our affiliative tendencies for cooperation and personal attachment. But these are the very tendencies that, as this paper has stressed, dehumanization can so seriously undermine.

Lorenz speaks of a natural balance within a species—essential to its preservation—between the capacity for killing and inhibition. In that sense, perhaps, man jeopardizes survival by disturbing, with his invention of nuclear bombs, such a balance as has been maintained throughout his long history of periodic "old-style" wars. Such a dire imbalance would be increased by any shift on the part of the "human animal" toward a society essentially devoid of mutual relationships. For this would vitiate the very tendencies toward emotional involvement and cooperation which are the source of our most reliable inhibitions against "over-killing." Therefore, in terms of the parallels suggested by Lorenz, in order to protect ourselves against the doom of extinction as a species, we must encourage and devise every possible means of safeguarding the "family of man" from becoming an uncaring crowd. Not merely the limiting or halting, but the reversing of maladaptive dehumanization emerges as a key to survival.

What can be done to counteract these dangers? Assuredly, there is no single or ready answer. The development of psychic antidotes of rehumanization must involve a multiplicty of variables, levels of discourse and sectors of human activity, commensurate in complexity with the factors that make for *de*humanization. Our attempt in this paper to identify this mental mechanism, and to alert others to its significance, its frequency and its inter-relatedness to nuclear risk, represents in itself a preliminary phase of remedial endeavor. For the very process of recognizing a psychosocial problem such as this, by marshaling, reordering and interpreting diverse sets of facts to find new significances in them, is a form of social action, and one that is especially appropriate to behavioral scientists. Beyond this initial posing of the problem, however, any chance of effectively grappling with it will require the converging efforts of those in many different professions and walks of life.

Rehumanization as a mode of neutralizing the dangerous effects that we have stressed should not be misconstrued as aiming at the reestablishment of pre-nuclear age psychology—which would be impossible in any case. We cannot set history back nostalgically to "the good old days" prior to automation and the other changes in contemporary society (nor were the conditions of those earlier days really so "good" for the self-realization of a large portion of the population). On the contrary, the process of rehumanization means to us a way of assimilating and re-integrating, emotionally and intellectually, the profound new meanings that have been brought into our lives by our own advances, so that a much fuller conviction than ever before of our own humanity and inter-dependence with all mankind becomes intrinsic to our basic frame of reference.

The imperative for speeding up such a universal process of psychological change is rooted in the new and *specific* necessity to insure survival in the face of the awesome irreversibility of nuclear annihilation. The most essential approaches toward achieving this goal, however, lead us into such *general* and only seemingly unrelated issues as the degree of political freedom and social justice; our patterns of child care and child-rearing; and our philosophy of education, as well as the quality of its implementation. For the process of dehumanization, which eventuates in indifference to the suffering implicit in nuclear warfare, has its beginnings in earlier periods and other areas of the individual's life. It is through these areas that influences conducive to rehumanization must be channeled.

We need to learn more, and to make more effective use of what is already known about how to strengthen people's capacity to tolerate irreducible uncertainty, fear, and frustration without having to take refuge in illusions that cripple their potential for realistic behavior. And we urgently need to find ways of galvanizing our powers of imagination (including ways of weakening the hold of the emotionally-based mechanisms that imprison it).

Imagination and foresight are among the highest functions of the human brain, from the evolutionary standpoint, and also among the most valuable. They enable us to select and extrapolate from previously accumulated experience and knowledge, in order to create guidelines for coping with situations never before experienced, whose nature is so far unknown.

• • •

Through imagination . . . a completely new situation can be projected in the mind in its sensate and vivid entirety, so that the lessons it contains for us can be learned without the necessity of going through it in real life. This form of "future-directed" learning, which creative imagination makes possible, is therefore uniquely advantageous in dealing with the problematic issues of thermonuclear war; it permits us to arrive at more rational decisions for preventing it without having to pay the gruesome price of undergoing its actuality.

The fact is that the "once-and-for-all" character of full-scale nuclear war renders the methods of "learning through experience"—our own or others'—not only indefensible (in terms of the human cost) but also utterly unfeasible. The empirical privilege of "profiting" from an experience of that nature would have been denied to most if not all of humanity by the finality of the experience itself.

Accordingly, it would seem that whatever can quicken and extend our capacity for imagination, in both the empathic and conceptual spheres, is a vital form of "civil defense." It requires . . . all the pedagogic ingenuity that we can muster to overcome the lag in our intellectual development that keeps us from fully comprehending the new dimensions of our existence. . . .

(1) Lifton, R., "Psychological effects of the atomic bomb in Hiroshima; the theme of death," *Daedalus, Journal of the Amer. Acad. of Arts and Sciences,* pp. 462–97, Summer, 1963.
(2) Koestler, A. "On disbelieving atrocities," in *The Yogi and the Commissar,* New York, Macmillan, 1945.
(3) *Yank, the Army Weekly,* New York, Duell, Sloane and Pearce, 1947, p. 282.
(4) Kahne, M. J., "Bureaucratic Structure and Impersonal Experience in Mental Hospitals," *Psychiatry,* 22, 4, pp. 363–75, 1959.
(5) Rosenthal, A. M., *Thirty-Eight Witnesses,* New York, McGraw-Hill, 1964.
(6) Lorenz, K., *Das Sogenännte Böse—Zur Naturgeschichte der Aggression,* Vienna. Dr. G. Borotha-Schoeler Verlag, 1963.

THE PURSUIT OF LONELINESS: AMERICAN CULTURE AT THE BREAKING POINT

Philip Slater

America, according to Philip Slater, is at its breaking point. Personal aggrandizement and gain are overshadowing social consciousness, and greed and competition have reached such pathological proportions that

Philip Slater, *The Pursuit of Loneliness: American Culture at the Breaking Point,* pp. 120–24, 126–39, 141–44, 154. Copyright © 1970 by Philip E. Slater. Reprinted by permission.

they are driving the society to destruction. To prevent catastrophe, a new consciousness and set of incentives must be acquired. Social consciousness must become the incentive for both production and consumption. America must become socially radical and technologically conservative, reversing the emphasis of the old culture and its antipathy to human life and human satisfaction. According to Slater, only through the acquisition of such new values can harmony between the individual and society be restored.

. . . C. Wright Mills coined the term "crackpot realism" to characterize the kind of short-run, parochial thinking that finds itself unable to reconsider an existing policy, no matter how disastrous. A crackpot realist is an administrator who throws away a million dollars because "you can't just junk a project we've put a hundred thousand dollars into." Crackpot realists cite "practical politics" to defend our support of tottering dictatorial regimes that have collapsed one after the other (indeed, our policy of trying to outbid the Soviet Union for white elephants has made our greatest defeats look, in retrospect, like clever stratagems).

Crackpot realism also renders us incapable of guarding ourselves against the mortal domestic hazards we create. Although the devastation wrought by DDT, for example, has been firmly established for years, lawmakers even now talk of a "timetable" for phasing it out. (If we discovered arsenic in our flour bin would we construct a "timetable" for phasing out the flour?) And when a miscalculation at Dugway caused nerve gas to drift halfway to Salt Lake City, killing 6000 sheep en route, government officials did not reassess the desirability of manufacturing such poisons and spraying them into our atmosphere.[1] Finally, crackpot realism argues that we must move slowly in handling urban problems, despite the fact that ghetto conditions annually manufacture thousands of stunted minds, burnt-out cases, and killers. The middle-class "realist's" neglect nurtures today the disturbed freak who will kill his child tomorrow. But it is not "practical" in America to make drastic changes, even to save lives.

Yet there is a sense in which all change is gradual. There is an illusory element in revolutionary change—a tendency to exaggerate the efficacy of the revolutionary moment by ignoring the subtle and undramatic changes leading up to that moment, and the reactions, corruptions, and

---

1. Another feature of crackpot realism is the policy of automatic lying adopted by public officials and corporation executives when caught with their fingers in the cookie jar. The Pentagon and the State Department are the most incorrigible in this respect, but the automobile executives who tried to "get something on" Ralph Nader showed a cinematic knowledgeability that appealed to aficionados of old Bogart films. On the whole, however, the when-in-doubt-lie-for-a-while approach has been an important source of youthful hostility to old-culture leaders.

compromises that follow it. The revolutionary moment is like a "break-through" in scientific discovery, or in psychotherapy. It is dramatic and exciting and helps motivate the dreary process of retooling society (or scientific thought, or the personality structure) piece by tedious piece. It may be necessary for any real change to occur at all—even the kinds of changes that liberal reformers seek. The only reason for stressing the latent gradualism in revolution is that revolutionaries typically expend much of their energy attacking those very groups that undertake the "softening-up" work that makes revolution possible.

Such internecine warfare often revolves around the notion that correct radical strategy seeks to "make things worse" in order to encourage a revolutionary confrontation between the forces of reaction and the revolutionary saviors. In this view any liberal efforts at social amelioration are to be avoided as dampers on revolutionary fervor. One attempts instead to bring about a situation so repressive and disagreeable that the masses will be forced to call on the revolutionaries, waiting in the wings. . . . But provoking repression is an effective technique only if the repression itself is confused and anarchic. The result of "things getting bad enough" is usually to demoralize most of those who want change and to intimidate a good many more. Revolution does not occur when things get bad enough but when things get better—when small improvements generate rising aspirations and decrease tolerance for long-existing injustices. The "make things worse" approach is not only not strategic, it is not even revolutionary—it seeks unconsciously to preserve, while at the same time discrediting, parental authority. The emotional logic behind it might be expressed as: "if things get bad enough They will see that it is unfair." As every radical knows, radical movements are always plagued with people who want to lose, want to be stopped, want in effect to be put under protective custody.

• • •

Change can take place only when liberal and radical pressures are both strong. Intelligent liberals have always recognized the debt they owe to radicals, whose existence permits liberals to push further than they would otherwise have dared, all the while posing as compromisers and mediators. Radicals, however, have been somewhat less sensible of their debt to liberals, partly because of the rather single-minded discipline radicals are almost forced to maintain, plagued as they always are by liberal backsliding and timidity on the one hand and various forms of self-destructiveness and romantic posing on the other.

Yet liberal adjustments often do much to soften up an initially rigid *status quo*—creating just those rising expectations that make revolutionary change possible. Radicals often object that liberal programs generate an illusory feeling of movement when in fact little is changing. Their assumption is always that such an illusion slows down movement, but it is just as likely that the reverse is true. Radicals are so absorbed with the difficulties they have in overcoming inertia that they tend to assume that motionlessness is a comfortable state that everyone will seek with the slightest excuse. But even an illusory sense of progress is invigorating, and whets the desire for further advances. Absolute stagnation is enervating, and creates a feeling of helplessness and impotence. The "war on poverty" may have done very little to alleviate poverty and nothing at all to remove its causes, but it raised a lot of expectations, created many visions of the possibilities for change, alerted a large number of people to existing inadequacies in the system and to the relative efficacy of various strategies for eliminating them. One factor that radicals overlook, in other words, is the educative value of liberal reform, however insignificant that reform may be in terms of institutional change.

Liberal reform and radical change are thus complementary rather than antagonistic. Together they make it possible continually to test the limits of what can be done. Liberals never know whether the door is unlocked because they are afraid to try it. Radicals, on the other hand, miss many opportunities for small advances because they are unwilling to settle for so little. No one group can possibly fulfill both these functions—constant testing of the maximum prohibits constant testing of the minimum and vice versa.

• • •

STRANGERS IN PARADISE

We need now to consider seriously what the role of those over thirty is to be during the transition to and emergence of the new culture. Many will of course simply oppose it, with varying degrees of violence. A few will greet it with a sense of liberation, finding in it an answer they have long sought, but will experience a sense of awkwardness in trying to relate themselves to what has been so noisily appropriated by the young. Many more will be tormented with ambivalence, repelled by the new culture but disillusioned by the old.

It is to this latter group that what follows is addressed, for I do not believe that a successful transition can be made without their participation. If the issue is left to generational confrontation, with new-culture adherents attempting simply to push their elders out of the way and into the grave, the results will probably be catastrophic. The old culture will not simply fall of its own weight. It is not rotten but wildly malfunctioning, not weak and failing but strong and demented, not a sick old horse but a healthy runaway. It no longer performs its fundamental task of satisfying the needs of its adherents, but it still performs the task of feeding and perpetuating itself. Nor do the young have the knowledge and skill successfully to dismantle it. If the matter is left to the collision of generational change it seems to me inevitable that a radical-right revolution will occur as a last-ditch effort to stave off change.

Only those who have participated fully in the old culture can prevent this. Only they can dismantle the old culture without calamity. Furthermore, no revolution produces total change—much of the old machinery is retained more or less intact. Those intimate with the machinery are in the best position to facilitate the retooling and redirection.

But why should they? Why should they tear down what they have built? What place is there for them in the new culture? The new culture is contemptuous of age and rejects most of the values by which moderates have ordered their lives. Yet it must be remembered that the contempt for age and tradition, the worship of modernity, is not intrinsically a new-culture trait but a foundationstone of a technology-dominated culture. It is the old culture that systematically invalidates learning and experience, that worships innovation and turns its back on the past, on familial and community ties. The new culture is preoccupied with tradition, with community, with relationships—with many things that would reinstate the validity of accumulated wisdom. Social change is replete with paradox, and one of the most striking is the fact that the old culture worships novelty, while the new would resuscitate a more tradition-oriented way of life. The rhetoric of short-run goals, in which the young shout down the present and shout up the future, masks the fact that in the long run there is more room for the aged in the new culture than in the old. This is something about which new-culture adherents, however, are also confused, and old-culture participants will have much to do to stake out a rightful place for age in the new culture. If they fail the new culture will be corrupted into a reactionary parody of itself.

My main argument for rejecting the old culture is that it has been unable to keep any of the promises that have sustained it for so long, and as it struggles more and more violently to maintain itself, *it is less and less able to hide its fundamental antipathy to human life and human satisfaction.** It spends hundreds of billions of dollars to find ways of killing more efficiently, but almost nothing to enhance the joys of living. Against those who sought to humanize their physical environment in Berkeley the forces of "law and order" used a poison gas outlawed by the Geneva Conventions. The old culture is unable to stop killing people —deliberately in the case of those who oppose it, with bureaucratic indifference in the case of those who obey its dictates or consume its

---

*Our italics, M. S. W. and E. R.

products trustingly. However familiar and comfortable it may seem, the old culture is threatening to kill us, like a trusted relative gone berserk so gradually that we are able to pretend to ourselves he has not changed.

But what can we cling to—what stability is there in our chaotic environment if we abandon the premises on which the old culture is based? To this I would answer that it is precisely these premises that have generated our chaotic environment. I recognize the desperate longing in America for stablity, for some fixed reference point when all else is swirling about in endless flux. But to cling to old-culture premises is the act of a hopeless addict, who, when his increasingly expensive habit has destroyed everything else in his life, embraces his destroyer more fervently than ever. The radical change I am suggesting here is only the reinstatement of stability itself. It may appear highly unappealing, like all cold-turkey cures, but nothing else will stop the spiraling disruption to which our old-culture premises have brought us.

I am arguing, in other words, for a reversal of our old pattern of technological radicalism and social conservatism. Like most old-culture premises this is built upon a self-deception: we pretend that through it we actually achieve social stability—that technological change can be confined within its own sphere. Yet obviously this is not so. Technological instability creates social instability as well, and we lose both ways. Radical social change *has* occurred within the old culture, but unplanned and unheralded. The changes advocated by the new culture are changes that at least some people desire. The changes that have occurred under the old culture were desired by no one. They were not even foreseen. They just happened, and people tried to build a social structure around them; but it has always been a little like building sand castles in heavy surf and we have become a dangerously irritable people in the attempt. We have given technology carte blance, much in the way Congress has always, in the past, given automatic approval to defense budgets, resulting in the most gigantic graft in history.

How long is it since anyone has said: "this is a pernicious invention, which will bring more misery than happiness to mankind?" Such comments occur only in horror and science-fiction films, and even there, in the face of the most calamitous outcomes that jaded and overtaxed brains can devise, the audience often feels a twinge of discomfort over the burning laboratory or the lost secret. Yet who would dare to defend even a small fraction of the technological innovations of the past century in terms of human satisfaction? The problem is that technology, industrialism, and capitalism have always been evaluated in their own terms. But it is absurd to evaluate capitalism in terms of the wealth it produces, or technology in terms of the inventions it generates, just as it would be absurd for a subway system to evaluate its service in terms of the number of tokens it manufactured. We need to find ways of appraising these systems in terms of criteria that are truly independent of the systems themselves. We need to develop a human-value index—a criterion that assesses the ultimate worth of an invention or a system or a product in terms of its total impact on human life, in terms of ends rather than means. We would then evaluate the achievements of medicine not in terms of man-hours of prolonged (and often comatose) life, or the volume of drugs sold, but in terms of the overall increase (or decrease) in human beings feeling healthy. We would evaluate city planning and housing programs not in terms of the number of bodies incarcerated in a given location, or the number of millions given to contractors, but in terms of the extent to which people take joy in their surroundings. . . .

Lest I be accused of exaggeration, let me quote from a recent newspaper article: "How would you like to have your very own flying saucer? One that you could park in the garage, take off and land in your own driveway or office parking lot. . . . Within the next few years you may own and fly just such an unusual aircraft and consider it as common as driving the family automobile. . . ." The writer goes on to describe a newly invented vertical-takeoff aircraft which will cost no more to own and operate than a sports car and is just as easy to drive. After an enthusiastic description of the design of the craft he attributes its development to the inventor's "concern for the fate of the motorist," citing the inability of the highways and city streets to handle the increasing number of automobiles. The inventor claims that his saucer "will help solve some of the big city traffic problems"![2]

The inventor is so confident of the public's groveling submission to every technological command that he does not even bother to defend this outlandish statement. Indeed, it is clear that he does not believe it himself, since he brazenly predicts that every family in the future will own a car *and* a saucer. He even acknowledges rather flippantly that air traffic might become a difficulty, but suggests that "these are not his problems," since he is "only the inventor."[3] He goes on to note that his invention would be useful in military operations (such as machine-gunning oriental farmers and gassing students, functions now performed by the helicopter) and in spraying poisons on our crops.

How can we account for the lack of public resistance to this arrogance? Why does the consumer abjectly comply with every technologic-

2. Alvin Smith, *Boston Sunday Globe,* January 5, 1969.
3. One is reminded of Tom Lehrer's brilliant song about the rocket scientist:

"Once they are up who cares where they come down:
That's not my department," says Werner Von Braun.

The Nuremberg and Eichmann trials were attempts to reverse the general rule that those who kill or make wretched a single person are severely punished, while those (heads of state, inventors, weapons manufacturers) who are responsible for the death, mutilation, or general wretchedness of thousands or millions are generally rewarded with fame, riches, and prizes. The old culture's rules speak very clearly: if you are going to rob, rob big; if you are going to kill, kill big.

al whim, to the point where the seller scarcely bothers to justify it, or does so with tongue in cheek? Is the man in the street so punchdrunk with technological propaganda that he can conceive of the saucer as a solution to *any* problem? How can he greet with anything but horror an invention that will blot out the sky, increase a noise level which is already intense to unbearable levels, pollute the air further, facilitate crime immeasurably, and cause hundreds of thousands of horrible accidents (translating our highway death toll to the saucer domain requires the addition of bystanders, walking about the city, sitting in their yards, sleeping in their beds, or strolling in the park) each year? Is the American public really so insane or obtuse as to relish the prospect of the sky being as filled with motorized vehicles as the ground is now?

● ● ●

Furthermore, Americans are always hung over from some blow dealt them by their technological environment and are always looking for a fix—for some pleasurable escape from what technology has itself created. The automobile, for example, did more than anything else to destroy community life in America. It segmented the various parts of the community and scattered them about so that they became unfamiliar with one another. It isolated travelers and decoordinated the movement of people from one place to another. It isolated and shrank living units to the point where the skills involved in informal cooperation among large groups of people atrophied and were lost. As the community became a less and less satisfying and pleasurable place to be, people more and more took to their automobiles as an escape from it. This in turn crowded the roads more which generated more road-building which destroyed more communities, and so on.

The saucers will simply extend this process further. People will take to their saucers to escape the hell of a saucer-filled environment, and the more they do the more unbearable that hell will become. Each new invention is itself a refuge from the misery it creates—a new hero, a new heroin.

How far can it go? What new inventions will be offered the staggering American to help him blow up his life? Will he finally flee to outer space, leaving the nest he has so industriously fouled behind him forever? Can he really find some means to propel himself so fast that he will escape his own inventive destructiveness? Is the man in orbit—the true Nowhere Man, whirling about in his metal womb unable to encounter anyone or anything—the destiny of all Americans?

The old-culture American needs to reconsider his commitment to technological "progress." If he fails to kick the habit he may retain his culture and lose his life. . . .

Some resistance comes from the old culture's dependence upon the substitutes and palliatives that its own pathology necessitates. "Without all these props, wires, crutches, and pills," its adherents ask, "how can I function? Without the 'extensions of man' I am not even a person. If you take away my gas mask, how can I breathe this polluted air? How will I get to the hospital without the automobile that has made me unfit to walk?" These questions are serious, since one cannot in fact live comfortably in our society without these props until radical changes have been made—*until the diseases that necessitate these palliatives have been cured.** Transitions are always fraught with risk and discomfort and insecurity, but we do not enjoy the luxury of postponement. No matter how difficult it seems to engage in radical change when all is changing anyway, the risk must be taken.

Our servility toward technology, however, is no more dangerous than our exaggerated moral commitment to the "virtues" of striving and individual achievement. The mechanized disaster that surrounds us is in no small part a result of our having deluded ourselves that a motley scramble of people trying to get the better of one another is socially useful instead of something to be avoided at all costs. *It has taken us a long time to realize that seeking to surpass others might be pathological, and trying to enjoy and cooperate with others healthy, rather than the other way around.**

The need to triumph over each other and the tendency to prostrate ourselves before technology are in fact closely related. . . .

The essentially ridiculous premises of a competitive society are masked not only by technology, but also by the complexity of our economic system and our ability to compartmentalize our thinking about it. . . .

Our refusal to recognize our common economic destiny leads to the myth that if we all overcharge each other we will be better off.

This self-delusion is even more extraordinary when we consider issues of health and safety. Why are executives living in cities indifferent to the air pollution caused by their own factories, since it is the air they and their families breathe? Or do they all live in exurbia? And what of oil company executives: have they given up ocean beaches as places of recreation? Do they all vacation at mountain lakes? Do automobile manufacturers share a secret gas mask for filtering carbon monoxide out of the air? Are the families of canning company executives immune to botulism? Those of farming tycoons immune to insecticides?

These questions are not entirely facetious. To some extent wealth does purchase immunity from the effects of the crimes perpetrated to obtain it. But in many of the examples above the effects cannot be escaped even by those who caused them. When a tanker flushes its tanks

*Our italics, M. S. W. and E. R.

at sea or an offshore well springs a leak the oil and tar will wash up on the most exclusive beach as well as the public one. The food or drug executive cannot tell his wife not to purchase his own product, since he knows his competitors probably share the same inadequate controls. We cannot understand the irresponsibility of corporations without recognizing that it includes and *assumes* a willingness on the part of corporate leaders to endanger themselves and their families for the short-run profit of the corporation. Men have always been able to subordinate human values to the mechanisms they create. They have the capacity to invest their libido in organizations that are then viewed as having independent life and superordinate worth. Man-as-thing (producer) can then enslave man-as-person (consumer), since his narcissism is most fully bound up in his "success" as a producer. What is overlooked, of course, is that the old-culture adherent's success as a producer may bring about his death as a consumer. Furthermore, since the Nuremberg and Eichmann trials there has been a gradual but increasing reluctance to allow individuals to hide behind the fiction of corporate responsibility.

One might object at this point that the preceding discussion places so much emphasis on individual motivation that it leaves us helpless to act. We cannot expect, after all, that everyone will arise one morning resolved simultaneously to act on different premises, and thus miraculously change the society. Competitive environments are difficult to modify, since whoever takes the first step is extremely likely to go under. "The system" is certainly a reality, no matter how much it is composed of fictions.

An action program must thus consist of two parts: (1) a long-term thrust at altering motivation and (2) a short-term attempt to redirect existing institutions. As the motivational underpinnings of the society change (and they are already changing) new institutions will emerge. But so long as the old institutions maintain their present form and thrust they will tend to overpower and corrupt the new ones. During the transitional period, then, those who seek peaceful and gradual change should work toward liberal reforms that shift the incentive *structure* as motivations in fact change.

• • •

Let me give a concrete example of adjusting institutions to match motivational changes. It seems quite clear that a far smaller proportion of college graduates today are interested in careers of personal aggrandizement, compared with twenty years ago. Far more want to devote themselves to social problems of one kind and another, or to helping individuals who are disadvantaged in some way. This is surely a beneficial shift in emphasis—we perhaps do not need as many people as we once did to enrich themselves at our expense, and we have no place to put the overpriced junk we already have. But our old-culture institutions continually place obstacles in the path of this shift. Those who seek to provide services are often prevented by established members of the professions—such as doctors, teachers, and social workers—since the principle behind any professional organization is (a) to restrict membership and (b) to provide minimum service at maximum cost. . . .

We need to reward everyone *except* the money-hungry—to reward those who are helping others rather than themselves. Actually, this could be done very easily by simply eliminating the entire absurd structure of deductions, exemptions, and allowances, and thus taxing the rich and avaricious instead of the poor and altruistic. This would have other advantages as well: discouraging overpopulation and home ownership, and saving millions of man-hours of senseless and unrewarding clerical labor.

Reforms in the kinds of priorities involved in the disbursement of federal funds would also help. At present, almost 80 percent of the federal budget is devoted to life-destroying activities, only about 10 percent to life-enhancing ones. The ending of the war should be the first item on everyone's agenda, but even without the war there is much to be done in the way of priority changes. At present most government spending subsidizes the rich: defense spending subsidizes war contractors, foreign aid subsidizes exporters, the farm program subsidizes rich farmers, highway and urban redevelopment programs subsidize building contractors, medical programs subsidize doctors and drug companies, and so on. Some programs, like the poverty program, subsidize middle-class service-oriented people to some extent, and this is helpful. It is probably impossible to subsidize the poor themselves with existing techniques—such a profound reversal of pattern requires a more radical approach, like the negative income tax or guaranteed employment.

It must be made clear that we are not trying to make money-grubbers out of those who are not, but rather to restore money to its rightful place as a medium of exchange—to reduce the role of money as an instrument of vanity. . . .

Such a profound transformation is not likely to occur soon. Yet it is interesting that it is precisely the reversal of the incentive structure that is most feared by critics of such plans as the negative income tax. Why would people want to work and strive, they ask, if they could get all they wanted to eat without it? Why would they be willing to sell out their friends, sacrifice family ties, cheat and swindle themselves and everyone else, and disregard social problems and needs, if in fact they could obtain goods and services without doing these things? "They would have to be sick," we hear someone say, and this is the correct answer. Only the sick would do it—those who today when they have a million dollars keep striving for more. *But the non-sick would be free from the obligation to behave as if they were sick—an obligation our society presently enjoins.* It would not be made so difficult, if these proposals were carried out, for Americans to be motivated by something other than greed. People engaged in helping others, in making communities viable, in making the environment more attractive, would be able to live more comfortably if they wished. Some people would of course do nothing at all but amuse themselves, like the idle rich, and this seems to disturb people: "subsidized idleness," they call it, as if thus to discredit it. Yet I personally would far rather pay people *not* to make nerve gas than pay them to make it; pay them *not* to pollute the environment than pay them to do it; pay them *not* to inundate us with instant junk than pay them to do it; pay them *not* to swindle us than pay them to do it; pay them *not* to kill peasants than pay them to do it; pay them *not* to be dictators than pay them to do it; pay them *not* to replace communities with highways than pay them to do it, and so on. One thing must be said for idleness: it keeps people from doing the Devil's work. The great villains of history were busy men, since great crimes and slaughters require great industry and dedication.

Those skilled in social and political action can probably devise many more profound programs for defusing the perverse incentive structure our society now enjoys, but the foregoing will at least serve to exemplify the point I wish to make. As a general rule it can be said that every institution, every program in our society should be examined to determine whether it encourages social consciousness or personal aggrandizement.

Let us now turn to the question of long-range modifications in motivation. For no matter how much we try to eliminate scarcity assumptions from the incentive structures of our institutions, they will continue to reemerge if we do not devote some attention to reforming the psychic structures that our family patterns generate in children.

• • •

It is difficult . . . not to repeat patterns that are as deeply rooted in primary emotional experiences as these are, particularly when one is unprepared. The new parents may not be as absorbed in material possessions and occupational self-aggrandizement as their own parents were. They may channel their parental vanity into different spheres, pushing their children to be brilliant artists, thinkers, and performers. But the hard narcissistic core on which the old culture was based will not be dissolved until the parent-child relationship itself is de-intensified, and this is precisely where the younger generation is likely to be most inadequate. . . .

Breaking the pattern means establishing communities in which (a) children are not socialized exclusively by their parents, (b) parents have lives of their own and do not live vicariously through their children, hence (c) life is lived for the present, not the future, and hence (d) middle-aged and elderly people participate in the community. This constellation of traits forms a coherent unit, as does its opposite.

• • •

What the new culture seeks is wholeness, and obviously it cannot achieve this by exclusion. A community that does not have old people and children, white-collar and blue-collar, eccentric and conventional, and so on, is not a community at all, but the same kind of truncated and deformed monstrosity that most people inhabit today.

What I have been saying may sound excessively utopian even to those adults who feel drawn to the new culture. Can any middle-aged person, trained as he is in the role considered appropriate to his age, find anything in the new culture to which he can attach himself without feeling absurd? Can he "act his age" in the new culture? There are indeed severe contradictions between the two, but syntheses are also to be found. Adults in encounter groups usually discover that much of what is new-culture is not at all alien or uncomfortable for them. There are many roles that can and must be carved out for older people, for otherwise we will still have the same kind of ice-floe approach to the aged that we now have.

• • •

Americans have always entertained the strange fantasy that change can occur easily and without pain. This pleasant idea springs from a confusion between change (the alteration of behavior patterns) and novelty (the rotation of stimuli within a pattern). Americans talk about social change as if it involved nothing more than rearranging the contents of a display window. But real change is difficult and painful, which perhaps explains why Americans have abandoned all responsibility for initiating it to technology and the rotation of generations.

Given general recognition by old-culture adherents of the necessity for change, and equally general commitment to it, there is no particular reason why the United States could not become the center of the most beautiful, benign, and exciting culture the world has ever known. We have always been big, and have done things in big ways; having lately become in many ways the worst of societies we could just as easily become the best. No society, after all, has ever solved the problems that now confront us. Potentiality has always been our most attractive characteristic, which is one reason why we have always been so reluctant to commit ourselves to finally realizing it. But perhaps the time has come to make that commitment—to abandon our adolescent dreams of omnipotentiality and demonstrate that we actually *can* create a palatable society. . . .

INTIMATE BEHAVIOUR
Desmond Morris

In the next reading, Desmond Morris argues that tactile contact with people is natural and necessary for healthy personal development. Yet in many ways our society and cultural beliefs inhibit such intimacy. Parents are, for example, afraid of spoiling their children; and friends are afraid of implying sexual interest. In addition, conditions of increasing social density breed interpersonal hostility and distrust, feelings not conducive to intimacy. As a result, the need for various palliatives for human contact are sought. Morris sees these artificial substitutes as ineffectual, however, and their proliferation as pathological. How can we as a society overcome these inhibitions and obtain the intimate contact we need? Morris suggests that today's freer attitudes toward affectionate child-rearing is one step. Another is the encounter group movement, which encourages adults to shed their inhibitions to touch and reach out to their companions.

We are born into an intimate relationship of close bodily contact with our mothers. As we grow, we strike out into the world and explore, returning from time to time to the protection and security of the maternal embrace. At last we break free and stand alone in the adult world. Soon we start to seek a new bond and return again to a condition of intimacy with a lover who becomes a mate. Once again we have a secure base from which to continue our explorations.

If, at any stage in this sequence, we are poorly served by our intimate relationships, we find it hard to deal with the pressures of life. We solve the problem by searching for substitutes for intimacy. We indulge in social activities that conveniently provide us with the missing body contacts, or we use a pet animal as a stand-in for a human partner. Inanimate objects are enlisted to play the vacant role of the intimate companion, and we are even driven to the extreme of becoming intimate with our own bodies, caressing and hugging ourselves as if we were two people.

These alternatives to true intimacy may, of course, be used as pleasant additions to our tactile lives, but for many they become sadly necessary replacements. The solution seems obvious enough. If there is such a strong demand for intimate contact on the part of the typical human adult, then he must relax his guard and open himself more easily to the friendly approaches of others. He must ignore the rules that say, "Keep yourself to yourself, keep your distance, don't touch, don't let go, and never show your feelings." Unfortunately, there are several powerful factors working against this simple solution. Most important of these is the unnaturally enlarged and overcrowded society in which he lives. He is surrounded by strangers and semi-strangers whom he cannot trust, and there are so many of them that he cannot possibly establish emotional bonds with more than a minute fraction of them. With the rest, he must restrict his intimacies to a minimum. Since they are so close to him physically, as he moves about in his day-to-day affairs, this requires an unnatural degree of restraint. If he becomes good at it, he is likely to become increasingly inhibited in *all* his intimacies, even those with his loved ones.

In this body-remote, anti-intimate condition the modern urbanite is in danger of becoming a bad parent. If he applies his contact restraint to his offspring during the first years of their life, then he may cause irreversible damage to their ability to form strong bonds of attachment later on. If, in seeking justification for his inhibited parental behaviour, he (or she) can find some official blessing for such restraint, then it will, of course, help to ease the parental conscience. Unhappily, such blessings have occasionally been forthcoming and have contributed harmfully to the growth of personal relationships within the family.

One example of this type of advice is so extreme that it deserves special mention. The Watsonian method of child-rearing, named after its perpetrator, an eminent American psychologist, was widely followed earlier in this century. In order to get the full flavour of his advice to parents, it is worth quoting him at some length. Here are some of the things he said:

> Mothers just don't know, when they kiss their children and pick them up
> and rock them, caress them and jiggle them upon their knee, that they are

slowly building up a human being totally unable to cope with the world it must later live in. . . . There is a sensible way of treating children. Treat them as though they were young adults. . . . Never hug or kiss them, never let them sit on your lap. If you must, kiss them once on the forehead when they say goodnight. . . . Can't a mother train herself to substitute a kindly word, a smile, in all of her dealings with the child, for the kiss and the hug, the pickup and the coddling? . . . If you haven't a nurse and cannot leave the child, put it out in the backyard a large part of the day. Build a fence around the yard so that you are sure no harm can come to it. Do this from the time it is born. . . . If your heart is too tender and you must watch the child, make yourself a peephole so that you can see it without being seen, or use a periscope. . . . Finally, learn not to talk in endearing and coddling terms.

Since this was described as treating a child like a young adult, the obvious implication is that the typical Watsonian adults never kiss or hug one another either, and spend their time viewing one another through metaphorical peepholes. This is, of course, precisely what we are all driven to do with the *strangers* who surround us in our daily lives, but to find such conduct seriously recommended as the correct procedure between parents and their babies is, to say the least, remarkable.

The Watsonian approach to child-rearing was based on the behaviourist view, to quote him again, that in man "There are no instincts. We build in at an early age everything that is later to appear . . . there is nothing from within to develop." It therefore followed that to produce a well-disciplined adult it was necessary to start with a well-disciplined baby. If the process was delayed, then "bad habits" might start to form which would be difficult to eradicate later.

This attitude, based on a totally false premise concerning the natural development of human behaviour in infancy and childhood, would merely be a grotesque historical curiosity were it not for the fact that it is still occasionally encountered at the present day. But because the doctrine lingers on, it requires closer examination. The main reason for its persistence is that it is, in a way, self-perpetuating. If a tiny baby is treated in this unnatural manner it becomes basically insecure. Its high demand for bodily intimacy is repeatedly frustrated and punished. Its crying goes unheeded. But it adapts, it learns—there is no choice. It becomes trained and it grows. The only snag is that it will find it hard ever to trust anyone again, in its entire life. Because its urge to love and be loved was blocked at such a primary stage, the mechanism of loving will be permanently damaged. Because its relationship with its parents was carried on like a business deal, all its later personal involvements will proceed along similar lines. It will not even enjoy the advantage of being able to behave like a cold automaton, because it will still feel the basic biological urge to love welling inside it, but will be unable to find a way of letting it out. Like a withered limb that could not be fully amputated, it will go on aching. If, for conventional reasons, such an individual then marries and produces offspring, the latter will stand a high chance of being treated in the same way, since true parental loving will now, in its turn, have become virtually impossible. This is borne out by experiments with monkeys. If an infant monkey is reared without loving intimacies with its mother, it later becomes a bad parent.

For many human parents the Watsonian regime appeared attractive, but far too extreme. They therefore employed a softened, modified version of it. They would be stern with their baby one moment, then give in the next. In some ways they applied rigid discipline, in others they coddled it. They left it to cry in its cot, but they gave it lots of expensive toys and cooed over it at other times. They forced it into early toilet training, but they kissed and cuddled it. The result, of course, was a totally confused baby which grew into what was called a "spoilt child." The fundamental error was then made of ascribing the "spoiltness," not to the confusion, or to the early baby-stage disciplinary elements, but entirely to the moments of "softness." If only they had stuck to the rigid regime and not given in so often, the parents told themselves, then all would have been well. The growing child, now being awkward and demanding, was therefore told to "behave itself," and discipline was strengthened. The result, at this stage and later, was tantrum and rebellion.

Such a child had seen what love was, in those early "softer" moments, but, having been shown the entrance, had then had the gate repeatedly slammed in its face. It knew how to love, but it had not been loved enough, and in its later rebellions it repeatedly tested its parents, hoping to prove at last that they loved it no matter what it did—that they loved it for itself and not for its "good behaviour." All too often it got the wrong answer.

Even when it got the right answer, and the parents forgave its latest outrage, it still could not believe that all was well. The early imprints were too deeply engraved, the early, intermittent disciplines too unloving for a baby's mind. So it tested them again, going further and further in its desperate attempt to prove that, after all, they really did love it. Then the parents, faced with chaos, either finally applied strict discipline and confirmed the child's darkest fears, or they gave in over and over again, condoning increasingly anti-social acts out of a sense of dawning guilt—"Where did we go wrong, how have we failed? We have given you everything."

All this could have been avoided if only the baby had been treated as a baby in the first place, instead of a "young adult." During the first years of life, an infant requires total love, nothing less. It is not "trying to get the better of you," but it does need the best of you. If the mother is unstressed, and has not herself been warped in infancy, she will have a natural urge to give her best, which is why, of course, the disciplinarian has to repeatedly warn mothers against giving in to those tender "weaknesses" that "tug at their heart-strings," to use a favourite Watsonian phrase. If the mother *is* under pressure, as a result of our modern way of life, it will not be so easy; but even so, without an artificially imposed regime, it is still not impossible to come close enough to the ideal to produce a happy and well-loved baby.

Far from growing into a "spoilt child," such an infant will then be able to mature into an increasingly independent individual, remaining loving, but with no inhibitions about investigating the exciting world around it. The early months gave it the assurance that there is a truly safe and secure base from which to venture forth and explore. . . . Experiments with monkeys bear this out. The infant of a loving monkey mother readily moves off to play and test the environment. The offspring of a non-loving mother is shy and nervous. This is the exact opposite of the Watsonian prediction, which expects that an "excess" of early loving, in the intimate, bodily sense, will make for a soft, dependent creature in later years. The lie to this can even be seen by the time the human child has reached the third year of life. The infant that was lavished with love during its first two years already begins to show its paces, launching out into the world with great, if unsteady, vigour. If it falls flat on its face it is not more, but less, likely to cry. The infant that was less loved and more disciplined as a tiny baby is already less adventurous, less curious about what it sees, and less inclined to start making the first fumbling attempts at independent action.

In other words, once a totally loving relationship has been established in the first two years of life, the infant can readily move on to the next stage in its development. As it grows, however, its headlong rush to explore the world *will,* at this later phase, require some discipline from the parents. What was wrong at the baby stage now becomes right. The Watsonian distaste for the doting, over-protective parents of *older* children has some justification, but the irony is that where protection of this type occurs to excess, it is probably a reaction against the damage caused by earlier Watsonian baby-training. The child that was a fully loved baby is less likely to provoke such behaviour.

During later life the adult who, as a baby, formed a strong bond of attachment with its parents in the primary phase of total love, will also be better equipped to make a strong sexual bond of attachment as a young adult and, from this new "safe base," continue to explore and lead an active, outgoing, social life. It is true that, in the stage before an adult bond of attachment has formed, he or she will be much more sexually exploratory as well. All exploring will have been accentuated, and the sexual sphere will be no exception. But if the individual's early life has been allowed to pass naturally from stage to stage, then the sexual explorations will soon lead to pair-formation and the growth of a powerful emotional bond, with a full return to the extensive body intimacies typical of the loving baby phase.

Young adults who establish new family units and enjoy uninhibited intimacies within them will be in a much better position to face the harsh, impersonal world outside. Being in a "bond-ful," rather than a bond-starved, condition, they will be able to approach each type of social encounter in its own terms and not make inappropriate, bond-hungry demands in situations which, inevitably, will so often require emotional restraint.

One aspect of family life that cannot be overlooked is the need for privacy. It is necessary to have private space in order to enjoy intimate contacts to the full. Severe overcrowding in the home makes it difficult to develop any kind of personal relationship except a violent one. Bumping into one another is not the same as performing a loving embrace. Forced intimacy becomes anti-intimate in the true sense, so that, paradoxically, we need more space to give body contact greater meaning. Tight architectual planning that ignores this fact creates unavoidable emotional tension. For personal body intimacy cannot be a permanent condition, like the persistent impersonal crowding of the urban world outside the home. The human need for close bodily contact is spasmodic, intermittent, and only requires occasional expression. To cramp the home-space is to convert the loving touch into a suffocating body proximity. If this seems obvious enough, then it is hard to understand the lack of attention that has been given to private home-space by the planners of recent years.

In painting this picture of the "intimate young adults," I may have given the impression that, if only they can acquire an adequate private home-space, have a loving infancy behind them, and have formed strong new bonds of attachment to one another, then all will be well. Sadly, this is not the case. The crowded modern world can still encroach on their relationship and inhibit their intimacies. There are two powerful social attitudes that may influence them. The first is the one that uses the word "infantile" as an insult. Extensive body intimacies are criticized as regressive, soft or babyish. This is something that can easily deter a potentially loving young adult. The suggestion that to be too intimate constitutes a threat to his independent spirit, summed up in such sayings as "the strongest man is the man who stands alone," begins to make an impact. Needless to say, there is no evidence that for an adult to indulge in body contacts typical of the infant stage of life necessarily means he will find his independence impaired at other times. If anything, the contrary is the case. The soothing and calming effects of gentle intimacies leave the individual freer and better equipped emotionally to deal with the more remote, impersonal moments of life. They do not soften him, as has so often been claimed; they strengthen him, as they do with the loved child who explores more readily.

The second social attitude that tends to inhibit intimacies is the one which says that bodily contact implies sexual interest. This error has been the cause of much of the intimacy restraint that has been needlessly applied in the past. There is nothing implicitly sexual about the intimacies between parent and child. Parental love and infantile love are not sexual love, nor need the love between two men, two women, or even between a particular man and a particular woman be sexual. Love is love — an emotional bond of attachment — and whether sexual feelings enter into it or not is a secondary matter. In recent times we have somehow come to overstress the sexual element in all such bonds. If a strong, primarily non-sexual bond exists, but with minor sexual feelings accompanying it, the latter are automatically seized upon and enlarged out of all proportion in our thinking. The result has been a massive inhibition of our non-sexual body intimacies, and this has applied to relationships with our parents and offspring (beware, Oedipus!), our siblings (beware, incest!), our close same-sex friends (beware, homosexuality!), our close opposite-sex friends (beware, adultery!), and our many casual friends (beware, promiscuity!). All of this is understandable, but totally unnecessary. What it indicates is that in our true sexual relationships we are, perhaps, not enjoying a sufficiently erotically exhausting degree of body intimacy. If our pair-bond sexual intimacies were intensive and extensive enough, then there should be none left over to invade the other types of bond relationships, and we could all relax and enjoy them more than we seem to dare to do at present. If we remain sexually inhibited or frustrated with our mates, then of course the situation is quite different.

The general restraint that is applied to non-sexual body contacts in modern life has led to some curious anomalies. For example, recent American studies have revealed that in certain instances women are driven to use random sex simply for the purpose of being held in someone's arms. When questioned closely, the women admitted that this was sometimes their sole purpose in offering themselves sexually to a man, there being no other way in which they could satisfy their craving for a close embrace. This illustrates with pathetic clarity the distinction between sexual and non-sexual intimacy. Here there is no question of body intimacy leading to sex, but of sex leading to body intimacy, and this complete reversal leaves no doubt about the separation between the two.

These, then, are some of the hazards facing the modern intimate adult. To complete this survey of intimate human behaviour, it remains to ask what signs of change there are in the attitudes of contemporary society.

At the infant level, thanks to much painstaking work by child psychologists, a greatly improved approach to the problems of child-rearing is being developed. A much better understanding now exists of the nature of parent/offspring attachments, and of the essential role that warm loving takes in the production of a healthy growing child. The rigid, ruthless disciplines of yesterday are on the wane. However, in our more overcrowded urban centres, the ugly phenomenon of the "battered baby syndrome" remains with us to remind us that we still have a long way to go.

At the level of the older child, constant gradual reforms are taking place in educational methods, and a more sensitive appreciation is growing of the need for social as well as technical education. The demands for technological learning are, however, heavier than ever, and there is still a danger that the average schoolchild will be better trained to cope with facts than with people.

Amongst young adults, the problem of handling social encounters seems, happily, to be solving itself. It is doubtful whether there has ever before been a period of such openness and frankness in dealing with the intricacies of personal interaction. Much of the criticism of the conduct of young adults, on the part of the older generation, stems from a heavily disguised envy. It remains to be seen, however, how well the new-found freedom of expression, sexual honesty and disinhibited intimacies of present-day youth survive the passage of time and approaching parenthood. The increasingly impersonal stresses of later adult life may yet take their toll.

Amongst older adults there is clearly a growing concern about the survival of resolved personal life inside the ever-expanding urban communities. As public stress encroaches more and more on private living, a mounting alarm can be felt concerning the nature of the modern human condition. In personal relationships, the word "alienation" is constantly heard, as the heavy suits of emotional armour, put on for social battle in the streets and offices, become increasingly difficult to remove at night.

In North America, the sounds of a new rebellion against this situation can now be heard. A new movement is afoot, and it provides an eloquent proof of the burning need that exists in our modern society for a revision of our ideas concerning body contact and intimacy. Known in general terms as "Encounter Group Therapy," it has appeared only in the last decade, beginning largely in California and spreading rapidly to many centres in the United States and Canada. Referred to in American slang as "Bod Biz" (for "show business" read "body business"), it goes under a number of official titles, such as "Transpersonal Psychology," "Multiple Psychotherapy" and "Social Dynamics."

The principal common factor is the bringing together of a group of adults for sessions lasting from roughly one day to one week, in which they indulge in a wide variety of personal and group interactions. Although some of these are largely verbal, many are non-verbal and concentrate instead on body contacts, ritual touchings, mutual massage, and games. The aim is to break down the facade of civilized adult conduct, and to remind people that they "do not *have* bodies; they *are* bodies."

The essential feature of these courses is that inhibited adults are encouraged to play like children again. The avant-garde scientific atmosphere licenses them to behave in an infantile manner without embarrassment or fear of ridicule. They rub, stroke and tap one another's bodies; they carry one another around in their arms and anoint one another with oil; they play child-like games and they expose themselves naked to one another, sometimes literally, but usually metaphorically.

This deliberate return to childhood is explicitly expressed in the following words, in connection with a four-day course entitled "Become as You Were":

> The adjusted American achieves a dubious state of "maturity" by burying many child parts under layers of shame and ridicule. Relearning how to be a child may enrich the man's experience of being masculine and the woman's experience of being feminine. Re-experiencing being child with mother may shed light on one's approaches to loving, love-making and love-seeking. Paradoxically, making contact with childish helplessness releases surges of power and contacting childish tears opens the channels for expression and joy.

Other similar courses called "Becoming More Alive through Play" and "Sensory Reawakening: Rebirth" also emphasize the need to return to the intimacies of childhood. In some cases the process is taken even further with the use of "womb-pools" kept at precisely uterine temperature.

The organizers of these courses refer to them as "therapy for normal people." The visitors are not patients; they are group members. They go there because they are urgently seeking some way of finding a return to intimacy. If it is sad to think that modern, civilized adults should need official sanction to touch one another's bodies, then it is at least reassuring that they are sufficiently aware that something has gone wrong to actively do something about it. Many of the people who have been through such sessions repeatedly return for more, since they find themselves loosening up emotionally and unwinding in the course of the ritual body contacts. They report a sense of release and a growing feeling of warmth in connection with their personal interactions at home.

Is this a valuable new social movement, a passing fad, or a dangerous, new, drugless addiction? With dozens of new centres opening up every month, expert opinions are varied. Some psychologists and psychiatrists vigorously support the encounter-group phenomenon, others do not. One argues that group members "don't improve—they just get a maintenance dose of intimacy." If this is true, then even so the courses may at least see certain individuals through a difficult phase in their social lives. This puts group attendance at the intimacy level of going dancing, or going to bed with a cold and being comforted there, but there is nothing wrong with that. It merely adds one more string to the bow of a person seeking a "licensed to touch" context. Other criticisms, however, are more severe. "The techniques that are supposed to foster real intimacy sometimes destroy it," says one. A theologist, no doubt sensing a new form of serious competition, comments that all that people learn in encounter groups is "new ways to be impersonal—a new bag of tricks, new ways to be hostile and yet appear friendly."

It is certainly true that, listening to the leaders of the movement talking to the general public about their methods and their philosophy, there is sometimes an unmistakable air of smug condescension. They give the impression of having discovered the secret of the universe, which they are gracious enough to impart to other, lesser mortals. This point has been stressed as a serious criticism by some, but it is probably no more than a defence against anticipated ridicule. It is reminiscent of the tactics of the world of psycho-analysis in earlier days. Like encounter-group veterans, those who had been through analysis could not help smiling smugly down at those who had not. But analysis is past this stage now, and if encounter groups survive the novelty phase, the attitude will no doubt change, as the new cult matures to become an accepted pattern.

The more severe criticism that the group sessions actually do serious harm has yet to be proved. "Instant intimacy," as it has been called, does, however, have its hazards for the returning devotee when he steps back, fully or partially "reawakened," into his old environment. He has been changed, but his home companions have not, and there is a danger that he may make insufficient allowance for this difference. The problem is essentially one of competing relationships. If an individual visits an encounter group, has himself massaged and stroked by total strangers, plays intimate games with them, and indulges in a wide variety of body contacts, then he is doing more with them than he will have been doing with his true "intimates" in his home setting. (If he is not, then he had no problem in the first place.) If—as will inevitably happen—he later describes his experiences in glowing detail, he is automatically going to arouse feelings of jealousy. Why was he prepared to act like that at the encounter centre, when he was so remote and untouching at home? The answer, of course, was the official, scientific sanction for such acts in the special atmosphere of the centre, but that is no comfort to his "real life" intimates. Where couples attend intimacy sessions together, the problem is greatly reduced, but the "back home" situation still requires careful handling.

Some have argued that the most distasteful aspect of the encounter groups is the way in which they are converting something which should be an unconscious part of everyday life into a self-conscious, highly organized, professional pursuit, with the act of intimacy in danger of becoming an end in itself, rather than as one of the basic means by which we can intuitively help ourselves to face the outside world.

Despite all these understandable fears and criticisms, it would be wrong to scorn this intriguing new trend. Essentially, its leaders have seen an increasing and damaging shift towards impersonality in our personal relationships and have done their best to reverse this process. If, as so often happens, by the "law of reciprocal errors," they are swinging the pendulum rather wildly in the opposite direction, then this is a minor fault. If the movement spreads and grows to a point where it becomes a matter of common knowledge, then, even for the non-enthusiasts, it will exist as a constant reminder that something is wrong with the way in which we are using—or, rather, not using—our bodies. If it does no more than make us aware of this, it will be serving its purpose. Again, the comparison with psycho-analysis is relevant. Only a small proportion of the general population have ever been directly involved in analysis, and yet the basic idea that our deepest, darkest thoughts are not shameful or abnormal, but are probably shared by most others, has permeated healthily throughout our culture. In part, it is responsible for the more honest and frank approach to mutual personal problems in young adults today. If the encounter-group movement can provide the same indirect release for our inhibited feelings concerning intimate bodily contact, then it will ultimately have proved to have made a valuable social contribution.

The human animal is a social species, capable of loving and greatly in need of being loved. A simple tribal hunter by evolution, he finds himself now in a bewilderingly inflated communal world. Hemmed in on all sides, he defensively turns in on himself. In his emotional retreat, he starts to shut off even those who are nearest and dearest to him, until he finds himself alone in a dense crowd. Unable to reach out for emotional support, he becomes tense and strained and possibly, in the end, violent. Lost for comfort, he turns to harmless substitutes for love that ask no questions. But loving is a two-way process, and in the end the substitutes are not enough. In this condition, if he does not find true intimacy—even if it is only with one single person—he will suffer. Driven to armour himself against attack and betrayal, he may have arrived at a state in which all contact seems repellent, where to touch or to be touched means to hurt or be hurt. *This in a sense, has become one of the greatest ailments of our time, a major social disease of modern society that we would do well to cure before it is too late.* If the danger remains unheeded, then—like poisonous chemicals in our food—it may increase from generation to generation until the damage has gone beyond repair.

In a way, our ingenious adaptability can be our social undoing. We are capable of living and surviving in such appallingly unnatural conditions that, instead of calling a halt and returning to a saner system, we adjust and struggle on. In our crowded urban world, we have battled on in this way, further and further from a state of loving, personal intimacy, until the cracks have begun to show. Then, sucking our metaphorical thumbs and mouthing sophisticated philosophies to convince ourselves that all is well, we try to sit it out. We laugh at educated adults who pay large sums to go and play childish games of touch and hug in scientific institutes, and we fail to see the signs. How much easier it would all be if we could accept the fact that tender loving is not a weakly thing, only for infants and young lovers, if we could release our feelings, and indulge ourselves in an occasional, and magical, return to intimacy.

THE GREENING OF AMERICA
Charles A. Reich

America is a Corporate State, Charles Reich argues, structured for the benefit of the business establishment, whose interests control the political structure, formal institutions, and the law. It pursues economic and technological progress, profits, maximum production, and consumption in opposition to such humanitarian ends as conservation, peace, safety, and liberty.

Reich calls for a revolution—for dismantling the Corporate State and for radically reordering our priorities and concerns. This revolution, however, must come not from altering formal structures but from altering our own lives and the values we hold. For the power of the Corporate State lies in our own subscription to its values. Once we re-educate ourselves to effect a "revolution of consciousness," the established structures of society will have to change in response.

*Our italics, M. S. W. and E. R.

From Charles A. Reich, *The Greening of America,* pp. 299–304, 306–8, 316–19, 336–43, 343–44, 346, 347, 348. Copyright © 1970 by Charles A. Reich. Reprinted by permission of Random House, Inc. and Penguin Books Ltd.

How can our society be changed? No matter how many people join the ranks of [a new] consciousness . . . the Corporate State seems likely to go on as before. There is no convincing plan, no political strategy, for turning new consciousness into something effective in structural terms. Quite the contrary: there is every reason to fear that the State is growing ever more powerful, more autonomous, more indifferent to its own inhabitants. But the liberals and radicals who despair because there is no plan or strategy are simply looking for the wrong thing. They would not recognize the key to dismantling the Corporate State even if they saw it. The Corporate State cannot be fought by the legal, political, or power methods that are the only means ever used up to now by revolutionists or proponents of social change. We must no longer depend wholly upon political or legal activism, upon structural change, upon liberal or even radical assaults on existing power. Such methods, used exclusively, are certain to fail. The only plan that will succeed is one that will be greeted by most social activists with disbelief and disparagement, yet it is entirely realistic—the only means that is realistic, given the nature of the contemporary State: revolution by consciousness.

Any discussion of the means of change must start with a recognition that our present course, including nearly a century of liberal and radical struggles by orthodox means, has brought us to the brink of an authoritarian or police state. Liberals and radicals both assume that this proves only that more of such efforts are needed. Is it not possible that they are wrong? Despite all efforts at reform by legal and political means, for the past twenty years we have helplessly watched the coming of a closed society. One mark of it has been the institutionalization of war. The Cold War, Korea, the Dominican Republic, Vietnam, are wars without beginnings or endings. They fade into one another. Perhaps the Vietnam War will "end," but more likely it will drag on and slowly merge into a broader but less flagrant pattern involving semipermanent hostilities in Southeast Asia—one aspect of a worldwide defense system for Fortress America. Inside our borders, our country may be a fortress as well. The National Commission on the Causes and Prevention of Violence has predicted a pattern of urban life in which cities will become places of terror and widespread crime, work and public activities will be conducted only under substantial police protection, and middle- and upper-class people will live either in fortified apartment buildings or suburbs, in either case protected by private guards, security devices, electronic surveillance devices, and armed citizens in cars supplementing the police.

One of the most clearly marked trends for over twenty years has been the decline in civil liberties. The condition of the Bill of Rights cannot accurately be measured by Supreme Court decisions; the real situation depends upon surveillance and arrest procedures, attitudes of public and private employers, the scope of free discussion on television and in the press, and other factors embedded deeply in the day-to-day working of society. At this level, there has been a steady increase in surveillance, wiretapping, spying, police actions that are "political" in nature; there has been a gradual acceptance of loyalty-security criteria for more and more jobs. There has been a steady monopolization of media of communication. The Bill of Rights is less and less of a shield between the citizen and the State.

An equally significant pattern is the growing aggressiveness of government toward its own citizens. The politicization of police across the country is an index of this; they have become a major political force, with an interest in promoting "law and order." Police, led by the FBI, seem to be independent of their civilian supervisors. With the support of government, repression is carried on in an ever more aggressive manner—with technology used against the populace, random arrests and clubbings, and politically motivated treatment in prison. Government, notably the Nixon and Reagan administrations, has become more partisanly militant, aggressively taking sides against one portion of the population. It seems eager to promote a polarization of America—a division in which a majority will feel bound by loyalty and patriotism to support the State.

The trend is toward our becoming two nations. The two nations will be separated from each other by mutual fear, by differences in consciousness and culture so deep that even communication will be impossible. California seems to be two nations already—a nation of the old and a nation of the young. The young feel that government might as well represent a foreign country, they are so detached from it. This pattern of two nations is becoming a familiar one in the world—two Germanies, two Chinas, two Koreas, two Vietnams, a United Nations that does not include the largest nation in the world. Why not two nations here in America—the nation of the peace marchers and the nation of the headlights?

This is the point we have reached after more than three decades of the liberal welfare state, after all the hard-fought battles for civil liberties, for civil rights, for reforms in government administration, for a more just society based on law. This is where we are after the liberals, the radicals, the humanitarians have tried to make a better nation by making a better political structure and by dedicating their own lives to this greater public interest. The political activists have had their day and have been given their chance. They ask for still more activism, still more dedication, still more self-sacrifice, believing more of the same bad medicine is needed, saying their cure has not yet been tested. It is time to realize that this form of activism merely affirms the State. Must we wait for fascism before we realize that political activism has failed?

All orthodox liberal and radical thinking about social change or revolution concludes that there are two main approaches to translating consciousness into effective action. The first is favored by the liberal establishment: using the existing legal, administrative, and democratic procedures to advance change. These are the "lawful channels" through which students and radicals have been advised to work. The second approach is based upon power. At one end of the spectrum, it merges with politics such as the Gene McCarthy movement—elect people who will change the course of society. At the other end of the spectrum is the radical concept of revolution, street fighting, mobilization of the Left. Under this approach, the State must be changed by getting together more power—political or physical—than now is in the hands of the "Establishment" or the "ruling class."

The experience of new consciousness people with established procedures has made clear what should have long been obvious: these procedures are not designed for social change except within the terms of the existing system; for more radical change they are a dead end. There remained the alternative of power—the revolutionary tactics of the New Left. But how could power succeed against the State? Power, in the second half of the twentieth century, resides in organization, in technology, in the machine. Whether or not we postulate a "ruling class" in Marxist terms, power is a function of organization, not merely of economic position. How, then, can those who oppose organization and the machine expect to win a fight where the field of battle is power? It is a fight on the enemy's ground. a fight which the Corporate State is sure to win. It is the street fighters against the tank, the automatic rifle, the helicopter. It can only come to disaster and defeat.

Neither lawful procedures nor politics-and-power can succeed against the Corporate State. Neither can prevent the steady advance of authoritarian rule. If the new consciousness sticks to these tactics, it will throw itself away on an ideology that fails to take account of its real power. The power is not the power of manipulating procedures or the power of politics or street fighting, but the power of new values and a new way of life.

For the road to a new society is there nonetheless. Consciousness is capable of changing and of destroying the Corporate State, without violence, without seizure of political power, without overthrow of any existing group of people. The new generation, by experimenting with action at the level of consciousness, has shown the way to the one method of change that will work in today's post-industrial society: changing consciousness. It is only by change in individual lives that we can seize power from the State.

Can this really work? Have we not said that the Corporate State is subject to no controls whatever, even by a majority of the people? And isn't there evidence of this in the continuance into 1970 of the Vietnam War, which was already so unpopular years earlier that President Johnson was forced to retire, and both candidates promised peace? Moreover, almost all New Left theorists, from Marcuse on down, agree that no revolution is possible in the United States at the present time. And many people believe that if anything happens, it will be a right-wing reaction that will smash whatever there is of the New Left. In the light of all of this, what power can we expect a new consciousness to have? How, after all we have said about the invulnerable power of the Corporate State, could change possibly be so simple?

•   •   •

The revolution must be cultural. For culture controls the economic and political machine, not vice versa. Consider production. Now the machinery turns out what it pleases and forces people to buy. But if the culture changes, the machine has no choice but to comply. For the willing buyer of whatever the machine produces is replaced by a buyer who buys only what he chooses. The machine is forced to obey, and the market power of buyers is restored. The machine has to turn out Beatles records, bell-bottom pants, or better hospitals. But to gain this power, the buyer must free himself from the power of advertising by developing a different consciousness. Once he does, the machine is his slave. Similarly, the employee liberates himself by turning his back on the institutional goals of advancement in the hierarchy, status, and security. He makes himself independent of the organization by a change of values, and the organization then loses the power over his individuality which it formerly had. Thus the machine can be mastered.

The essential point is that the political structure, the law, and the formal institutions of society are not the creative part of the Corporate State. They are merely its *administrative* department, and they administer whatever values there are to be administered. They do not have the power to change values; for one interested in basic change, law and political institutions are virtually irrelevant (except as theatres in which to stage exemplary battles of consciousness). Even a great political change, such as the New Deal, can accomplish nothing if there is no accompanying change of consciousness. On the other hand, the government of the Corporate State has proven unable to do anything whatever to stem the great cultural changes coming about with the appearance of [the new] consciousness. . . . The case of marijuana illustrates the government's complete lack of power over culture, *once it loses the ability to create false consciousness.* Government, then, is mere management (it is significant that President Nixon has seen it in this light). Culture is the substantive part of society. Thus social change, instead of beginning at the palace, comes up from below. The law and the government are not the first things to be changed, they are the last. Should [the new] consciousness . . . sweep the country, the federal government could simply be ignored until it became completely isolated from the people of the nation, and had no choice but to change. At that point, the President would have to don bell bottoms and a dirty T-shirt and go looking for his constituents.

The fact is that America still has, despite all we have said, a democratic form. Power is not exercised in this country by force of arms, as in some dictatorships. Power rests on control of consciousness. If the people are freed from false consciousness, no power exists that could prevent them from taking the controls.

Our form of government may be antiquated in many ways, but it still has enough flexibility to permit a determined people to make the necessary changes. Elected officials show a remarkable ability to change when their constituencies change; New York's Senator Goodell, a backward-looking man when he represented an upstate constituency, grew sideburns and became a vocal liberal as he became the representative of the entire state; whether this was mere necessity, a genuine case of education, or privately held principles finally emerging, matters less than the fact of change. The machinery of government is also capable of change once political power has shifted. A change in *public opinion* is not enough to accomplish this at any but the superficial level of liberal reform. But a change of consciousness can strike deeper; it need not abolish the State; it can master it, and require it to submit to new values and a new vision.

• • •

To bring the concept of revolution by consciousness from the level of theory to the level of action, we must return to our analysis of how the Corporate State actually works. As we have said, its motive power is supplied by a willing producer and a willing consumer. Thus the motivating power of the machine is found *within each of us.* More specifically, the motivating power is that portion of each individual's life in which he acts as a machine-part, namely, where he acts as a motivated producer or consumer. Revolution by consciousness can be accomplished when enough individuals change that part of their lives.

Let us first consider a change in the "consumer" motive force. Here the crucial point is that a mere change of opinion is not enough, nor is a change at the level of politics. Suppose that, noting that the national environment is being steadily destroyed by the works of man, we decide that there should be more conservation. If at the same time we continue to believe in the basic values of economic and technological "progress" no program for conservation will be effective; conservation will always be "too expensive" or contrary to the public interest. The values of technology and progress, which remain unquestioned, are the real destroyers of the environment, rather than man's carelessness or wantonness. Suppose, on the other hand, we subordinate "progress" to the value of conservation, as is now just beginning to happen in this country. Genuine victories for conservation will follow. For there has been a genuine change in values, not merely a surface change.

Other illustrations suggest the same conclusion. If we want auto safety but continue to believe in auto profits, sales, styling, and annual obsolescence, there will be no serious accomplishments. The moment we put safety ahead of these other values, something will happen. If we want better municipal hospitals but are unwilling to disturb the level of spending for defense, for highways, for household appliances, hospital service will not improve. If we want peace but still believe that countries with differing ideologies are threats to one another, we will not get peace. What is confusing is that up to now, while we have wanted such things as conservation, auto safety, hospital care, and peace, we have tried wanting them without changing consciousness, that is, while continuing to accept those underlying values that stand in the way of what we want. The machine can be controlled at the "consumer" level only by people who change their whole value system, their whole world view, their whole way of life. One cannot favor saving our wildlife and wear a fur coat.

The "producer" motive force operates within organizations and institutions. To change it one must change the way in which one performs one's role. Those who act in such a way as to seek promotion, expansion of the organization, increasing monetary rewards, and professional success and recognition are causing the wheel to turn. The professional who fights for good causes outside his role, but dutifully performs his function during the working day, is defeating his own efforts. He may favor more money for hospitals, but as a member of a business organization, he helps make his organization grow, at the expense of hospitals if necessary. What he should do is take the position, in his official capacity, that further growth of his organization is undesirable because of competing social needs. If he is in a company that makes cars or jets, he should take the position that corporate growth cannot be justified if it contributes to air and noise pollution. He does not have to be at the top of the hierarchy for his views to be felt. Galbraith, in *The New Industrial State,* has shown that power is not at the top of organizations; decisions come up from below. In acting in this way, the organization man may not earn himself a promotion or a bonus, but he probably will not get fired either. And he will have helped significantly to rechannel the power of the Corporate State.

We are suggesting a vital distinction between attempts to change the State from "inside" and from "outside." By "inside" we refer to any action that affects the motive power of the State—"consumer" or "producer." By "outside" we refer to efforts to change the State without slowing down its motive power. A campaign to save the redwoods, to ban the SST, or to improve public welfare administration, is an "outside" effort unless it either reaches people at the level of their way of life as consumers, or influences their way of life as producers, professionals, and members of organizations. Outside efforts have little effectiveness; the machine rolls on. Inside efforts—"consumer" or "producer"—*are* effective. The maxim is, act where you have power. When Americans refuse to buy what the State wants to sell—economically or politically—and refuse to produce by striving for the goals set by the State's organizations, the wheel will have no power to turn, and revolution by consciousness will have become a reality. A change in one's own way of life is an "inside" change.

•   •   •

The reason that "established procedures" presented these obstacles goes to the very essence of the liberal welfare state—what we have called the Corporate State. As we tried to show, the State rejects "conflict" in favor of administration; it defines only a small area as "political" and calls the outside area "deviance" that must be administered, controlled, treated, given therapy, cured, or if necessary, punished; but it cannot be recognized as "legitimate." Use of marijuana, occupation of "private" property for a public park, a sit-in in a university building, demand for non-faculty members as teachers, long hair, or the insistence on making an individual, nonreligious decision about the draft, were not issues that could find adequate expression within "established procedures." These procedures simply refused to recognize new consciousness attitudes or activities.

The political process was just as closed as "established procedures." The Vietnam War and the 1968 election furnish the best example, for it was not merely the younger generation, but a large segment of the country that wanted peace; but the political process produced opposing candidates who were equally unresponsive to this demand; the people never got a chance to vote for Gene McCarthy. An example that is even clearer, because more specific, is that of inequities in the draft laws; here a presidential commission of leading citizens made some very moderate proposals for reform to the Congress, proposals that surely could have won the support of a majority of the voters, but no action was taken. In short, even if the students could get "public opinion" on their side of a particular issue, it would make no substantial difference. What the students found was that America's political system, supposedly the sector of the State most subject to popular influence, is perhaps the most rigid and least "democratic" of all. It is far easier to get a change in mass-produced product or a change in religious ceremonies than a change in government policy. They began to feel that the people were not sovereign after all, that there was a power structure that blocked off democracy; they began to be aware of their own subjugation.

But these same "established procedures," which seem so impassable, may become a route to change if they are accompanied by even a partial change of consciousness. Sometimes the liberals *have* succeeded by working through structure. One example is in conservation. For a long time, it appeared that no legal safeguards could accomplish much for conservation. The forces of "progress" were just too powerful; the "lawful procedures" bent with the prevailing forces. For example, the Federal Power Commission, with jurisdiction over hydroelectric projects on rivers, was supposed to protect conservation values, but normally ignored them. Thus, when Consolidated Edison of New York applied to the FPC for approval of its plans to construct a facility on the Hudson River near Storm King Mountain, the FPC approved the facility, ignoring the pleas of conservationists based on damage to aesthetic and historical values. The conservationists appealed to the courts; under established precedents they should have lost. Instead, the Court of Appeals reversed the FPC. It held that the agency should have given greater weight to conservation values. The structure of the Corporate State gave way to a degree, and an era of greater legal deference to conservation began.

We could cite a catalogue of similar changes through established procedure, from the school segregation decision of 1954, to cases involving the rights of welfare recipients, to the setting up of black studies departments in some universities without any prior demonstration or protest efforts. On the other hand, we could also cite many structural changes which have accomplished virtually nothing. The New Deal is full of examples; to some extent the school segregation decision is an example; we are all familiar with examples of new student governments that are powerless, new television regulations that are meaningless, codes of procedure that are ignored by the police. The liberals then, produced all sorts of results: sometimes no change in structure, sometimes a change that had no meaning, sometimes a change that had profound meaning and signalled a major trend.

It should be clear by now that the controlling factor is consciousness. The liberals won when they influenced consciousness, or when consciousness was changing at the time of their victory. The Storm King case came at a time of changing consciousness regarding environmental values. In the United States Court of Appeals, the conservationists argued that environmental values should have been given more weight in the FPC's decision; they based this on their interpretation of the governing concept of "public interest." Thus their argument was explicitly an appeal for a change in consciousness with respect to "the public interest" and the relative weight of economic and environmental factors. To call it a "legal" argument merely means that it was addressed to a court, that it cited what Congress' original intention in passing the FPC Act must have been, that other court decisions were cited, and that it was claimed that the FPC failed to consider evidence put forward by the conservationists, all in an effort to show that environment was a factor that should be weighed.

The entire legal structure that we described as the backbone of the Corporate State is changeable once consciousness changes. Welfare administrators regarded unannounced midnight searches of recipients' homes as necessary to enforce the welfare laws; accordingly they deemed the searches reasonable and no violation of the constitutional prohibition against "unreasonable" searches. But arguments pointing out the importance of privacy and dignity to the individual welfare recipient succeeded in changing consciousness in this respect, and courts began to hold the midnight searches illegal. In the area of occupational licensing and other public benefits, the old theory was that denial or revocation required only the most abbreviated of procedures, because the license or benefit was a "gratuity." But after it was realized that such benefits were in fact extremely important and valuable, and that government actions such as revocation could be arbitrary and oppressive, the "law" began to change to require stricter hearing procedures, and more exacting substantive rules. In each of the above cases, it is possible to give a "legal" explanation of the change. But our point is that "legal" changes occur in precisely the same way as non-legal changes. The present concern and anxiety over domestically based nuclear missile systems is a marked change from previous acceptance of anything proposed by the military as "necessary" for the public interest. No courts and no laws are involved as of the present writing. But the process of argument is remarkable for its similarity to the Storm King case. The same process can be seen at work on the debate over money for domestic needs versus money for defense needs such as the missile system. The controlling concepts of "need" and "public interest" are given a new meaning as awareness and values change.

Changes in attitude with regard to conservation values, or privacy for welfare recipients, or defense spending, represent partial changes of consciousness. . . . As such they give us valuable data, almost on a par with scientific experiments, on how particular changes of consciousness can affect structure. The changes are mostly small and ineffectual, but the process is revealed. When a federal judge holds that the draft laws cannot discriminate against non-religious conscientious objectors, when the Howard Hughes organization begins to question underground testing by the Atomic Energy Commission, when oil pollution is viewed as a possible ground for halting offshore drilling, when the necessity of the Vietnam War begins to be questioned, we can start to gauge the power of changes in consciousness.

To work within established procedures thus can succeed only when a change of consciousness is caused by or accompanies the work. This is the hard test that must be met by those who choose this method of seeking change, as distinguished from trying to change people's way of life by direct means. Self-deception is easy. To work within established procedures without changing consciousness merely affirms the existing system. Yet revolution by consciousness can take place in the court room, the administrative hearing chamber, the committee meeting, as well as in a private home or on the streets.

One of the most potent means of revolution during the 1970's is "subversion" through culture. There are two aspects of this "subversion," and both are already evident throughout the mass media. The first approach is the most obvious: those who create the mass culture simply start introducing radical ideas. Music, the theatre, and the plastic arts have become major avenues of ideas critical of our society, and there seems to be nothing the state can do to prevent this. At least in the case of pop music, the radicalism of Dylan, of the Rolling Stones, of the Jefferson Airplane reaches a vast audience in a meaningful way. Even television is vulnerable, if the creative people who write and edit television shows are becoming radical. News broadcasts begin suggesting that something is wrong with our foreign policy, dramas and advertising imply a radical life style, hip and "suggestive" language appears in dialogue. The television censors may successfully keep "controversial" political discussions off the air, but there is little they can do against a changing culture, which flows into every cell of any cultural medium, even the media which are the main purveyors of false culture.

The second aspect of cultural subversion follows the lead of Pop Art, and simply begins making new uses of existing mass culture. These new uses do not need to be obviously satirical. It is not necessary to make fun of comic strip heroes. All that is necessary is to stop taking them seriously, and begin enjoying them on a new level. To paint a Campbell's Soup can is to transcend that particular aspect of culture, to see it objectively rather than be dominated by it. That does not make the object "beautiful" but it does take away the object's power over man, and perhaps man may even learn something from it, or get a little enjoyment from it. One can watch television, the news, the ads, the commentators, the dramas, and just laugh and laugh and laugh; all the power of television turns impotent and absurd.

Thus each individual who wants to see change come about has a wide choice of personal means. He can concern himself only with his own life. He can try to influence the "consumer" way of life and values. He can take a job or profession and try to bring about change from there. Or, in a position such as that occupied by a lawyer, he may attempt the complex and subtle task of introducing new consciousness directly into existing structure. Each individual must choose and experiment. What is common to all the choices is this: none involve assaults on the machine from "outside." All depend upon changing consciousness. All require, as their one indispensable element, changing one's own life first.

In contrast to the efforts of radicals to attack and remake structure, up to now an almost total failure, stands the success of those who have simply changed their lives. These people have started to live in their own way without waiting for structure, politics, or ideology to "be right." And as they have done this, structure and politics have begun to seem utterly irrelevant and absurd. The newspapers make their front page news, day after day, out of the speeches and actions of a few men in Washington whose thoughts are ludicrous, predictable, stereotyped, banal, and above all, boring; who are utterly out of touch with American society; who deserve, beyond anything else, to be ignored. Those who simply change their lives feel a magnificent sense of detachment. . . .

"Stoned" refers to the drug experience, but it also expresses an attitude toward life, a way of life, that has found the immense power inherent in changing one's own life, the power that comes from laughter, looseness, and the refusal to take seriously that which is rigid and nonhuman. To fight the machine is to experience powerlessness. To change one's life is to recapture the truth that only individuals and individual lives are real.

To the sincere and dedicated liberal or radical, especially the one who has spent many years, perhaps his whole life, in battling for liberty and against the State, the idea that massive, authoritarian power can best be fought by changing one's own life must seem puny and absurd. It must seem like lying down in front of a tank, or, worse yet, the weak and watery moralism of some frightened, timid, sycophantic preacher who enjoins us to reform ourselves while, outside, rampant evil rages unchecked. It is difficult for anyone who believes in action and social responsibility not to feel this; but even the most courageous battle is senseless if it mistakes the source of evil. We must answer the doubters by saying that their methods have failed and failed and failed, and that only changing one's own life confronts the real enemy.

• • •

How is changing one's way of life different from Christianity, which has failed over and over again for two thousand years? There is one crucial difference. Christianity asks men to give up power, aggression, and materialism for a promise of something better in another world, a world after death. And men have always chosen the here-and-now instead of the promise, no matter how real it was made to seem. Unlike Christianity, the new way of life proposes a better life now. It offers something that is immediately more satisfying—the sensual beauty of a creative, loving, unrepressed life. It offers something that is real, not remote. Christianity is just another form of giving up the present for some goal—a religious form of the very repression that characterizes technological man in the Corporate State. Perhaps Christianity was not always that way, but for most people that is what it has come to mean in practice. The state tells man to give up happiness in order to serve the State in one or another function, the church tells him to give up his present interest for something that will "serve all mankind."

· · ·

And so the way to destroy the power of the Corporate State is to live differently now. The plan, the program, the grand strategy, is this: resist the State, when you must; avoid it, when you can; but listen to music, dance, seek out nature, laugh, be happy, be beautiful, help others whenever you can, work for them as best you can, take them in, the old and the bitter as well as the young, live fully in each moment, love and cherish each other, love and cherish yourselves, stay together.

· · ·

Perhaps there are bad times ahead. Perhaps it will be necessary to seek shelter, to avoid unnecessary exposure, to struggle, to form small communes and communities away from the worst pressures, or to take jobs within the Establishment and try to preserve one's freedom nevertheless. But the whole Corporate State rests upon nothing but consciousness. When consciousness changes, its soldiers will refuse to fight, its police will rebel, its bureaucrats will stop their work, its jailers will open the bars. Nothing can stop the power of consciousness.

To the realists, the liberals and radicals and activists who are looking for a program and a plan, we say: this is the program and the plan.

There is a great discovery awaiting those who choose a new set of values—a discovery comparable to the revelation that the Wizard of Oz was just a humbug. The discovery is simply this: there is nobody whatever on the other side. Nobody wants inadequate housing and medical care—only the machine. Nobody wants war except the machine. And even businessmen, once liberated, would like to roll in the grass and lie in the sun. There is no need, then, to fight any group of people in America. They are all fellow sufferers. There is no reason to fight the machine. It can be made the servant of man. [The new] consciousness . . . can make a new society.

QUESTIONS FOR DISCUSSION

1. Do you agree with the depiction of societal dehumanization and pathology provided in these selections? Do you think the proposed solutions are feasible in industrial society? Why or why not?

2. How are the arguments of Bernard *et al.* and Morris related?

3. What do you think of Slater's position on the nature of social change? How does this differ from some of the folk theories of change heard on college campuses?

4. What are the apparent differences between Slater's and Reich's arguments? Regarding these differences, which argument do you support?

5. Do you agree with Reich that a "revolution by consciousness" would be effective? Why or why not?

6. The social pathology perspective presupposes that the well-being of a society can be judged objectively. Can it be cogently argued that such judgments only reflect the arbitrary values and interests of the analyst?

7. Do you think social pathologists idealize what society once was or could be? Are their solutions consequently unrealistic?

8. Summarize what you think are the major strengths and weaknesses of the social pathology perspective and the solutions it suggests.

SELECTED REFERENCES

Agel, Jerome, *The Radical Therapist: The Radical Therapist Collective,* New York: Ballentine Books, 1971.

Implications of the contemporary pathology perspective for the counseling profession are succintly delineated in a "Manifesto."

Chilman, Catherine S., *Growing Up Poor,* Washington, D. C.: U. S. Government Printing Office, 1966.

The traditional social pathology perspective is still popular among social workers. This book illustrates their use of the perspective in conceptions of the poor and the subsequent form that their proposed programs take.

Fromm, Erich, *The Revolution of Hope: Toward a Humanized Technology,* New York: Harper & Row, 1968.

Fromm assesses the pathology produced by modern technology, bureaucracy, and consumption, examining modern man's unfulfilled needs and the resulting symptoms. He suggests that a solution is possible through introspection, education, and the development of a new set of values in which a marketing orientation is replaced by a humanistic one.

Henderson, Charles Richmond, *Introduction to the Study of the Dependent, Defective, and Delinquent Classes and of Their Social Treatment,* Boston: D. C. Heath and Co., 1909.

This early book is important and influential in the development of the pathology perspective on social problems and their solutions.

Platt, Anthony M., *The Child Savers: The Invention of Delinquency,* Chicago: The University of Chicago Press, 1969.

This is a sociological history of how middle-class women in the late nineteenth century, oriented by the early pathology perspective, established a new legal institution, the juvenile court, and a new correctional institution, the reformatory, to accommodate the needs of youth.

Rosenberg, Bernard, Israel Gerver, and F. William Howton, *Mass Society in Crisis: Social Problems and Social Pathology,* New York: Macmillan, 1971 (2nd ed.).

This book of readings on social problems is organized around the viewpoint of contemporary social pathology. "Part Four: Solutions" (pp. 459–526) exemplifies how problems may be diagnosed from one perspective but solved from another.

3 SOCIAL DISORGANIZATION

Routine makes the business of daily living possible. It allows people to take for granted much of what they do and how they do it. Whatever is routine after a while usually comes to be viewed as morally warranted. Consequently, many people are morally offended when a particular routine is disrupted. They usually define the situation as a problem and try to solve it by devising a new routine.

Like social pathology, the social disorganization perspective deals with the regulation of behavior, but in a less individualistic manner. The social disorganization perspective locates social problems in the social structure. Thus, if behavior seems to be unregulated, the social disorganization perspective places responsibility not on the people involved but on the inadequacy of the rules which guide them.

Rules can be inadequate in a number of ways. Without rules, it is difficult to sustain a routine and go about the business of living. If rules exist but plainly contradict one another, a regulated social routine cannot survive either. Or if people follow clearly stated rules only to be frustrated rather than rewarded, then trouble is sure to follow. All of these situations can produce social problems. From the social disorganization perspective, then, difficulty in regulation is the major source of social problems.

GENERAL FEATURES OF THE SOCIAL DISORGANIZATION PERSPECTIVE

The place. It is possible that a primary, secondary, and advanced perspective on social disorganization exists in daily life, in government, and in academic sociology, respectively. Expressions such as "the best laid plans of mice and men gang aft a-gley" attest to the universal experience of social disorganization. Similarly, in government circles as well as in public media, the sociological concept of bureaucracy is employed to signify the case where complex organizations designed to achieve specific goals fail to do so. Though phenomena noted by the perspective of social disorganization are discussed and reacted to both in everyday life and in government circles, sociologists have elaborated upon the phenomena by giving it a name and a corresponding perspective. This is understandably the case since it is their task to find the common and general factors in a host of seemingly different kinds of problematic situations.

The attitude.   Social disorganization, as a refined sociological perspective, rests upon the *systemic* attitude. According to this, society consists of a complex whole made up of a number of interdependent parts. The part-whole relationship is the core of the systemic attitude. From this vantage point, it follows that problematic situations themselves are but indicators of larger changes taking place in the shifting part-whole complex. Given this concern with understanding the relationship in such a large social field, comprising a set of complex entities in a state of mutual dependence, there is little room for personalizing events. The analyst searches for generalizations describing how parts change in their relations to the whole and, reciprocally, how changes in the whole affect the parts. The very abstract notion of a social system aids the analyst in this search. And so the stance of the person who studies social problems from the perspective of social disorganization is purportedly objective, abstract, and nonevaluative.

The content.   Disturbances in the part-whole complex produce the content in the social disorganization perspective. Certain violated expectations produce a sense of unpredictability, disorder, frustration, discontent, disorientation, and meaninglessness. This sense of violated expectations comes from recurrent or sporadic disturbances in the rule-result relationship. Rules are assumed to produce intended results. In a state of social disorganization, the common-sense relationship between rules and results is disturbed in one of three ways: *normlessness, culture conflict,* or *breakdown.*

In normlessness, relevant rules are absent. In these circumstances, anything goes. The predictability that stems from recurrent correspondence between conformity with social rules and attainment of cultural goals is lacking. In a situation of normlessness people sense a loss of guidelines for action. They find they cannot count on themselves, their neighbors, the larger corpus of rules, and the usual results of social action. In situations such as natural disasters, panics, and riots, people experience momentary normlessness.

In culture conflict, rules are plentiful. Rules here cannot produce desired results, however, because the rules for a given situation are contradictory. Given the human strain toward consistency, one typical response to norm conflict is either inaction or withdrawal. Such conflicts accrue at points where cultures intersect. One example appears when there is mass immigration from one country to another.

In breakdown, although people may behave according to existing rules, they do not get the promised rewards. The customs of waiting and of taking turns hinge on rewards for conformity. Breakdown occurs when doubts are cast on the delivery of goods and services for which one has waited. Three examples are: middle-class women may shoplift because they have to wait too long for a salesclerk, recipients may riot in New York welfare centers when checks do not appear at their expected times and places, and people at rock concerts may riot when promoters sell more tickets than the number of seats.

Inconsistency exists in each of the three forms of social disorganization. In normlessness, the absence of social rules is inconsistent with one's past experience of social life; in culture conflict, rules are inconsistent with each other; and in breakdown, the rules are inconsistent with rewards. In all of these forms of disorganization, there is a reconstitution of the relations of the parts to the whole. Unless steps are taken to readjust an inconsistent rule-result relationship, disorganization is very apt to spread, calling into question the effectiveness of rules in other situations.

THE FORMULA

When all parts are in good working relation with one another and with the complex whole, there is social order. As any of these parts get out of phase with one another or with the whole, however, a number of disturbing situations—social problems when interpreted according to the social disorganization perspective—begin to occur. Restoration of order follows when the parts are brought into alignment with the whole. Language, doctrine, and recipe are all geared to accomplish this end.

The vocabulary. Key terms useful in describing and diagnosing problems according to the disorganization perspective are: *abrupt change, accelerating change, breakdown, complexity, conflict, consistency, control, coordination, cultural lag, demoralization, disaster, disintegration, disorder, disorientation, entropy, integration, lag, malfunction, malintegration, meaninglessness, normlessness, rapid change, rate of change, social change, social control, technological change.* The vocabulary of social disorganization seeks to capture the sense of violated expectations and lack of control, to call attention to the experience of inconsistency, and to suggest that contradictions between parts and whole define the source of social problems.

The beliefs and doctrines.   Sociologists, in developing the abstract perspective of social disorganization, have formalized a perspective of everyday life. The beliefs and doctrines of the social disorganization perspective rest on a widely shared set of tacit assumptions. The assumptions are:

a. There is no organized conduct without social rules.

b. Predictability in social life thus rests on social rules.

c. Social order requires consensus on rules.

d. Some consistency between ideas and actions is also essential.

e. Persistent inconsistency between ideas and actions leads to problem situations.

Consequently, the principal belief of those who regard social problems as signs of social disorganization is that life in society must be based on shared and consistent sets of meanings.

The recipe.   Prescriptions for remedial action follow from the assumptions of social disorganization. The remedial action works toward reestablishment of consistency between ideas and actions. Normlessness disappears with the appearance of a clear set of rules to govern the problem situations. Communities exposed to frequent natural disasters have reduced panic and looting by instituting procedures for maintaining order.

Culture conflict often results from rapid change, social or technological. One remedy is to slow down the rate of change. Another is to take steps to bring the parts of culture that are out of phase into mutual readjustment with the other changing parts. For example, immigrants can band together and set up rules for deciding what aspects of the host culture to integrate with their own. In this fashion, they can slowly assimilate into the host culture without forfeiting the culture they brought with them. Thus, they can maintain their ethnic identity and pride.

Breakdown appears to be soluble, at least theoretically, by centralization, coordination, and communication. For instance, when jurisdictions overlap or are unclear, services are either duplicated or not performed at all. The development of metropolitan governments, as Mitchell Gordon points out in one of the readings to follow, can streamline administration and deliver more and better municipal services at much less cost.

The recipe for resolving any social problem in accordance with the disorganization perspective can take one or more of the forms outlined above. Proposed solutions derived from this perspective involve assumptions, implications, justifications, and consequences. The principal assumption, of course, is that since social order is ultimately based on rules, inconsistency between ideas and actions lies at the heart of social problems. The main implication for any recipe is that it must strain toward a re-establishment of consistency in social relations. The justification is that such disturbing social situations require intervention if the desired consequence, the restoration of social order, is to be achieved.

THE HISTORY OF THE SOCIAL DISORGANIZATION PERSPECTIVE

Although laymen, writers, and statesmen have formulated ideas on the social world which are close to the style of thought of social disorganization, it remained for sociologists to formulate and develop a systematic conception of social disorganization, under which rubric could be subsumed numerous forms and varieties of social problems.

As sociology evolved in America, the social disorganization perspective was developed in an attempt to formulate a set of truly sociological concepts. As the sociologists were developing concepts to understand the structure and function of human groups, they came to see that these concepts also could be used to make some sense out of the bewildering array of social problems they saw about them. In applying their concepts, sociologists came to see that the source of social problems and their solutions does not simply lie in the moral character of individuals. Rather, they came to believe that the majority of social problems could be best understood by examining the elements of social order. Sociologists saw social rules as the basic constituent of social order. They went on to study the phenomena of rules as the critical aspect of social problems.

W. I. Thomas and Florian Znaniecki, major theorists of social disorganization, signaled the importance of rules when they said, "We can define social disorganization briefly as a *decrease of the influence of existing social rules of behavior upon individual members of the group.*"[1] For a generation or more, this definition was popular among American sociologists. Then other sociologists refined the concept of disorganization—for example, by distinguishing its various forms as culture conflict, breakdown, and normlessness.

Thomas and Znaniecki, for example, reported culture conflict to be the cause of high rates of alcoholism, crime, juvenile delinquency, mental disorder, and suicide among Polish immigrants. The rules that immigrants had brought with them were in sharp conflict with the rules of their new locale, and this produced numerous frustrations in the

---

1. W. I. Thomas and Florian Znaniecki, *The Polish Peasant in Europe and America,* Vol. 4, Boston: Richard G. Badger, 1918, p. 2.

course of daily life. Charles H. Cooley shaped the thought of numerous sociologists by discussing how secondary contacts in urban areas led the traditional primary groups of families and neighbors to lose hold on their members. In addition, his notion of formalism antedated current concerns with organizational disorganization that frustrates enterprise, members, and clients alike.[2] William F. Ogburn, in his concept of cultural lag, noted that technological changes outran the ability of groups and institutions to keep up and to adapt.[3] Consequently, the later ideas of lack of coordination and institutional malintegration derive from Ogburn's early concern with the effect of technology on social rules. These four men laid down the principal arguments and basic ideas that underlie the social disorganization thesis as we know it today.

At the present time, several points about this perspective seem clear. Fewer textbooks are now titled *Social Disorganization,* and the notion receives only passing mention in textbooks on social problems. This is largely because the concept is abstract and difficult to treat scientifically. At the same time, the phenomena highlighted by the social disorganization perspective seem to be increasing. Thus, social disorganization is still a viable perspective because its key terms, doctrine, content, and recipe continue to organize thinking about social problems and to give form to proposals for solving them. Ultimately, of course, the effectiveness of the social disorganization perspective in solving social problems can only be determined when programs formulated according to its recipe are instituted and their outcomes are systematically evaluated.

SUMMARY AND CONCLUSION

From the social disorganization perspective, social problems are considered against a backdrop of systemic social organization in which individuals and institutions act according to rules, in a predictable and coordinated way. When organized structures of guiding rules are absent or fail, behavior becomes unregulated, unpredictable, and uncoordinated, and social problems arise. This happens especially in situations of rapid social or technological change. In a situation of normlessness, there are no relevant rules of behavior one can look to for guidance. In a situation of culture conflict, different sets of competing and contradictory rules make coordination and accomplishment impossible, and leave one confused as to which set of rules to follow. In a situation of

2. Charles Horton Cooley, *Human Nature and the Social Order,* New York: Charles Scribner's Sons, 1902; *Social Organization,* New York: Charles Scribner's Sons, 1927.
3. William F. Ogburn, *Social Change,* New York: B. W. Huebush, 1922.

breakdown, guiding rules are available but following them does not bring the expected result.

From the social disorganization perspective, solutions consist of establishing a clear system of rules which are appropriate, consistent, and effective in coordinating action and producing desired results. From this perspective, it is assumed that direct intervention to establish these rules is justified, that the people involved will be disposed to adopt the new set of rules in their quest for predictability, and that as the social disorganization disappears so will the social problem.

THE POPULATION EXPLOSION

Kingsley Davis

The soaring rate of population growth in most parts of the world is recognized today as an imminent threat. In many countries concerned governments and private agencies, such as Planned Parenthood, have initiated programs for controlling population growth. Kingsley Davis predicts, however, that these attempts will fail because population control is being approached through "private solutions" (e.g. helping a family space their children) rather than through a reorganization of the societal features that compete with such attempts. In effect, a classic situation of culture conflict exists—norms regarding population control are juxtaposed with institutional norms that encourage traditional family structure and, concomitantly, childbirth. Thus, as Davis points out, more general changes in the economy, social structure, and culture are necessary to forestall the dismal projections regarding population. Davis provides specific recommendations that would help to avert disaster.

Throughout history the growth of population has been identified with prosperity and strength. If today an increasing number of nations are seeking to curb rapid population growth by reducing their birth rates, they must be driven to do so by an urgent crisis. My purpose here is not to discuss the crisis itself but rather to assess the present and prospective

From Kingsley Davis, "Population Policy: Will Current Programs Succeed," *Science,* 158 (10 November 1967), pp. 730–39. Copyright © 1967 by the American Association for the Advancement of Science. Reprinted by permission of the author and publisher.

measures used to meet it. Most observers are surprised by the swiftness with which concern over the population problem has turned from intellectual analysis and debate to policy and action. Such action is a welcome relief from the long opposition, or timidity, which seemed to block forever any governmental attempt to restrain population growth, but relief that "at last something is being done" is no guarantee that what is being done is adequate. On the face of it, one could hardly expect such a fundamental reorientation to be quickly and successfully implemented. I therefore propose to review the nature and (as I see them) limitations of the present policies and to suggest lines of possible improvement.

THE NATURE OF CURRENT POLICIES

With more than 30 nations now trying or planning to reduce population growth and with numerous private and international organizations helping, the degree of unanimity as to the kind of measures needed is impressive. The consensus can be summed up in the phrase "family planning." President Johnson declared in 1965 that the United States will "assist family planning programs in nations which request such help." The Prime Minister of India said a year later, "We must press forward with family planning. This is a programme of the highest importance." The Republic of Singapore created in 1966 the Singapore Family Planning and Population Board "to initiate and undertake population control programmes."[1]

As is well known, "family planning" is a euphemism for contraception. The family-planning approach to population limitation, therefore, concentrates on providing new and efficient contraceptives on a national basis through mass programs under public health auspices. . . .

What is wrong with such programs? The answer is, "Nothing at all, if they work." Whether or not they work depends on what they are expected to do as well as on how they try to do it. Let us discuss the goal first, then the means.

GOALS

Curiously, it is hard to find in the population-policy movement any explicit discussion of long-range goals. By implication the policies seem to promise a great deal. This is shown by the use of expressions like *population control* and *population planning*. . . . It is also shown by the characteristic style of reasoning. Expositions of current policy usually start off by lamenting the speed and the consequences of runaway population growth. This growth, it is then stated, must be curbed—by

1. *Studies in Family Planning*, No. 16 (1967).

pursuing a vigorous family-planning program.That family planning can solve the problem of population growth seems to be taken as self-evident.

• • •

When the terms *population control* and *population planning* are used, as they frequently are, as synonyms for current family-planning programs, they are misleading. Technically, they would mean deliberate influence over all attributes of a population, including its age-sex structure, geographical distribution, racial composition, genetic quality, and total size. No government attempts such full control. By tacit understanding, current population policies are concerned with only the *growth* and *size* of populations. These attributes, however, result from the death rate and migration as well as from the birth rate; their control would require deliberate influence over the factors giving rise to all three determinants. Actually current policies labeled population control do not deal with mortality and migration, but deal only with the birth input. This is why another term *fertility control,* is frequently used to describe current policies. But, as I show below, family planning (and hence current policy) does not undertake to influence most of the determinants of human reproduction. Thus the programs should not be referred to as population control or planning, because they do not attempt to influence the factors responsible for the attributes of human populations, taken generally; nor should they be called fertility control, because they do not try to affect most of the determinants of reproductive performance.

• • •

The actual programs seem to be aiming simply to achieve a reduction in the birth rate. Success is therefore interpreted as the accomplishment of such a reduction, on the assumption that the reduction will lessen population growth. In those rare cases where a specific demographic aim is stated, the goal is said to be a short-run decline within a given period. The Pakistan plan adopted in 1966[2] aims to reduce the birth rate from 50 to 40 per thousand by 1970; the Indian plan[3] aims to reduce the rate from 40 to 25 "as soon as possible"; and the Korean aim[4]

2. *Hearings on S. 1676, U.S. Senate, Subcommittee on Foreign Aid Expenditures, 89th Congress, Second Session, April 7, 8, 11* (1966), pt. 4, p. 889.
3. B. L. Raina, in *Family Planning and Population Programs,* B. Berelson, R. K. Anderson, O. Harkavy, G. Maier, W. P. Mauldin, S. G. Segal, Eds. (Univ. of Chicago Press, Chicago, 1966).
4. D. Kirk, *Ann. Amer. Acad. Polit. Soc. Sci.* **369,** 53 (1967).

is to cut population growth from 2.9 to 1.2 percent by 1980. A significant feature of such stated aims is the rapid population growth they would permit. Under conditions of modern mortality, a crude birth rate of 25 to 30 per thousand will represent such a multiplication of people as to make use of the term *population control* ironic. A rate of increase of 1.2 percent per year would allow South Korea's already dense population to double in less than 60 years.

One can of course defend the programs by saying that the present goals and measures are merely interim ones. A start must be made somewhere. But we do not find this answer in the population-policy literature. Such a defense, if convincing, would require a presentation of the *next* steps, and these are not considered. One suspects that the entire question of goals is instinctively left vague because thorough limitation of population growth would run counter to national and group aspirations.

• • •

Goal peculiarities inherent in family planning. Turning to the actual measures taken, we see that the very use of family planning as the means for implementing population policy poses serious but unacknowledged limits on the intended reduction in fertility. The family-planning movement, clearly devoted to the improvement and dissemination of contraceptive devices, states again and again that its purpose is that of enabling couples to have the number of children they want. "The opportunity to decide the number and spacing of children is a basic human right," say the 12 heads of state in the United Nations declaration. . . .

Logically, it does not make sense to use *family* planning to provide *national* population control or planning. The "planning" in family planning is that of each separate couple. The only control they exercise is control over the size of *their* family. Obviously, couples do not plan the size of the nation's population, any more than they plan the growth of the national income or the form of the highway network. There is no reason to expect that the millions of decisions about family size made by couples in their own interest will automatically control population for the benefit of society. On the contrary, there are good reasons to think they will not do so. At most, family planning can reduce reproduction to the extent that unwanted births exceed wanted births. In industrial countries the balance is often negative—that is, people have fewer children as a rule than they would like to have. In underdeveloped countries the reverse is normally true, but the elimination of unwanted births would still leave an extremely high rate of multiplication.

Actually, the family-planning movement does not pursue even the limited goals it professes. It does not fully empower couples to have only the number of offspring they want because it either condemns or disregards certain tabooed but nevertheless effective means to this goal. One of its tenets is that "there shall be freedom of choice of method so that individuals can choose in accordance with the dictates of their consciences,"[5] but in practice this amounts to limiting the individual's choice, because the "conscience" dictating the method is usually not his but that of religious and governmental officials. Moreover, not every individual may choose: even the so-called recommended methods are ordinarily not offered to single women, or not all offered to women professing a given religious faith.

Thus, despite its emphasis on technology, current policy does not utilize all available means of contraception, much less all birth-control measures. The Indian government wasted valuable years in the early stages of its population-control program by experimenting exclusively with the "rhythm" method, long after this technique had been demonstrated to be one of the least effective. A greater limitation on means is the exclusive emphasis on contraception itself. Induced abortion, for example, is one of the surest means of controlling reproduction, and one that has been proved capable of reducing birth rates rapidly. It seems peculiarly suited to the threshold stage of a population-control program — the stage when new conditions of life first make large families disadvantageous. It was the principal factor in the halving of the Japanese birth rate; a major factor in the declines in birth rate of East-European satellite countries after legalization of abortions in the early 1950's, and an important factor in the reduction of fertility in industrializing nations from 1870 to the 1930's.[6] Today, according to *Studies in Family Planning,* [7] "abortion is probably the foremost method of birth control throughout Latin America." Yet this method is rejected in nearly all national and international population-control programs. American foreign aid is used to help *stop* abortion.[8] The United Nations excludes abortion from family planning, and in fact justifies the latter by presenting it as a means of combating abortion.[9] Studies of abortion are being made in Latin America under the presumed auspices of popula-

5. J. W. Gardner, Secretary of Health, Education, and Welfare, "Memorandum to Heads of Operating Agencies" (Jan. 1966), reproduced in *Hearings on S. 1676 (5),* p. 783.
6. C. Tietze, *Demography* **1,** 119 (1964); *J. Chronic Diseases* **18,** 1161 (1964); M. Muramatsu, *Milbank Mem. Fund Quart.* **38,** 153 (1960); K. Davis, *Population Index* **29,** 345 (1963); R. Armijo and T. Monreal, *J. Sex Res.* **1964,** 143 (1964); Proceedings World Population Conference, Belgrade, 1965; Proceedings International Planned Parenthood Federation.
7. *Studies in Family Planning, No. 4* (1964), p. 3.
8. D. Bell (then administrator for Agency for International Development), in *Hearings on S. 1676 (5),* p. 862.
9. *Asian Population Conference* (United Nations, New York, 1964), p. 30.

tion-control groups, not with the intention of legalizing it and thus making it safe, cheap, available and hence more effective for population control, but with the avowed purpose of reducing it.[10]

Although few would prefer abortion to efficient contraception (other things being equal), the fact is that both permit a woman to control the size of her family. The main drawbacks to abortion arise from its illegality. When performed, as a legal procedure, by a skilled physician, it is safer than childbirth. It does not compete with contraception but serves as a backstop when the latter fails or when contraceptive devices or information are not available. As contraception becomes customary, the incidence of abortion recedes even without its being banned. If, therefore, abortions enable women to have only the number of children they want, and if family planners do not advocate—in fact decry—legalization of abortion, they are to that extent denying the central tenet of their own movement. The irony of anti-abortionism in family-planning circles is seen particularly in hair-splitting arguments over whether or not some contraceptive agent (for example, the IUD) is in reality an abortifacient. . . .

The questions of sterilization and unnatural forms of sexual intercourse usually meet with similar silent treatment or disapproval, although nobody doubts the effectiveness of these measures in avoiding conception. Sterilization has proved popular in Puerto Rico and has had some vogue in India (where the new health minister hopes to make it compulsory for those with a certain number of children), but in both these areas it has been for the most part ignored or condemned by the family-planning movement.

On the side of goals, then, we see that a family-planning orientation limits the aims of current population policy. Despite reference to "population control" and "fertility control," which presumably mean determination of demographic results by and for the nation as a whole, the movement gives control only to couples, and does this only if they use "respectable" contraceptives.

THE NEGLECT OF MOTIVATION

By sanctifying the doctrine that each woman should have the number of children she wants, and by assuming that if she has only that number this will automatically curb population growth to the necessary degree, the leaders of current policies escape the necessity of asking why women

10. R. Armijo and T. Monreal, in *Components of Population Change in Latin America* (Milbank Fund, New York, 1965), p. 272; E. Rice-Wray, *Amer. J. Public Health* **54**, 313 (1964).

desire so many children and how this desire can be influenced.[11,12] Instead, they claim that satisfactory motivation is shown by the popular desire (shown by opinion surveys in all countries) to have the means of family limitation, and that therefore the problem is one of inventing and distributing the best possible contraceptive devices. Overlooked is the fact that a desire for availability of contraceptives is compatible with *high* fertility.

Given the best of means, there remain the questions of how many children couples want and of whether this is the requisite number from the standpoint of population size. That it is not is indicated by continued rapid population growth in industrial countries, and by the very surveys showing that people want contraception—for these show, too, that people also want numerous children.

The family planners do not ignore motivation. They are forever talking about "attitudes" and "needs." But they pose the issue in terms of the "acceptance" of birth control devices. At the most naive level, they assume that lack of acceptance is a function of the contraceptive device itself. This reduces the motive problem to a technological question. The task of population control then becomes simply the invention of a device that *will* be acceptable.[13] The plastic IUD is acclaimed because, once in place, it does not depend on repeated *acceptance* by the woman, and thus it "solves" the problem of motivation.[14]

But suppose a woman does not want to use *any* contraceptive until after she has had four children. This is the type of question that is seldom raised in the family-planning literature. In that literature, wanting a specific number of children is taken as complete motivation, for it implies a wish to control the size of one's family. The problem woman, from the standpoint of family planners, is the one who wants "as many as come," or "as many as God sends." Her attitude is construed as due to ignorance and "cultural values," and the policy deemed necessary to change it is "education." No compulsion can be used, because the movement is committed to free choice, but movie strips, posters, comic books, public lectures, interviews, and discussions are in order. These supply information and supposedly change values by discounting superstitions and showing that unrestrained procreation is harmful to both

11. J. Blake, in *Public Health and Population Change,* M. C. Sheps and J. C. Ridley, Eds. (Univ. of Pittsburgh Press, Pittsburgh, 1965), p. 41.
12. J. Blake and K. Davis, *Amer. Behavioral Scientist* 5, 24 (1963).
13. See "Panel discussion on comparative acceptability of different methods of contraception," in *Research in Family Planning,* C. V. Kiser, Ed. (Princeton Univ. Press, Princeton, 1962), pp. 373–86.
14. "From the point of view of the woman concerned, the whole problem of continuing motivation disappears, . . ." [D. Kirk, in *Population Dynamics,* M. Muramatsu and P. A. Harper, Eds. (Johns Hopkins Press, Baltimore, 1965)].

mother and children. The effort is considered successful when the woman decides she wants only a certain number of children and uses an effective contraceptive.

In viewing negative attitudes toward birth control as due to ignorance, apathy, and outworn tradition, and "mass-communication" as the solution to the motivation problem,[15] family planners tend to ignore the power and complexity of social life. If it were admitted that the creation and care of new human beings is socially motivated, like other forms of behavior, by being a part of the system of rewards and punishments that is built into human relationships, and thus is bound up with the individual's economic and personal interests, it would be apparent that the social structure and economy must be changed before a deliberate reduction in the birth rate can be achieved. As it is, reliance on family planning allows people to feel that "something is being done about the population problem" without the need for painful social changes.

• • •

We thus see that the inadequacy of current population policies with respect to motivation is inherent in their overwhelmingly family-planning character. Since family planning is by definition private planning, it eschews any societal control over motivation. It merely furnishes the means, and, among possible means, only the most respectable. Its leaders, in avoiding social complexities and seeking official favor, are obviously activated not solely by expediency but also by their own sentiments as members of society and by their background as persons attracted to the family-planning movement. Unacquainted for the most part with technical economics, sociology, and demography, they tend honestly and instinctively to believe that something they vaguely call population control can be achieved by making better contraceptives available.

THE EVIDENCE OF INEFFECTIVENESS

If this characterization is accurate, we can conclude that current programs will not enable a government to control population size. In countries where couples have numerous offspring that they do not want, such programs may possibly accelerate a birth-rate decline that would occur anyway, but the conditions that cause births to be wanted or un-

---

15. "For influencing family size norms, certainly the examples and statements of public figures are of great significance . . . also . . . use of mass-communication methods which help to legitimize the small-family style, to provoke conversation, and to establish a vocabulary for discussion of family planning." [M. W. Freymann, in *Population Dynamics,* M. Muramatsu and P. A. Harper, Eds. (Johns Hopkins Press, Baltimore, 1965)].

wanted are beyond the control of family planning, hence beyond the control of any nation which relies on family planning alone as its population policy.

• • •

IS FAMILY PLANNING THE "FIRST STEP" IN POPULATION CONTROL?

To acknowledge that family planning does not achieve population control is not to impugn its value for other purposes. Freeing women from the need to have more children than they want is of great benefit to them and their children and to society at large. My argument is therefore directed not against family-planning programs as such but against the assumption that they are an effective means of controlling population growth.

But what difference does it make? Why not go along for awhile with family planning as an initial approach to the problem of population control? The answer is that any policy on which millions of dollars are being spent should be designed to achieve the goal it purports to achieve. If it is only a first step, it should be so labeled, and its connection with the next step (and the nature of that next step) should be carefully examined. In the present case since no "next step" seems ever to be mentioned, the question arises: Is reliance on family planning in fact a basis for dangerous postponement of effective steps? To continue to offer a remedy as a cure long after it has been shown merely to ameliorate the disease is either quackery or wishful thinking, and it thrives most where the need is greatest. Today the desire to solve the population problem is so intense that we are all ready to embrace any "action program" that promises relief. But postponement of effective measures allows the situation to worsen.

Unfortunately, the issue is confused by a matter of semantics. "Family *planning*" and "fertility *control*" suggest that reproduction is being regulated according to some rational plan. And so it is, but only from the standpoint of the individual couple, not from that of the community. What is rational in the light of a couple's situation may be totally irrational from the standpoint of society's welfare.

The need for societal regulation of individual behavior is readily recognized in other spheres—those of explosives, dangerous drugs, public property, natural resources. But in the sphere of reproduction, complete individual initiative is generally favored even by those liberal intellectuals who, in other spheres, most favor economic and social planning. Social reformers who would not hesitate to force all owners of rental property to rent to anyone who can pay, or to force all workers in an industry to join a union, balk at any suggestion that couples be permitted to have only a certain number of offspring. Invariably they interpret societal control of reproduction as meaning direct police supervision of individual behavior. Put the word *compulsory* in front of any term describing a means of limiting births—*compulsory sterilization, compulsory abortion, compulsory contraception*—and you guarantee violent opposition. Fortunately, such direct controls need not be invoked, but conservatives and radicals alike overlook this in their blind opposition to the idea of collective determination of a society's birth rate.

That the exclusive emphasis on family planning in current population policies is not a "first step" but an escape from the real issues is suggested by two facts. (i) No country has taken the "next step." The industrialized countries have had family planning for half a century without acquiring control over either the birth rate or population increase. (ii) Support and encouragement of research on population policy other than family planning is negligible. It is precisely this blocking of alternative thinking and experimentation that makes the emphasis on family planning a major obstacle to population control. The need is not to abandon family-planning programs but to put equal or greater resources into other approaches.

NEW DIRECTIONS IN POPULATION POLICY

In thinking about other approaches, one can start with known facts. In the past, all surviving societies had institutional incentives for marriage, procreation, and child care which were powerful enough to keep the birth rate equal to or in excess of a high death rate. Despite the drop in death rates during the last century and a half, the incentives tended to remain intact because the social structure (especially in regard to the family) changed little. At most, particularly in industrial societies, children became less productive and more expensive.[16] In present-day agrarian societies, where the drop in death rate has been more recent, precipitate, and independent of social change,[17] motivation for having children has changed little. Here, even more than in industrialized nations, the family has kept on producing abundant offspring, even though only a fraction of these children are now needed.

If excessive population growth is to be prevented, the obvious requirement is somehow to impose restraints on the family. However, because family roles are reinforced by society's system of rewards, punishments,

16. K. Davis, *Population Index* **29,** 345 (1963). For economic and sociological theory of motivation for having children, see J. Blake [Univ. of California (Berkeley)], in preparation.
17. K. Davis, *Amer. Economic Rev.* **46,** 305 (1956); *Sci. Amer.* **209,** 68 (1963).

sentiments, and norms, any proposal to demote the family is viewed as a threat by conservatives and liberals alike, and certainly by people with enough social responsibility to work for population control. One is charged with trying to "abolish" the family, but what is required is selective restructuring of the family in relation to the rest of society.

The lines of such restructuring are suggested by two existing limitations on fertility. (i) Nearly all societies succeed in drastically discouraging reproduction among unmarried women. (ii) Advanced societies unintentionally reduce reproduction among married women when conditions worsen in such a way as to penalize childbearing more severely than it was penalized before. In both cases the causes are motivational and economic rather than technological.

It follows that population-control policy can de-emphasize the family in two ways: (i) by keeping present controls over illegitimate childbirth yet making the most of factors that lead people to postpone or avoid marriage, and (ii) by instituting conditions that motivate those who do marry to keep their families small.

POSTPONEMENT OF MARRIAGE

Since the female reproductive span is short and generally more fecund in its first than in its second half, postponement of marriage to ages beyond 20 tends biologically to reduce births. Sociologically, it gives women time to get a better education, acquire interests unrelated to the family, and develop a cautious attitude toward pregnancy.[18] Individuals who have not married by the time they are in their late twenties often do not marry at all. For these reasons, for the world as a whole, the average age at marriage for women is negatively associated with the birth rate: a rising age at marriage is a frequent cause of declining fertility during the middle phase of the demographic transition; and, in the late phase, the "baby boom" is usually associated with a return to younger marriages.

Any suggestion that age at marriage be raised as a part of population policy is usually met with the argument that "even if a law were passed, it would not be obeyed." Interestingly, this objection implies that the only way to control the age at marriage is by direct legislation, but other factors govern the actual age. Roman Catholic countries generally follow canon law in stipulating 12 years as the minimum *legal* age at which girls may marry, but the actual average age at marriage in these countries (at least in Europe) is characteristically more like 25 to 28 years. The actual age is determined, not by law, but by social and economic conditions. In agrarian societies, postponement of marriage (when post-

18. J. Blake, *World Population Conference [Belgrade, 1965]* (United Nations, New York, 1967), vol. 2, pp. 132–36.

ponement occurs) is apparently caused by difficulties in meeting the economic prerequisites for matrimony, as stipulated by custom and opinion. In industrial societies it is caused by housing shortages, unemployment, the requirement for overseas military service, high costs of education, and inadequacy of consumer services. Since almost no research has been devoted to the subject, it is difficult to assess the relative weight of the factors that govern the age at marriage.

ENCOURAGING LIMITATION OF BIRTHS WITHIN MARRIAGE

As a means of encouraging the limitation of reproduction within marriage, as well as postponement of marriage, a greater rewarding of non-familial than of familial roles would probably help. A simple way of accomplishing this would be to allow economic advantages to accrue to the single as opposed to the married individual, and to the small as opposed to the large family. For instance, the government could pay people to permit themselves to be sterilized[19]; all costs of abortion could be paid by the government; a substantial fee could be charged for a marriage license; a "child-tax"[20] could be levied; and there could be a requirement that illegitimate pregnancies be aborted. Less sensationally, governments could simply reverse some existing policies that encourage childbearing. They could, for example, cease taxing single persons more than married ones; stop giving parents special tax exemptions; abandon income-tax policy that discriminates against couples when the wife works; reduce paid maternity leaves; reduce family allowances[21]; stop awarding public housing on the basis of family size; stop granting fellowships and other educational aids (including special allowances for wives and children) to married students; cease outlawing abortions and sterilizations; and relax rules that allow use of harmless contraceptives only with medical permission. Some of these policy reversals would be beneficial in other than demographic respects and some would be harmful unless special precautions were taken. The aim would be to reduce the number, not the quality, of the next generation.

A closely related method of de-emphasizing the family would be modification of the complementarity of the roles of men and women. Men are now able to participate in the wider world yet enjoy the satisfaction of having several children because the housework and childcare fall

19. S. Enke, *Rev. Economics Statistics* **42,** 175 (1960); ———, *Econ. Develop. Cult. Change* **8,** 339 (1960); ——, *ibid.* **10,** 427 (1962); A. O. Krueger and L. A. Sjaastad, *op. cit.,* p. 423.

20. T. J. Samuel, *J. Family Welfare India* **13,** 12 (1966).

21. Sixty-two countries, including 27 in Europe, give cash payments to people for having children [U.S. Social Security Administration, *Social Security Programs Throughout the World, 1967* (Government Printing Office, Washington, D.C., 1967), pp. xxvii–xxviii].

mainly on their wives. Women are impelled to seek this role by their idealized view of marriage and motherhood and by either the scarcity of alternative roles or the difficulty of combining them with family roles. To change this situation women could be required to work outside the home, or compelled by circumstances to do so. If, at the same time, women were paid as well as men and given equal educational and occupational opportunities, and if social life were organized around the place of work rather than around the home or neighborhood, many women would develop interests that would compete with family interests. Approximately this policy is now followed in several Communist countries, and even the less developed of these currently have extremely low birth rates.[22]

That inclusion of women in the labor force has a negative effect on reproduction is indicated by regional comparisons.[23,24] But in most countries the wife's employment is subordinate, economically and emotionally, to her family role, and is readily sacrificed for the latter. No society has restructured both the occupational system and the domestic establishment to the point of permanently modifying the old division of labor by sex.

• • •

THE DILEMMA OF POPULATION POLICY

It should now be apparent why, despite strong anxiety over runaway population growth, the actual programs purporting to control it are limited to family planning and are therefore ineffective. (i) The goal of zero, or even slight, population growth is one that nations and groups find difficult to accept. (ii) The measures that would be required to implement such a goal, though not so revolutionary as a Brave New World or a Communist Utopia nevertheless tend to offend most people reared in existing societies. As a consequence, the goal of so-called population control is implicit and vague; the method is only family planning. This method, far from de-emphasizing the family, is familistic. One of its stated goals is that of helping sterile couples to *have* children. It stresses parental aspirations and responsibilities. It goes along with most aspects of conventional morality, such as condemnation of abortion, disapproval of premarital intercourse, respect for religious teachings and cultural taboos, and obeisance to medical and clerical authority. It deflects hostility by refusing to recommend any change other than the one it stands for: availability of contraceptives.

22. Average gross reproduction rates in the early 1960's were as follows: Hungary, 0.91; Bulgaria, 1.09; Romania, 1.15; Yugoslavia, 1.32.
23. Footnote 11, p. 1195.
24. O. A. Collver and E. Langlois, *Econ. Develop. Cult. Change* **10**, 367 (1962); J. Weeks, [Univ. of California (Berkeley)], unpublished paper.

The things that make family planning acceptable are the very things that make it ineffective for population control. By stressing the right of parents to have the number of children they want, it evades the basic question of population policy, which is how to give societies the number of children they need. By offering only the means for *couples* to control fertility, it neglects the means for societies to do so.

Because of the predominantly pro-family character of existing societies, individual interest ordinarily leads to the production of enough offspring to constitute rapid population growth under conditions of low mortality. Childless or single-child homes are considered indicative of personal failure, whereas having three to five living children gives a family a sense of continuity and substantiality.[25]

• • •

It follows that, in countries where contraception is used, a realistic proposal for a government policy of lowering the birth rate reads like a catalogue of horrors: squeeze consumers through taxation and inflation; make housing very scarce by limiting construction; force wives and mothers to work outside the home to offset the inadequacy of male wages, yet provide few child-care facilities; encourage migration to the city by paying low wages in the country and providing few rural jobs; increase congestion in cities by starving the transit system; increase personal insecurity by encouraging conditions that produce unemployment and by haphazard political arrests. No government will institute such hardships simply for the purpose of controlling population growth. Clearly, therefore, the task of contemporary population policy is to develop attractive substitutes for family interests, so as to avoid having to turn to hardship as a corrective. The specific measures required for developing such substitutes are not easy to determine in the absence of research on the question.

In short, the world's population problem cannot be solved by pretense and wishful thinking. The unthinking identification of family planning with population control is an ostrich-like approach in that it permits people to hide from themselves the enormity and unconventionality of the task. There is no reason to abandon family-planning programs; contraception is a valuable technological instrument. But such programs must be supplemented with equal or greater investments in research and experimentation to determine the required socioeconomic measures.[26]

25. Roman Catholic textbooks condemn the "small" family (one with fewer than four children) as being abnormal [J. Blake, *Population Studies* **20,** 27 (1966)].

26. Judith Blake's critical readings and discussions have greatly helped in the preparation of this article.

TOO MANY GOVERNMENTS

Mitchell Gordon

"Too Many Governments" discusses the integration of scattered, over-lapping, and uncoordinated governmental units in urban areas. Such a governmental proliferation has grown steadily; as a result, the city as an entity has become increasingly disorganized. Confusion has followed from the welter of conflicting and confusing codes and regulations. In a word, cities have lost control over themselves. Several solutions— annexation, metropolitan area government, and the consolidation of municipalities—are discussed along with their positive and negative features.

One of the most inspiring sights one could witness is the panorama of light and color of the spreading cities and populated county area of the Los Angeles basin when observed from a point on the partially surrounding mountain formation, especially from Mount Wilson on a smogless night. To the uninformed in local government matters, this is Los Angeles; to those who have been interested in metropolitan problems there is only a checkerboard of governmental areas in the third largest metropolitan area in the United States.

The words appear in a volume entitled *Metropolitan Los Angeles: Its Governments,* one of a series of studies on the area sponsored by the city's philanthropic Haynes Foundation. The volume was published in 1949. Today, the lights are spread even more broadly across the plains and amid the mountains which punctuate that vista.

The governments, too, are more numerous. Los Angeles County contained fewer than fifty cities in 1949. Today it has well over seventy, and more are being formed all the time. Counting school, water, mosquito-abatement, and hundreds of other districts and agencies which infest this once halcyon scene, there are presently over 600 different taxing bodies within the confines of the county.

Los Angeles' patchquilt of local governments is particularly interesting for the bizarre variety of its origins, but the pattern of administrative and fiscal frustration is repeated in practically every metropolitan area in the land. And it is getting considerably worse as sprawling growth knits existing cities together, physically if not politically, and governments, if they do little else, proliferate. Dr. Luther Gulick, Chairman of the Institute of Public Administration of New York's first City Administrator, recently counted the number of local governments operating in various metropolitan areas around the United States. He found the Pittsburgh area had even more than Los Angeles and that Chicago's was higher still: over 950. New York's total was even higher: 1,100, some 550 of them cities, towns, and villages.

In the San Francisco Bay area, which has half the population of metropolitan Los Angeles, there were, at a recent date, 13 more cities and some 250 more governmental units than in Los Angeles. Bergen County, in New Jersey, has roughly half the land area of Los Angeles—but almost as many incorporated towns and cities. Bergen County had 70 at the time Los Angeles County had 73. Four of Bergen County's incorporated municipalities are less than a square mile; its largest is just over 25 square miles.

The mosaic of local authorities in a single metropolitan area should be of more than statistical interest to those who live among it or who one day might. It results in increasingly wasteful duplications of local services, conflict and confusion in their execution, inequities in taxation, and, in many instances, complete paralysis in the solution of more and more urgent areawide needs, from the provision of a single metropolitan transit system to effective policing, and from the control of air and water pollution to the execution of regional planning.

Probably no aspect of the modern metropolitan scene is more thoroughly criticized and lamented among students of local government and practical administrators than the multiplicity of local governmental units, many of them obsolete but almost all of them indestructible. As Dr. Gulick puts it: "Our system of local government in America was set up in the 1700's and 1800's to fit conditions existing then. And it was a marvelous and brilliant invention. But the conditions have changed. The living city is no longer within the old city limits. The problems we are asking local governments to wrestle with now sprawl all over the map.

> Take any problem, like water or traffic, says he; not only does it reach beyond the lines of any one organized governmental body, but it falls in several independent and often competing jurisdictions. Thus, you have problems which cannot even be thought about except on a comprehensive and unitary basis, fractionated among a score of separate political action units.

Professor William A. Robson, of the London School of Economics and Political Science and past president of the International Political Science Association, in a volume entitled *Great Cities of the World*, declares: "It is obvious that a large municipality, surrounded by a multiplicity of small local authorities of various kinds, cannot hope to meet the social, political or administrative needs of a great metropolitan area. A medley of scattered and disintegrated local authorities cannot provide the unity required for a coherent scheme of development."

Catherine Bauer Wurster, author and lecturer on housing and city planning at the University of California in Berkeley, maintains that "after a century dominated by the growth of enormous cities and the resulting increase of urban functions and responsibilities, the city is weaker as an entity than it has ever been in its history. It controls neither its shape, its function, nor its density. It is smothered and paralyzed by its own offspring: the suburbs and satellite towns. The latter are themselves equally weak and helpless."

Consider, for a moment, the confusion produced by this welter of government. The city of La Mirada, which straddles the Los Angeles and Orange County lines, provided a poignant example not long ago. Residents of the city with "LAwrence" telephone exchanges generally were getting their fire service from the Los Angeles County Fire Department, but they weren't all doing so. New and nervous telephone operators occasionally became confused between which did and which did not. One day, a fire was reported in the two-year-old home of the John Broadbents. The operator mistakenly put the call through to the Orange County Fire Department. The department decided the call was outside its jurisdiction and passed it along to the police department of nearby Buena Park for action. The Buena Park Police desk made some quick checks and turned the call back to the Orange County Fire Department. Eventually, the call got to where it was supposed to go in the first place: the Los Angeles Fire Department. The LAFD had a station only two blocks from the Broadbent residence, but the house was wholly engulfed in flames by the time its engines arrived. A Los Angeles fire official testified later that the home could have been saved if the engines were dispatched correctly the moment the call was turned in.

Shortly after the incident, the Los Angeles Fire Station—Engine Company Number 29—distributed cards among residents of the area suggesting that next time they have a fire to report they should dial FAirview 8-7366. It was subsequently pointed out that the number could not be dialed from LAwrence exchanges in La Mirada but would have to go through an operator first, which could easily set the train of confusion back into motion again. An official of the nearby Buena Park Fire Department noted at the time: "This is a bad situation, and everyone in the area is aware of it. We get reports every time La Mirada has a fire."

The effect of "balkanized" government on police service, where its debilitation is especially serious, has already been described.

For the most part, the price of governmental confusion is paid unknowingly by the average citizen. He suffers it in such forms as time lost in trying to find an address as the name of a street and even its numbers vary as it crosses imperceptibly from one jurisdiction to another, or through the receipt of a traffic ticket innocently incurred as the regulations of one city vary from another. In Orange County, California, motorists are subjected to five different speed limits on a single two-mile stretch of street. In nearby Los Angeles County, one major artery changes names three times as it moves through three different cities— Claremont, Pomona, and La Verne.

Conflict, as well as confusion, results from the profusion of local government. A former battalion chief of the Las Vegas Fire Department tells of orders he once received to take an engine to the city line and let it sit there while a fire blazed in a house just on the other side: "Our station was only two and a half blocks from the scene, and Clark County's was a good deal further but the fire was in County jurisdiction. We arrived nine minutes before they did with orders to act only if the fire threatened city property. Some of the residents got angry and started throwing stones at the truck. It cost us more to repair the truck than it would have cost to fight the fire, but maybe they got the idea: if they wanted city services, they had to join the city."

"The Battle of Alameda Street," as it was known, raged for nine years before the city of Los Angeles finally succeeded in getting the industrial city of Vernon to help pay for a traffic light on an intersection of that heavily traveled street which divides the two cities. Los Angeles had been trying to get a traffic light installed there since 1939, but failed to get the city of Vernon to go along until a court order forced it to do so in 1948.

Conflicting codes and other municipal regulations penalize all manner of economic enterprise, which burdens business and makes for costlier products and services to consumers. An electrical contractor in the greater Miami area must obtain separate permits to work in different municipalities, permits that are not always easy to get. Gasoline distributors in the greater Los Angeles area are allowed to use aluminum delivery trucks in the cities of Torrance and Santa Fe Springs but not in most other areas of the county. Highway contractors in the greater New York region have been clocked through as many as 187 procedural steps before they were able to get their specifications approved by every governmental body involved so they could begin to award contracts.

As it thickens, the jurisdictional jungle produces further duplication of facilities and services—and other costly waste. "It wasn't so bad when the snow plow stopped at the city limits and there was nothing beyond, but it seems a needless waste for the vehicle to turn around and go back to the garage now when it is just as built up on one side of the city as on the other," exclaims Samuel Resnic, Mayor of Holyoke, Massachusetts.

At least four municipalities in his area, Mr. Resnic maintains, could benefit by pooling their public works departments—Holyoke, Chicopee, South Hadley, and West Springfield—but years of talk have yet to produce results.

Tax inequities, as well as waste and confusion, flourish in the soil of fragmented government. "Eighty percent of the youngsters in Shelby County live in the city of Memphis, yet they get only 50 percent of the county's total educational tax money," declares Mayor Henry Loeb. "The other 50 percent goes to 20 percent of the county's schoolchildren. In fact, we have had to have a special city tax to make up deficiencies in the city school system."

Some communities, particularly those which are primarily industrial, set themselves up as incorporated municipalities largely for the purpose of ducking the tax burden they would otherwise have to help carry if they were part of a more residential city. The City of Industry in the eastern part of Los Angeles County is one of several such municipalities to be found around the country. Its origin is particularly interesting. Because California law required a minimum of 500 inhabitants before an area could qualify for incorporation as an independent municipality, industry's aspiring city fathers who otherwise could not muster the necessary number had to include some 173 inmates of a local mental institution, the El Encanto Sanitarium. A taxpayer inside the proposed city area who brought suit against the action was promptly bought out; the new property owner asked for withdrawal of the action and the incorporation went through.

Sigfrid Pearson, Executive Secretary of the Center for Urban Studies at the University of Wichita in Kansas, maintains that voters in communities capable of bringing pressure to bear at the county or state level against "tax haven" cities are either being hoodwinked into tolerating them or neglecting their opportunities for achieving fiscal justice. Says he:

> Folks are scared off from mounting a campaign against this sort of thing when they're told that by compelling industry to bear a fair share of the community tax burden, they are going to chase it right out of the area and everyone will lose his job. On the whole, this is not true. And if that's the kind of industry that is being attracted to the area, the community shouldn't want it anyway.

The State of California has since amended its incorporation rules so no one can again include in its minimum of 500 inhabitants the inmates of a mental institution. Municipalities, however, continue to multiply in Los Angeles County as elsewhere. With only 16 percent of its land area still unincorporated by 1962, some authorities in the County of Los Angeles were predicting there would not be a square foot of unincorporated area remaining a decade hence. That phenomenon has long since come to pass in older, more heavily urbanized metropolises of the country, not alone in the East but in the Midwest as well, around such cities as St. Louis and Cleveland, for instance.

One of the most ominous of all the effects of splintered government is the paralysis it brings to the provision of necessary metropolitan area-wide services. A special commission investigating government problems in the New York City area recently found control of water pollution and the development of an adequate regional park system were suffering seriously from the failure of local governments in the area to take common action. It noted that vast sums had been spent by some municipalities on incinerators and sewage plants but that others were highly neglectful about where they dumped their refuse and raw sewage. Water conditions had become so bad in the region, it stated, that the city was faced with "having all its beaches closed by health authorities." It concluded: "Divided authority for planning and constructing sewers is a contributory cause preventing solution to the problem of pollution."

Highway planning is especially vulnerable to roadblocks thrown up by conflicting governments. The same New York study commission figured 33 years were consumed in the planning of the now-famous Sunrise Highway through wrangling among governmental units in the three counties involved, Brooklyn, Queens, and Nassau. The problem of obtaining coordinated action among local governments in the field of transportation is described as "the greatest one in the whole transportation difficulty" by Boyd T. Barnard, President of the Urban Land Institute, the Philadelphia-based nonprofit research group. . . .

The most serious of all problems connected with the balkanization of local government, perhaps, is the inability of the central city to extend its taxing jurisdiction any further while its wealthier citizens and new industry are taking to the suburbs. "The heart of the metropolitan problem, not only in the central city but in a good many suburban cities as well," says Mayor Henry W. Maier of Milwaukee, "is the taxing problem." Not only are the core cities saddled with greater servicing needs at a time when their tax revenues are faltering, but suburban cities once able to support themselves "suddenly find they've a lot of kids to educate, so they start raising property taxes—and make it more difficult than ever to attract the industry they themselves vitally need to bolster their own revenues," maintains Mayor Maier.

A certain amount of conflict, waste, and confusion is probably inevitable in any system of decentralized government and, no doubt, in highly centralized systems as well. But there are ways to cope with and perhaps even reverse the trend toward shattered local government. The most effective method of all, perhaps, for cities which can still do so, is annexation of surrounding areas before they develop and incorporate themselves. That device, which has its political problems, is fully discussed in the following. . . . There are other methods, however—each with political debilities of their own.

METRO OR SUPERGOVERNMENT?

One which has received a good deal of attention of late and must inevitably come increasingly into the public eye is "metro." The term signifies "metropolitan area government," generally consisting of an upper tier of local government to exercise control over a variety of areawide problems, such as transit, sewage, recreation, and planning. As such, metro is similar to federal government on a national level, which handles such problems as defense and international trade and whose purpose would otherwise be less effectively served were each state free to administer those functions as it saw fit.

The concept comes in for a good deal of criticism from those who view it altogether too simply as the great big bad bogey of "supergovernment." The label is too facile a substitute for the closer study that students of the subject, with rather striking unanimity, feel it warrants. Nor is it unique, as many of its critics make it out to be. Under attack most commonly in Florida's Metropolitan Dade County, where it has been struggling for survival since it came into being in 1957, it has been accepted in the United States over a much longer period of time in such forms as the Metropolitan District Commission, which operates in the Boston area, the city-parish government of Baton Rouge, Louisiana, which is a city-county government of the Miami-Dade County type and, above all, in New York City with its borough system.

New York City's "metro" government, in fact, came into being back in 1898, when the old city of New York was transformed into two boroughs—Manhattan and the Bronx—and three counties were also turned into boroughs, Kings County (which became the borough of Brooklyn), Richmond County (which became the borough of Richmond), and Queens County (which became the borough of Queens). Though the main functions of metropolitan-wide government were vested in the new municipality of Greater New York, certain local powers continued to reside in the county or "borough" governments. The city government has become more centralized over the course of time through various changes in the city charter, especially that of 1935.

The tendency toward centralization of local government is one of the most serious criticisms opponents level at "metro" government. Yet the governmental structure of New York City, possibly because it has experienced that centralization gradually, is rarely criticized on this account today. Indeed, it is perhaps more often criticized for not having kept abreast of the times: when Greater New York was created, its boundaries encompassed almost all of what was then the metropolitan area; those boundaries take in about 60 percent or less of that vastly expanded metropolitan area today. . . .

Metros are becoming more common outside the United States, in such areas as that of London, Manchester, Paris, and, particularly, in Canada. Canada's first metro government came into being four years before that of Dade County, when the Metropolitan Toronto Corporation was formed by decree of the Ontario Legislature in 1953. Originally, it was to perform seven major functions for an area consisting of 13 independent municipalities, including Toronto: the provision of water supply, sewage disposal, arterial highways, parks, school financing, certain welfare services, and coordinated planning. In 1956 its functions were expanded to include policing, business licensing, and air-pollution control as well. The corporation has no power to tax directly, but gets its funds through assessments on each municipality based on the ratio their property assessments bear to the area's total. The corporation assesses all property in the region, which ensures uniformity. . . .

Dade County's metro was voted into being to tackle such problems as traffic control, sewage, zoning, and water for an area consisting of twenty-six municipalities, including Miami. Some of those municipalities, however, have fought metro tooth and nail, with the result that metro has yet to operate in the manner its founders originally envisioned. In some respects, it has become just another party in the governmental free-for-all. Nevertheless, it is showing some gradual, if painful, progress, particularly in the standardization of traffic laws and signs, the invigoration of its port authority, and in the assembly of a nucleus for areawide mass transit.

Nowhere are the difficulties of Dade County's metro better demonstrated than in its attempted reorganization of the courts. Under the provisions creating metro, traffic court administration was to become the exclusive domain of Dade County, though the cities were to be permitted to retain their courts for penal purposes if they chose to do so. By mid-1962, only three cities had handed metro their penal cases: Opa Locka, Hialeah, and Homestead. A number of other cities, particularly well-heeled Miami Beach, however, stoutly resisted metro's takeover even of the traffic courts. The city of Miami Beach, in fact, turned its traffic records over to metro only after the United States Supreme Court handed down a ruling compelling it to do so. One reason for Miami Beach's reluctance: the last year it operated its own traffic courts it took in approximately $1 million in fines, nearly half the $2.5 million collected by traffic courts throughout the county.

Actually, metro is supposed to return the traffic fines it collects to the cities where they are collected, two-thirds of the sum within 30 days and the remainder, less the county's administrative costs, shortly thereafter. Cities like Miami Beach object to the system, nevertheless, on two accounts: first, because they feel the county's administrative take is an additional cost to them because their court systems are operating anyway to handle penal cases. And, second, they object because the county does not seem to be garnering as much revenue from its traffic-court operation as cities like Miami Beach were collecting. Judge Charles H. Snowden of the Metropolitan Court of Dade County pleads guilty to the latter charge with pride: "We are interested not only in punching a cash register. If suspension of a driver's license promises to be more effective than a fine, we prefer the suspension." Judge Snowden contends he would rather have a violator appear in court when an "accident-producing" violation is involved than have him mail in his fine, even if it is costlier to the court. Driver education, he contends, is more important than court revenue.

City officials of Miami Beach are generally well regarded, but there is no doubt that some municipal officials do not like to lose control over traffic courts for a very practical reason: when they do so, they also lose much of their ability to fix a ticket, a very valuable resource for any politician interested in perpetuating himself in office in the traditional manner. Indeed, the charter of the city of Hialeah permits the mayor to overrule a city judge if he chooses to do so, so he doesn't even have to bother fixing a ticket; the right became academic when the county took over operation of the traffic court, however.

The traffic-court tussle provides another insight into metro's difficulties: as of mid-1962, metro's cities still had some 37 judges on their payrolls, only three fewer than they had before metro came along. Metro itself had 13 judges. Thus, the metropolitan area actually had ten more judges three years after the metro traffic court came into being than it had before. Had the cities chosen to deliver up their penal courts as well, there would likely have been many fewer judges over metro than before metro came along—but they have yet to do so. In other words, metro afforded the means for economy if the cities chose to use it, but it imposed still another unit of government to discharge the functions where they chose not to do so. . . .

Is metro, then, the solution to the problem of fragmented government in areas in which annexation is no longer possible?

Students of local government, almost to a man, believe it is certainly a remedy worth serious study in many metropolitan areas. They recognize, however, that it is not very salable to voters. And its complexities, along with some preconceived notions and basic fears, make it difficult to merchandise.

• • •

ALTERNATIVES

One of the more appealing of these remedies to theorists of government, except that it is even less salable to the electorate than metro, is
the consolidation of municipalities into one another or into the county.
The device proved highly successful in ultimately solving the problems
of Passe-a-Grille and St. Petersburg Beach in Florida when, in 1957, they
and two adjoining municipalities—Bella Vista Beach and Don-Ce-Sar
—consolidated into the single city of St. Petersburg Beach so they
could get on with their urgent urban tasks. Shortly after consolidation,
the enlarged city, though it contained but 6,000 persons even then,
succeeded in selling $2.1 million worth of bonds for a sewer system
and $1.5 million for new roads.

Though consolidation efforts are under way almost continually in
some part of the nation, they rarely succeed except where the area that
would thus be absorbed is in desperate need of urban services such as
water or sewers, and sees no other way of getting them, or in that
rare instance where a single areawide vote will decide the issue rather
than separate elections which have to be won in each separate jurisdiction. The metros of Baton Rouge and Dade County rode to victory on
single areawide votes, while Canada's have been decreed mostly by
provincial legislatures.

Consolidation efforts have been made in recent years in such metropolitan areas as Pittsburgh, Cleveland, Milwaukee, Detroit, and St.
Louis, only to be beaten, usually in the outlying area. Of three consolidations that carried in 1961, Virginia Beach with Princess Anne
County in Virginia, the town of Winchester with the city of Winsted
in Connecticut, and the city of Port Tampa with the city of Tampa
in Florida, not one matched partners where both were as large as 10,000
in population. Two relatively large consolidations failed altogether
at the polls that year: Henrico County with Richmond, Virginia, and
Durham with Durham County, North Carolina. In 1962, voters moved
to create the nation's third largest city, in terms of area, by approving
the consolidation of the city of South Norfolk (1960 population: 22,000)
with the county of Norfolk (over 73,000); the new city, which was to
come into being in January, 1963, was to have an area of 371 square
miles—smaller at the time only than the area of Oklahoma City and
the City of Los Angeles, though its population was to be considerably
smaller than either. Virginia is hardly typical in its consolidation climate,
however, since its courts have authority to order annexation even over
objections on the part of the annexees. Thus, there is considerably more
fear in outlying areas of big-city annexation ambitions. In the case of the
Norfolk County-South Norfolk merger, the fear of further expansion

by the areas dominant city, Norfolk, is considered to have eased the consolidation effort.

If metro conjures fears of supergovernment and a loss of control over local affairs, consolidation makes those prospects certainties. Municipalities that can manage to obtain necessary urban services without having to surrender their identity or their prerogatives naturally shy away from consolidation. As long as state laws require consolidation measures to pass individually in each political entity involved in the proposed consolidation, as practically every state law does, the smaller municipality can, in effect, exercise veto rights over any such attempt.

Consolidation, however, need not be effected on a total basis; it can be effected on a functional basis as well, and still leave municipal entities intact, much the way metro does. One commonly employed device for accomplishing this purpose is the special district or public authority. The special district is customarily tax-supported, where public authorities generally obtain their support from revenue bonds paid off by user fees on their services. Special districts for schools, water, sanitation, refuse disposal, and other such functions are common; public authorities are more likely to be found in transportation, operating toll roads, bridges, ports, and parking lots. Like the special district, however, the Public Authority is a single-purpose type of agency which, quite naturally, has its own objectives at heart to the exclusion of all others. A city official in Los Angeles County who serves on the boards of five special districts confesses: "There's absolutely no coordination between them. They fight each other to get the most money out of the County of Los Angeles." . . .

One device for straightening out the spaghetti of local government, and getting rid of some costly, unwanted functions as well without midwifing a prospective governmental rival, is for one level of government to transfer those functions to another. In recent years county governments have taken over such services as civil defense from the city of Detroit, boiler and elevator inspection from the city of Nashville, and the jailing of alcoholics from the city of Los Angeles. County governments, often even more financially strapped than the cities themselves, generally resist such efforts, but the municipalities manage to bring political pressures to bear, through their respective state municipal leagues, for example. Such pressures are not generally difficult to amass, since the logic of government often calls for the function to be performed over a wider area anyway. Nor is the effort always stoutly resisted: weak county governments are sometimes only too happy for the opportunity to enhance their stature with additional tasks.

The strengthening of taxing and other authority at the county level in recent years by such states as California, Maryland, and New York places counties in a better position to assume these and other metropolitan-wide functions. The device may ultimately prove among the more attainable of solutions to the problem of metropolitan-wide local government, if for no other reason than because it lets metro in through the back door. Back-door metro, however, is likely to differ from front-door metro in one significant respect: it is bound to accumulate many more unrelated and largely undesirable services. If it is to serve as something more than a receptacle of unwanted governmental functions, metro must encompass services whose areawide performance is vital or more efficiently and effectively performed, though municipalities may wish to retain them for reasons of revenue, the dispensation of special privilege, or other reasons.

• • •

PUERTO RICAN IMMIGRANTS IN NEW YORK CITY

Puerto Rican Forum

Unlike earlier American immigrants, Puerto Ricans do not come to the United States to flee oppression. Rather, they experience it after their arrival. From citizen to foreigner, from racial acceptance to racial rejection, from work to unemployment, from strong to weak family ties— these are some of the changes and difficulties that the Puerto Rican immigrant experiences. The foundations of tradition and family which in the past provided the Puerto Rican with security are lost, and the new locale does not provide viable substitutes. The sense of normative breakdown, culture conflict, and normlessness makes adjustment difficult. To help in alleviating these problems, the Puerto Rican Community Development Project has established a self-help program. It seeks to aid the immigrant in fortifying his cultural patterns and in protecting him from the debilitating effects of migration. Moreover, the Project helps the Puerto Rican become integrated into his new environment,

From Puerto Rican Forum, *A Study of Poverty Conditions in the New York Puerto Rican Community,* New York: Puerto Rican Forum, Inc., 1964, pp. 10–11, 11–12, 12–13, 66, 68, 69–70, 70–71, 71–72, 72–75, 75–76, 76–77, 78. Reprinted by permission.

for example, by helping to orient him to his new locale and its resources, through job training and job opportunities, and through means of dealing with his language problems.

This great disparity between the values the Puerto Rican brings with him to New York and the realities that are forced upon him by the city lies at the heart of the fate that so often overtakes him . . . the Puerto Rican is an individual . . . not a blank piece of paper awaiting the stamp of the city's rules and regulations. The Puerto Rican is a complete human being with a language, a culture, a way of perceiving life that date back centuries; he comes with a knowledge of his place in the universe, of his duties to himself, his family, to authority, to God; he comes with a morality, a belief in his own innate dignity as a man and as a member of the human race. And nearly everything that he believes in and cherishes is threatened by the conflicts he encounters in the city.

• • •

In Puerto Rico, the mores of the family are strictly delineated and are scrupulously observed. A father is the unquestioned head of the family, accorded respect by his wife and children. He provides for them, furnishes the home, supervises their activities, offers them security and leadership. Second in magnitude to the racial issue confronting the Puerto Rican in New York is the plight of the Puerto Rican male.

The lines of kinship in Puerto Rico are spread generously; life is shared with aunts, cousins, relatives by marriage, neighbors, godparents, friends. No matter how little a family may possess, its members never hesitate to share with a less-fortunate relative. This family closeness, with its concomitant warmth and generosity, cushions the harsher aspects of life for the islander. If mothers must work, their children are cared for by loving hands. If a father loses his job, there is a relative who will help the family over hard times. If a person is too old and ill to take care of himself, he need never fear that he will be abandoned.

In New York, the Puerto Rican tries to keep up the strength of this family circle, but there are many things going against him. The American ethic, quickly apprehended, is "fend for yourself"—and the many pressures of wresting a livelihood from the hostile, hurried, overpowering city tend to harden a person's sensitivity to the needs of others. The salary dollar, so laboriously earned, must be spread out over so many more necessities of life than in Puerto Rico. Life in an already overcrowded apartment is not so easy to share as life in one's own small house where, whatever the shortcomings, there is all of the outdoors to live in all day, every day. Then, too, the whole circle of family is so geographically spread out, that the whole burden of supporting a new-comer or a relative who is out-of-work now may fall on one member, where before it would have been shared. It is little wonder that the warmth of family relationships may cool somewhat in the rougher New York climate, and the cushion that the family provided against the shocks and disappointments of the outside world may wear thin. Still, an effort is generally made to retain some semblance of the family circle, and it is a rare newcomer who cannot look forward to a place to stay, at least for awhile, and some help, however limited, in finding a job and learning the ways of the city.

Earlier immigrants were sustained and strengthened in their battle with the city by their national protective societies—the B'nai B'rith, the Irish Emigrant Society, the Croatians and Slovenian Benevolent Soci-eties, the National Order of the Sons of Italy, the Ancient Order of Hibernians, the Hebrew Immigrant Aid Society. These functioned some-what like "super" family circles; they might give charity, arrange burials, create a social life, publish a newspaper, exert political and social pressure for their members, protect and pass on the traditions and memories of the old country, preserve the language, the music, and the handcrafts, keep alive the pride and the independence of their country-men, function as unions, political clubs, counselors, employment agencies, insurance companies, banks, translators, "family." At least partly because of the supportive influence of these societies, the suc-cessive immigrations to the city achieved a certain social cohesion and strength and often attained great political impact. The Puerto Ricans in New York have only started to form such groups.

• • •

For the Puerto Rican, with his background of male dignity, taking welfare money is an admission to the world that he is a failure as a man, a husband, and a father; it shames and humiliates him; the acceptance of this token monies creates deeper and more corrosive problems than it solves.

One of the great anomalies of the Puerto Rican migration arises out of the special circumstances of our age, in which the voyage, literally be-tween two worlds, can be accomplished in three hours. The Puerto Rican from the country goes in three hours, out of a life virtually un-changed from the nineteenth-century village life the Spaniards founded when they populated the island, into a space-age New York. Although the Puerto Rican arriving from the city is perhaps more prepared for this encounter, there is nevertheless a "time travel" quality to his journey. Not unlike the European immigrants, he is skilled in operations that require of him strength, willingness to work, patience and ability to take orders. But unlike them, the new migrant is faced with a paucity of jobs, and those available do not require what he has to offer. . . . The affluence of the city magnifies his poverty and only contributes to make his life, on a mere subsistence level, almost unendurable.

Some who achieve financial success move away from the city to melt comfortably into the milieu of suburbia. There are those who gain a foothold in the entertainment world, in politics, sports and the professions, and those who have achieved seniority and skill at their jobs. Others have had their most-cherished dream of sending their children through college and on to a professional career realized. And there are some who sustain their goal of returning to the island, and manage to return with their families and establish businesses there.

• • •

However, despite the attainments of the Puerto Ricans in the history of their migration to the city, studies reveal that half of the group has been caught in the inexorable cycle of poverty. It is tragic for the City of New York, that so many of the Puerto Ricans who have come in search of a better life have found instead slums, poverty, inadequate education, *the destruction of cultural patterns and absence of viable substitutes,** exploitation, and meager incomes.

• • •

The program plan developed by the Puerto Rican Community Development Project represents the first major attempt by the Puerto Rican community of New York City to affect significantly the lives of more than 600,000 Puerto Ricans. It aims to mobilize the total strengths and resources of a cultural minority in a comprehensive self-help effort. . . .

The program plan proposed reflects a belief that the critical problems that impede the successful integration of Puerto Ricans into New York City can be overcome only if Puerto Ricans themselves are engaged in devising the means of overcoming them. Goals, priorities and objectives must be determined by Puerto Ricans; techniques used must reflect the culture and the character of the Puerto Rican people; and programs must build upon the strengths of the Puerto Rican community, and must relate to its needs.

Another cardinal principle in developing a program plan is that the entire Puerto Rican community must be served since the very fact of its being a cultural minority places it in a position of need. Furthermore,

*Our italics, M. S. W. and E. R.

the only effective way to utilize the rich human resources in the Puerto Rican community in a massive self-help effort is to design programs that relate to the cultural ways and the organizational life of the Puerto Rican. *Only by fortifying cultural patterns and protecting them against the debilitating effects of migration can Puerto Ricans retain their health as social beings, and find the strength to adapt successfully to a new environment.* *

. . . (The) major problems facing Puerto Ricans are in the areas of education, employment and youth development. It is our contention that the greatest strengths in the Puerto Rican community stem from its cultural institutions and organizational life. A program plan has, therefore, been designed to address itself to these needs and strengths.

• • •

A. TO RAISE FAMILY INCOME AND REDUCE POVERTY AND DEPENDENCY

• • •

Job Development Program.   Language and cultural barriers . . . hamper many in projecting themselves as employees.

A job development program will be established in which job advancement for qualified Puerto Ricans into higher salaries and supervisory levels within their existing place of employment will be sought. Social agencies and private institutions will be approached to create new jobs for Puerto Ricans. Large corporations such as IBM will be asked to develop on-the-job training programs in new fields for the placement of qualified Puerto Ricans. Youths could be paid from funds secured from Federal agencies. Cooperation will be sought from city departments to create openings for the employment of needed bilingual Spanish-speaking personnel.

• • •

Selective Work-Training Programs for Adults and Youth.   Training programs will be created for those unemployed youth and adults who are capable of benefiting from such training. Programs would be geared to:

1. Teaching basic skills in English and arithmetic
2. Giving specialized training for a variety of work situations
3. Offering group and individual counseling in both Spanish and English.

* Our italics, M. S. W. and E. R.

Help on problems peculiar to a cultural group will be given heavy emphasis.

• • •

Enrichment programs will be developed to improve earning capacity and to raise income of youth and adults who are already employed but who can advance readily with additional training. Basic skills will be taught in new fields with a greater demand for workers and offering higher salaries. Preparation courses for civil-service examinations as well as group orientation sessions will be offered. Placement services will be coordinated with the job-development program and with existing agencies such as the State Youth Employment Service.

• • •

B. TO RAISE THE EDUCATIONAL LEVEL
For youth

1. ASPIRA. (an existing educational and leadership development agency serving 500 youths.) An extensive educational ASPIRA program will be developed to serve capable youths who have the potential to achieve but who are hampered because of poor guidance, lack of financial resources, family difficulties, and poor motivation. Youth in the junior high, senior high, college and graduate school levels between the ages of approximately 12 and 25 will be given remedial tutoring, educational and career guidance, [and] leadership training. . . .

a. After-school youth centers will be established in neighborhoods with high concentrations of Puerto Ricans. The centers will offer remedial tutoring; group and individual guidance; club activities (with an educational emphasis); language classes (Spanish and English); youth forums; dramatic presentations; courses on Puerto Rican history, literature, folklore, and art (aimed at motivation through positive self-identity); and leadership training through formal courses and service to community.

b. . . . An extensive work-study program will be developed in which youths doing well in school can work as paid tutors. These high-achievers would not only be able to relieve financial burdens at home, which might make higher education more feasible, but they would also become models for younger Puerto Ricans to emulate. Qualified youngsters needing after-school employment could also be referred to other nonprofit agencies under the work-study plan.

• • •

c. A scholarship center will be established to secure scholarships, fellowships, grants, and loans for qualified Puerto Rican students. Universities, foundations, private donors, industries, unions, and governmental agencies will be approached for funds so that a significantly large number of Puerto Ricans might get financing for higher education. Capable students will be given guidance, supportive help, and remediation needed to successfully qualify and retain scholarships or loans.

d. A "godparents" program will be developed in which interested adults—Puerto Rican and non-Puerto Rican—will serve as counselors, contacts, and sponsors for young Puerto Ricans, helping them to enter professions and careers. They will serve as positive images to follow and will in many ways offer the personal "helping hand" so important to young and insecure adolescents.

2. Bilingual Experimental Projects. Bilingual Block Nursery School and Child Care Centers. An experimental demonstration program for preschool Puerto Rican children between the ages of 3 and 6 will be established, probably in East Harlem, an area of most severe Puerto Rican deprivation.

The aim will be to raise the educational level, the learning potential and motivation of Puerto Rican children by teaching them in two languages (Spanish and English) in the very early years; by broadening their base of experiences through directed play and early training; by strengthening their cultural identity and establishing a positive image of Puerto Ricans; and by fostering an adaptation to two cultures with different social patterns, thus preventing the culture-conflict of later years.

The project will continue, in cooperation (not yet arranged) with the Board of Education when the children enter elementary school. Special educational materials would be used to supplement the standard ones: for example, books in Spanish along with names, pictures, and examples that would reflect Puerto Rican experiences and cultural patterns. In order to prevent segregation, the children could be assigned to a regular class for half or most of the day and could be instructed as a group (in Spanish) for the rest of the day. The project will be continued at least through the third grade. . . . If the results are positive, an attempt will be made to continue the experiment through the elementary school period; to establish it in other preschool nurseries; and to expand it within the public-school system and into the junior and senior high school levels.

• • •

3. Youth Service Corps. A youth service program to recruit and train youths between the ages of about 9 to 11, 12 to 15, and 16 to 19 will be developed in eight neighborhoods of high Puerto Rican concentration. Dropouts and potential dropouts who do not relate to other programs such as ASPIRA or work-training will be the target group. . . . An organization will be developed in which rank and status would be achieved through a merit system of community service. . . .

The educational aspect of the program will be stressed, and the learning of basic skills, such as reading and arithmetic, will be basic to "corps" functioning. . . . Culture building and ego building activities and materials will be introduced to mitigate tendencies toward self-hate and negative attitudes toward themselves and other Puerto Ricans.

For adults

1. Consumer Education Program.   A consumer education program will be developed in the South Bronx as a prototype for other neighborhoods.

a. A consumer clinic open several nights a week to receive complaints, to offer consumer information and advice and give legal counsel (and if needed, provide legal services.)

b. Publications and informative materials will be distributed in Spanish and English, and reports and directories will be made available regarding local, as well as city-wide business establishments and their selling practices. Lectures and courses will be given on how to buy articles such as furniture, food, drugs, medicines and clothing—and on how to make loans and buy on credit.

c. Comparative shopping will be done by citizens' committees with staff help. Chain stores, small neighborhood stores, and other business establishments will be visited to examine prices, quality of merchandise, conditions of the store, and services and employment practices. Poor quality, price differentials, and poor practices will be corrected through discussions and negotiations with owners of business establishments.

d. Credit unions and food cooperatives for local residents will be encouraged. Some success has been seen in ventures of this type with Puerto Rican families in New York. Mothers on welfare in East Harlem have been known to save up to $400 a year by pooling monies and making cooperative purchases.

• • •

2. Leadership Development and Community Education Project.   A leadership development program, now operated by the Puerto Rican Forum will be expanded and broadened with the following aims:

a. Developing informed and effective Puerto Rican leadership by teaching essential skills, group functioning, the role of a chairman, the role of boards of directors, how to administer and direct programs, etc.

b. Providing orientation about the New York community—its institutions, formal and informal power structure, financial and community resources, social, political, economic, religious, and ethnic organizations, and government and city agencies.

c. Seeking and identifying potential leaders, (especially among the second generation) and instilling in them a pride and dedication to their community and a desire to serve New York City; preventing the pattern of rejection of one's background and of turning away from community problems; utilizing the needed skills and talents of the professional and middle-class Puerto Rican for the welfare and enrichment of the city as a whole.

The Program will consist of:

1. Training institutes, courses, seminars and forums for Puerto Rican leaders. These programs will involve the learning in depth of certain subject areas, as well as general orientation in a variety of subjects and issues. They will also be geared to acquiring leadership skills.

2. An Information Bureau with specialists in the areas of education, health and welfare, intergroup relations, housing, youth problems, employment and business, analyzing and interpreting issues and problems in those areas that most critically affect the Puerto Rican community. Reports, digests, and summaries will be prepared and issued not only to Puerto Ricans, but also to the general population, in order to foster maximum understanding of the effect of those problems on the Puerto Rican population. Recommendations will be made for remedying problems and instituting change.

3. Development of educational materials; educational material such as books, pamphlets, weekly or monthly publications, posters, etc., will be developed and distributed. These will be on a wide range of subjects important for the healthy integration of Puerto Ricans into the New York society. They would rely heavily on the knowledge of cultural patterns and value systems, folkways, outlook, experiences, language and usages peculiar to the Puerto Rican migrant.

Educational, artistic, and documentary films will be made in Spanish to illustrate problems of Puerto Ricans in New York and approaches to handling them. This has been done successfully in Puerto Rico. Educational radio programs will be prepared.

A central library on Puerto Rican affairs, Puerto Rican history, literature, folklore, music and art will be established for the public's use. Youths, as well as adults, will be encouraged to use it.

4. Puerto Rican Folk Theatre; a community Puerto Rican Theatre will be established. It will be located in one of the areas of high Puerto Rican concentration such as East Harlem and at the same time will be

a moving theatre sent to other areas of the city. A bilingual theatre group, already in formation, will portray the true image of the Puerto Rican and make known the patterns of Puerto Rican culture to both Puerto Rican and non-Puerto Rican audiences. The theatre will be used as an educational tool in presenting social problems, solutions, and civic responsibilities. Youth will be trained in all facets of theatre (playwrighting, scenic design, etc.) and the talents of Puerto Ricans in music, the dance, writing, painting, etc., will be fostered consciously.

C. TO STRENGTHEN FAMILY LIFE AND CULTURAL INSTITUTIONS

1. The Puerto Rican Family. The Puerto Rican Family Institute (already existing as a volunteer agency of the Puerto Rican community) offers a service with a creative approach to orientation and counseling. The service is set up on the principle of one Puerto Rican family already integrated into the life of New York serving as a "big sister" family to a newly-arrived migrant family. The idea for this program was conceived out of the observation and concern of Puerto Rican social workers in the traditional agencies giving services to migrant families. When Puerto Rican families knocked at the door for services, it was usually too late to deal effectively with the multiplicity of problems they brought to the agency. The impact of family breakdown was such that little could be accomplished in treatment.

Some families well-adjusted within the extended family structure in Puerto Rico, in migrating north, develop feelings of loneliness, inadequacy and failure.

They bring with them a set of values that they are forced to drop in the new environment. *This often leads to social and psychological disorganization.**

Part of this deterioration can be remedied if, upon arrival, these individuals are provided with a supporting family to emulate and a receptive community in which to grow.

● ● ●

2. Padres de Crianza (Puerto Rican Foster Care Guidance and Orientation Agency). A Puerto Rican Foster Care Guidance and Orientation Agency will be instituted, wherein adjusted Puerto Rican New York families would be encouraged to take in Puerto Rican youngsters now in institutions and temporary shelters and to serve as foster parents. This would relieve the tremendous burden now experienced by private and

---

* Our italics, M. S. W. and E. R.

public social welfare institutions unable to place Puerto Rican young-sters. It would provide compatible homes for many neglected and aban-doned children.

. . . Lack of understanding and language barriers between social agencies and qualified families often serve as deterrent to the successful recruitment of these families.

Foster parentage is a well-established social institution in Puerto Rico, and this cultural pattern could serve a useful social purpose in New York, as it does on the island.

3. Institute for Puerto Rican Culture.   We propose to establish in New York City a chapter of the Puerto Rican "Instituto de Cultura." The major goal of the institute is the advancement and enrichment of Puerto Rican culture . . . the preservation of Puerto Rican folklore and folk arts, and the recognition, development and encouragement of the Puerto Rican artist. Existing Puerto Rican cultural organizations will be brought together to form a sponsoring card for an Institute on Puerto Rican Culture in New York City. Attempts will be made to secure tech-nical and financial aid from the Government of Puerto Rico for the purpose of establishing such an institute.

• • •

D. TO STRENGTHEN PUERTO RICAN ORGANIZATIONAL LIFE IN NEW YORK CITY

1. Aid to Existing Puerto Rican Organizations.   In order that the rich resources of Puerto Rican organized life in New York may be tapped for maximum benefit to the Puerto Rican and the total New York communi-ty, "subsistence" contracts will be provided to the Puerto Rican organi-zations that offer a service to the community. There is a vital need for the continued existence of these groups since they are an expression of the health, stability and constructive efforts of the Puerto Rican com-munity.

• • •

2. Puerto Rican Neighborhood Boards.   Although the organizational patterns of Puerto Ricans are city-wide in nature, it is essential that neighborhood associations be established in order to foster neighbor-hood ties and begin a process by which Puerto Rican residents of an area can begin to relate to local institutions, concern themselves with local problems, and accelerate the process of their integration into the large community.

Puerto Rican Neighborhood Planning Boards will be established in eight neighborhoods of highest Puerto Rican concentration. . . . A center large enough for community meetings and for housing neighborhood programs will be secured and staff needed to conduct local programs will be hired. Working relationships and cooperative activities with existing agencies and institutions in the area will be fostered as a means toward accelerating integration and broadening the base for mutual understanding.

3. Neighborhood Orientation Centers. Neighborhood centers will be opened in eight neighborhoods where Puerto Rican concentrations are largest. The centers will be operated by Neighborhood Planning Boards. . . . Each will be autonomous and will deal with the city-wide project in establishing needed programs at the neighborhood level. . . . Community residents—non-professionals, by and large, will be given part-time and full-time employment.

The centers will remain open all day and in the evenings. During the day, work-training programs could be conducted, and groups in the community would have space to meet and to conduct special activities. In the evening, adult education classes could be given in vital areas such as English, health counseling, parent education and consumer education. Forums, conferences, and meetings could be held for general orientation on important problems such as housing, discrimination, education and drug addiction. Service would be given for specific needs such as legal aid, social service and referrals, and family counseling. City departments and other social agencies that have field services—for example, the City Commission on Human Rights, Department of Labor, and Department of Health—could be invited to send field staff to give direct service at the center.

Meetings will be conducted in Spanish whenever possible, for maximum effectiveness. A fundamental objective would be to foster interest and participation by Puerto Rican residents in the life of the community at large, and to contribute to its total welfare.

In addition, a *Research Center for Puerto Rican Studies* will be proposed as a means of uncovering vital information about Puerto Ricans, Puerto Rican social patterns, culture, history, migration, needs, and problems as well as other vital data about the Puerto Rican community that would be important to deal effectively with a large cultural minority of New York City.

• • •

In all the programs proposed, an overriding and fundamental principle is that the limitations of a cultural minority, within a majority culture which is new and different, must be considered. The social patterns, family strengths, language, and outlook of the Puerto Rican must also be taken into account. The character and approach of services given will add another broader dimension to the content of the programs—a dimension that emanates from the manner, style and values of Puerto Ricans.

• • •

FUTURE SHOCK

Alvin Toffler

The tempo of change in modern society has accelerated so rapidly that it has gotten out of hand. No longer is there a sense of control over where we are going, and efforts to exert control merely end in a proliferation of ineffective, uncoordinated programs which seem only randomly and vaguely related to the ends they are supposed to serve. Alvin Toffler calls this sense of normlessness "future shock." According to Toffler, we need to develop a keen consciousness of the future, images and predictions of the future states which are possible and probable, and channels for the public to debate and choose the future conditions which society should pursue. Change could then be comprehended, organized, and controlled, rather than being a major source of disorientation and disorganization.

Can one live in a society that is out of control? That is the question posed for us by the concept of future shock. For that is the situation we find ourselves in. If it were technology alone that had broken loose, our problems would be serious enough. The deadly fact is, however, that many other social processes have also begun to run free, oscillating wildly, resisting our best efforts to guide them.

Urbanization, ethnic conflict, migration, population, crime—a thousand examples spring to mind of fields in which our efforts to shape change seem increasingly inept and futile. Some of these are strongly related to the breakaway of technology; others partially independent of

From Alvin Toffler, *Future Shock,* pp. 446–47, 458–59, 462–63, 463–64, 465, 466–67, 467–68, 469–70, 470–71, 472–73, 475–76, 478–79, 480, 485–86. Copyright © by Alvin Toffler. Reprinted by permission of Random House, Inc. and The Bodley Head.

it. The uneven, rocketing rates of change, the shifts and jerks in direction, compel us to ask whether the techno-societies, even comparatively small ones like Sweden and Belgium, have grown too complex, too fast to manage?

How can we prevent mass future shock, selectively adjusting the tempos of change, raising or lowering levels of stimulation, when governments—including those with the best intentions—seem unable even to point change in the right direction?

Thus a leading American urbanologist writes with unconcealed disgust: "At a cost of more than three billion dollars, the Urban Renewal Agency has succeeded in materially reducing the supply of low cost housing in American cities." Similar debacles could be cited in a dozen fields. Why do welfare programs today often cripple rather than help their clients? Why do college students, supposedly a pampered elite, riot and rebel? Why do expressways add to traffic congestion rather than reduce it? In short, why do so many well-intentioned liberal programs turn rancid so rapidly, producing side effects that cancel out their central effects? No wonder Raymond Fletcher, a frustrated Member of Parliament in Britain, recently complained: "Society's gone random!"

If random means a literal absence of pattern, he is, of course, overstating the case. But if random means that the outcomes of social policy have become erratic and hard to predict, he is right on target. Here, then, is the political meaning of future shock. For just as individual future shock results from an inability to keep pace with the rate of change, governments, too, suffer from a kind of collective future shock —a breakdown of their decisional processes.

With chilling clarity, Sir Geoffrey Vickers, the eminent British social scientist, has identified the issue: "The rate of change increases at an accelerating speed, without a corresponding acceleration in the rate at which further responses can be made; and this brings us nearer the threshold beyond which control is lost."

• • •

TIME HORIZONS

Technocrats suffer from myopia. Their instinct is to think about immediate returns, immediate consequences. They are premature members of the now generation.

If a region needs electricity, they reach for a power plant. The fact that such a plant might sharply alter labor patterns, that within a decade it might throw men out of work, force large-scale retraining of workers, and swell the social welfare costs of a nearby city—such considerations are too remote in time to concern them. The fact that the plant could trigger devastating ecological consequences a generation later simply does not register in their time frame.

In a world of accelerant change, next year is nearer to us than next month was in a more leisurely era. This radically altered fact of life must be internalized by decision-makers in industry, government and elsewhere. Their time horizons must be extended.

To plan for a more distant future does not mean to tie oneself to dogmatic programs. Plans can be tentative, fluid, subject to continual revision. Yet flexibility need not mean shortsightedness. To transcend technocracy, our social time horizons must reach decades, even generations, into the future. This requires more than a lengthening of our formal plans. It means an infusion of the entire society, from top to bottom, with a new socially aware future-consciousness.

• • •

We are . . . witnessing a perfectly extraordinary thrust toward more scientific appraisal of future probabilities, a ferment likely, in itself, to have a powerful impact on the future. It would be foolish to oversell the ability of science, as yet, to forecast complex events accurately. Yet the danger today is not that we will overestimate our ability; the real danger is that we will under-utilize it. For even when our still-primitive attempts at scientific forecasting turn out to be grossly in error, the very effort helps us identify key variables in change, it helps clarify goals, and it forces more careful evaluation of policy alternatives. In these ways, if no others, probing the future pays off in the present.

Anticipating *probable* futures, however, is only part of what needs doing if we are to shift the planner's time horizon and infuse the entire society with a greater sense of tomorrow. For we must also vastly widen our conception of *possible** futures. To the rigorous discipline of science, we must add the flaming imagination of art.

Today as never before we need a multiplicity of visions, dreams and prophecies — images of potential tomorrows. Before we can rationally decide which alternative pathways to choose, which cultural styles to pursue, we must first ascertain which are possible. Conjecture, speculation and the visionary view thus become as coldly practical a necessity as feet-on-the-floor "realism" was in an earlier time.

This is why some of the world's biggest and most tough-minded corporations, once the living embodiment of presentism, today hire intuitive futurists, science fiction writers and visionaries as consultants. . . .

Corporations must not remain the only agencies with access to such services. Local government, schools, voluntary associations and others

---

*Our italics, M. S. W. and E. R.

also need to examine their potential futures imaginatively. One way to help them do so would be to establish in each community "imaginetic centers" devoted to technically assisted brainstorming. These would be places where people noted for creative imagination, rather than technical expertise, are brought together to examine present crises, to anticipate future crises, and to speculate freely, even playfully, about possible futures.

What, for example, are the possible futures of urban transportation? Traffic is a problem involving space. How might the city of tomorrow cope with the movement of men and objects through space? To speculate about this question, an imaginetic center might enlist artists, sculptors, dancers, furniture designers, parking lot attendants, and a variety of other people who, in one way or another, manipulate space imaginatively. Such people, assembled under the right circumstances, would inevitably come up with ideas of which the technocratic city planners, the highway engineers and transit authorities have never dreamed.

Musicians, people who live near airports, jack-hammer men and subway conductors might well imagine new ways to organize, mask or suppress noise. Groups of young people might be invited to ransack their minds for previously unexamined approaches to urban sanitation, crowding, ethnic conflict, care of the aged, or a thousand other present and future problems.

• • •

The rushing stream of wild, unorthodox, eccentric or merely colorful ideas generated in these sanctuaries of social imagination must, after they have been expressed, be subjected to merciless screening. Only a tiny fraction of them will survive this filtering process. These few, however, could be of the utmost importance in calling attention to new possibilities that might otherwise escape notice. . . .

While imaginetic centers concentrate on partial images of tomorrow, defining possible futures for a single industry, an organization, a city or its subsystems, however, we also need sweeping, visionary ideas about the society as a whole. Multiplying our images of possible futures is important; but these images need to be organized, crystallized into structured form. In the past, utopian literature did this for us. It played a practical, crucial role in ordering men's dreams about alternative futures. Today we suffer for lack of utopian ideas around which to organize competing images of possible futures.

Most traditional utopias picture simple and static societies—i.e., societies that have nothing in common with super-industrialism. B. F. Skinner's *Walden Two,* the model for several existing experimental communes, depicts a pre-industrial way of life—small, close to the earth, built on farming and handcraft. Even those two brilliant anti-utopias, *Brave New World* and *1984*, now seem oversimple. Both describe societies based on high technology and low complexity: the machines are sophisticated but the social and cultural relationships are fixed and deliberately simplified.

Today we need powerful new utopian and anti-utopian concepts that look forward to super-industrialism, rather than backward to simpler societies. These concepts, however, can no longer be produced in the old way. First, no book, by itself, is adequate to describe a super-industrial future in emotionally compelling terms. . . . Second, it may now be too difficult for any individual writer, no matter how gifted, to describe a convincingly complex future. We need, therefore, a revolution in the production of utopias: collaborative utopianism. We need to construct "utopia factories."

One way might be to assemble a small group of top social scientists— an economist, a sociologist, an anthropologist, and so on—asking them to work together, even live together, long enough to hammer out among themselves a set of well-defined values on which they believe a truly super-industrial utopian society might be based.

Each member of the team might then attempt to describe in nonfiction form a sector of an imagined society built on these values. What would its family structure be like? Its economy, laws, religion, sexual practices, youth culture, music, art, its sense of time, its degree of differentiation, its psychological problems? By working together and ironing out inconsistencies, where possible, a comprehensive and adequately complex picture might be drawn of a seamless, temporary form of super-industrialism.

● ● ●

Meanwhile, other groups could be at work on counter-utopias. While Utopia A might stress materialist, success-oriented values, Utopia B might base itself on sensual, hedonistic values, C on the primacy of aesthetic values, D on individualism, E on collectivism, and so forth. Ultimately, a stream of books, plays, films and television programs would flow from this collaboration between art, social science and futurism, thereby educating large numbers of people about the costs and benefits of the various proposed utopias.

Finally, if social imagination is in short supply, we are even more lacking in people willing to subject utopian ideas to systematic test. More and more young people, in their dissatisfaction with industrialism, are experimenting with their own lives, forming utopian communities, trying new social arrangements, from group marriage to living-learning communes. Today, as in the past, the weight of established society comes down hard on the visionary who attempts to practice, as well as merely preach. Rather than ostracizing utopians, we should take advantage of their willingness to experiment, encouraging them with money and tolerance, if not respect.

Most of today's "intentional communities" or utopian colonies, however, reveal a powerful preference for the past. These may be of value to the individuals in them, but the society as a whole would be better served by utopian experiments based on super- rather than pre-industrial forms. Instead of a communal farm, why not a computer software company whose program writers live and work communally? Why not an education technology company whose members pool their money and merge their families? Instead of raising radishes or crafting sandals, why not an oceanographic research installation organized along utopian lines? Why not a group medical practice that takes advantage of the latest medical technology but whose members accept modest pay and pool their profits to run a completely new-style medical school? Why not recruit living groups to try out the proposals of the utopia factories?

In short, we can use utopianism as a tool rather than an escape, if we base our experiments on the technology and society of tomorrow rather than that of the past. And once done, why not the most rigorous, scientific analysis of the results? The findings could be priceless, were they to save us from mistakes or lead us toward more workable organizational forms for industry, education, family life or politics.

• • •

Indeed, with these as a background, we must consciously begin to multiply the scientific future-sensing organs of society. Scientific futurist institutes must be spotted like nodes in a loose network throughout the entire governmental structure in the techno-societies, so that in every department, local or national, some staff devotes itself systematically to scanning the probably long-term future in its assigned field. Futurists should be attached to every political party, university, corporation, professional association, trade union and student organization.

We need to train thousands of young people in the perspectives and techniques of scientific futurism, inviting them to share in the exciting venture of mapping probable futures. We also need national agencies to provide technical assistance to local communities in creating their own futurist groups. And we need a similar center, perhaps jointly funded by American and European foundations, to help incipient futurist centers in Asia, Africa, and Latin America.

We are in a race between rising levels of uncertainty produced by the acceleration of change, and the need for reasonably accurate images of what at any instant is the most probable future. The generation of reliable images of the most probable future thus becomes a matter of the highest national, indeed, international urgency.

As the globe is itself dotted with future-sensors, we might consider creating a great international institute, a world futures data bank. Such an institute, staffed with top caliber men and women from all the sciences and social sciences, would take as its purpose the collection and systematic integration of predictive reports generated by scholars and imaginative thinkers in all the intellectual disciplines all over the world.

Of course, those working in such an institute would know that they could never create a single, static diagram of the future. Instead, the product of their effort would be a constantly changing geography of the future, a continually re-created overarching image based on the best predictive work available. . . .

Only when decision-makers are armed with better forecasts of future events, when by successive approximation we increase the accuracy of forecast, will our attempts to manage change improve perceptibly. For reasonably accurate assumptions about the future are a precondition for understanding the potential consequences of our own actions. And without such understanding, the management of change is impossible.

•   •   •

ANTICIPATORY DEMOCRACY

In the end, however, social futurism must cut even deeper. For technocrats suffer from more than econothink and myopia; they suffer, too, from the virus of elitism. To capture control of change, we shall, therefore, require a final, even more radical breakaway from technocratic tradition: we shall need a revolution in the very way we formulate our social goals.

•   •   •

Intermittently, a change-dazed government will try to define its goals publicly. Instinctively, it establishes a commission. In 1960 President Eisenhower pressed into service, among others, a general, a judge, a couple of industrialists, a few college presidents, and a labor leader to "develop a broad outline of coordinated national policies and programs" and to "set up a series of goals in various areas of national activity." In due course, a red-white-and-blue paperback appeared with the commission's report, *Goals for Americans*. Neither the commission nor its goals had the slightest impact on the public or on policy.

The juggernaut of change continued to roll through America untouched, as it were, by managerial intelligence.

A far more significant effort to tidy up governmental priorities was initiated by President Johnson, with his attempt to apply PPBS (Planning-Programming-Budgeting-System) throughout the federal establishment. PPBS is a method for tying programs much more closely and rationally to organizational goals. Thus, for example, by applying it, the Department of Health, Education and Welfare can assess the costs and benefits of alternative programs to accomplish specified goals. But who specifies these larger, more important goals? The introduction of PPBS and the systems approach is a major governmental achievement. It is of paramount importance in managing large organizational efforts. But it leaves entirely untouched the profoundly political question of how the overall goals of a government or a society are to be chosen in the first place.

President Nixon, still snarled in the goals crisis, tried a third tack. "It is time," he declared, "we addressed ourselves, consciously and systematically, to the question of what kind of a nation we want to be. . . ." He thereupon put his finger on the quintessential question. But once more the method chosen for answering it proved to be inadequate. "I have today ordered the establishment, within the White House, of a National Goals Research Staff," the President announced. "This will be a small, highly technical staff, made up of experts in the collection . . . and processing of data relating to social needs, and in the projection of social trends."

• • •

Behind all such efforts runs the notion that national (and, by extension, local) goals for the future of society ought to be formulated at the top. This technocratic premise perfectly mirrors the old bureaucratic forms of organization in which line and staff were separated, in which rigid, undemocratic hierarchies distinguished leader from led, manager from managed, planner from plannee.

Yet the real, as distinct from the glibly verbalized, goals of any society on the path to super-industrialism are already too complex, too transient and too dependent for their achievement upon the willing participation of the governed, to be perceived and defined so easily. We cannot hope to harness the runaway forces of change by assembling a kaffee klatsch of elders to set goals for us or by turning the task over to a "highly technical staff." A revolutionary new approach to goal-setting is needed.

• • •

In complex, differentiated societies, vast amounts of information must flow at even faster speeds between the formal organizations and subcultures that make up the whole, and between the layers and substructures within these.

Political democracy, by incorporating larger and larger numbers in social decision-making, facilitates feedback. And it is precisely this feedback that is essential to control. To assume control over accelerant change, we shall need still more advanced—and more democratic—feedback mechanisms.

The technocrat, however, still thinking in top-down terms, frequently makes plans without arranging for adequate and instantaneous feedback from the field, so that he seldom knows how well his plans are working. When he does arrange for feedback, what he usually asks for and gets is heavily economic, inadequately social, psychological or cultural. Worse yet, he makes these plans without sufficiently taking into account the fast-changing needs and wishes of those whose participation is needed to make them a success. He assumes the right to set social goals by himself or he accepts them blindly from some higher authority.

• • •

Let us convene in each nation, in each city, in each neighborhood, democratic constituent assemblies charged with social stock-taking, charged with defining and assigning priorities to specific social goals for the remainder of the century.

Such "social future assemblies" might represent not merely geographical localities, but social units—industry, labor, the churches, the intellectual community, the arts, women, ethnic and religious groups, students, with organized representation for the unorganized as well. There are no sure-fire techniques for guaranteeing equal representation for all, or for eliciting the wishes of the poor, the inarticulate or the isolated. Yet once we recognize the need to include them, we shall find the ways. Indeed, the problem of participating in the definition of the future is not merely a problem of the poor, the inarticulate and the isolated. Highly paid executives, wealthy professionals, extremely articulate intellectuals and students—all at one time or another feel cut off from the power to influence the directions and pace of change. Wiring them into the system, making them a part of the guidance machinery of the society, is the most critical political task of the coming generation. Imagine the effect if at one level or another a place were provided where all those who will live in the future might voice their wishes about it. Imagine, in short, a massive, global exercise in anticipatory democracy.

Social future assemblies need not—and, given the rate of transience—

cannot be anchored, permanent institutions. Instead, they might take the form of ad hoc groupings, perhaps called into being at regular intervals with different representatives participating each time. Today citizens are expected to serve on juries when needed. They give a few days or a few weeks of their time for this service, recognizing that the jury system is one of the guarantees of democracy, that, even though service may be inconvenient, someone must do the job. Social future assemblies could be organized along similar lines, with a constant stream of new participants brought together for short periods to serve as society's "consultants on the future."

• • •

All social future assemblies . . . could and should be backed with technical staff to provide data on the social and economic costs of various goals, and to show the cost and benefits of proposed trade-offs, so that participants would be in a position to make reasonably informed choices, as it were, among alternative futures.

• • •

Most important of all . . . social future assemblies would help shift the culture toward a more super-industrial time-bias. By focusing public attention for once on long-range goals rather than immediate programs alone, by asking people to choose a preferable future from among a range of alternative futures, these assemblies could dramatize the possibilities for humanizing the future—possibilities that all too many have already given up as lost. In so doing, social future assemblies could unleash powerful constructive forces—the forces of conscious evolution.

By now the accelerative thrust triggered by man has become the key to the entire evolutionary process on the planet. The rate and direction of the evolution of other species, their very survival, depends upon decisions made by man. Yet there is nothing inherent in the evolutionary process to guarantee man's own survival.

Throughout the past, as successive stages of social evolution unfolded, man's awareness followed rather than preceded the event. Because change was slow, he could adapt unconsciously, "organically." Today unconscious adaptation is no longer adequate. Faced with power to alter the gene, to create new species, to populate the planets or depopulate the earth, man must now assume conscious control of evolution itself. Avoiding future shock as he rides the waves of change, he must master evolution, shaping tomorrow to human need. Instead of rising in revolt against it, he must, from this historic moment on, anticipate and design the future.

This, then, is the ultimate objective of social futurism, not merely the transcendence of technocracy and the substitution of more humane, more far-sighted, more democratic planning, but the subjection of the process of evolution itself to conscious human guidance. For this is the supreme instant, the turning point in history at which man either vanquishes the processes of change or vanishes, at which, from being the unconscious puppet of evolution he becomes either its victim or its master.

• • •

QUESTIONS FOR DISCUSSION

1. How would you evaluate Davis' analysis of the population problem and his proposals for solution? How might an analysis and solution of the population explosion using the social pathology perspective differ from Davis'?

2. Gordon's proposed solution for the problem of multiple, uncoordinated urban governments is one of centralization and consolidation. How does this compare with the kind of solution Toffler would suggest?

3. What do you think of the program of the Puerto Rican Forum? Would you revise it in any way? What implications does it have for the solution of other social problems?

4. Alvin Toffler in *Future Shock* suggests we plan "utopias" in terms of a super-industrial model rather than the preindustrial model usually proposed by contemporary social pathologists. Which model appeals most to you? Why? Are they mutually exclusive? What seems most realistic?

5. What do you think of Toffler's suggestions regarding "popular democratization" and "social future assemblies"?

6. Is it realistic to think we can predict how the various parts of society are interrelated and how intervention in one part will affect another part or the whole system? Explain your position.

7. Is "social disorganization" an objective, neutral expression or does it mask a value judgment about the nature of the organization or values of some segment of society? In light of your answer, do you think active intervention into the problem situation, which is suggested by this perspective, is justified?

8. Summarize what you think are the major strengths and weaknesses of the social disorganization perspective and the solutions it suggests.

SELECTED REFERENCES

McCorkle, Lloyd W. and Richard Korn, "Resocialization within Walls," *The Annals of the American Academy of Political and Social Science,* 293 (May 1954), pp. 88–98.

McCorkle and Korn portray culture conflict, normlessness, and normative breakdown among inmates, treatment personnel, and custodial staff within the prison. To become true resocializing agencies, prisons need clear, consistent, enforced rules.

McHugh, Peter, "Social Disintegration as a Requisite of Resocialization," *Social Forces,* 64 (March 1966), pp. 355–63.

In a sophisticated theoretical argument, McHugh points out that social reorganization is probably possible only through induced social disorganization. His position owes much to ethnomethodology, a branch of sociology which maintains that perhaps the best way of finding out the basis of current order is by creating social disorder.

Sennett, Richard, *The Uses of Disorder: Personal Identity and City Life,* New York: Alfred A. Knopf, 1970.

If urban neighbors will come into contact and conflict, Sennett suggests, they will come to know one another as individuals. The resulting accommodations they make will produce a new state of social organization in urban areas to replace the current state of social disorganization.

Von Eckardt, Wolf, "Urban Design," in Daniel P. Moynihan (ed.), *Toward a National Urban Policy,* New York: Basic Books, 1970, pp. 107–18.

Urban research, urban planning, and urban design are all needed to decrease the disorganization of cities and their pattern of change. The author discusses the nature of these aspects of organized change and how they can prevent programs from inadvertently heightening rather than diminishing disorganization.

4 VALUE CONFLICT

Some see the present state of culture and society, current modes of interpersonal relations, and the development of nuclear weapons as manifestations of a "sick society." They define society, its institutions, and its structures as social problems. And some believe that these social problems can be resolved by changing human nature through moral re-education. Many people, however, do not define these situations as social problems. And of those who do agree with the definition, there are probably just as many who fail to see how moral or characterological changes will solve the problems.

Many people may spend very little time worrying about world population, technological change, the assimilation of immigrants, and the costs and benefits of city services. They may very well feel that they have more than enough personal troubles to keep them occupied. And even if many of them did give some thought to these situations and agreed upon their being bona fide social problems, it is doubtful that they would also agree on what steps should be taken toward their solution.

It is obvious, then, that there is widespread disagreement over whether certain situations are social problems. It is also obvious that just as much disagreement exists over what to do about situations defined as social problems. Since the United States is a pluralistic society, there is no monolithic system of beliefs, norms, and values to which the population of over 200 million people completely subscribe. A diversity rather than a unity of interpretations is more often the case because members of the population differ by age, sex, income, education, occupation, ethnicity, race, religion, residence, community, and region. Since all have different combinations of these social statuses, so do all exhibit different combinations of beliefs, norms, and values.

This very obvious fact, however, if looked at in a new way, actually provides yet another perspective on social problems—situations are social problems when people say they are. They become manifest when conflict exists either over the definition of the situation as a problem or

135

over the appropriate solution to the problem. Since values pertain to preferences, this way of looking at social problems has come to be known as the value conflict perspective.

CENTRAL FEATURES OF THE VALUE CONFLICT PERSPECTIVE

An important characteristic of all groups is that they seek interests in accordance with their values. In pursuing their own interests they frequently come into conflict with other groups who are similarly pursuing their interests. The analyst delineates what groups are fighting with one another, what they are fighting about, what interests and values are at stake, and what is the likely outcome of the battle. The central features of the value conflict perspective provide a framework for answering these questions.

The place.   Value conflict, as a perspective on problems and their solutions, is always very close to the scene of action—i.e. the problem situation itself. To a very large extent this seems to be true because so many of the problems encompass, as well as arise in, the course of some pattern of social interaction. As a result, two points can be made about the social location of this perspective. First, it is more apt to be found in the course of everyday struggles between groups than in the rhetoric of our government or our academic writings. Second, the perspective is apt to be voiced most clearly and sharply by the leaders of the respective groups who are contesting against one another.

This is not to say that officials in government are strangers to the rhetoric of value conflict or that sociologists do not include the concept in their intellectual tool kit. Far from it. But there are some important differences that need to be taken into account in the respective roles that persons and groups take in the social-problem-solution process. These roles afford the location from which a particular attitude of mind comes into being for viewing and responding to problem situations. For example, the leaders of groups involved in a struggle over interests and values act as ideologists for their constituents, while government officials, for the most part, prefer to take the role of administering the conflict process itself, seeking the neutrality of referee as far as humanly possible. By the same token, sociologists and others in academia perform an intellectual function. They formulate a broader view, to ascertain of what larger generalization the problem under discussion may be an instance, and, if at all possible, to fit it to some set of principles. While the sociologist, for instance, may work hard to account for the existence of the problem in the light of a particular sociological theory, the leaders of the opposed groups must take immediate action on the problem.

Different positions within the problem process are thus acquired in the course of social life, and these positions constrain participants to examine the merits of the problem from their special locations.

The attitude. The attitude of the value conflict perspective has four characteristics. It is *naturalistic, group-centered, specific,* and *evaluative.* It is naturalistic in that persons who appraise problem situations from the perspective of value conflict do so in terms of everyday life. The viewpoint of the speaker or writer is quite clear. Most of the time, he talks about the situation from personal experience in a way that suggests intimate contact with persons caught up in the problem situation.

It is group-centered in that reports on the situation and the experiences are one-sided according to the group's values. Such reports explicitly include a remark to the effect that "this is how things look to the group."

It is specific in describing how the group's interests and values have been affected by the problem situation. The spokesman talks about details of the immediate situation and limits his discussion and analysis to these details, treating them as the "facts" of the case.

Finally, the view is evaluative in that the group's interests have been jeopardized and its values threatened. In reaction to this definition of the situation, any spokesman regards the situation as disturbing and as wrong according to the group's value scheme. Saul Alinsky, theorist and practitioner of social conflict, sums up the attitude quite well, "All of life is partisan. There is no dispassionate objectivity."[1]

The content. Typical content in the value conflict perspective includes: *the recital of grievances, the expression of moral indignation, the interest-value assessment, identity by opposition,* and *the declaration of group duty.*

a. The recital of grievances. Communications about the problem situation, regardless of the media, contain grievances, such as actual injuries experienced by the members of the group and continued potential dangers or threats. Persistent failure of tenement landlords to keep apartments in good repair is an example.

b. The expression of moral indignation. Complaints issued give voice to feelings of moral indignation. These strong feelings arise from the sense of unmet expectations and unfulfilled obligations. Some agents or agencies have failed to perform duties required of them, or they have engaged in actions that are violations of some set of social rules. Inter-

---

1. Saul Alinsky, *Rules for Radicals,* New York: Random House, 1971, p. 10.

estingly, moral indignation varies inversely with the expectations held
and the degree to which they are violated. That is, the better off people
are, the less offense they will tolerate. And, conversely, the worse off
people are, the more offense they will take. Nonetheless, deprived
people also have their limits. And when these are reached, they experience and express their moral indignation.

c. The interest-value assessment.   Some assessment of the probable
course of events is necessary. An inventory of the consequences for the
group is outlined, indicating what may be expected should the situation continue. Assessment itemizes the relevant group interests
and values at stake. The assessment closes generally with the report
that losses to the group, both in a material and moral sense, are the
cardinal features of the situation.

d. Identity by opposition.   A new group identity develops out of the
assessment. The assessment indicates to the group what sort of collective identity it now has in the eyes of others and how that collective
identity may be changed when the group opposes its oppressors.

e. Declaration of group duty.   This declaration is an agenda that sets
forth what the group is obliged to do if it is to realize its new identity or
to gain or regain power, status, or wealth. Once the group's humanity
has been compromised and put at stake, action to redress grievances
and to institute a fundamental change in the situation is necessary. The
agenda tries to make clear to the group that it really has no other set of
options.

   Thus, in summary, the value conflict perspective most often appears
close to the scene of the social problem, reflects a group-based attitude,
and contains both a definition of the situation as a problem and a
determination to seek redress in some way.

THE FORMULA

The central features narrate the circumstances of the problem and make
the case for collective action. Unless the steps noted above are completed, such action is most unlikely. Should they be completed, a plan
of action in terms of form, doctrine, and recipe can then be formulated.

The vocabulary.   Terms describing the form of value conflict come
mainly from everyday language and deal with the means and ends of
social contests. Because there are so many possible kinds of contests,

the list to follow is only representative, not exhaustive: *action, aliena-*
tion, bargain, community control, deal, demands, demonstration, dis-
crimination, domination, equality, exploitation, fight, freedom, identity,
issues, justice, militancy, movement, negotiation, oppression, over-
throw, polarization, politics, power, protest, radical, reform, rights,
self-interest, sides, strategy, strike, struggle, and tactics.

The beliefs and doctrines. The basic assumptions of the value conflict perspective are closely tied to the personal experience of social
conflict. From this experience a philosophy of conflict, together with
strategy and tactics, has evolved. Given the philosophy, conficts can be
interpreted, programs for change fashioned, and struggles carried out.
The assumptions are:

  a. Ideas and values represent group interests.

  b. Since there are so many groups, conflicts of interest are inevitable.

  c. Order in society is maintained by resolving these conflicts according to some system of institutionalized compromise between conflicting
interests.

  d. Institutions, such as the courts, seek to resolve disputes that cannot
be settled by the prevailing system of compromise.

  e. When social institutions fail, the conflict becomes more manifest
and more visibly a social problem.

  f. That group which brings to bear the strongest combination of
moral, economic, and political sanctions controls the terms of the new
compromise that will redress or stabilize the situation.

The principal assumption is that conflict really is the rule rather than
the exception, but so long as it is bound up in a socially sanctioned system of compromise, social order prevails. This order, however, is more
often in keeping with the interests of dominant groups. When different
values and interests can no longer be managed according to rules of
compromise, a state of conflict can ensue.

The recipe. After a realistic solution is pointed out, the conflict becomes more socially apparent. This recipe for solution follows the three
stages of *arousal, mobilization,* and *enactment.*

a. Arousal. Arousal consists of two paradoxical parts. The first
part calls attention to the pattern of violated expectations, showing members of the group that the actual situation exists and is worse
than they had thought it was. The greater the apathy and resigned
acceptance of the troublesome state, the greater the effort required to
produce awareness. The second part instills hope by calling attention
to how they might respond to ameliorate or resolve the problem.

b. Mobilization. Mobilization consists of spreading the word and organizing a social base. The word is a message which says the limits of tolerance have been reached. All people exposed to the oppressive features of the situation should then join together. Once they have met, the next task is organizing for social action. The procedure here is to recruit as many people as possible to join the incipient movement. In order to form a strong base, recruits should include those directly affected by the problem, those indirectly affected, and sympathizers. All three form a coalition that constitutes the mobilized social base.

c. Enactment. Enactment, the final phase, consists of drawing up the set of demands that will best serve the interests of the group and support their threatened values. Here, leaders draw up a plan of attack, set forth a list of demands, and suggest a set of slogans or symbols that neatly summarizes what the group seeks and why. Tactics consist essentially of putting the demands and the plan of action into operation. Demonstrations, marches, picketing, strikes, sit-ins, and teach-ins are some examples of tactics that have become formalized in recent years on the part of specific social movements formed around conflict over such issues as peace, poverty, and racial injustice.

If the recipe is viewed as an organizational process in its own right, then it is clear that it is most complex and contingent in character. Several points should be briefly noted with regard to organization, complexity, and contingencies. Organizing groups on behalf of their own threatened values becomes more difficult the longer they have accepted the situation as unchangeable. Once expectations rise, however, the possibility of organizing discontented persons on behalf of threatened or unrealized values increases. Moreover, inaction on social problems is more likely as the number of interrelated values that are in conflict increases. Such complexity calls attention to the fact that certain proposed solutions would actually jeopardize other values; consequently, many persons are willing to live with the situation without solving it. Finally, the variety of contingencies which affect social conflict have yet to be worked out fully. It is clear, however, that as a result of various contingencies, some solutions based on value conflict have failed while others have succeeded.

THE HISTORY OF THE VALUE CONFLICT PERSPECTIVE

The value conflict perspective has been fashioned from the observations of sociologists about the conflicts among nations and among groups within a society.

Governments. Value conflict, throughout recorded history, has described the relations that ensue among nations. Alliances, treaties, negotiations, and warfare indicate the several ways that nations and their governments have tried to deal with persistent value conflicts. Because of the long experience of our own country with such features of international relations, the character of value conflict became apparent.

Intrasocietal groups. Because of the increased prevalence of overt group conflict in American society in the last decade, the value conflict perspective provides perhaps the best framework for reading and interpreting the news. We see more and more groups fighting for their rights and beliefs. Disaffected with their lot in life, they organize, obtain a power base, and contest their own or other's definitions and evaluations. As a result, the black, Chicano, homophile, Indian, Puerto Rican, and women's rights movements have adopted the techniques of the labor movement. Many of these movements, of course, have given rise to countermovements, thereby intensifying the conflict. The value conflict perspective delineates such movement and countermovement.

Because it deals with social power this perspective is also extremely useful in describing and analyzing a number of social problems that are somewhat less visible than the ones noted above. If much of the exercise of power is visible, a good deal more is less so. Thus, the fate of many laws, whether passed or defeated, enforced or neglected, could well be explained in terms of conflicting values and interests among various groups in the society.

Sociological students of conflict. Among the masters of European sociological thought, conflict theorists abound. Franz Oppenheimer, for one, saw warfare as the basis for the origin of the state and society.[2] Ludwig Gumplowicz, for another, held that racial conflict was the key to understanding social and historical development.[3] For American sociology the two most important theorists have been Karl Marx and Georg Simmel. Marx described history as the result of struggles between social classes.[4] Given the character of tension and conflict in the world at present, more and more sociologists are returning to the works of Marx. Simmel examined conflict as a feature of interpersonal relations, and his work also makes it possible to understand problems within society according to a system of formal principles.[5]

2. Franz Oppenheimer, *Der Staat,* Frankfurt, Germany, 1908; *System der Soziologie,* Vol. 1, Jena, Germany, 1923; Vol. 2, 1926.
3. Ludwig Gumplowicz, *Der Rassenkampf,* Innsbruck, Austria, 1883.
4. Karl Marx and Friedrich Engels, *Selected Works,* 2 Vols., Moscow: Foreign Languages Publishing House, 1965.
5. Georg Simmel, "The Sociology of Conflict," translated from the German by Albion W. Small, *American Journal of Sociology* 9 (1903–4), pp. 490–525, 672–89, 798–811.

Robert E. Park and Albion Small brought Simmel's theories to the attention of American sociologists.[6] Their work, however, did not include giving special attention to social problems as instances of social conflict. It remained for L. K. Frank and Willard Waller to suggest that numerous social problems exist by reason of a conflict between what people know to be right and what they also know to be best for themselves.[7] Because of the very natural tension between culture and social organizations, Waller, for instance, was convinced that people just do not really want to solve certain social problems.

The major theorist on the conflict of values as the source of social problems in American sociology is Richard C. Fuller.[8] He coined the phrase and showed how values were involved in natural disasters and in moral and economic problems. Values determine, he said, whether or not groups agree on the definition of a situation as a problem and on the solution to the problem. Groups commonly clash over the definition of a problem or over its solution. In this clash between group interests and values, Fuller located the heart of social problems. He charted three stages of problems—awareness, policy determination, and reform—and indicated that values are in conflict at each of these stages. Fuller favored a realistic approach to the teaching of social problems: "If the student is to understand why these old established problems persist and defy solution, he must examine the values of our social organization which bring the undesirable conditions into existence and which obstruct efforts to remove them."[9]

In their textbook, Cuber, Kenkel, and Harper set forth Fuller's framework, asking students to treat values as data and to try to assess all the groups and all the values involved in specific social problems.[10] A number of books, monographs, and papers have also appeared which study specific social problems and the social movements they have generated in what might be loosely described as a conflict-of-values perspective.

6. Albion W. Small and George E. Vincent, *An Introduction to the Study of Society,* New York: American Book Co., 1894. Robert E. Park and Ernest W. Burgess, *Introduction to the Science of Sociology,* Chicago: The University of Chicago Press, 1921.

7. Lawrence K. Frank, "Social Problems," *American Journal of Sociology* 30 (January 1925), pp. 463–75. Willard Waller, "Social Problems and the Mores," *American Sociological Review* 1 (December 1963), pp. 924–33.

8. Richard C. Fuller, "Sociological Theory and Social Problems," *Social Forces* 15 (May 1937), pp. 496–502, Richard C. Fuller, "The Problem of Teaching Social Problems," *American Journal of Sociology* 44 (November 1938), pp. 415–28. Richard C. Fuller, "Social Problems," Part I, in R. E. Park (ed.), *An Outline of the Principles of Sociology,* New York: Barnes and Noble, 1939, pp. 3–61. Richard C. Fuller and Richard R. Myers, "Some Aspects of a Theory of Social Problems," *American Sociological Review* 6 (February 1941), pp. 24–32, Richard C. Fuller and Richard R. Myers, "The Natural History of a Social Problem," *American Sociological Review* 6 (June 1941), pp. 320–28.

9. Richard C. Fuller and Richard R. Myers, *op. cit.* (June 1941), p. 327.

10. John F. Cuber, William F. Kenkel, and Robert A. Harper, *Problems of American Society: Values in Conflict,* 4th ed., New York: Holt, Rinehart and Winston, 1964.

There have yet to appear, however, any funded research proposals in which sociologists seek to sketch out specific plans for solving problems involving conflicting values. Sociologists may well wish to be political activists, but as sociologists their first task has been to analyze the conflict situations.

SUMMARY AND CONCLUSION

The value conflict perspective deals with different groups' conflicting interpretations of what the world is and should be. When groups have confronted one another about these conflicting interpretations, the conditions for the development of a social problem have emerged. When interested parties—group leaders, agitators, students, or citizens —continually call attention to the values in conflict, set forth an alternative, mobilize a social base, and seek to achieve what they see as a solution, the social problem becomes most apparent. It is in the actual social struggle ensuing from the attempt to solve the problem that a much wider public becomes aware of the existence of the problem itself.

BLACK POWER

Stokely Carmichael and Charles V. Hamilton

Racism is ingrained in our society. Whether individual or institutional, it expresses itself in inequality, exploitation, discrimination, and the like. According to Stokely Carmichael and Charles Hamilton, the only answer for black people is to organize politically, take control of their own institutions, and obtain the interests of the black community. Only in this way can the black community trade powerlessness for power in directing its own destiny. The story of New York City School I.S. 201 is presented as a case in point. In addition, recommendations and illustrations are given regarding the needed economic and political restructuring of the black community.

We are aware that it has become commonplace to pinpoint and describe the ills of our urban ghettos. The social, political and economic

problems are so acute that even a casual observer cannot fail to see
that something is wrong. While description is plentiful, however, there
remains a blatant timidity about what to *do* to solve the problems.

Neither rain nor endless "definitive," costly reports nor stop-gap
measures will even approach a solution to the explosive situation in
the nation's ghettos. This country cannot begin to solve the problems
of the ghettos as long as it continues to hang on to outmoded structures
and institutions. A political party system that seeks only to "manage
conflict" and hope for the best will not be able to serve a growing body
of alienated black people. An educational system which, year after
year, continues to cripple hundreds of thousands of black children
must be replaced by wholly new mechanisms of control and management. We must begin to think and operate in terms of entirely new
and substantially different forms of expression.

It is crystal clear that the initiative for such changes will have to
come from the black community. We cannot expect white America
to begin to move forcefully on these problems unless and until black
America begins to move. This means that black people must organize
themselves without regard for what is traditionally acceptable, precisely because the traditional approaches have failed. It means that
black people must make demands without regard to their initial "respectability," precisely because "respectable" demands have not been
sufficient.

The northern urban ghettos are in many ways different from the
black-belt South, but in neither area will substantial change come
about until black people organize independently to exert power. As
noted in earlier chapters, black people already have the voting potential to control the politics of entire southern counties. Given maximum registration of blacks, there are more than 110 counties where
black people could outvote the white racists. These people should concentrate on forming independent political parties and not waste time
trying to reform or convert the racist parties. In the North, it is no less
important that independent groups be formed. It has been clearly
shown that when black people attempt to get within one of the two
major parties in the cities, they become co-opted and their interests
are shunted to the background. They become expendable.

We must begin to think of the black community as a base of organization to control institutions in that community. Control of the
ghetto schools must be taken out of the hands of "professionals," most
of whom have long since demonstrated their insensitivity to the needs
and problems of the black child. These "experts" bring with them
middle-class biases, unsuitable techniques and materials; these are, at
best, dysfunctional and at worst destructive. A recent study of New
York schools reveals that the New York school system is run by thirty

people—school supervisors, deputy and assistant superintendents and examiners. The study concluded: "Public education policy has become the province of the professional bureaucrat, with the tragic result that the status quo, suffering from many difficulties, is the order of the day."[1] Virtually no attention is paid to the wishes and demands of the parents, especially the black parents. This is totally unacceptable.

Black parents should seek as their goal the actual control of the public schools in their community: hiring and firing of teachers, selection of teaching materials, determination of standards, etc. This can be done with a committee of teachers. The traditional, irrelevant "See Dick, See Jane, Run Dick, Run Jane, White House, Nice Farm" nonsense must be ended. The principals and as many teachers as possible of the ghetto schools should be black. The children will be able to see their kind in positions of leadership and authority. It should never occur to anyone that a brand new school can be built in the heart of the black community and then given a white person to head it. The fact is that in this day and time, it is crucial that race be taken into account in determining policy of this sort. Some people will, again, view this as "reverse segregation" or as "racism." It is not. It is emphasizing race in a positive way: not to subordinate or rule over others but to overcome the effects of centuries in which race has been used to the detriment of the black man.

The story of I.S. 201 in New York City is a case in point. In 1958, the city's Board of Education announced that it would build a special $5-million school in District 4, whose pupils are 90 percent black, 8 percent Puerto Rican, with the remaining 2 percent white. The concept was that students from elementary schools in that district would feed into the new school at the fifth grade and after the eighth grade would move on to high school. This concept, at least according to official policy, was supposed to speed integration.

The parents of children who might be attending the school mobilized in an attempt, once and for all, to have a school adequate for the needs of Harlem. The Board had picked the site for I.S. 201: between 127th and 128th Streets, from Madison Avenue to Park Avenue—in the heart of Central Harlem. The parents argued against this location because they wanted an integrated school, which would be impossible unless it was located on the fringes, not in the heart, of Central Harlem. Their desire clearly points up the colonial relationship of blacks and whites in the city; they knew the only way to get quality education was to have white pupils in the school.

The Board of Education indicated that the school would be in-

1. Marilyn Gittell, "Participants and Participation: A Study of School Policy in New York City," New York: The Center for Urban Education. As quoted in the *New York Times,* April 30, 1967, p. E90.

tegrated, but the parents knew it could not be done and they demonstrated against the site during construction. When they saw that the school would have no windows, they also raised the question of whether this was merely a stylistic or practical innovation, or a means of closing out the reality of the community from the pupils for the hours they would be inside.

During the spring and summer of 1966, some six hundred pupils registered at I.S. 201—all of them black or Puerto Rican. Their parents then threatened that if the school wasn't integrated by fall, they would boycott it. The Board of Education, giving lip service to the parents, passed out and mailed 10,000 leaflets to the white community—in June!

Needless to say, few people go to a school on the basis of a leaflet received while getting off the subway or wherever, and even fewer (white) people want to send their children to school in Harlem. The request for "volunteers" had no effect, and on September 7, the Board of Education finally admitted its "apparent inability to integrate the school." It was the inability of that class . . . "whose primary interest is to secure objects for service, management, and control," the objects in this case being the mothers of I.S. 201. Threatened by a boycott, the school was not opened as scheduled on September 12, 1966.

At this point, the parents—who were picketing—moved in the only way they could: to demand some form of control which would enable them to break out of the old colonial pattern. In view of the fact that whites would not send their children to the school, one parent stated, "We decided we would have to have a voice to ensure that we got quality education segregated-style. We wanted built-in assurances." The parents knew that within a few years, given that pattern, this new school would be like all others which started with fine facilities and deteriorated under an indifferent bureaucracy. The parents' demands thus shifted from integration to control.

On September 16, Superintendent Bernard E. Donovan offered them a voice in screening and recommending candidates for supervisory and teaching positions at the school. An East Harlem community council would be set up with a strong voice in school affairs. The parents also wanted some control over the curriculum, the career guidance system, and financial matters, which the Board deemed legally impossible. Shortly afterward, the white principal—Stanley Lisser—voluntarily requested transfer. A black principal had been one of the parents' key demands. With these two developments, the parents announced that they would send their children to school.

At this point (September 19), however, the United Federation of Teachers bolted. The teachers at I.S. 201 threatened to boycott if Lisser did not stay. Within twenty-four hours, the Board had rescinded its agreement and restored Lisser. (It is contended by many that this was the result of planned collusion between the Board and the U.F.T.) Nine days late, the school opened. The parents became divided; some gladly began sending their children to school while others did the same because they were unaware that the agreement had been rescinded.

The parents' negotiating committee had moved to get outside help, while the city's top administrators, including Mayor Lindsay, entered the picture. A Harlem committee representing parents and community leaders proposed on September 29 that I.S. 201 be put under a special "operations board" composed of four parents and four university educators with another member selected by those eight. This board would pass on the selection of teachers and supervisors, and evaluate the curriculum at I.S. 201 as well as three elementary or "feeder" schools. But the U.F.T. attacked this proposal. As the struggle dragged on, it became clear that once again efforts by the community to deal with its problems had been laid waste.

Later, in October, the Board of Education offered the parents a take-it-or-leave-it proposal. It proposed a council of parents and teachers that would be purely advisory. The parents flatly rejected this. Father Vincent Resta, a Catholic priest and chairman of the local school board which covered I.S. 201, stated, "In theory the Board's proposal is something that could work. But an advisory role implies trust. And the community has absolutely no reason to trust the Board of Education." The local board later resigned en masse.

But the issue of community control did not end there. It had become clear to the parents that their problems were not restricted to School District 4. When the Board of Education met to discuss its proposed budget in December, 1966, I.S. 201 parents and others came to protest the allocation of resources. Unable to get any response, at the end of one session they simply moved from the gallery into the chairs of those meeting and elected a People's Board of Education. After forty-eight hours, they were arrested and removed but continued to meet in another location, with the Rev. Milton A. Galamison—who had led school boycotts previously in New York City—as President.

At one of its executive sessions on January 8, 1967, the People's Board adopted a motion which stated its goals as:

1. To seek to alter the structure of the school system . . . so it is responsible to our individual community needs, in order to achieve real community control. This may require legislative or state constitutional convention action. This means, of course, decentralization, accountability, meaningful citizen participation, etc.

2. To develop a program which will get grassroots awareness for,

understanding of, and support for the goal stated above. It is suggested that we give up top priority to organizing and educating parents and citizens in the poverty areas (approximately 14).

3. That we recognize that power should not rest in any central board, including our own, and that by every means possible we should encourage the development and initiative of local people's groups.

The parents at I.S. 201 failed because they are still powerless. But they succeeded in heating up the situation to the point where the dominant society will have to make certain choices. It is clear that black people are concerned about the type of education their children receive; many more people can be activated by a demonstrated ability to achieve results. One result has already been achieved by the I.S. 201 struggle: the concept of community control has now rooted itself in the consciousness of many black people. Such control has long been accepted in smaller communities, particularly white suburban areas. No longer is it "white folks' business" only. Ultimately, community-controlled schools could organize an independent school board (like the "People's Board of Education") for the total black community. Such an innovation would permit the parents and the school to develop a much closer relationship and to begin attacking the problems of the ghetto in a communal, realistic way.

· · ·

Virtually all of the money earned by merchants and exploiters of the black ghetto leaves those communities. Properly organized black groups should seek to establish a community rebate plan. The black people in a given community would organize and refuse to do business with any merchant who did not agree to "reinvest," say, forty to fifty percent of his net profit in the indigenous community. This contribution could take many forms: providing additional jobs for black people, donating scholarship funds for students, supporting certain types of community organizations. An agreement would be reached between the merchants and the black consumers. If a merchant wants customers from a black community, he must be made to understand that he has to contribute to that community. If he chooses not to do so, he will not be patronized, and the end result will be *no* profits from that community. Contractors who seek to do business in the black community would also be made to understand that they face a boycott if they do not donate to the black community.

Such a community rebate plan will require careful organization and tight discipline on the part of the black people. But it is possible, and has in fact already been put into effect by some ethnic communities. White America realizes the market in the black community; black America must begin to realize the potential of that market.

Under the present institutional arrangements, no one should think that the mere election of a few black people to local or national office will solve the problem of political representation. There are now ten black people on the City Council in Chicago, but there are not more than two or three (out of the total of fifty) who will speak out forcefully. The fact is that the present political institutions are not geared to giving the black minority an effective voice. Two needs arise from this.

First, it is important that the black communities in these northern ghettos form independent party groups to elect their own choices to office when and where they can. It should not be assumed that "you cannot beat City Hall." It has been done, as evidenced by the 1967 aldermanic elections in one of the tightest machine cities in the country: Chicago. In the Sixth Ward, an independent black candidate, Sammy Rayner, defeated an incumbent, machine-backed black alderman. Rayner first ran in 1963 and missed a run-off by a mere 177 votes. He then challenged Congressman William L. Dawson in 1964 and lost, but he was building an image in the black community as one who could and would speak out. The black people were getting the message. In 1967, when he ran against the machine incumbent for the City Council, he won handily. Precincts in the East Woodlawn area that he had failed to carry in 1963 (23 out of 26), he now carried (19 out of 26). The difference was continuous, hard, day-to-day, door-to-door campaigning. His campaign manager, Philip Smith, stated: "Another key to Sammy's victory was the fact that he began to methodically get himself around the Sixth Ward. Making the black club functions, attending youth meetings and all the functions that were dear to the hearts of Sixth Ward people became the order of the day."[2]

The cynics will say that Rayner will be just one voice, unable to accomplish anything unless he buckles under to the Daley machine. Let us be very clear: we do not endorse Rayner nor are we blind to the problems he faces. It is the job of the machine to crush such men or to co-opt them before they grow in numbers and power. At the same time, men like Rayner are useful only so long as they speak to the community's broad needs; as we said . . . black visibility is not Black Power. If Rayner does not remain true to his constituents, then they should dislodge him as decisively as they did his predecessor. This establishes the principle that the black politician must first be responsive to his constituents, not to the white machine. The problem then is to

2. Philip Smith, "Politics as I See It," *The Citizen,* Chicago (March 22, 1967).

resist the forces which would crush or co-opt while building community strength so that more of such men can be elected and compelled to act in the community's interest.

(It should be noted that Rayner is one of numerous black leaders who have rejected the term Black Power although their own statements, attitudes and programs suggest that they endorse what we mean by Black Power. The reason for this, by and large, is a fear of offending the powers-that-be which may go by the name of "tactics." This again exemplifies the need to raise the level of consciousness, to create a new consciousness among black people.)

The very least which Sammy Rayner can give the black community is a new political dignity. His victory will begin to establish the *habit* of saying "No" to the downtown bosses. In the same way that the black Southerner had to assert himself and say "No" to those who did not want him to register to vote, now the Northern black voter must begin to defy those who would control his vote. This very act of defiance threatens the status quo, because there is no predicting its ultimate outcome. Those black voters, then *accustomed* to acting independently, could eventually swing their votes one way or the other—but always for *their* benefit. Smith signaled this when he said: "The disbelievers who felt that you could not beat City Hall are now whistling a different tune. The victory of Sammy Rayner in the Sixth Ward should serve as a beacon light for all who believe in independent politics in this city. . . . Rayner is going to be responsible for the aldermanic position taking on a new line of dignity. Black people are going to be able to point with pride to this man, who firmly believes that we need statesmanlike leadership instead of the goatsmanship we have been exposed to."[3]

Let no one protest that this type of politics is naive or childish or fails to understand the "rules of the game." The price of going along with the "regulars" is too high to pay for the so-called benefits received. The rewards of independence can be considerable. It is too soon to say precisely where this new spirit of independence could take us. New forms may lead to a new political force. Hopefully, this force might move to create new national and local political parties—or, more accurately, the first *legitimate* political parties. Some have spoken of a "third party" or "third political force." But from the viewpoint of community needs and popular participation, no existing force or party in this country has ever been relevant. A force which is relevant would therefore be a first—something truly new.

The second implication of the political dilemma facing black people is that ultimately they may have to spearhead a drive to revamp completely the present institutions of representation. If the Rayners are

3. *Ibid.*

continually outvoted, if the grievances of the black community continue to be overlooked, then it will become necessary to devise wholly new forms of local political representation. There is nothing sacred about the system of electing candidates to serve as aldermen, councilmen, etc., by wards or districts. Geographical representation is not inherently right. Perhaps political interests have to be represented in some entirely different manner—such as community-parent control of schools, unions of tenants, unions of welfare recipients actually taking an official role in running the welfare departments. If political institutions do not meet the needs of the people, if the people finally believe that those institutions do not express their own values, then those institutions must be discarded. It is wasteful and inefficient, not to mention unjust, to continue imposing old forms and ways of doing things on a people who no longer view those forms and ways as functional.

We see independent politics (after the fashion of a Rayner candidacy) as the first step toward implementing something new. Voting year after year for the traditional party and its silent representatives gets the black community nowhere; voters then get their own candidates, but these may become frustrated by the power and organization of the machines. The next logical step is to demand more meaningful structures, forms and ways of dealing with long-standing problems.

We see this as the potential power of the ghettos. In a real sense, it is similar to what is taking place in the South: the move in the direction of independent politics—and from there, the move toward the development of wholly new political institutions. If these proposals also sound impractical, utopian, then we ask: what other real alternatives exist? There are none; the choice lies between a genuinely new approach and maintaining the brutalizing, destructive, violence-breeding life of the ghettos as they exist today. From the viewpoint of black people, that is no choice.

DISRUPTING CITY SERVICES TO CHANGE NATIONAL PRIORITIES

Frances Piven and Richard Cloward

Frances Piven and Richard Cloward argue that only massive subsidies can help the poor, but that funds for such subsidies have been diverted to the Vietnam War. At the same time, slum landlords have been skimping or speculating with their funds, also to the detriment of the poor, and millions of people eligible for welfare benefits have been unaware of their rights.

Thus, the poor need to organize and work together on behalf of their interests. For example, rent strikes could force landlords to repair houses and improve services, or to abandon houses to municipal take-over. Too, the poor should be mobilized to demand welfare benefits which have been withheld from them. A resulting fiscal crisis for city governments, the fear of urban ghetto violence, and the fact that the national administration needs votes—as does the city administration—mean that such a dramatization of issues could compel a Federal release of monies to ease the situation.

We often say that the nation's poor, especially the black poor, are carrying the main burdens of the war in Vietnam. Yet little is being done to make the poor an effective force in shifting national priorities from war to domestic programs. Mass demonstrations such as the Poor People's Campaign, which rely on "moral confrontation," are at best a limited form of pressure, and then only when conditions are ripe for new political accommodations. So far, the Administration has shown itself to be capable of absorbing countless demonstrations staged in the capitol itself.

The Administration is most vulnerable, we think, in the cities, especially if tactics more politically disruptive than demonstrations are employed. It is in the cities that the national Democratic Party has its base, and it is there that most of the black poor now live. Whatever happens in the cities reverberates on national Democratic leaders. Indeed, the growing demand from a wide variety of groups that the Administration give priority to trouble in the cities is becoming a major encumbrance on war policies. Trouble has been brewing over a number of years as masses of black poor have been forced off the land and into

From Frances Piven and Richard Cloward, "Disrupting City Services to Change National Priorities," *Viet-Report,* 3:8–9; 27–31 (Summer 1968).

the cities, where they aggravate municipal fiscal problems because of the public services they need, and aggravate the white working class by competing for scarce housing and jobs. Riots have further escalated tensions within urban Democratic constituencies, pushing municipalities nearer bankruptcy and worsening black-white electoral cleavages. Except for the war, massive federal grants-in-aid for welfare, health, housing, education, and employment could be used to ease this divisiveness between groups in the Democratic coalition, but that money now goes to the military establishment. If strategies can be found which substantially worsen tensions in the cities, the Administration might be forced to alter these priorities.

Disruptive strategies to produce this result are available. The cities are peculiarly vulnerable to disruption at this time, for city agencies serve older Democratic constituents at the expense of blacks who are a vast new electoral force in the cities. The key to disrupting services—and to exposing this anachronism—is to mobilize the poor either to withhold payments to a system from which they do not receive fair services because the system defers to other groups, or to mobilize people to claim benefits which have been withheld, again out of deference to other groups. First, we propose massive rent stoppages to bankrupt slum landlords and to force municipal takeover of slum buildings. Second, we will describe current efforts to organize actual and potential welfare recipients to claim hundreds of millions of dollars which are withheld from them, usually illegally. These strategies could force city governments into fiscal crisis, exacerbating already evident political strains in the cities, and escalating pressure on the Administration to bail out its urban political apparatus with massive subsidies for the poor.

DISRUPTING THE SLUM HOUSING SYSTEM

The slum is the underbelly of the real-estate market: tenants who cannot compete for housing elsewhere are preyed on by entrepreneurs who lack the capital or competence to compete for profit elsewhere. More prosperous and stable real-estate investors put their capital in the regular market, where money can be made in less demeaning ways, leaving the slum to be exploited by men who seek to gain on speculative exchanges or who, restrained by rent-control laws from levying large increases, shore up their declining profits by skimping on repairs and services. The result is inflated prices and deteriorated buildings—a situation that can be remedied only by public subsidies and public action.

But there is little political pressure for housing subsidies for the poor —only for affluent groups. And although deteriorated housing is illegal, public agencies make no effort to enforce housing codes, for a crackdown would produce massive dislocation of landlords and tenants. Repairs are extremely expensive, and building income is limited by the poverty of the captive tenant market. Slum landlords often do not have the funds to rehabilitate their buildings—not, at least, without substantial increases in rents. Just a modest step-up in enforcement activity under a new administration in New York City recently resulted in a rapid upsurge in the number of foreclosures, tax delinquencies and vacate orders. If slumlords were pushed out, government would have to house the minority poor. So the enforcement agencies use their powers gingerly and selectively, usually paying heed only when tenants have the tenacity or the "pull" to compel enforcement. In other words, slum profits depend on collusion between city agencies and landlords: in return for nonenforcement of the codes, the slumlord takes the blame for the slum and enables the city to evade the political ire of the ghetto.

To disrupt these collusive arrangements, the funds that fuel the slum system must be cut off. Tenants should be told to keep the rent money, and to spend it rather than put it aside for later payment to the landlord.

Some liberal jurisdictions have laws which authorize tenants in buildings with code violations to hold their rents in escrow accounts while they pursue an elaborate set of procedures culminating in a court action. But legalistic rent strikes have been a failure. Low-income tenants cannot secure redress in housing agencies and courts. At worst, the agencies and courts are corrupt instruments of real estate interests; at best, they are hamstrung by elaborate statutes and regulations written to safeguard private property. Even if this were not so, the sheer volume of tasks involved in pursuing a court case is overwhelming: canvassing buildings for violations; filling out complaint forms, arranging appointments for housing inspectors; checking to make sure that the inspectors file reports and that violations have been recorded; arranging for lawyers; chauffeuring tenants to trials—not once, but repeatedly as landlords successfully obtain adjournments. In short, everything we know about the failure of past legalistic rent strikes points to the futility of attempts to solve a widespread problem by making use of cumbersome procedures for individual legal redress.

Phase I: ending evictions.   The great obstacle to mounting a disruptive rent strike is the danger that tenants may be evicted. Fear of eviction will make tenants reluctant to withhold rent in the first place, and evictions later can break the morale of a rent-strike movement, causing its collapse. Thus the first phase of organizing should concentrate on resisting evictions. During this first phase, the momentum for a strike movement can also be built.

During a campaign to "Stop All Evictions!" in a particular neighborhood, resistance squads could be organized and tactics for dealing with marshals and police could be tested without exposing tenants to risk. In the meantime, organizers could talk up the idea of a rent strike. The key problem in this phase is to develop a neighborhood communications system for reporting evictions. One way is to leaflet a neighborhood, asking tenants threatened by eviction to call a central telephone number so that organizers can be dispatched to watch the apartment. Another way is to have organizers hang around the block, telling people to let them know the moment the marshal appears in the vicinity.

There are several tactics for resisting evictions. For example: organizers can mass both in front of the building and within the threatened apartment to block the marshal. They can sit on the furniture, return the furniture to the apartment as quickly as it is carried out, or neighborhood people could be deployed along the hallways and stairways through which the furniture must pass. To overcome even such simple tactics, a marshal must call for the police, who then must contemplate mass arrests in order to carry out a routine eviction. (So far, when these tactics have been tried, the police have been very reluctant to do the landlord's job.)

If resistance works, many more neighborhood people may be emboldened to join in. And when more people join, organizers can capitalize on the public's fear of riots. City officials are now extremely sensitive to the temper of ghettoes and exert themselves to avoid the minor incidents which have often set off conflagrations. Mayors have emergency power to halt evictions by executive order, and under the threat of riot would be likely to do so. Even tough-talking Mayor Daley of Chicago ordered all evictions halted during July and August of last year.

Phase II: rent revolt. Aside from reasonable assurances that they will not be evicted, tenants need an incentive to strike. The rent money is such an incentive, but only if the tenant can pocket it or spend it. Tenants who in past rent strikes were called upon to place their rent in escrow derived some satisfaction in just keeping the rent from the landlord, but the satisfaction would be far greater if that money could also be spent on family needs, particularly since rent absorbs so large a percentage of the typical slum family's income—sometimes more than half. At least as important, only the massive denial of rent will bankrupt the slum system; if the money is left to accumulate in escrow accounts, it will eventually be returned to landlords by the courts (or by tenants themselves, frightened by either the reality or the rumor that court cases are being lost).

The spread of rent-strike action must be controlled. If those withholding rent are dispersed over too wide an area, the logistics of resisting evictions may become overwhelming. It is probably preferable for organizers to work intensively on a few blocks at first, concentrating their energies to ensure complete coverage of eviction threats. As the area of strike action expands, organizers will need to make sure that a viable communication system exists, and that there are neighborhood cadres capable of resisting evictions. In addition, reserve forces— perhaps sympathetic student groups—should be available for quick mobilization to protect a particular block if public officials decide to try to break the strike by a dramatic show of force. (If some money is available, leaders of the strike may want to rent several vacant apartments, holding them in reserve in the event that a few evictions do in fact occur.)

Phase III: dealing with responses to the rent revolt. The response of landlords and municipal housing agencies to a successful rent revolt will vary depending on local conditions. Where landlords have little equity in their buildings, many may simply abandon them. In other situations, landlords may try to wait out the strikers, exerting counter-pressure by turning off utilities and discontinuing services. But there is nothing a landlord can turn off that tenants can't turn back on. And if marshals can be successfully resisted, so can utility men threatening to turn off gass and electricity.

When landlords terminate services or abandon the buildings, tenants may want to take over the task of providing minimum services. If they have the organizational capability to do so, they can then settle down to rent-free living until politicians decide to institute programs for refurbishing housing or subsidizing the construction of new housing.

But if a neighborhood does not or cannot take over the servicing of buildings, the consequences might turn into a political advantage for the strikers. Under such circumstances, dangerous conditions would quickly develop: hazards to health, threats of fire, the spread of disorder and suffering. Political leaders can ill afford to ignore these conditions in dense urban communities, where disease and fire can readily spread beyond the boundaries of the slum and ghetto.

Warm-weather months afford many tactical advantages. Lack of heat, the most serious inconvenience to tenants, is not a problem, and even the fear of eviction loses some of its force: hot pavements are not so fearsome as ice-covered ones. More important, people are much more likely to be on the streets in warm weather, making it easier to assemble crowds at the sites of attempted evictions. And until now, at least, the potential for riots and mass violence has been greatest in the summer, so that official repression of strikes is not so likely then.

Municipal political leaders, it should be stressed, possess the powers to act in emergencies. They can take over buildings, institute emergency repairs, and otherwise divert public funds from programs for other groups to cope with a crisis in the slum and ghetto. The question is, what will it take to force these actions. The answer, we suggest, is nothing short of a major crisis in the slum system.

DISRUPTING THE PUBLIC WELFARE SYSTEM

The growing national movement of welfare recipients is already revealing the fiscal punch of tactics which upset the longstanding practices by which local welfare systems withhold lawful benefits from the poor. In New York City, for example, organizing drives to claim benefits have forced the welfare rolls up by 50 percent in less than two years and doubled costs (to $1.3 billion). And this has been accomplished by a movement which has no support at all from civil rights or peace groups, and scarcely any funds or organizers of its own.

Americans regard every dollar spent for public relief to the unemployed and the unemployable as a sign that something is wrong. Many in the middle class are convinced that poverty should be dealt with by "rehabilitating" the poor rather than by redistributing income; the working class is preoccupied with taxes and hostile toward those below them; and many black leaders seem embarrassed to fight for "handouts," even for those who should not or cannot work, or for those who cannot get a decent job at a decent wage. It is in deference to these widespread sentiments that administrators of public-welfare agencies design policies and procedures to keep their budgets low, an objective achieved by keeping the poor ignorant of their eligibility, by erecting a tangle of bureaucratic barriers against those who do apply, by arbitrarily and illegally rejecting many applicants, and by refusing to allot the full benefits provided by law to those who do get on the rolls. The result is that only half of those who are eligible actually get on the rolls, and most of these are cheated out of full allowances.

Phase I: breaking the secrecy barrier. Welfare organizing across the nation has usually begun with efforts to inform people of their rights.

1. Organizers obtain the official manual of welfare regulations. Welfare administrators ordinarily will not release this manual, but a sympathetic welfare worker can usually be found who will steal a copy. Otherwise, recipients can hold a sit-in or, since manuals are public documents, initiate litigation to obtain copies.

2. A simplified handbook for the use of clients and organizers is prepared on the basis of the manual.

3. Thousands of copies are distributed in ghetto neighborhoods, through churches, stores and other outlets.

The handbook is especially useful if it is written to alert organizers and clients to the ways in which the system withholds benefits from people—e.g., giving illegal grounds for rejecting applicants, describing typical forms of underbudgeting, telling people about the availability of special grants for heavy clothing which are ordinarily kept secret. Overcoming the secrecy barrier is a crucial step in organizing: people cannot fight what they do not understand.

Phase II: developing cadres of recipients. The national welfare movement has been built largely by indigenous leaders (usually mothers on the Aid to Dependent Children rolls). Once information gets around regarding the extent to which recipients are being cheated out of various benefits, groups form quickly. In the early stages, these groups usually focus on settling the individual grievances of their members. Since negotiations with welfare officials over the intricacies of individual cases consume enormous amounts of time and energy, groups which continue to concentrate on settling individual grievances do not tend to grow. Other tactics, noted in the next phase, are necessary to produce mass action. But grievance work has had the useful consequence of developing cadres of recipients who are confident of their knowledge about the system and of their ability to stand up to it. These cadres, in turn, have often become the spearhead of efforts to mount mass campaigns against the system.

Phase III: mass claims for benefits. Large-scale campaigns are based on identifying a benefit to which many people are entitled but which few receive. Most welfare regulations, for example, allow grants for special purposes, but people are rarely told about them and generally don't get them. Staging a "mass benefit campaign" is much simpler than adjusting individual grievances and has far greater impact. Once the particular benefit is identified as the focus of the campaign (such as demands for school clothing), a check-list is mimeographed and distributed widely through the ghetto, together with an announcement of a demonstration. When several hundred people assemble to demand a common benefit, welfare departments usually release the grants, particularly in cities with large ghettoes, where public officials fear violence. In New York City, for example, campaigns staged by welfare groups around special grants for household items, clothing, and emergencies have released some 50 million dollars in extra allowances over the past year.

One of the most useful tactics learned from these campaigns is to make the waiting rooms in the welfare center the locus of organizing activity. In the big cities these waiting rooms are constantly jammed with people, many of whom will respond to on-the-spot offers of aid in getting on the rolls or in obtaining special allowances. In a number of places organizers are beginning to go into the centers with leaflets about welfare rights, with checklist forms for special grants, and with simplified eligibility forms which people can fill out before being called to the interviewing cubicle for an initial interview. If organizers are barred from waiting rooms by the police, they set up tables on the sidewalks outside to distribute literature and talk with people moving in and out of the centers.

Similar issues could be raised by mobilizing unemployed and underpaid black men who are kept off the rolls despite jurisdictions which allow some to obtain benefits under a "home relief" or "general relief" category, and others whose wages are less than they would receive on welfare to receive supplementary payments.

Some groups are contemplating mass advertising to inform people of their possible eligibility for welfare, or to inform those who are already on the rolls of the special allowances they are probably not receiving. The actions being considered include:

1. taking ads in newspapers or making spot announcements on radio stations that reach the ghetto;

2. placing posters in supermarkets and other stores in slum neighborhoods;

3. enlisting ghetto clergymen to preach on welfare rights;

4. mass leafletting of neighborhoods.

Advertising techniques should be especially effective in reaching the millions of poverty-stricken people who are still not on the rolls, sometimes for reasons of pride, but more often because of ignorance produced by secrecy about eligibility barriers.

In summary, strategies to bankrupt the cities have a double thrust. First, rising municipal costs mean that the poor are getting money, whether it's the rent money they keep or the higher welfare payments they receive. The promise of money is a powerful incentive in mobilizing mass action; the continued flow of money is a powerful force in sustaining it. Protest and demonstration tactics, by contrast, depend on the much less certain and usually less compelling appeal of ideology or momentary drama.

Second, the more money the poor get, the greater the leverage on the national Administration. Urban political leaders, already on the brink of fiscal disaster because they are squeezed between the services needed by an enlarging ghetto constituency and the indignation of their white taxpaying constituents, are becoming insistent lobbyists for increased federal subsidies. It will not be easy for a national Administration that depends on the cities to ignore these claims, or to ignore the worsening divisions in their urban constituency which these strategies can generate.

WOMEN'S LIBERATION

Ellen Cantarow, Elizabeth Diggs, Katherine Ellis, Janet Marx, Lillian Robinson, and Muriel Schein

Marx and Engels' view of society is employed by Ellen Cantarow et al. in an analysis of the oppression of women. In short, women are exploited to do labor rather than to perform work and are degraded in terms of the qualities attributed to them. Consequently, women are self-alienated, unable to fulfill themselves, and unable to obtain a satisfactory identity. Freedom can come to them only through an overthrow of the male-controlled system. Thus, women must become aware of their oppression and, once awakened, organize a struggle to change these oppressive realities.

> . . . though both Not equal, as their sex not equal seemed; for contemplation he, and valour formed, For softness she and sweet attractive grace; He for God only, she for God in him.
>
> MILTON, *Paradise Lost,* IV (11: 295 ff.)

The ultimate goal of a radical women's movement must be revolution. This is because the condition of female oppression does not "depend on," is not "the product of," is not "integral to" the structure of society; it *is* that structure. The oppression of women, though similar to that of blacks, differs from it in that it depends not on class division but rather on a division of labor premised on private property and resulting in the primary unit for the functioning of the economy. "The modern family," says Marx, "contains in embryo not only slavery . . . but serfdom also, since from the very beginning it is connected with agricultural services. It contains within itself in miniature all the antagonisms which later develop on a wide scale within society and its state" (quoted in Engels, *The Origin of the Family, Private Property, and the State*).

Engels, moreover, explains that "the word *familia* did not originally signify the ideal of our modern philistine, which is a compound of sentimentality and domestic discord." Among the early Romans it referred to the totality of slaves belonging to one individual and then became incorporated in a legal term to describe "a new social organism, the head of which had under him wife and children and a number of slaves" *(ibid.)*. Engels notes as well that the shift of inheritance from female to male lineage among the Shawnees, Miami and Delaware Indians, involved a mere semantic change in legal phraseology.

We begin with such allusions because they illustrate that the enslavement of women, like any sociological phenomenon, is a cultural and not a divinely arbitrated fact, proceeding by small, mundane human acts. The beginning of radical consciousness is recognizing cultural development for what it is. That it is the product of human history and not of cataclysm or immutable law means that it is within our power to understand it without bowing meekly before it. It is the revolutionary's tasks to seize those realities he has understood as oppressive, and to dare to change them.

The conditions of female servitude prevail today, and remain, in miniature, the basis for, if not the exact embodiment of, the contradictions that divide all of us in order to preserve the smooth functioning of the system.

A small, light, readily transported family unit is just the thing. IBM, General Motors, and our corporate universities depend on a highly mobile and docile labor force for their perpetuation and furthering. They own men—that is, they set down rules regulating men's labor and thus the structure of their lives. In turn the structure of men's lives determines what women's lives will be. A woman, once married, goes where her husband goes. Whether or not she herself works, it is understood that her real and legitimate vocation is child-rearing. The mythology that society has constructed to make female subjection a positive good is massive and profoundly rooted. In America this has been carried to the point of cultural hyperbole: for the first time in human history motherhood has become a full-time, 12 to 14 hour a day occupation. This development is in fact extremely recent, having occurred only since the second World War.

According to Marx there are two modes of productivity: labor and work. Labor is activity that renews itself cyclically—daily, monthly, or yearly. All janitorial, maintenance, secretarial and assembly-line work are included here. In a capitalist society, labor is always alienated. Work, by contrast, is activity that involves mental creation. Its results are public, while those of labor are private. The work of politics, art, and science involves the public employment of the mind's resources. Since it is an individual expression, work fulfills individual potential and creates individual identity, but its ultimate use is public. Labor is needed for survival, and physical survival depends on essentially private activity. One must care for one's body, wash it, comb it, feed it, wipe it, if one is to survive.

In capitalist society, the activities considered to be women's realm fall into the sphere of labor. Woman is seen as the modern "expert" in matters having to do with caring for children and servicing the family's environment. She is increasingly denied existence in the realm of work, for she is chained to male preconceptions of her being as essentially physical. Man conceives of woman primarily as a sexual object: she is the means by which the species reproduces itself. Therefore it is her *a priori* duty to subjugate all impulses toward public action to the interests of private labor in the home.

Marx observes that "the proletarians, if they are to achieve recognition as persons, will be obliged to abolish their own former conditions of existence, which are at the same time those of society as a whole, that is, to abolish labour. They are, consequently, in direct opposition to the State as the form in which the members of society have so far found their collective expression, and in order to develop as persons they must overthrow the State" *(German Ideology)*. This analysis is particularly relevant to women because we are oppressed in two ways, according to class and according to sex. In order to abolish the conditions of our existence which oppress us (and prevent us from developing as persons) we must recognize specific institutions and prejudices which must be overcome.

In a liberated, post-revolutionary society, women will have both time and energy to function fully. As long as a woman's time is subject to the demands of others, she is not free even in the most minimal sense. A man's time is not entirely his own either, since eight hours belong to his employer, but however degrading his servitude may be, it ends after eight hours. For a woman, on the other hand, the demands of others define her every waking moment. Her energy is channeled into a narrow round of activities which must be endlessly repeated in order to produce no change whatsoever.

The effectiveness of this full-time conditioning is difficult to exaggerate. Years of preparation have preceded it. From puberty on, girls are encouraged to make use of the "freedom" they have in order to prepare themselves for a future in which they will no longer want it. A woman who cannot or will not make this surrender of her time and energy forfeits the right of her caste and becomes, quite literally, untouchable. This is the price she pays for being an "unproductive" member of society, a fact which makes it clear that, despite the prevalence of Virginia Slims and other signs of the times, the realm of female productivity is limited to the most "socially useful" product of all.

Yet society provides women with many socially acceptable means of self-fulfillment. Achievement in any of these activities is enthusiastically praised and a woman who seeks self-realization through them is complacently patronized as "creative," "enterprising," "vital." These acceptable activities include all kinds of creative work which can be done in isolation, such as writing, painting, and music, as well as the "arts and crafts" activities such as potting, weaving, sewing, and making hand-printed place mats and Christmas cards. It becomes obvious at once that these occupations have several things in common: (1) they are solitary, and can therefore be performed in the home; (2) they are recognized as being activities which release frustrations by channelling the human need to be productive and creative; (3) they fall within the framework of traditionally "feminine" activities because they imply and affirm sensitivity, introspection, and emotional expression rather than the rationality, intellectual rigor, and the precision implied by traditionally "male" activities.

What is the larger social function of these activities? Most important, they perpetuate the status-quo by stabilizing the function and position of woman in society. Any frustrations she may feel are co-opted if she can express them in these accepted ways. The heretical alternative is for a woman to assert herself in the male world, the public world, in which fulfillment involves communication, social interchange, self-assertion (i.e., aggression, undoubtedly the most unacceptable trait in a female) and implies the exercise of the masculine traits of organizational ability, rational analysis, and the application of theory to practice.

• • •

Women today are no more than custodians of consumer goods, vacuuming the latest thing in wall-to-wall carpeting with the latest thing in vacuum cleaners. People don't need her . . . but those ugly stains on the kitchen sink require her constant vigilance. Objective conditions (dirty dishes, children's clutter, cavities, clean clothes every day for everyone) combine with the pressures generated by advertising (for whiter washes, softer hands, streak-free windows, odorless armpits) to wear women down to a point where change becomes literally inconceivable.

Until this is changed, there will be no revolution.

Consumerism serves as an agent of sexual oppression, and thus of counter-revolution, in that it seeks to tie the totality of women's energies to the care of products through which she is supposed to feel "fulfilled." She feels fulfilled when she looks at herself in the mirror and sees that those grey hairs have vanished. She feels fulfilled when the kids go off to school in their tumble-dried clothes and come home with fewer cavities. She feels this way because she has been too tired for too long (what is boredom, after all, but a symptom of repression?) to do anything other than what she is told by those who control her time.

Revolution will not take place until women reject and redefine their position in a society that must keep them in control by directing their search for fulfillment into the inexhaustible realm of consumption. Nothing could be more beneficial to a profit-based economy than a large population whose sole measure of its own worth lies in internalizing the concept of "marketable goods." It pays to keep the little woman alone at home with her children, visiting and being visited by other women against whom she can measure her "progress" by the yardstick of accumulation. What keeps her there is the sense of power she derives from her position in the family, the sense that it is she and she alone who teaches the children to brush after every meal, she and she alone whose market preferences determine what is on the supermarket shelf, she and she alone who feeds them their portion of "culture," she and she alone who can have babies. And for this she is exalted above the God who makes a tree. Who could ask for anything more?

Not she, that's for sure. Not when everything she associates with "becoming a woman" fills her with gratitude toward her oppressors. What has she done to deserve all these things? Her husband even washes the dishes for her sometimes, and takes the kids to the park on Saturdays so that she can do her hair and her nails in peace. What will it take to turn her against those who exploit her by offering, for no money down, all the things through which she has been taught to find her fulfillment? What is it that a liberated, post-revolutionary society must offer in their stead? Our goal must be to rediscover our real needs now, if in fact we have ever known what they are, and make these the basis of actions that would serve as a model for the movement as a whole.

No one knows what female nature really is. What are "feminine" characteristics? Is there any scientific reason to associate female qualities with weakness, dishonesty, stupidity, and mindless labor except for the fact that male domination has forced women into centuries of humiliation? These qualities are neither male nor female but qualities of the oppressed. White male imperialism always has its eager white male intellectuals to create lies justifying the "inferiority" of oppressed peoples. Because labor is necessary to human survival, yet by its very nature alienating in a capitalist society, it is relegated to "inferior" types—Third World peoples, blacks, and women. This leaves the realm of work as the unchallenged realm of white males, whether they be right or left wing in political persuasion. But work is necessary to human fulfillment; this is the essence of the Black Liberation struggle. We don't want a piece of the capitalist pie; we don't want to be integrated into a system that offers us little beyond the labor awaiting us in the nuclear family, but rather we want freedom to realize our identities as women and as individuals. This freedom, for us and for Blacks, can come only through transforming the white male economic system.

The transformation of society which Women's Liberation movements are seeking is more far-reaching that merely overthrowing capitalism and establishing socialism in its place. Before capitalism existed, oppression of slaves and women formed the economic basis for society. Slavery has been expanded to *de facto* apartheid and imperialism by capitalist societies. Women have been systematically made empty, commercial products whose only human function is to flatter, feed, and f — the imperialist white male. Not only must the distribution of wealth be made just, but also distribution of labor: property-based relationships between the sexes result in the oppression of women. If female oppression is incorporated into the "revolutionary" state, fundamental property relationships remain the same, and thus the abuses of capitalism reassert themselves. Any revolution based on male chauvinism is doomed to failure, as is any revolution based on racism. The untapped revolutionary potential of this country (the untapped hatred for the white men who run the society) resides in women.

Obviously, Women's Liberation movements do not cite the male per se as the enemy. For "to treat comrades like enemies is to go over to the side of the enemy" (Mao). A tendency among some Women's Liberation groups is to treat all men in the movement as enemies, or to advocate "making it" professionally—a concept conceived of and dictated by men. This tendency works against women's liberation in the long run because it means certain co-optation. But Mao's dictum works the other way around: for men to treat women in Women's Liberation as enemies is to go over to the side of the system. Male "supremacy" is in many ways the basis of capitalism, and it is as important to the cause of revolution in this country to root out this as it is to root out racism. Just as blacks are the initiators of the anti-racist movement, having known its oppression in their daily lives, so women must instigate the struggle against male chauvinism, since they experience daily its oppressive power. Women must realize that their own real interest lies not only with individual "success," but with transforming and finally overthrowing the oppressive regime. Only when struggle comes out of conscious political self-interest can it succeed.

Discussion of objective economic and social conditions implies collective solutions to social problems. However, capitalism both causes and feeds on alienation, on a false consciousness of individuality. For women, the situation is underlined by isolation and fragmentation in our lives as workers—whether at home or on the job. Economic forces are bolstered by cultural forces that serve to stabilize the system of oppression.

• • •

Socialists recognize the economic basis of both black and female oppression. Not only is racial and sexual oppression coetaneous with private property, but both groups have historically been property themselves. Under capitalism, both groups constitute a "marginal" source of cheap labor on which the system feeds. When capitalism becomes strained, both groups swell the ranks of the unemployed and the allegedly unemployable. Both are channeled into alienated labor, service jobs with no intrinsic meaning and little material gain. Exploitation of both women and blacks is necessary to support the contradictions of the capitalist system, which cannot produce both profits and full employment, let alone provide meaningful work for all members of society.

The psychic consequences of economic conditions are also similar for members of both groups. For most of us, our race and our sex are unequivocal, objective facts, immediately recognizable to new acquaintances. Thus, an immediate reaction occurs, as whatever stereotypes one has about either group go into operation mechanically, without regard to whether an individual conforms to the stereotype. Self-hatred in both groups derives not from anything intrinsically inferior about us, but from the treatment we are accustomed to. For middle-class white women, that treatment takes a less ugly form—at least there are material comforts along with the degradation—but that doesn't increase self-respect. The self-images of both groups are defined and manipulated by the cultural media, and both are made the victims of the consumer mentality, so that capitalism exploits us at both ends of the productive process.

Women and blacks have been alienated from their own culture, they have no historical sense of themselves because study of their condition has been suppressed. We understand that our historical function has been that of pawns, but we are given no basis on which to construct any other view of what people like us have done, no tools with which to destroy the existing mythologies about ourselves. Both women and blacks are expected to perform a social function as entertainers similar to our economic function as service workers. Thus, members of both groups have been taught to be passive and to please white male masters in order to get what we want.

Unusually gifted members of an oppressed race or sex are treated as exceptional and made to feel their "superiority" to the group of which they must remain an inalienable part by virtue of an objective fact. Similarly, we all recognize that racial conflict between black and white workers redounds chiefly to the benefit of those who exploit labor. A racist white worker is substituting his "white-skin privileges" and the sense of superiority they entail for real economic progress. Similarly, the male chauvinism that is most blatant in the working class provides the exploiter with an immediate and permanent division in that class. Oppressed groups are thus cut off from some of their potential leaders and from their natural allies.

Perhaps the greater irony in the situation is that so many black men— including most workers in the black liberation movement—are hostile to Women's Liberation. They have looked at the matriarchical history of American Negro society and blamed black women for destroying their manhood, rather than their true castrator, the white man. They have thus attempted to replace black women in their "natural," that is, oppressed, condition. But both they and the white men who reject the race-sex analogy seem to forget that more than half the black race is female and that you cannot liberate a people by deliberately keeping half of it in bondage. Black male chauvinism, supposed by many to be more tolerable on political grounds than white, is counter-revolutionary. While ignoring the potential strength of black women, it also maintains the myth of "the white man's woman" as most desirable. This caters to white supremacist conceptions of the Black while damaging the political power of the black movement. Even Eldridge Cleaver, who is responsible for the male chauvinist phrase, "pussy power," arrives at this conslusion in *Soul on Ice*. White women are oppressed because of their sex; those who are workers are oppressed because of class and sex. Black women are oppressed because of race, sex, and class. We cannot struggle for the liberation of society by tolerating, much less encouraging, the greatest injustices of the existing order.

Too much movement activity has been based on organizing about other people's needs. For instance, ERAP failed because it was founded on if not false, at least misdirected, consciousness: while correctly recognizing and assessing the effects of an exploitative society on poor people, it incorrectly assumed that outsiders not of the same class could organize them. In many places in the country SDS is now up against the same fact. In order to build a strong and profound movement, it is the task of all of us to begin to consider the difficult realities of our own circumstances.

The revolution we seek is very far off. But we can begin to act on our ideas in our own lives, *now*. We must begin now, because we must raise consciousness in all males and females of the objective conditions of their oppression. We have formulated immediate and specific goals related to our roles as college and university students and teachers, but we must realize and remember that these "goals" are only tools, a means to the ultimate goal of real liberation for all people. The immediate aims are the means of survival which will give us time and space in which to begin our struggle. We must enunciate and work for immediate ends. The radical movement has often been confused on this point. We are so afraid of being co-opted by satisfaction of demands that can be met that we refuse to tempt our purity by articulating immediate goals at all. But if we trust our own ideology, we must realize that the capitalist system cannot provide justice for all. By struggling for our demands, we will increase our awareness of the nature of the system and our position within it. By winning them, we will have increased consciousness of the contradictions in the system and the way to use them to escalate our struggle.

We are not formulating these goals as demands in the context of this NUC convention; but we should transform them into standards in our own lives and demands for our own universities.

1. The most important and indispensable goal, without which no others can be achieved, is that *women must become aware of male oppression and organize to fight it.** NUC members active in Women's Liberation groups must seek to make these groups centers of radical politics. The universities should be made to offer compensatory courses in the suppressed studies of women's history and culture.

2. The property-based nuclear family must be abolished and arrangements providing freedom equally for all must be brought into being. Every "radical" male and female living together *must divide labor equally** so that they can become equally free for action.

The Universities must establish, finance, and staff day-care centers for all preschool children of any man or woman connected with the university and the surrounding community.

3. *Women must have jurisdiction over their own bodies.** The health services of the universities must provide free birth control information and contraceptives and free abortions for all women they serve.

4. *Women must have equal control of and access to their professional lives.** The number of women in the student population should be proportionate to their number in the whole population. Women should be represented on boards of trustees, in the administrations, in teaching positions (tenured and nontenured), in all employment positions of the university, in proportion to their representation in the "adjusted" student body.

5. *No unit of the university should refuse to hire a man and woman of ability and promise on the grounds that they are married or living together.** There should be an end to the rules against the employment of spouses in the same institution, faculty, or department.

6. All education should be of equal quality for both sexes. The only way to ensure this is to have it at the same time and place. The single-sex college should be used now as a revolutionary forum, but eventually *separate women's and men's colleges should be abolished.**

7. *No territory in the university should be restricted on grounds of sex**—e.g., faculty clubs, toilets, gymnasia. Dormitories should be fully integrated. Phrased as a "demand," this sounds trivial, but that is because even radicals are conditioned to accept certain aspects of an oppressive system as normal. Actually, *it is our acceptance of abnormal segregations on biological grounds that is the aberration.** In its internal

*Our italics, M. S. W. and E. R.

and external relations alike, the university is a bastion of privilege, and we must attack class privileges within the academic community as well as the bias that excludes many people from the community. No, the revolution won't come when we integrate the Men's Faculty Club. But an attack on such institutions reveals to us all our dangerous habits of taking certain inequities for granted.

THE POLITICS OF ECOLOGY

Barry Weisberg

"The Politics of Ecology" concerns itself with the rampant and continuing destruction of natural resources and the imminent threat this poses. This is viewed as a part of the larger problem of the domination and control of society—of the political, social, and economic structures—by only a few, who exploit both man and nature for their own interests. Ecological problems, Barry Weisberg indicates, cannot be solved by appealing to this dominant minority. Rather, the social order must be radically revised and control taken by the people. Only through polarization and confrontation, and the inclusion of ecology in a politics of total liberation, will solution be possible. The spirit of revolution is necessary; bombing corporate headquarters and sabotaging industrial despoilers of natural resources will dramatize the issues, the values at stake, and the sides people must take in the struggle for a new social order.

The critical importance of ecology as a developing source of political opposition in America stems from the realization that politics in our age has acquired an absolute character. While political decision-making and control is steadily concentrated in the hands of a very few—the arena of control is steadily expanding. Fewer and fewer people control more and more—so that the very conditions which support life on this planet: the land we walk upon, the air we breathe and the water we drink, are now the subject of political management on a scale beyond normal comprehension. The politics of ecology must start from the premise that present-day reality is increasingly the product of a struc-

From Barry Weisberg, "The Politics of Ecology," *Liberation Magazine* (January 1970). Reprinted by permission of the author.

ture of economic and political power that consolidates and sustains itself through the systematic destruction of man and his physical world. The exploitation of man by man and nature by man are merely two sides of the same coin.

It is then folly to think that the destruction of our global life-support systems under advanced industrial capitalism or communism is merely a by-product of progress, a case of bad management, the result of insufficient esthetic sensibilities on the part of business and engineers, or simply a matter of who owns the means of production. In an historical sense, we have reached the point where we can totally violate the processes and structures of the natural world; hence our relationship to nature is no longer determined by the forces of nature but by the rule of political management. The deterioration of the natural environment all around us is therefore clearly a product of the nature of production and consumption, of cultural values and social relationships that today hold sway over industrial technological society—American or Soviet.

In short, our present technical manipulation of the life-support capacity of the planet now threatens the totality of physical conditions which nurture life itself. The oxygen content in the atmosphere, the metabolism of our own bodies, food chains and the relationship between populations and the resources needed to support them, conditions upon which the existence of all plant and animal life today depends, are the products of evolutionary processes extending over billions of years. Our industrial civilization is now destroying them in a matter of decades. We are talking about processes which may well have worked their irrevocable consequences within a decade or two—after which there will be nothing within the human potential to restore their life-giving capacity.

The culture itself is aware of the explosive potential of the imbalances between society and nature. Government and industry through the media have begun to manage these issues on a daily basis. Scientists speak out, reports are called for and committees created. In fact the pattern of action and language emerging around pollution parallels exactly the failures of civil rights and poverty—"a war on pollution," the calling for a "pollution pentagon." Even new bureaucratic offices to replace the Department of Interior are suggested. What such proposals miss is that it is not the control of the land, air and water that is at stake but the control of man.

The obvious question resulting from this brief survey is whether or not these are matters of bad management, dysfunction or the like, as mentioned earlier. The origins of our present destruction of the life-support capacity of this planet are rooted in the very fabric of our civilization, reaching their most insane dimensions in the present corporate America. The Greek rationalism of Aristotle, the Roman Engineering mentality, the biblical anthropomorphic injunctions to "have dominion over the land and subdue every creeping thing," the post-Enlightenment notions of growth and progress, the present technical corporate economic systems motivated by competition—all dominate the Western mentality of man against nature. Where nature works toward harmony, cooperation and interdependence, advanced industrial society works toward growth, competition and independence. The advanced nation-state works in direct opposition to those basic life-giving instincts which have nourished our billion year evolution. To repeat, the domination of man by man and man over nature are two sides of the coin. The precondition of our survival requires the most basic transformation of the cultural, social, political and economic mentalities and structures which dominate the developed nations and hang as a carrot over the never-to-be developed nations.

In view of the sudden flurry of government-initiated programs . . . it is especially chilling to contemplate the performance of government, industry and their conservationist junior partners. Here's a rundown:

GOVERNMENT

The proportion of the National Budget spent on all natural resource programs has declined steadily since 1959.

1965	2.3%
1966	2.2%
1967	2.0%
1968	1.9%
1969	1.9% est.
1970	1.8% est.

In other words, for fiscal 1969, we spent only 3.6 billion on all natural resource programs, of some 202 billion dollars, spending more (4 billion) to reach outer space than to make the earth habitable. The gap between authorization and appropriation on programs such as air and water pollution has widened every year. This is merely to demonstrate the inability of the Congress to achieve its own stated objectives—not that those objectives would have successfully dealt with any major issue. In fact, there is every reason to believe that more spending would have produced merely more pollution. Add to this a government which at the same time subsidizes the supersonic transport, maintains the depletion allowance for continued off-shore drilling, undermines efforts at consumer protection—and one begins to understand the meaning of federal efforts. While there are more committees, more reports, more research and more attention, less and less is actually done. The frightening conclusion, however, is not that government should do more, for the more it does the worse our ecological systems get.

INDUSTRY

What are we to make of the flurry of industrial ads depicting everything from Standard Oil to Dow Chemical to the American Rifle Association as conservation-minded people? Of the recent Business of Pollution Control Technology of the investment of industry in conservation organization? The answer I think is to be found, for instance, in the words of Robert Anderson, chairman of the board of Atlantic Richfield. In a recent address before a State Department-sponsored conference on Man and His Environment, Anderson argued that the costs of pollution control should be passed on to the consumer and that oil should remain the base of energy supply. In short, industry has made of the environmental crisis a commodity. Recent financial reports indicate that the business of pollution control will in fact make a profit out of pollution while at the same time generating more pollution; more growth will be the remedy applied to the perils of growth. In short, that advertising will continue to cost more for business than research, that the consumers will be passed on any costs of "pollution control," and that federal agencies, new or old, will continue to operate as captives of the industry they are to regulate.

CONSERVATION

More than any single element of the present collage of conservation activity, the conservation organizations themselves, to varying degrees, lead the public to believe that the emperor has no clothes when in fact they serve as clothes for the emperor. Such organizations act in the most fragmentary ways, attacking isolated problems and not complex patterns of social and political behavior. They save a nature area and fail to address the entire land use patterns of that region. They save a seashore from development when that seashore is threatened with the biological destruction of its wildlife. As such, their victories are at best stop gaps, always provisional. They foster the existence of centralized forms of authority through the support they lend to present elective procedures—"get the good guys in office." They have virtually no critical understanding of the governments of oil, agri-business, public utilities or chemicals. The conservationists frequently violence-bait the Left or shun it as revolutionary. "The country is tired of SDS and ready to see someone like us come to the forefront," a young conservationist recently noted. Increasingly motivated and supported by various governmental machinations, these people work in total isolation to the civil rights and peace movements, with no relationship to the varied forces of opposition and liberation in the society today—the revolutionary young, women's liberation, labor, and oppressed minorities. They seek private solutions to what more correctly are public issues—picking up litter rather than attacking the production of junk, refusing to use autos rather than struggling against oil and the auto manufacturers, to be merely suggestive.

But most important, the "new breed of young conservationists" fail to see that the crisis of the environment truly is but a reflective of the crisis of this culture itself, of the values, institutions, and procedures which have for some 200 years systematically guided the slaughter of human and all other forms of life at home and abroad. These tendencies were demonstrated too well by a recent selection of "youth" hand-picked by the Department of State to participate in the U.S. Commission for UNESCO Conference on Man and His Environment in San Francisco last month. Virtually all "program" suggested by these participants lent credence to the status quo by advocating "better" candidates, new ecology colleges, yet additional "research," and more jobs for conservation-minded college kids.

The barrage of petitions and letters to the president was greeted by the conference "adults" with adulation, for the kids turned out to be "reasonable men" just as their parents. The popular press billed their performance as revolutionary—defined as "nonviolent," get-your-man-in-office, and increased student participation. But the role of our benign media goes much further.

By and large, the media has purposely obscured the political and social content of the environmental crisis by confining problems as well as solutions solely to the realm of science and technology. The result is that blind faith in the omnipotence of expertise and technocracy wholly dominates current thinking on ecological issues. Technological innovation and more reasonable methods of resource allocation cannot possibly reverse the present logic of the environment unless the overriding political, social and economic framework which has actually generated that trend is radically rebuilt. Such a transformation cannot reside solely in the realm of culture and values—as most often proposed by the youthful elites of conservation. The critical task today is to raise the issue of pollution/destruction, imperialistic styles of consumption, and of overpopulation to a political status in order to reveal an arena of political opposition in America which the Left has hitherto ignored. That is not to say that the Left can simply absorb the ecological crisis into its own kind of "business as usual" behavior. For the patterns of life in which most of us partake are not much different than those of the ruling class. This is not to say that true solutions reside in private action, but that public transformation without an entirely different style of life is futile. Thus the development of an ecological politics on a practical level may provide the only framework in which the alienated and oppressed can achieve true liberation.

That potential for liberation doesn't lie in the Save the Bay Campaigns, the protection of a redwood grove or planned parenthood. It does not reside alone in the culturally symbolic acts of many ecology action groups around the country. The true origin of what has yet to become an authentic movement is in the People's Park episode, in militant actions against corporate despoilers (including sabotage) and in the private as well as public attempts to create ecologically sound lives.

While the traditional conservationists have made no imaginative attempt to understand what our cities would look like without autos, with decentralized agriculture or power, with neighborhood control and rationed resources, save for few scant efforts, the Left, with few exceptions, has been equally derelict. "Radical" economists still contemplate growth-motivated economies grounded in false notions of affluence and unlimited resources.

The New Left has at this point made little serious effort to understand or relate to the politics of ecology. While the battles in the streets appear more pressing and more direct, it ought to be understood that unless something very basic and very revolutionary is done about the continued destruction of our life support system, there may well be no wind to weather in the near future.

Dismissing overpopulation as simply a matter of genocide, efforts to take back the land as bourgeois or the necessity for clean air and water as a luxury completely fails to grasp what can only properly be understood as a matter of life or death.

The task of ecological radicals is to continually raise those issues which sort those which seek to patch up the status quo from those who struggle for basic transformation. *The polarization of the rulers and the ruled is the authentic growth of any true movement for liberation.** When conservationists argue that everyone is in the same boat (or on the same raft), that everyone must work together, tempering their actions to suit the imperatives of coalition, they are in fact arguing for the further consolidation of power and profit in the hands of those responsible for the present dilemma.

There is no easy way to summarize exactly how the movement must respond to the growing politics of ecology. Publishing special magazine editions and flimsy attacks on "sewermen" will not do. Few models exist to lend direction to organizing efforts. Already throughout the country people have been organized around industrial accidents and health hazards, consumer boycotts, women's liberation and the nuclear family,

*Our italics, M. S. W. and E. R.

the extinction of animal species or the struggle against a new highway. This is just the beginning. This winter and spring we can expect a series of radical ecological actions: the bombing of more corporate headquarters, sabotage to the industrial machinery that pollutes and obstruction at airports and other transportation corridors.

It is safe to suggest that organizing around environment issues that fails immediately to lead to the political causes and implications of that peril is misguided. For too long eco news and reports have begun and ended with nature—without understanding that nature itself is today the product of manipulation by man. We should have learned from the People's Park that the road ahead will be perilous and paved with a life and death struggle. If the state of California would defend a parking lot with the life of one person and the shooting of another 150, imagine the cost of taking back a forest, preventing an off-shore drilling rig from being placed, blocking the construction of a nuclear power plant or tampering with the power/communication/food/transport systems which make America grow. But the sooner this happens the better. The sooner the spirit of the People's Park infuses every ecological action, the brighter will be our chances to insure the conditions for our survival and, beyond that, a decent society.

Educating "the people about the impending ecological disaster" without pointing to possible forms of action available is at this point a disservice to the movement. As people engage in direct struggle against the Con Edisons, the Standard Oils, the pollution control agencies, and the United Fruit companies of the world, more and more new insights for strategy will develop. What has been happening to poor whites and blacks for several hundred years, what America has done to the Vietnamese, America is now doing to its own population, en masse. The organizing implications of this single fact may be profound. In a world of total biological slavery, liberation is the very condition of life itself. To fail does not mean growing up absurd, but not growing up at all.

QUESTIONS FOR DISCUSSION

1. Compare Carmichael and Hamilton's proposals for blacks to those of the Puerto Rican Forum for Puerto Ricans. What advantages and disadvantages accrue from each? Which type of program do you favor? Why?

2. Do you agree with Piven and Cloward that disrupting city services would change national priorities? Explain your position.

3. Piven and Cloward advocate what Slater calls a "make things worse" strategy to force governmental accommodations to slum residents' demands. Do you think Slater's criticisms of such strategies apply to Piven and Cloward's proposal?

4. What is your response to the reading on Women's Liberation? To the Women's Liberation movement in general? How would you feel about a more holistic "gender liberation movement"? Do you think a strategy seeking such liberation from the traditional assumptions of both male and female roles would be more or less successful than the polarization approach suggested in this article?

5. Evaluate Weisberg's proposed solution to the problem of pollution. What is your evaluation of alternative approaches, including the ones he criticizes?

6. Compare Reich's "revolution by consciousness" with the "revolution by confrontation" advocated by the authors in this section. Which seems more feasible to you?

7. Does the value conflict emphasis on confrontation to solve social problems imply that "might" determines "right"? How do you feel about such a position?

8. Do you think the tactic of forcing change by confronting the opponent (rather than trying to convince him without pressure) is likely to succeed in producing a balance of power more favorable to the protesting parties and a concomitant shift in attitudes on the part of their oppressors? Or is it likely that the confronted party will eventually rally superior power and reassert its dominance even more forcefully?

9. Summarize what you think are the major strengths and weaknesses of the value conflict perspective and the solutions it suggests.

SELECTED REFERENCES

Alinsky, Saul A., *Rules for Radicals: A Practical Primer for Realistic Radicals,* New York: Random House, 1971.

This is a handbook for organizing a community in order to protect or realize its interests and values. Alinsky clearly states the need for a community to develop a spirit of partisanship and then to fight for its values.

Buckout, Robert and eighty-one concerned Berkeley students (eds.), *Toward Social Change: A Handbook for Those Who Will,* New York: Harper & Row, 1971.

This text-reader diagnoses many contemporary social problems and prescribes remedies for them from the value conflict perspective.

Daniels, Arlene Kaplan, "From Lecture Hall to Picket Line," in *Academics on the Line,* Arlene Kaplan Daniels, Rachel Kahn-Hut, and associates, San Francisco: Jossey-Bass, 1970, Chap. 3.

This fascinating personal chronicle presents the unfolding history of the San Francisco State University strike of 1969 and a faculty member's involvement in it.

Love, Sam (ed.), *Earth Tool Kit: A Field Manual for Citizen Activists,* New York: Pocket Books, 1971.

This is a handbook of techniques in the solution of ecological problems from the value conflict perspective. Strategies range from the traditionally acceptable to the traditionally unacceptable. The tactics are easily generalized to other problem areas.

O. M. Collective. *The Organizer's Manual,* New York: Bantam Books, 1971.

During the national student strike in May 1970, Boston University students organized and wrote this book. Clearly in the value conflict tradition, it deals with the principles of organizing and the constituencies to be organized.

Silberman, Charles E., "Up From Apathy—The Woodlawn Experiment," *Commentary,* 37 (May 1964), pp. 51–58.

This is the stirring story of Saul Alinsky's organization of the Chicago slum of Woodlawn.

5 DEVIANT BEHAVIOR

Latter-day pathologists diagnose the society as "sick" and urge individuals to re-educate themselves in order to humanize the society. Disorganization theorists locate social problems in the failure of the social system to work according to cultural prescriptions and seek ways of redressing these inconsistencies. Students of value conflict see social problems as the result of people in groups acting rationally and on behalf of their own group interests and values when they engage each other in conflict. The solution entails the organization and use of power to realize their interests and values.

Much like value conflict theorists and practitioners, deviant behaviorists accept social problems as a natural, expected part of life. They consider it possible that some people who behave in a deviant manner might well be doing so in some kind of systematic rather than irrational fashion. They look upon social problems as instances of repeated, systematic departures from social norms. While deviant behaviorists regard problem behavior, such as crime and delinquency, as a natural, expected part of society, they do not say that there is little one can do about social problems. They ask that others help them to find what underlies the recurrent pattern. Once that is obtained, it may then become possible to eliminate the unacceptable behavior and replace it with more acceptable behavior.

CENTRAL FEATURES OF THE DEVIANT BEHAVIOR PERSPECTIVE

Culture contains a body of ideas on what to think and feel, what to prefer and seek, and what to do. These elements comprise beliefs, values, and norms, respectively. Social organization refers to the actual situation—how people living in society actually think, feel, and act, what alternatives really exist, and so on. If culture refers to the "ought," or the normative order, then social organization refers to the "is," or the factual order. Within all societies there is some tension between these realms. And many state that social problems arise primarily when the

179

discrepancy between the "is" and the "ought" goes beyond the limits of tolerance. For deviant behaviorists, social problems arise when, in response to this situation of frustration, there is some systematic and patterned behavior which jeopardizes the wider community.

The place.   Governments in mass democratic societies must be responsive to such discrepancies between culture and social organization. In recent years, the development of the welfare state indicates that such pervasive social problems require the intervention of the public sector of the society. And, more recently, programs like the Job Corps, Headstart, and Mobilization for Youth, exemplify this trend. These programs share in common the notion that alternate outlets must be made available to persons who by reason of their location in society are overexposed to discrepancies between cultural promises and the realities of social organization. These programs have been adopted as possible solutions to such problems as poverty, racial injustice, juvenile delinquency, and unemployment.

In addition, members of the public have developed self-help programs. Deriving much of their inspiration from early Christian sects, these movements seek converts to their cause. In banding together they provide their followers with a systematic and patterned response to their shared situation of frustration. The most outstanding example of such a world-wide movement is Alcoholics Anonymous. Its success is interpreted by many as an indication of the utility of the deviant behavior perspective. Numerous other self-help movements among deviant minorities, such as drug addicts, ex-convicts, and mental patients, have modeled their own organizations after the pattern of A.A. In doing so, organizations such as Synanon, the Fortune Society, and Recovery, Inc., carry out their remedial work in accordance with the principles of this perspective.

The deviant behavior view of social problems has, moreover, challenged sociologists to develop theories, concepts, and methods for both understanding and ameliorating discrepant situations. Of all the sociological perspectives on social problems, this perspective has influenced and produced more theorizing and empirical study of social problems than any of the other perspectives.

The attitude.   Within the deviant behavior perspective, different attitudes are represented by the practitioner of self-help and by the sociologist of deviance.

a. The practitioner of self-help.   Practitioners of self-help, twice-born people themselves for the most part, focus upon the solution of the social problem. As a result, though they work within the frame of the deviant behavior perspective, their attitude is essentially *experimental, anti-*

intellectual, pragmatic, and *dogmatic.* The principles which they apply in the course of their work are often based upon their own experiences before and after a career in personal deviation. In the terms of William James, they have *knowledge about* the problem. Their attitude toward the truth of their own experience and how it may apply in the solution of the social problem is intuitive and anti-intellectual. They are pragmatic, satisfied to know if something works and to use it on that basis alone. Finally, they are often dogmatic in expecting others to accept without question the program that may have worked for them.

b. The sociologist of deviance.   The sociologist of deviance, bound by the norms of his discipline, is *condition-centered, theoretical, developmental,* and *empirical* in his attitudes toward both cause and solution of social problems. He is condition-centered in that he seeks to ascertain the conditions under which the problem behavior takes place (the "essence" of the experience is usually of less importance to him than the circumstances in which it occurs). He is theoretical in that the case is of interest primarily to the degree that it can be understood as an instance of a generalization. He is developmental in that he is most anxious to find the reasons why a person continues to engage in a course of deviant behavior. Finally, he is empirical in that he seeks to test his statements by observation, research, and experimentation.

The content.   The sociologist of deviance has *theoretical knowledge of* deviant behavior while the practitioner of self-help has personal *knowledge about* deviant behavior. Despite this, there is some agreement in the facts and the ideas that both employ in making sense of social problems. The practioner is primarily interested in solutions and the sociologist in causes, but both may view the problem situation similarly, although the terms they use may differ somewhat.

The common notions are as follows. Social problems center on roles, not acts. The actions leading to these problems are patterned responses to a condition of discrepancy. And the behaviors are directed through primary group association and the learning and reinforcement of deviant ways.

Sociologists have been most instrumental in developing this point of view for explaining how persons become involved in departures from social norms. Self-help practitioners draw upon the same etiological model for designing a program to change the behavior of their followers.

THE FORMULA

In applying the deviant behavior perspective as a means of solving social problems, both the layman and the sociologist agree on two fundamental points. First, the perspective cannot be employed as a solving device for all social problems. It is applicable only to persons who risk becoming career deviants because of their overexposure to discrepancy and to other deviants. Second, because it is a social rather than an individual solving device, it requires application in and through human groups.

The vocabulary.   The terms used in this perspective include technical sociological concepts as well as lay discourse. A representative listing includes such terms as *access, alienation, anomie, bad company, commitment, companions, conformity, conversion, cultural goals, delinquent subculture, deviant subculture, deviation, differential association, differential identification, ends, example, frustration, function, goals, group, life chances, means, moral support, opportunities, outlets, partners, peers, recidivism, relapse, relief, resocialization, risk, role model, self-image, significant others, socialization, social structure, status, strain, stress,* and *tension.*

The beliefs and doctrines.   The solution to some social problems is to be found in human groups set up specifically for that purpose. However, according to the deviant behavior perspective, to be eligible for such social-problem-solving groups (preventive as well as therapeutic) clients must have had some prior experience in human groups other than deviant groups; be amenable to peer influence; have acquired status, role, self-image, and skills in deviant groups; and seek or require group support for resocialization.

Along with these requirements, there is another set of assumptions which indicates that personality change is not a requirement for solution.

a. Since deviant behavior is a property of roles rather than personality, only roles require change.

b. A given behavior occurs only under given conditions; therefore, if conditions change, then behavior changes.

c. Change can only come about through membership in a primary group which specifically seeks such change.

d. Change will thus come about if the person is removed from other groups and becomes a member of a primary group of persons in similar circumstances who seek to change their deviant roles.

The central presumption, of course, is that all behavior, conformist as well as deviant, is learned in the course of participation in human groups. If persons have learned to perform deviant behavior as a result of their participation in deviant groups, then they can unlearn that pattern of deviant behavior and simultaneously learn or relearn a pattern of conformist behavior in the course of their participation in a conformist group.

The recipe.   Both sociologists and lay practitioners of self-help draw upon these basic assumptions in constructing programs. The common factors for solving social problems according to the deviant behavior perspective are reduction of contact with illegitimate patterns of conduct, increase of contact with legitimate patterns, opportunities for exhibiting conformist skills, and a group that will provide new roles, stauses, and self-images in exchange for developing and maintaining expertise in conformity. In these circumstances of changed social conditions, deviant role behavior subsides and conformity prevails.

Given the differences in attitude between lay practitioners and sociologists, however, there are some important differences in the form of their programs. In order to harness the set of tripartite pressures (groups, norms, and goals) on behalf of conformist values, practitioners of self-help construct a primary group. This group must establish a set of highly specific goals, and it must devise and then prescribe norms for the achievement of these goals. Implicitly, the recipe suggests that something very compulsive drives persons to persist in a pattern of deviant behavior. If that compulsion can be employed for conformist uses, the content of behavior changes. Charismatic leaders established Alcoholics Anonymous and later Synanon in accordance with these basic ideas.

Whereas practitioners evolve their recipes in informal, charismatic, and crescive ways, sociologists do so in formal, routinized, and enacted ways. For instance, it is hard to imagine a group of stigmatized deviants devising a primary group for their own resocialization and re-entry into conventional society, and, at the same time, withholding this treatment from a comparable number of similarly situated deviants in order to determine through comparison whether or not their program is truly effective. Nonetheless, sociologists have learned and borrowed freely from these unique self-help movements. They have sought to replicate the conditions under which these groups come into being, thereby formalizing the creation of such informal groups. Such programs, designed and studied by sociologists, abound in the field of juvenile delinquency. Outstanding examples are Essexfields, Highfields, Provo, and Silverlake. In each of these programs, sociologists have created the organizational conditions in which primary groups may develop among inmates for the purpose of resocializing their members without too much assistance from professionals.

In devising programs for the prevention of deviant behavior (see Cloward's paper in this chapter for one very good example), sociologists may draw up a blueprint based on the theoretical principles of the deviant behavior perspective. In that sense, the blueprint conforms to the formal, routinized, and enacted model.

THE HISTORY OF THE DEVIANT BEHAVIOR PERSPECTIVE

The theme of discrepancy between goals and means is found in the writings of many philosophers and historians. The most important work on this endemic situation occurs in the writings of Emile Durkheim (1858–1917), particularly in his concept of anomie (which means norm-lessness) developed in his study of suicide.[1] Robert K. Merton in his classic paper "Social Structure and Anomie," published in 1938, general-ized the concept of anomie so that it might account for a wide assort-ment of deviant behaviors.[2] Developing one line of Durkheimian theory, Merton argued that anomie could be the normal state of affairs for persons in certain segments of society; for example, lower-class persons who may aspire to the widely held goal of material success but for whom legitimate opportunities for achieving that goal are blocked. Merton then shows how this discrepancy between goals and legitimate means for achieving those goals can generate patterned deviant responses to the resulting frustration.

Since, according to Merton, these states of discrepancy are more often found in the situation of the lower classes, the rates of deviant behavior are higher for the lower classes. Thus, the theory attempts to explain why there is more deviant behavior in one sector of the society rather than another. It does not, however, answer the question of why some people in those sectors become deviant while others do not.

Edwin H. Sutherland's principles of differential association, first set forth in 1939, provide this explanation.[3] In the course of intimate group life, persons can learn deviant ways. This form of learning from one's associates is common for all people, but the content of one's learning depends on the nature of one's group affiliations. In 1955, Albert K. Cohen synthesized the anomie and differential association theories with a theory of the rise of the delinquent subculture. Lower-class adolescent boys, denied status in the middle-class high school, devised their own status system in which status, role, and self-image were based on one's delinquent achievements.[4]

Another synthesis of the anomie and differential association theories, the one with most direct application to the solution of social problems, is Richard Cloward and Lloyd Ohlin's "opportunity theory," which first

1. Emile Durkheim, *Suicide,* translated from the French by John A. Spaulding and George Simpson, New York: The Free Press, 1951.
2. Robert K. Merton, "Social Structure and Anomie," *American Sociological Review,* 3 (October 1938), pp. 672–82.
3. Edwin H. Sutherland, *Principles of Criminology,* Philadelphia: J. B. Lippincott, 1939, pp. 4–9.
4. Albert K. Cohen, *Delinquent Boys,* New York: The Free Press, 1955.

appeared in 1960.[5] This theory maintains that the distribution of illegitimate as well as legitimate opportunities is of critical importance in determining the form deviation will take. Thus, criminal gangs are most often found in sectors of the city where there is a well-organized underworld, with membership in such a gang providing training for entry into the rackets. Conflict or fighting gangs emerge where slums are so disorganized that there are few, if any, opportunities to enter either the legitimate or the illegitimate social world. Retreatist gangs, devoted to drug use, develop in response to "double failure"; that is, when young adolescents fail to "make it" in either the legitimate or the illegitimate world.

As noted above, this theory provided the rationale for a number of attempts at solving some of the urban social problems of the '60's, for example, juvenile delinquency, poverty, racial injustice, and unemployment. Whether it be the Job Corps, Mobilization for Youth, Headstart, or Upward Bound, all of these programs have in common the fact that they seek, in the situation of a primary group of peers, to increase contact with legitimate patterns of behavior and to decrease contact with illegitimate ones.

SUMMARY AND CONCLUSION

The deviant behavior perspective treats the unexpected, namely, the violation of expectations, as if it were expected. Following Durkheim's observation that deviance is normal and to be expected in all societies, this point of view seeks to establish the conditions under which deviant behavior makes its appearance. Once these conditions become known, programs of intervention are possible. Departures from social norms, which constitute social problems from this perspective, arise as patterned responses to states of tension between culture and social organization. In the situation of company, persons may learn deviant alternatives which in time become systematic and form the basis of a deviant role, status, and self-image. Both lay and professional visions of intervention agree that a primary group can reverse the situation and ultimately teach its formerly deviant members to become conformists by adhering to the group's norms and pursuing what it regards as important goals. This most systematic of perspectives on social problems combines Merton's anomie theory with Sutherland's theory of differential association; and, in their synthesis in opportunity theory, a way to solve social problems on a large scale makes its appearance.

---

5. Richard A. Cloward and Lloyd E. Ohlin, *Delinquency and Opportunity,* New York: The Free Press, 1960.

THE PREVENTION OF DELINQUENT SUBCULTURES

Richard Cloward

A discrepancy between culturally defined success-goals and access to opportunities for achieving these goals has been theorized to be responsible for the emergence of delinquent subcultures among lower-class youth. Given this social force to deviate from cultural norms, the kind of community and the illegitimate opportunities available then determine which form the violations will take. The remedies proposed by Richard Cloward involve measures for opening legitimate avenues of opportunity and at the same time channeling discontent into collective actions that can work against the societal inequities that exist.

Delinquency has many forms. In this paper, I shall be concerned solely with delinquent subcultures—that is, with groups in which some type of law-violating activity is required in the performance of group roles. It is not the commission of collective delinquent acts that distinguishes the delinquent subculture from other groups; this definition excludes the many groups that occasionally commit collective delinquencies but do not construe such activities as required forms of role behavior (4). I shall also limit my remarks to delinquent subcultures composed of lower-class, adolescent males.

There appear to be three more or less distinct types of delinquent subculture among male adolescents in the slums of large urban areas. One is essentially a "criminal subculture," a type of gang devoted to theft, extortion, and other illegal methods of obtaining income. Another is the "conflict subculture," a type of gang in which the manipulation of violence predominates as a way of winning status. The third is the "retreatist subculture," a type of gang in which the consumption of drugs and other illicit experiences are stressed. Although these subcultures are rarely found in pure form, they generally exhibit sufficient differentiation to warrant being classified separately.

In this paper, I am concerned with some of the issues and problems which face us in trying to construct programs for the prevention of delinquent subcultures, and I shall try to identify some of the related problems calling for research. Unfortunately, there is little research to

From *Role of the School in Prevention of Juvenile Delinquency,* edited by William R. Carriker, Washington, D.C., United States Department of Health, Education, and Welfare, 1963, pp. 69–84. Reprinted by permission of the author.

draw upon. Previous studies have generally focused on the individual delinquent or on particular types of delinquent acts rather than on the delinquent subculture.

• • •

REGULATING ACCESS TO LEGITIMATE ADAPTATIONS

What we do about a particular type of deviance depends, in part, on our assumptions about the forces that give rise to it. The theory of culture conflict, for example, states that delinquent groups arise either as a way of managing conflicting identifications resulting from the simultaneous internalization of two divergent cultural codes (14) or as a consequence of internalizing a cultural code which so deviates from the prevailing middle-class values that conformity with it creates tension and conflict (6, 8, 10). If we accept this theory in either form, then the school, depending on its approach, can either heighten the conflict or help young people develop skills in managing it. According to another theory delinquent subcultures are a response to barriers in the transition from adolescence to adulthood (1). Our society, according to this theory, encourages the young to want to achieve adult status but places obstacles in the way of their achieving this goal. The gang arises to perform the functions served by *rites de passage* in more ordered societies. This theory also has implications for the school; it suggests, for one thing, that the school may have to be reorganized in order to afford young people better channels of integration with adult roles. Still another theory suggests that delinquent gangs in our society arise in response to barriers to masculine identification among boys. These barriers are said to be particularly strong in female-centered households, such as those prevailing among lower-class Negroes. The delinquent group, which is said to arise by a process of reaction formation, represents a "protest" against the femininity of these households; it serves as a structure within which masculine modes of adaptation can be tested and adopted (9). This theory also has implications for education, for there is a tendency in many sectors of our society to regard the school and those who are successful in school as "unmasculine." Thus we might want to be concerned with the sex distribution in school faculties and the relative masculinity of the curriculum.

My own view of the origins of pressure toward delinquent subcultures stems principally from what I call, together with Lloyd E. Ohlin, the theory of differential opportunity systems (4). This theory states that deviance is a result of the systems of forces governing the accessibility of culturally approved goals by legitimate means (7) and by illegitimate means (2). Limitations on the accessibility of cultural goals by legitimate means are, in this theory, the principal source of pressures toward deviance; the relative accessibility of cultural goals by *illegitimate* means is the principal determinant of the *content* of the resulting deviant adaptation. In this section, I shall briefly discuss the availability of legitimate opportunity in our society and the pressures which it exerts toward deviance. In the next section, I shall consider illegitimate opportunity systems and their impact upon types of delinquent subculture. In both instances, implications for prevention will be noted.

Discrepancies between definitions of success-goals and access to opportunities for achieving these goals create great pressure for the emergence of delinquent subcultures. In Western democratic societies, people are universally enjoined to orient themselves toward making marked improvements in their social and economic position. The ideology of equality of opportunity buttresses these high aspirations and gives hope to the dispossessed that a better way of life can be achieved. Difficulties arise in the pursuit of this goal, however, because of the differential distribution of opportunities and resources for achievement. In other words, for many people there is no connection between the ends to which they orient themselves and the means at hand for achieving those ends. This disjunction is greater at some points in the social structure than at others. It appears, for example, that lower-class youngsters are at a disadvantage in the competitive struggle to improve their social and economic position by legitimate means. Access to higher educational facilities—one of the most widely sanctioned routes for upward mobility—is partly dependent upon economic resources. Even in the primary and secondary grades, it costs several hundred dollars a year to send a child to school, for he must have adequate clothes, transportation, lunches, and pocket money for extracurricular activities. Those in the lower strata of society therefore experience acute frustration, which may lead to delinquency among adolescents and other forms of deviance among adults.

I am not saying here that delinquent subcultures are a product of poverty. Quite the contrary: responses to poverty vary considerably, according to the way in which people define this state. In American society, poverty is defined as a temporary condition from which the individual can reasonably expect to rise. Channels of mobility are said to be available to every aspirant, regardless of his social origins. But when people find that such factors as socioeconomic background and racial affiliation *do* materially influence the possibility of becoming mobile, discontent and frustration result. It is not poverty as such that produces these frustrations but objective discrepancies between culturally induced aspirations and socially structured possibilities of achievement.

Coupled with objective differentials is the accessibility of success-goals. There are cultural patterns which hinder lower-class young people from making effective use of the opportunities they do have. It appears, for example, that academic skills are more closely integrated with middle-class than with lower-class socialization; the middle-class child is encouraged to develop verbal fluency, a capacity for deferred gratification, a sustained attention span, and other attributes which facilitate academic achievement. The result is that many lower-class young people eventually compare themselves invidiously with middle-class youngsters, who are more likely to succeed in school. Lower-class adolescents may subsequently become estranged from the school and join the ranks of the dropouts (11).

Members of the lower class are doubtless aware of the general importance assigned to education in our society and of the relationship between education and social mobility. But they are doubtless also very much aware of economic barriers in access to educational facilities. It is my view that social-class differences in the value placed on education in large part reflect objective differentials in the availability of educational opportunities. Educational attainment and related forms of goal-striving are eschewed not so much because they are inherently devalued as because access to them is relatively restricted. And once these adaptive patterns arise in a particular community, young people may be exposed to them directly and thus exhibit little interest in education from an early age.

Although I have been focusing upon *class* differentials in pressures toward deviant behavior, it should also be noted that these pressures affect males more than females and adolescents more than younger or older people. It is primarily the male who must go into the marketplace to seek employment, make a career for himself, and support a family. Adolescence is a time when preparation for these roles is greatest. The adolescent male in the lower class is therefore particularly vulnerable to pressures toward deviance arising from discrepancies between aspirations and opportunities for achievement. These pressures are especially acute among adolescents in slum communities, which are populated largely by adults who have themselves failed to become mobile. Delinquent subcultures represent specialized forms of adaptation to this problem of adjustment. The criminal and conflict subcultures provide illegal avenues to success-goals that are unavailable by legitimate means. The retreatist subculture is a loosely structured group of persons who have withdrawn from the competitive game, who anticipate defeat and seek escape from the burden of failure.

Some of the implications stemming from this theory seem clear. First, efforts must be made to expand the structure of legitimate opportunity for those segments of the population which now suffer from restrictions.

Education in particular must be made more accessible regardless of race or socioeconomic status. We must also be concerned with the restrictions on access to skilled vocations. Perhaps we should re-examine our laws governing work among minors in order to permit lower-class adolescents to earn the money they need for future training. Methods of overcoming traditional adaptive responses to limited opportunity, such as apathy and hedonism, must also be found and put into effect. An approach involving both the provision of greater opportunity and the modification of adaptive, defeatist attitudes should have an important impact upon the problem of delinquent subcultures.

This theory implies, further, that we must be concerned with the social regulation of aspirations. The task is not, however, to persuade lower-class young people to lower their levels of aspiration but to induce them to join in efforts to expand legitimate opportunities for people in their social category as a whole. Excessive individualism has always been the greatest deterrent to the development among dispossessed groups of organized efforts to improve their lot in life, and the case of our lower classes certainly constitutes no exception. The task is one of demonstrating, as in the case of labor movements, that the likelihood of one's social advancement is partly dependent upon the elevation of the whole social category to which the individual belongs. But now I am intruding upon a subject which should more properly be discussed in connection with the special problem of social alienation and delinquent subcultures, one of the subjects to which I shall now turn.

REGULATING ACCESS TO ILLEGITIMATE ADAPTATIONS

Pressures toward deviance can probably be reduced; however, it is doubtful that they can or should be completely eliminated. Stress between various parts of the society (i.e. between adolescent and adult, between different socioeconomic groups, etc.) is inherent in every society and often performs useful functions. Thus, the task of prevention is not simply to enlarge opportunities for legitimate adaptations but, as I shall now try to show, to restrict access to certain illegitimate adaptations as well. Most attempts to explain delinquency stop once the sources of pressure have been identified, and most programs of prevention are limited to trying to modify these forces. But the forces that lead people to violate social norms do not necessarily determine the *content* of the violations. A given problem of adjustment can have a variety of deviant outcomes. Thus one cannot predict the outcome of pressures toward deviance simply by identifying these pressures. New variables intervene to channel pressures toward deviance into one or another form of deviant behavior.

To illustrate this point, consider two people who occupy the same position in the social structure except that one is male and the other female. Despite the similarity in their positions, we would not ordinarily expect them to respond in the same way to equivalent problems of adjustment. Types of deviant behavior, like types of conforming behavior, are differentiated along a dimension of masculinity-femininity. Some forms of deviance, such as armed robbery, are characteristically masculine; others, such as prostitution, are characteristically feminine. We would consider it "inappropriate" for a female to become an armed robber or for a male to become a prostitute. When people become deviant, in other words, the selection of deviant adaptations is partly controlled by cultural values. This, then, is one sense in which the social structure regulates the outcome of pressures toward deviance.[1]

The crucial regulatory function of the social structure has been overlooked not only in the development of etiological theories but in the construction of programs of action as well. Yet it represents an area of research which, in my opinion, is of paramount importance. To explain any form of deviance, we must know not only why pressures toward deviance arise but also why these pressures result in different outcomes throughout the social structure. And to prevent any form of deviance, we must not only reduce pressures toward deviance but also modify the social forces that channel these pressures into a given type of deviance.

Alienation and Deviant Behavior.   One of the crucial ways in which the social structure regulates the outcome of pressures toward deviance is by influencing the actor's definition of his problems of adjustment. This is an important determinant of his response to these problems (4). Some persons who experience disjunction between their aspirations and the possibilities of achievement look outward, attributing their dilemma to unjust and arbitrary institutional practices, such as racial discrimination. Others look inward, attributing their difficulties to personal deficiencies, such as a lack of discipline, zeal, intelligence, or persistence. Whether the "failure" blames the social order or himself is of central importance to the understanding of delinquent conduct (if not of all forms of deviance), for the one form of attribution leads to alienation from the social order and the other to self-depreciation. Once he is alienated from conventional rules and ideologies, the deviant is free to experiment with illegitimate ways of securing access to success-goals—for example, searching for status through conflict behavior or for money through participation in groups organized for thievery.

In our society, success and failure are explained in essentially individ-

---

1. For a further example of this regulatory influence see Cloward's discussion of inmate adaptations (3).

ualistic terms. Success is formally attributed to ambition, perseverance, talent, and the like; failure, on the other hand, is said to result from a lack of these traits. In explaining occupational achievement or failure, we do not ordinarily refer to "life chances" or "objective opportunities"; we tend, rather, to ask whether people have made the most of their chances, whether they have been diligent, industrious, and imaginative in the pursuit of success-goals. This tendency to equate success with individual merit and failure with individual inferiority contributes to the stability of existing social arrangements by deflecting criticism from the institutional order. Those who attribute failure to their own shortcomings in effect accept the prevailing ideology of the society. They explain their adjustment problems on the basis of socially accepted criteria. Such persons are not at odds with society; on the contrary, self-blame is an important index of attitudinal conformity, for it is essentially an affirmation of the fairness and moral validity of the prevailing ideology. Individuals who explain failure in this way then have the problem of coping with the psychological consequences of regarding themselves as unworthy or inferior. It is unlikely, however, that they will join with others to develop collective solutions, for they see their adjustment problems as essentially personal.

Those who feel that they are victims of arbitrary institutional arrangements, however, are at odds with the social order. This alienation generates a great deal of tension in their dealings with the carriers of the dominant ideology, such as teachers, policemen, and judges. To some extent, tension can be relieved if alienated persons gain support from others who are in the same position and who share the view that their misfortunes are due to unjust social arrangements. Collective support can provide reassurance, security, and validation for a frame of reference toward which the world at large is hostile and disapproving.

If alienation is an important factor in the development of delinquent subcultures, then the implication for prevention is clear. Approaches to lower-class youth generally and to participants in delinquent subcultures particularly must entail a frank recognition of the objective barriers to opportunity which they face. Too often we act as if our object is to lead dissident adolescents to account for their circumstances by questioning their own adequacy rather than by questioning the adequacy of institutional arrangements. Indeed, this seems to be the implicit goal in many current clinical approaches to delinquent subcultures.[2] The tendency is

2. A considerable amount of clinical opinion holds that many of the participants in delinquent subcultures, unlike most "lone" delinquents, are not distinguished by personality disorganization or pathology. Perhaps for this reason, the problem of delinquent subcultures has not generally attracted the attention of clinicians, although they have had much to do with individualistic delinquents. This may also account for what I believe to be a fact; namely, that there is no systematic psychological theory of the origins, evolution, and maintenance of delinquent subcultures.

to explore the motivations underlying the individual's membership in a deviant group, and to assess the ways in which he has learned to satisfy his needs through such deviant activity. The result, whether intended or not, is often to define the delinquent subculture as the product of individual maladjustment, without acknowledging the influence of the social order. The projected remedies are thus of a psychological nature, and the ideological and structural bases of the social order are left unchallenged.

I believe, however, that our approach to the management of delinquent subcultures would be much more successful if we did not so often focus upon personality issues to the exclusion of issues of social justice. Many participants in delinquent subcultures are bright and alert; they may be underachievers, poor readers, or school failures, but they are not lacking in basic intelligence. In Negro neighborhoods in large urban centers adolescents are aware not only that many legitimate economic channels are restricted or closed to them but that even the various stable illegitimate economic channels (e.g., the "rackets") are controlled exclusively by other racial and socioeconomic groups. This situation would pose somewhat less of a problem in a society which sought to make a virtue of poverty or which otherwise controlled the aspirations of its participants. But in a society which systematically inculcates discontent with one's social position and which emphasizes the doctrine of equality of opportunity, barriers to opportunity based on race, nationality, or socioeconomic status create a pervading sense of defeat and despair among the dispossessed.

I contend, in short, that we must give much greater attention to problems of social structure and social justice than has generally been the case in previous approaches to prevention. Dispossessed young people are entitled to have their views of the world given a fair appraisal by professionals. We should acknowledge to them that there *are* marked inequalities in access to opportunity in our society and that one's life chances are materially affected by the vicissitudes of birth. Unless we can convince them that we understand what it is to live in despair, without goals and without hope, large numbers of these young people will be disaffected from the outset.

Further, it seems to me that we must offer these young people an ideology of hope based on the assumption that people can do something about their social conditions. The major institutions with which the urban lower-class adolescent comes in contact—the school, the church, the settlement house—have been greatly at fault in failing to make available programs in which adolescents can come to grips with the issues that affect their lives and can develop skill in collectively acting upon these issues. The school and settlement house and church tend, for the most part, to insulate lower-class young people from any channels through which they might express legitimate grievances against the social order. The problem of dealing with delinquent subculture is not simply to reduce pressures toward deviance or to dissuade individual delinquents, by therapeutic and other means, to relinquish deviant ways of behaving. If they are to be asked to give up forms of adjustment that they find satisfying, they must be given functional alternatives. If they harbor a deep, inarticulate sense of resentment against existing institutional arrangements, they must be shown not that their alienation is without basis but that there are nondeviant, though perhaps controversial, ways of expressing such sentiments. This may mean that those of us working in schools, churches, settlement houses, and other institutional spheres of lower-class life will have to reorganize our programs in order to create realistic opportunities for collective efforts against racial discrimination, slum housing, and the like. The task is not to subtly persuade these young people that their grievances are imaginary or to help them adjust to unfortunate social realities but to provide legitimate ideologies and channels for the collective expression of alienation and discontent and to teach them how to use these channels. This may be one of the most crucial ways in which the social milieu can be altered to prevent delinquent subcultures. To put such an approach into practice, however, it will be necessary to make some basic changes in the organization of services and in our concept of power and its uses.

Limiting Access to Deviant Adaptations.   Attempts to regulate the outcome of pressures toward deviance by providing the young with functional alternatives, such as opportunities for collective social action, should be coupled with efforts to reorganize the social milieu to remove the social supports and resources for various forms of deviance. . . . For this reason, I shall use conflict subcultural behavior to illustrate the proposition that access to deviant adaptations is controlled by the social milieu.

To understand the emergence of conflict subcultures as opposed to other types of delinquent subculture, let us compare the social conditions under which the fighting gang develops with those that give rise to criminally oriented subcultures. Criminal and conflict subcultures do not arise in the same types of urban neighborhood. Where the criminal adaptation prevails, one finds strong counter-pressures against conflict behavior, and where the conflict adaptation prevails, one finds that the social milieu is unfavorable to stable criminal forms of adaptation.

Slum communities, a number of observers have noted, are not necessarily disorganized simply because they are slums (13). Sometimes they exhibit forms of social organization which, although different in many respects from middle-class forms of organization, are extremely stable and give unity, direction, and cohesion to community life. Slum communities, like other communities, can therefore be placed on a continuum ranging from a high degree of organization to little or none (5). Such differences are of great significance, for different types of delinquent subculture tend to be associated with variations in slum organization.

It should be noted that the successful performance of deviant social roles, like that of conforming social roles, requires more than the volition of the actor. One cannot simply decide to make a career of crime and then do so, any more than one can merely *will* a successful career in law; in both instances, certain social supports must be present. For the development of a criminal, two types of social support are essential. One is integration between the carriers of conventional and criminal values: patterns of accommodation and cooperation among police, politicians, racketeers, professional criminals, businessmen, and other local residents. The second is integration among offenders of different age-levels: close relationships among criminal apprentices, semisophisticated young adult criminals, and mature members of the underworld (4).

These two features of social organization exert a crucial influence upon the evolution of delinquent subcultures. Unless the society seeks the services performed by the occupants of a social role, the role will not be likely to persist. Criminals, especially those engaged in organized crime, provide many services which are more or less in demand—gambling, sexual outlets, narcotics, strong-arm squads, and the like. If these services are to be provided in an orderly, continuous way, the activities of criminals must be protected from scrutiny by elements in the society who would like to suppress them. Thus coalitions of groups who have an interest in the preservation of these services grow up to defend them. In communities where these coalitions exist, we have the integration of carriers of criminal and of conventional values. Such integration is a functional prerequisite for the existence of stable, organized criminal enterprises. Communities which exhibit this form of integration can provide illegitimate career opportunities for young people who feel that legitimate channels to success-goals are restricted or closed to them. Because integration of the carriers of both the criminal and the conventional values produces a stable criminal opportunity structure, the young in such communities may orient themselves toward careers in crime as alternatives to the inaccessible legitimate careers which might otherwise have commanded their allegiance.

The opportunity to engage in a criminal career does not account for the actual emergence of such a career. Persons who orient themselves toward criminal careers must be inducted into criminal groups; they must be exposed to situations in which the prerequisite criminal values and skills can be acquired. This learning function is performed by the integration of different age-levels of offender. In slum communities which exhibit such integration, a young man finds older offenders after whom to pattern himself and from whom to learn the ways of crime. Each age-level is connected to a higher level so that young offenders are, through intervening age-grades, ultimately linked to the adult criminal system. Knowledge, values, skills, and attitudes are transmitted through this age hierarchy. For those who excel in learning, upward passage is assured, and a position in a stable adult criminal enterprise may be the eventual reward (12). These are communities, then, which provide both criminal learning and criminal opportunity; they are characterized by the criminal type of delinquent subculture, a subculture composed of adolescents gradually coming to occupy positions of apprenticeship in organized or professional crime.

Purposeless, undisciplined, aggressive behavior is not sanctioned in communities which exhibit these particular forms of integration. This is not to say that violence has no place in their scheme of life; there are occasions when violent behavior is appropriate, but street combat between gangs in search of status is generally discouraged. What inter-gang conflict occurs in these areas is generally defensive, as when local gangs defend their territory against "invasion" by foreign, marauding gangs. The young are made aware by their elders that street warfare not only has little point but tends to bring unfavorable public scrutiny to the neighborhood and thus endangers the various illegitimate community enterprises. Thus the social groups of the community, *illegitimate as well as legitimate,* constantly exert pressure to restrain aggressive behavior among the adolescents. In effect, illegitimate norms support and buttress the conventional prohibitions.

These norms against violence are known to dissident adolescents and are enforced by powerful community sanctions, controlled by various adults in the distribution of illegitimate rewards. In criminal opportunity systems, as in opportunity systems in general, there is a surplus of contenders for positions; not all who orient themselves toward a place in these structures can succeed. A process of selection takes place at every age level. Control of this selection process gives adults in the community enormous influence over the behavior of adolescents, for the adults are in a position either to make great rewards available or to withhold them. Thus the behavior of the young is encompassed within a system of social controls that originates in both legitimate and illegitimate sectors of the community. This point has been developed by Kobrin (5). This type of slum community, in short, is not a favorable environment for the emergence of the fighting gang.

The conflict subculture is principally a product of unstable communities. High rates of vertical and geographic mobility, massive housing projects, and changing patterns of land use (as in the case of residential areas that are encroached upon by adjacent commercial or industrial areas) are among the factors that keep a community off balance and check tentative efforts to develop social organization of any kind. Transiency and instability thus become the overriding features of social life.

Disorganized communities tend to produce a conflict form of delinquency for several reasons. They cannot provide alternative channels to success-goals, legitimate or criminal. Although there may be a good deal of criminal activity in these areas, it is sporadic, unorganized, and poorly protected. Because stable criminal opportunity structures do not exist, stable criminal careers cannot develop. To the extent that the adolescents also experience discrepancies between aspirations and legitimate avenues of social ascent, the absence of illegitimate channels heightens their frustration in these communities.

Furthermore, disorganized neighborhoods have virtually no means of controlling the expression of impulses to deviate. Not only the conventional institutions but also the illegitimate activities of the communities are disorganized. Hence social controls do not originate in either legitimate or illegitimate segments of community life. The combination of heightened frustration and simultaneously weakened social controls appears to give rise to the conflict form of subcultural behavior. Lacking institutionalized channels of social ascent, legitimate or illegitimate, and without effective patterns of social control, dissident adolescent groups seize upon violence as an avenue to status which *is* available and which *can* be utilized by them. Thus there grows up a network of gangs which compete for status on the basis of skills in street combat and other forms of violence.

This analysis has a number of implications for the prevention of conflict subcultures. Above all, the degree of community solidarity must be heightened in order to reduce conflict behavior. In this sense, the target in a program of prevention should be not the individual delinquent or even the conflict subculture but, rather, the community. If relationship patterns among adults can be strengthened, access to conflict behavior can be gradually restricted. The problem of prevention is therefore partly a problem of social control and partly a problem of reorganizing the social milieu so as to reduce the availability of a particular form of deviant behavior.

I am aware that it is not fashionable in professional circles today to speak of social control as a component of prevention. An emphasis on social control is generally regarded as punitive, primitive, and unresponsive to the needs of young people. I would agree if social control is the exclusive emphasis; the delinquency field has provided some dramatic illustrations of the futility of programs based solely on control. For example, it has been observed in a number of communities in New York City that when access to violence as a means of securing status is abruptly closed to delinquents, drug use increases sharply. Many areas in which organized, systematic harassment and suppression by the police and other agencies have forced conflict groups to relinquish violence have subsequently exhibited a disconcerting rise in drug use and other forms of passive, retreatist delinquency. The point is that by restricting access to one form of deviance *without providing functional but conforming alternatives,* we run the risk of simply converting one form of deviance into another. But where conforming alternatives are provided, where the social milieu is reordered so that the means and resources for conforming adaptations are made more accessible, various measures of social control will also be useful.

It should be noted that social control is probably more effective when it is an internal feature of a community than when it is externally imposed, and when access to the conflict subcultural adaptation is restricted by building indigenous institutional forms in a slum community, by increasing the observability of community prohibitions against violence and by enhancing the capacity of a community to impose sanctions. In the long run, young people will be far more responsive to an adult community which exhibits the capacity to organize itself, to manage its problems, and to mobilize indigenous resources than to a community which must have these functions performed by external agents.

The task of generating institutions in disorganized communities poses a variety of problems. Among other things, we need new concepts of the institutional forms most appropriate in an age of rapid social change. Some of the older forms—such as the nationality or ethnic organizations characteristic of the traditional but disappearing immigrant ghettos—may not be suitable in contemporary lower-class urban communities. Once we have decided upon appropriate models, we face a host of questions concerning the way in which to involve the residents of a community in the process of reconstruction. We need to know much more about concepts of leadership in the lower class and in different ethnic groups, about patterns of interpersonal relationships which are compatible to various groups, about the organization and use of power. We may, for example, have to become much more concerned about the role of indigenous groups in large urban communities with respect to the formulation of school policies and practices.[3] We cannot speak of reconstructing community organization without involving the school in this process. These, then, are some of the issues and problems that face us in the prevention of delinquent subcultures.

REFERENCES

1. Bloch, Herbert, and Niederhoffer, Arthur. *The Gang: A Study in Adolescent Behavior.* New York: Philosophical Library, 1958.

2. Cloward, Richard A. "Illegitimate Means, Anomie and Deviant Behavior," *American Sociological Review,* Vol. 24, No. 2, 1959.

3. ———. "Social Control in the Prison," *Theoretical Studies of the Social Organization of the Prison,* Bulletin No. 15, New York: Social Science Research Council, 1960.

4. ——— and Ohlin, Lloyd E. *Delinquency and Opportunity: A Theory of Delinquent Gangs.* Glencoe, Ill.: Free Press, 1960.

5. Kobrin, Solomon. "The Conflict of Values in Delinquency Areas," *American Sociological Review,* Vol. 16, 1951.

6. Kvaraceus, W. C., and Miller, W. B. *Delinquent Behavior: Culture and the Individual.* Washington, D. C.: National Education Association, 1959.

7. Merton, Robert K. *Social Theory and Social Structure,* (Rev. and Enl. Ed.) Glencoe, Ill.: Free Press, 1957.

8. Miller, Walter B. "Lower Class Culture as a Generating Milieu of Gang Delinquency," *Journal of Social Issues,* Vol. 14, No. 3, 1958.

9. Parsons, Talcott. *Essays in Sociological Theory,* (Rev. Ed.) Glencoe, Ill.: Free Press, 1954.

10. Sellin, Thorsten, *Culture Conflict and Crime,* New York: Social Science Research Council, 1938.

11. Sklare, Marshall (ed.); Toby, Jackson. "Hoodlum or Businessman: An American Dilemma," *The Jews: Social Patterns of an American Group,* Glencoe, Ill.: Free Press, 1958.

12. Sutherland, Edwin H. *The Professional Thief.* Chicago: University of Chicago Press, 1937.

13. Whyte, William. *Street Corner Society: The Social Structure of an Italian Slum.* Chicago: University of Chicago Press, 1955.

14. Wirth, Louis. "Culture Conflict and Misconduct," *Social Forces,* 9:484–92, June 1931.

---

3. The control of school systems in many urban areas has become so bureaucratized and centralized that local residents no longer feel that they can have any important role to play in school affairs. This is especially true in low-income areas where school officials often have virtually no contact with adult residents.

THE MARSHALL PROGRAM OF
DELINQUENCY REHABILITATION

Doug Knight

Correctional programs usually fail. Two reasons are generally given to account for this failure—the resistance of inmate culture to such change and the stake the inmate has in maintaining his present identity. Consequently, most inmate cultures sabotage correctional programs, and inmates leave the program more, rather than less, committed to deviant values.

To solve this problem, the Marshall Program incorporates delinquents into active engagement in, and responsibility for, the rehabilitation process. The inmates are placed in the role of resocializing agent in a way that works against inmate negativism and conformity to deviant values. Inmates work at resocializing one another to nondelinquent values through large and small group encounters, confrontations, and negative sanctions. Hence, inmate culture is designed to assist rather than resist treatment goals. In addition to these processes of differential association, the Program also works at providing practical social-living skills to help the inmate succeed vis-à-vis the legitimate opportunity structure.

(Since the time when this Program was described in the following article, an evaluation study has been conducted. Its findings show the Program to be most successful with persons who are not easily threatened, those with the personal and social strength to face the confrontation methods used in the Program. Because such techniques have the potential for arousing a great deal of anxiety, a sense of failure and social alienation sometimes resulted for threat-sensitive persons. Supportive programs, which de-emphasize confrontations and the probing of maladjustment are, therefore, preferable for such persons.*

The Marshall Program represents a distinct divergence from the traditional institutional approach to the rehabilitation of delinquents. But why embark on a new approach? What issues do old approaches fail to resolve? To begin with, institutional treatment programs have not been

From Doug Knight, *The Marshall Program: Assessment of a Short-Term Institutional Treatment Program,* Part 1, State of California, Department of the Youth Authority, Research Report No. 56, March 1969, pp. 6–13, 18–26, 26–28. Reprinted by permission.

*Doug Knight, *The Marshall Program: Assessment of a Short-Term Institutional Treatment Program, Part II: Amenability to Confrontive Peer-Group Treatment,* California: Department of the Youth Authority, Research Report No. 59, August 1970.

remarkable for their natural appeal to delinquent youth. Even where treatment programs have seemed relevant to the street behavior of the inmates, the inmates have still managed to nullify, or neutralize, the impact of activities deemed good for them. The inmate delinquent's resistance to treatment—his ability to evade it, to fend it off, or to neutralize its impact—can be viewed as a function of at least two interrelated influences. These two influences, the lack of peer support for real change and the disinclination of youth to seek potentially threatening rearrangements of life style, will be discussed briefly in order.

First, in many correctional institutions for youth, the impact of the formal, or planned, program is sharply diluted by the informal social organization of the resident population. William E. Dickerson (Marshall unit administrator during the study period) and others have elaborated part of the traditional dilemma:

> The traditional institutional approach results in a vicious cycle maximizing the conflict between captives and captors. The emphasis is on conformity. The captives must demonstrate to the captors their ability to conform to standards of behavior set by the captors. The captive is usually informed that he will remain a captive until he meets the captor's standards. Anxiety, feelings of inadequacy, suspicion, and resentment increase. Initiative and leadership are suppressed *and driven underground,* where they produce . . . a peer culture dedicated to sabotaging and negating the efforts of the captors. The . . . peer culture's destructive effectiveness is generally insured since the captor's culture consists of various disciplines, all more or less pursuing their own goals largely unencumbered, unfettered, and uninvolved with others who are also directly related to the treatment of the captive. The peer-group culture's success in thwarting the efforts of the captor's culture tends to increase the captor's anxiety, feelings of inadequacy, suspiciousness, resentment, etc. The captor then tends to increase the demand for conformity and becomes more punitive in his suppression of non-conformity—and the cycle continues. The sub-group culture always has control but is directed toward destructive goals.[1]

This is to say that adaptation to total institutional living reflects not only the personalities and attitudes delivered into the institution but the organizational character of the institutional setting as well. Institutions holding non-volunteers, or captives, suffer from built-in strains which militate against inmate allegiance to staff and program. Since delinquents generally do not like to be locked up in a situation of authoritar-

---

1. William E. Dickerson and others, "Operational Guide for the James Marshall Treatment Program" unpublished report, California Youth Authority, September, 1966. Emphasis added. Presumably this is not to suggest that delinquents do not feel some ambivalence about deviant behavior. The ward social system does, however, point up the need for inmates to maintain a sense of autonomy and self-esteem while being managed (call it treatment or not) in a social outcast status under authoritarian control.

ian control, the tendency for confined delinquents to react against the traditional setting should not be surprising. No matter the form or degree this negativism takes, what is observed is what Erving Goffman has termed "the practice of reserving something of oneself from the clutch of an institution. . . ."[2] And what is more, the circumstances which elicit this practice are largely *shared.* The inmate underlife thus represents, at least in part, a *collective* adaptation to those abasements of self which tend to be inflicted by this brand of involuntary institutional living.[3] In the traditional institution, the ward who might feel a sense of duty to the institution and its program would probably encounter little peer support for such feeling.

But, *second,* even beyond the problem of the inmate subculture, why should we expect to alter lives with our programs? In this regard we must at some juncture address ourselves to the relevance of programs in light of the *viability* of the human personality and value system. Should we really expect to intrude on these systems so readily? One might indulge the notion that the treatment professional's instinct for "program" is so overriding that he only infrequently pauses to check his implicit assumptions about people-changing. The history of corrections is, after all, largely a chronicle of sensible programs which have not worked. So coercive is the treator's instinct for programming (it might be argued), so profound his allegiance to the correctional image of malleable man, that he may often plunge into common sense programs without truly examining the relevance of program activities to that boy whom he intends to change. If a delinquent boy has a stake in who he is today, an investment in some tolerable and durable self (which at least avails him of a modicum of social reward), then it would seem rash to expect his eager participation in our people-changing programs.

Taken in this light, then, our programs can be seen as *competing* with the functional values which are already part of the boy's life style— values fundamental to a status system which validates (if only tenuously) the boy's worth. Adaptively uncommitted to convention (the boy has yet to experience any sustained sense of achievement, satisfaction, or worth from those activities which are intrinsic to a more conventional

2. Erving Goffman, *Asylums,* Garden City, New York: Doubleday Anchor Books, 1961, p. 319.
3. See Goffman, for example. The social organization of training schools and prisons is the focus of numerous studies and theoretical writings. The nature and function of inmate subcultures are discussed in many of the 46 references cited by Don C. Gibbons, *Changing the Lawbreaker,* Englewood Cliffs, New Jersey: Prentice-Hall, Inc., 1965, pp. 197–198 and p. 212. Other findings can be traced through the references in Thomas P. Wilson, "Patterns of Management and Adaptations to Organizational Roles: A Study of Prison Inmates," *American Journal of Sociology,* 74:146–157, September, 1968.

adolescent identity), he is unlikely to regard a "treatment program" as a promising route to a better life.

In short, the inmate delinquent's resistance to treatment can be viewed as a function of two interrelated influences: (1) the relative negativism of the inmate community to which the boy belongs and within which he strives for some acceptable status, and (2) the personal stake he has in preserving not only his conception of self but also the proving ground of that conception—the alternative status system which provides criteria of achievement and worth responsive to his life situation.

The problem is not easily solved. The Marshall effort is one attempt, nonetheless, at direct engagement of some of the forces of treatment neutralization: the task is first to diminish group resistance against treatment involvement and then, on the basis of a change orientation shared and supported by staff and wards alike, to begin to call into question the conflict between delinquent and conventional alternatives. The day-to-day atmosphere is crucial. As Empey and Rabow have observed, writing about the Provo Experiment:

> Delinquent ambivalence for purposes of rehabilitation can only be utilized in a setting conducive to the free expression of feelings, both delinquent and conventional. This means that the protection and rewards provided by the treatment system for candor must exceed those provided either by delinquents for adherence to delinquent roles or by officials for adherence to custodial demands for "good behavior."[4]

Relying on this assumption, Marshall Program staff have set about to mold a social situation in which wards are not only actively engaged in treatment but, requisite to that, even assume responsibility for its process. Hopefully, a system is built up at Marshall in which neither anti-social nor pro-social expression is suppressed as a result of staff or peer sanctions. The premise is that if the ward *group* can come to genuinely value change and if the change orientation is a focal concern within the total group-living process at Marshall, then significant numbers of Marshall boys can develop a bona fide personal stake in change. Ideally in that event, inmate negativism would not subvert treatment objectives, nor would the immediate status system (in which criteria of worth are often grounded) demand that social rewards be secured in terms of deviant values. With treatment neutralization or resistance thus reduced, real questioning could reveal considerable ambivalence toward delinquent behavior—and this ambivalence would become the basis for change.

That this ideal is not easily workable hardly needs stating. The Mar-

4. Empey and Rabow, "The Provo Experiment in Delinquency Rehabilitation," *op. cit.*, p. 683.

shall Program staff have nevertheless accepted this difficult challenge and have aspired to promote a setting in which the ward group culture itself fosters an orientation toward self-examination and growth. Everything considered, there can probably be no more difficult or crucial task in corrections; for, again, this job points at the essence of the correctional dilemma: the problem of changing the behavior of persons who may upon first contact possess neither the desire nor, in some cases, the immediate wherewithal to change.

Although the Marshall intervention strategy is not geared to a specific theory of etiology, certain relevant assumptions about delinquent behavior underlie treatment programming. These assumptions are:

1. The positive acceptance of conventional authority and limits are at least episodically devalued in delinquent group process.

2. While in interaction with delinquent peers, most delinquents rarely have the opportunity to question the utility of delinquent behavior.

3. Life styles conducive to delinquency often arise out of learning processes which have hindered:

    a. development of adequate conventional interpersonal relationships.

    b. acceptance of conventional responsibility for behavior.

    c. ability to experience and develop good work habits.

    d. capacity for conventional adjustment to stress.

A second set of assumptions connects the three statements about delinquent behavior to intervention strategy:

1. Negativism within the subculture of delinquency will subvert program objectives if the force of the ward social system is not strategically directed.

2. If wards share in the responsibility for their own treatment and other activities, staff and wards are more likely to develop a climate of interlocking interest. Correspondingly, treatment goals are more likely to be endorsed by wards when staff and wards share perspectives to a maximum extent.

3. Once subcultural resistance is effectively reduced, staff can help boys identify and confront cultural, academic, vocational, and social adjustment areas in which conventional achievement has been thwarted.

4. Under guidance by skilled group counselors, many delinquent boys can be stimulated to collectively question behavior in ways which would have elicited negative sanctions in peer-group "street talk." If questioning is in fact sincere and not mainly tactical, the ward subculture can discover redirection from within.

5. Parents of delinquent boys often need help in providing family life conducive to non-delinquent behavior.

At Marshall, therefore, treatment is designed to go beyond the mere administration of "help" (which, unless accepted by the "treated," may be no help at all). A program description summary in the January, 1967 *James Marshall Treatment Program Progress Report* (pp. 3-4) provides a succinct overview of the program and its orientation:

> In this intensive treatment and rehabilitation effort, the Marshall Program strives to apply the concepts of the "therapeutic community," in which the wards share in the responsibility for their own treatment and are involved in decisions relating to their own treatment. On Marshall, this approach includes small group counseling meetings, a daily community counseling meeting attended by all wards and Marshall staff, and weekly group counseling meetings with parents. The wards participate in special school, work, and religious programs. The Marshall Program recognizes the strength of the peer-group culture and is directed to the use of the peer-group culture and the staff all working together toward one major goal: the utilization of the strengths of each toward a basic common objective— positive growth and change.

Staff members on the Marshall unit have tried to forestall the boys' resistance to treatment (1) by institutionalizing self-responsibility and a change orientation throughout the entire ward social system, (2) by intensifying the use of change media (such as group counseling), and (3) by anchoring formal program elements as central features of the informal social life on the unit (for example, small group members are accountable to each other for their day-to-day attitudes and actions).

• • •

PROGRAM ELEMENTS[5]

This section's description of program elements indicates how staff have attempted to link formal treatment components to the ward group process itself. Essentially, the focus is on implanting the themes of behavior examination and behavior change into the ward norm and value systems—which is to say, into the *informal* social arrangement.

Indispensable to this effort, first of all, is the nurturance of a group living program which fosters ward responsibility. This matter of responsibility merits special mention, since it is an integral feature of Marshall Program group living. Even discipline is the responsibility of the entire Marshall community—staff and wards alike. Violators of living unit rules are not just summarily disciplined. Although a behavior "grade" or room restriction (for example) may ultimately be imposed, it is the responsibility of the offending ward's peers (as well as staff) to confront him with his infraction in large or small group meetings, provide him

5. This section is for the most part an edited and adapted version of *James Marshall Treatment Program Progress Report,* State of California, California Youth Authority, January, 1967, Part IV-A.

with feedback as to how others see him, help him improve his behavior, and determine that he will make the required effort before he is again considered a working member of the Marshall community.

"Community responsibility" extends to all aspects of the Marshall Program. The wards are given considerable freedom of movement in the Marshall unit, for example; and ordinarily they keep their appointments at their own initiative. The wards have gained this degree of independence as a result of their own proposals and initiative, and they understand that serious abuse of their independence may bring about its temporary loss. Marshall staff encourage wards to take responsibility and, correspondingly, staff are charged with tolerating the wards' experimentation with its acceptance.

Community meetings.   Hour-long large group meetings are held five times per week and are attended by all of the boys and all staff on duty. The meetings are scheduled for particular morning and afternoon shifts throughout the week so that as many staff members as possible can participate. Whenever the group decides that a one-hour discussion has been insufficient, an additional meeting is arranged. It is expected that a 30-minute critique will follow each regularly scheduled meeting so that staff can discuss the dynamics of the group. Not only is ward participation considered during this discussion but so is the participation of staff. Through self-examination and self-understanding, it is assumed, staff members can more effectively respond in a guidance, or enabling, role.

During large group meetings the staff and boys, acting as a democratic community, deal with problems that confront them. While a myriad problems arise out of the group-living experience and demand remedy, the most vital work of the meetings is to identify, discuss, and modify group-living problems which are related to irresponsible or delinquent behavior. The treatment philosophy of the Marshall Program requires that delinquent values held by individuals when they arrive on the unit (and reflected in the dynamics of the group itself) be questioned and contrasted with more socially acceptable values. Translated into the large group process, this rationale requires that the boys—as members of a *community*—be responsible enough to expose problems they see in others and, out of empathetic concern, go beyond confrontation to actively assist in the resolution of these problems. In many instances, once a "problem" is identifed by the large group, the subject individual's small group is requested to explore it with him in greater detail, seek resolution, and report back at a later date. Staff, who are also members of the community, are expected to intervene or guide when it appears the group is deviating from its purpose, but at the same time are expected to avoid subverting the democratic spirit of the meetings.

Dickerson and others have expressed the staff's view of what occurs in these community meetings:

> The impact of the institutional living experience is brought into focus daily. Interpersonal relationships and conflicts are examined and dealt with. The large group meetings provide a positive channel for dealing with behavior problems. The reality of the "here and now" of behavior and its applicability to positive community adjustment are examined. In addition the large group meetings develop rapport between residents and staff. An attempt is made to provide a social climate which encourages honest expression of feeling without fear of retaliation or recrimination from either staff or residents. Specialized areas of help needed by individual residents are identified and brought to the attention of the individual's small group for more intensive treatment. There is in the large group meeting a stimulation of concern for self and group with consistent demand and assistance to develop give and take relationships. Each resident is then required and provided the opportunity to become aware of the effects of his behavior on the total community. In summary, the large group meetings provide an opportunity structure for utilizing the positive strengths of the peer culture itself, under guidance of staff, to assume responsibility for their own behavior and learning. Instead of being made to account to adults, a role reversal takes place, and the resident finds he must now account to himself and his peers, as well as staff, working in the framework of a community.[6]

Small group meetings.   Each boy is also a member of a small group comprised of six or seven other boys and an adult leader. (During the period of this study the small group leaders were the group supervisors and the social worker, and their caseloads consisted of their small group members.) A minimum of three hour-long meetings per week are held at times consistent with the group leader's work schedule. Newly arrived boys are assigned randomly to groups having openings, and these boys remain members of their respective assigned groups until they leave the program.

The small group embraces the same treatment objectives as other elements of the Marshall Program, but because of the intimacy of the small group and the intensity of its interactions it is the locus of what staff consider to be some of the most decisive treatment experiences. It is here in these small group meetings, many staff members have observed, that the most relevant and probing encounters take place. Consequently, the meetings can be very anxiety-producing. Since a boy's irresponsible behavior on the Marshall unit is often perceived by his peers to be symptomatic of a well-entrenched personal problem, sometimes very personal material is touched upon in the process of dealing with it.

6. William E. Dickerson and others, "Operational Guide for the James Marshall Treatment Program," *op. cit.,* p. 7. Emphasis deleted.

Presumably, however, the support extended by the group permits individuals to tolerate a considerable measure of anxiety and to work toward change. Treatment progress is evaluated by the group and reported to the Unit Review Committee by the small group leader. The small group is also responsible for initiating specific recommendations regarding the disciplining of any of its members.

This small group interaction, staff have agreed, is a vigorous force for what the program is intended to accomplish:

> Within this setting a boy will have his most intensive and dynamic experience . . . in both being confronted with his own behavior as well as examining that of his peers. As the large group represents community, the small group represents family. This concept is reinforced through insisting that the majority of behavior problems, even though brought to light by the large group, be examined and worked through in the small group. Essentially, the small group experience offers the greatest opportunity for . . . involvement of the individual into a guided group experience with his peers. His peers demand that he participate in the rehabilitation process, and they are invested, through the guidance, consent and sometimes instigation of the small group leader, with sanctions in dealing with recalcitrant members.

> These sanctions are:

> 1. Holding back passes
> 2. Cutting the length of passes
> 3. Withdrawal of privileges

> Voting is discouraged and all decisions should be based on mutual discussion and agreement. The Small Group Leader is the ultimate source for resolving conflicts . . . .[7]

School. In planning the school curriculum, consideration was given to its potential role in the total treatment effort, to the availability of educational staff, and to scheduling limitations. As a result the curriculum stresses social and life adjustment—the development of practical social-living survival skills. A regular academic program was deemed unfeasible in view of the rapid turnover of wards at Marshall.

One position, that of school psychologist, was established to develop and carry out the Marshall school program. The school psychologist conducts two morning and two afternoon "life-adjustment" classes, each meeting three to four times a week. Each class group is made up of two small counseling groups. Classroom activities focus on certain life adjustment areas:

7. *Ibid.,* pp. 10–11.

1. Success in a school or training setting following release to the community.
2. Employment problems and realities.
3. Interpersonal relationships.
4. Sex education.
5. Practical consumer finance problems.
6. Constructive use of leisure time.
7. The role of emotions in our well-being.
8. Special adjustment areas.

These areas are explored through techniques such as group discussion, films, and role playing. All boys in Marshall attend life-adjustment and physical education classes, and if requirements are completed all receive five credits for each of the two courses.

"Self-study" courses in history, English, mathematics, and biology were also available during most of the study period but have subsequently been discontinued as unrealistic because of the boys' short stay.

Work.   Another important feature of the Marshall Program is its work experience program. Various work assignments involve the wards in the institution's maintenance work and in several other service trades. Under the supervision of tradesmen and other institution staff members, the wards are given an opportunity at least to begin to learn proper work habits. For many of these boys, it should be understood, a work assignment at Marshall is a first exposure to an organized work situation. Each ward works a half-day and spends the other half in other Marshall Program activities.

At the time a ward is accepted into the Marshall Program he is given a job assignment, usually to the painting crew or grounds maintenance crew. Later, boys are often reassigned to work for one of the tradesmen. If a ward does not perform properly on a job he may be "fired" by his "employer." If this happens the boy must work out his difficulties with his small group and, after that, with the community group. Once relevant issues are resolved, he must find a job on his own, either from his former boss or from one of the other "employers." If he does not locate a job he is subject to transfer from the Marshall Program, and this possibility—plus peer pressure—has prompted most of the wards to work diligently at keeping their jobs.

Activity groups.   Through special activity groups the Marshall residents endeavor to govern themselves to a degree, deal with disruptive individuals, publish a newspaper, arrange recreational activities, and carry out other seemingly constructive and useful functions. These groups not only contribute toward a healthy atmosphere within the unit but also provide at least some opportunity for personal and social development. Although boys must be elected or volunteer in order to participate, three-fourths or more do hold membership in at least one of these groups during their stay.

Passes and furloughs.   After 30 days' residence in the Marshall Program, boys become eligible for a series of passes and brief furloughs. Actual granting of passes in an individual case is the responsibility of the Unit Review Committee (to be described in this section) with the advice of the small group leader and, through him, with the recommendation of the entire small group. A boy's first passes are four hours long, and there is a gradual increase in duration until the 24- and 48-hour furloughs toward the end of his program. These outings serve more than a recreational purpose. Wards are expected to spend much of their time on passes with their parents attempting to resolve family conflicts. Upon returning to the Marshall unit, the boys are encouraged to discuss their "outside" experiences with staff and peers, usually in small group meetings. A boy's reluctance to report on his activities will normally elicit close questioning by the other members of his group who, as discussed earlier, share some responsibility for his progress. The parents have their opportunity for discussion in the parent group meetings.

Parent group meetings.   Operating in conjunction with the pass program is the parent group counseling program. Parents escorting their son back to the institution at the conclusion of leaves attend group meetings conducted by the unit social worker. A rather intricate schedule has been worked out whereby parents whose son is in the second month of his program meet separately from those whose son is in his third month. These meetings provide a forum for parents' feedback about conflicts and progress (particularly in the area of family relationships) based on their sons' brief stays at home. With the aid of the social worker the parents help each other by clarifying problems, suggesting and discussing solutions, offering support, and engaging in various other kinds of helping activities. Over the course of these meetings the social worker also presents a series of prepared talks dealing in various ways with the topics of delinquent behavior and family life. Questions and comments lead to further problem-solving discussions. After each meeting an hour is made available for those parents who want to consult privately with the worker in order to go more deeply into specific family problems.

• • •

Unit review committee.[8]   In keeping with the traditional functions of an institutional classification committee, a Unit Review Committee

---

8. The Unit Review Committee procedure was abandoned in September, 1967—following the study period of this evaluation—in favor of a "team staffing" concept.

meets once a month with each boy in order to evaluate his progress in all areas of the Marshall Program. An effort is made to assess movement toward the ward's specific treatment goals and sometimes to modify goals or to establish new goals. The appraisal itself is based largely on a monthly progress report prepared by the ward's small group leader. The Review Committee also acts as the final decision-making body for major dispositions within the program and for the approval of recommendations to the Youth Authority Board. Thus, the granting of passes, the placement of boys on a "critical list" of boys in danger of program failure, and the transfer of boys out of the program are all responsibilities of the Review Committee. In practice, however, the Committee tends strongly to affirm the recommendations made by the boy's small group leader.

The Review Committee is composed of two panels. The unit administrator participates on one panel, the unit social worker on the other; the school psychologist and senior group supervisor participate on either panel as their schedules permit. At least one day per week is devoted by these key staff members to the Committee meetings.

Parole involvement.   The function of bridging the gap between institutional treatment in the Marshall Program and parole supervision has never been translated into a parole workload and properly funded. The program was unfortunately developed without any augmentation of parole staff (1) to provide for parole agents' participation in the Marshall Program itself, and (2) to provide a transitional group program during the period of parole supervision.

Only a small proportion of parole agents having Marshall Program wards destined for their caseloads have been able to visit these boys in the program, even though the opportunity for parole agents to meet their future clients and establish early relationships would seem desirable for treatment continuity.

When a Marshall graduate is in danger of parole failure, his parole agent has the option of returning him to the program on a 30-day "guest" basis—an intermediate disposition which avoids, or at least defers, a longer confinement. During the "guest" stay the Marshall community (and particularly the appropriate small group) attempts to help the boy confront his course of conduct "on the outs." His irresponsible behavior and its likely contingencies are contrasted with the alternatives, with what else the boy can do given various problems and social situations. The entire Marshall community is also assumed to benefit from discussion about the returnee's predicament, since all of the boys must soon face the reality of "making it out there." Although only ten boys during the 18½-month study period were returned as "guests," the use of this option has increased since that period.

REHABILITATING THE CHRONIC
DRUNKENNESS OFFENDER

Earl Rubington

Half-way houses are intended to serve as a bridge in redirecting deviant careers. With regard to chronic drunkenness offenders, with their generally high rates of relapse, membership in a half-way house can help break their pattern of recurring relapse.

Ordinarily, chronic drunkenness offenders must associate with drinking companions to meet their needs for social and economic support and, subsequently, wind up intoxicated. Half-way houses serve as a legitimate alternative. A half-way house can provide shelter, association and fellowship with sober companions, and access to opportunities for gainful employment. The half-way house described in the following article is supportive in its "therapy" and encourages offenders to transfer their dependence on alcohol to the house, its norms, and its people.

This article reviews experience with relapse in a new program for chronic drunkenness offenders. Programs which attempt to change men who have been drinking heavily for over fifteen years cannot hope for great effectiveness by ordinary standards. Yet the program under review has attained a fair degree of success by standards adapted to the realities of the chronic drunkenness offender problem. The Compass Club, a pilot facility of the Connecticut Commission on Alcoholism established in New Haven, Connecticut, almost five years ago, owes its effectiveness to paradox. For the club puts the negatively valued traits of dependency and recidivism to good organizational uses.

MEETING THE RELEASE PROBLEM

Connecticut's typical offender depends upon alcohol, social agencies and other offenders to solve his problems of social and economic support. With advancing age, reliance on all three increase. After 45, most men in this deviant pattern of social life, finding it difficult to change, accept their fate. With increased reliance on alcohol, they often get drunk in public view. As arrests and jail sentences mount, they become known as "repeaters." Relapses become part of their way of life; agency help only sustains them between relapses.

From Earl Rubington, "Relapse and the Chronic Drunkenness Offender," *Connecticut Review on Alcoholism* (November 1960).

The "release problem," which offenders typically face on discharge from jail or hospital, reveals one source of economic and social waste. Effects of treatment or punishment vanish rapidly in the face of the offender's release crisis. Unlike most high-status problem drinkers, he is alone, without social or economic support. Jobless, homeless, he can turn to few groups for help. Without food, shelter or a job before night-fall, he rejoins a drinking group.

The evidence seems fairly clear that offenders have only a dilemma, no choice, at release. If the only groups open are drinking groups, these are the groups to which they return. These groups require heavy drink-ing. Social or solitary drinkers, men with social or technical skills— each meets the release problem a little differently, but achieves the same negative results. Both rejoin drinking groups to meet their needs for social and economic support, only to wind up intoxicated once again. Release, nine times out of ten, under these conditions means relapse for the chronic drunkenness offender.

If membership in one group quickens drinking, membership in an-other kind can slow it down. The "delaying action" in the present state of knowledge is the best strategy against inebriety. In the case of the chronic drunkenness offender, delay can come about through member-ship in a sober group. A break in the pattern of increasing relapse may ensue if they can join a sober group immediately after their release.

Stop-gaps offering this choice at the time of release go by the name of half-way houses. Places of social and economic support, they are in-tended as turning-points in offender careers. Some offenders, by means of half-way house "therapy" will transfer their dependence on alcohol to the house, its norms, its people. In this way, they can reverse the direction of a life headed for increased dependence, misery, ultimate degradation.

SHELTER HOUSE—"THE PROGRAM" AND HOW IT WORKS

In February of 1956 the Connecticut Commission on Alcoholism opened its own pilot half-way house called The Compass Club in New Haven. Action by the Connecticut legislature established The Compass Club as a facility for the purpose of studying, treating and caring for selected samples of chronic drunkenness offenders. In common with other half-way houses, the club started and continues on an exploratory basis; during its period of operation, there have been numerous changes in policies. And, in response to anticipated future developments, both internal and external, other changes will most likely take place.

Both staff and members of the club refer to it as "the program." The informal, almost amorphous "therapy" which goes on daily within its walls is referred to as "getting the program." Despite many policy changes, two ideas continue as the core of the program. Distilled from the wisdom of all past and present self-help movements among problem drinkers, major emphasis is on "sticking with" a group of people who have alcohol problems and who are trying to stay sober. And, because of the homeless and jobless circumstances of most offenders, the club, unlike Alcoholics Anonymous and most other treatment resources, provides shelter and opportunities for gainful employment. In the constant interplay between changing uses of its social and economic supports, some men "get the program," while others do not.

The Compass Club is a semi-protective environment in which demands on members are kept to a minimum. All are asked to abide by a simple set of rules, most outstanding and important of which is, staying sober just one day at a time. A group of 24 members live voluntarily under the supervision of a staff of five counselors all of whom are members of Alcoholics Anonymous. The members obtain outside employment as soon as they can, live at the club, and pay three dollars a day in "dues" after the first week which is free. They eat two meals a day, breakfast and dinner, in their special dining quarters, and occupy a 10-bed dormitory on the third floor and 14 private rooms on the second floor. Men "graduate" from the dormitory to the private rooms as openings occur.

The nature of the "therapy," as noted above, is most informal. After the initial interview, a physician examines each new member and prescribes medication as needed. After a brief period of "restriction," the men go in search of work. Two evenings a week, they attend a meeting —one for the entire membership held on Monday nights in which "gripes" are solicited, heard and discussed—the other for a regularly assigned group of eight men and a counselor in which all aspects of problem drinking come in for discussion and analysis.

The very informality of "the program" appears to be a source of strength. Although there are only two regularly scheduled meetings a week, the bulk of a member's time at the club is spent in public and private discussions with counselors and fellow-members. In many respects, the "program" resembles a kind of permanent, unstructured group therapy. During all of these discussions, membership and counselors exchange ideas, attitudes, exert diverse influences upon each other. Needless to say, all discussions center around alcohol problems and conditions which make for relapse.

Close contact under casual conditions makes for an atmosphere in which friendships may form and flourish. Moreover, because of the range of opportunities for intimate talks with counselors, intensive interpersonal relations between counselors and members frequently develop. These relationships seem quite comparable to those transactions which go on between psychiatrist and patient and are, many times, productive of real and lasting personality changes in some members.

Completion of the program is the major goal which the staff sets for the membership, to which the members, in turn, aspire. Formerly of three-months' duration, the program is now six months. Irrespective of its terminus, however, all concur, counselors and members alike, that if a man is to get anything at all from the program, if something is "to rub off on him," then he must complete the program, stay the limit.

Considering the past record of offenders in suddenly severing their memberships in groups, sticking to groups and rules presents a severe challenge. Thus, the program, on its face, gives every appearance of being an endurance contest. Members join the club, agree to renounce alcohol during the period of membership, to abide by the club's simple code of conduct. The abstinence norm, the source of all their past difficulties, in the club creates conditions where social learning may take place. All problem drinkers have had periods of sobriety. Most of these "dry" periods were actual endurance contests, sacrificial rituals, tests or self-imposed punishments. During these periods, tensions cumulated, for the drinker was "dry" not "sober." Ultimately, he resolved these mounting tensions in the usual manner. However, in the club, an opportunity exists for a man to go from the "dry" state to the "sober" state, a most difficult period of adjustment for most problem drinkers. Membership in a group who share common alcohol problems may increase the chances of a successful transition despite the many challenges which membership in groups have posed for most offenders.

In the "dry" state, most problem drinkers re-experience the kinds of personal discomfort for which only drinking gave relief. Once inner distress becomes unbearable, they "break out," and relapse into uncontrolled drinking. In the "sober" state, the problem drinker experiences as much personal discomfort, often a great deal more; the difference lies in acceptance of the proposition that drinking will only add to, rather than subtract from, the burden of discomfort. Social as well as problem drinkers have been quite aware of this sensible idea for years. Yet until it became a truly personal idea, its repetition never prevented relapse among problem drinkers.

Despite its easy atmosphere, a half-way house is not immune from those tensions which make for personal discomfort. Men who feel tension sooner than others are aware when it rises from within, from club incidents, from the outside world. They mount, when members, now "dry" for only a short period of time, suddenly desire to reverse the pattern of a lifetime overnight. Men, for example, who seek to regain status with wife and family expose themselves to rebuff. Unless they accede to cumulative group pressures from counselors, members or both, to "take it easy," to "go slow," they will relapse in the face of these status crises. For the first time, many members actually find themselves in the company of men who seem to understand their own feelings and experiences. Under these conditions, a form of "on-the-spot" therapy, designed to nip tension in the bud, makes it possible for some men to go from the "dry" state to the "sober" state. Sober periods which problem drinkers experience in isolation from their fellows rarely permit this type of social learning. Conditions in either jails, hospitals or welfare agencies are likewise unsuited to maximizing the influences which the group can have upon its members to remain abstinent.

TYPES OF EFFECTIVENESS

The Compass Club is a disruptive influence on the network of triple dependency in which most offenders become involved. Its purpose is that of the delaying action; to remake offenders overnight is out of the question. It succeeds and is effective to the degree that it interrupts the "revolving door," that it extends periods between relapses. As a wedge between the drawing power of alcohol, drinking men and the support of agencies, the club succeeds to the extent that it maintains a grasp upon its membership.

Consequently, the several types of effectiveness which have come out of Compass Club experience depend upon duration of membership. Recruitment and retention of clients are the problems of all types of treatment organizations; to change men it is first necessary to break their old ties to groups and their norms, then to bind them to the new group and its norms. Recruiting the membership and then holding it in the group constitute the two major problems of the club.

Since its opening, more than 600 admissions have gone through the club program. About half that number are first admissions. The remainder are "repeaters," who comprise a group of over a hundred men who have tried the program two times and a small number, around thirty, who have tried it three times, the maximum number permitted. The three major sources of admissions (all voluntary) have been and continue to be the Blue Hills Hospital, the New Haven State Jail, and self-referrals. The remainder of admissions come from a variety of sources, such as the state hospitals, Alcoholism Division clinics, Alcoholics Anonymous, Yale Hope Mission, court officers, clergy, etc.

Criteria for admission are minimal. Beyond a wish to gain sobriety by the methods of the "program," a man must qualify as an offender and state resident. If a man has had three or more arrests for drunkenness in the past five years, is between 30 and 55, and employable, he is eligible for membership in The Compass Club.

The facts noted above specify the conditions of entry; there are, in addition, four principal modes of departure from the program. Reasons for separation from the program are designated as follows: A-according to plan; B-with notice; C-without notice; and D-disciplinary action. As with all treatment programs, there are preferred as well as undesirable conditions of exit. The rate of relapse, naturally, is quite high; perhaps as much as 60% of all admissions revert to drinking and fail to complete the program. Obviously, these constitute undesirable conditions of departure. On the other hand, since the major criterion of effectiveness is in sheer "sticking to the program," those who remain for the full six months are separated "according to plan." These are the select group of preferred discharges. And, as with half-way houses around the country, members who "complete the program" (or "the course" as some have called it) are considered "graduates" and occupy honorific status.

Most of these men, of course, have done more than just endure a six months period without drinking. That, by itself, is no mean accomplishment, as counselors and members all will agree. For to date the "according to plan" discharge rate stands at 13%, sharp testimony to the difficulties of attaining "graduate" status, yet these results are comparable to those attained in other half-way houses where accurate records are kept.

Follow-up data indicate, however, that "graduates" navigate best in the new and difficult post-club waters if they continue to "stick to the program," or embrace Alcoholics Anonymous, for relapse is an ever present threat. Those graduates who do not develop group supports for the post-club period, relapse much sooner. Slightly more than half of the club's graduates have moved into private rooms in the Yale Hope Mission. These men have remained physically close to the program. Yet most of them have stayed sober longer than those who ventured immediately into the outside world. Of those graduates who sought private rooms outside, only those who joined Alcoholics Anonymous or took an active part in the Alumni Club, a group composed of club graduates, were able to extend the period of sobriety they had first established for themselves as club members.

Positive examples, however, are more numerous. For, in addition to renouncing the homeless alcoholic way of life, many show signs of increasing respectability. The evidence, of course, is the acquisition of material goods, feelings of enhanced self-respect, and, in several instances, wives and children. Others assumed jobs of considerable responsibility; most notable in this connection is the fact that two of the current staff of counselors are graduates of the club program themselves.

Irrespective of ultimate relapse, graduates are enormously important, far beyond their numbers in both social and economic spheres. Their influence on fellow-offenders and current and other graduates is much stronger than personnel in jails, hospitals, and agencies. For they are positive proof that it can be done; despite all the evidences to the contrary, the wishes for sobriety are strong in most offenders. When one of their own makes it, morale rises. In a field already swamped with paradox, another is the instance of affilation with Alcoholics Anonymous which occurs with some graduates. Day-to-day contact with counselors has broken down in some cases the almost universal, intense antagonism which offenders feel towards Alcoholics Anonymous. So far as these graduates have any influence in their former circle of drinking acquaintances, their example only serves to further break down barriers. When the news of a graduate's success spreads over the "grapevine," many of his friends seek admission to the program.

Economically, the "recoveries" of some graduates are frankly astounding. Reclaiming these men constitutes an enormous saving in dollars and cents to their community. When one considers the number of times that some of them have been in jail, alcoholism clinics, state mental hospitals, their complete reversal of form to self-supporting, sober citizens is amazing.

Graduates, then stand at the pinnacle of effectiveness. They regain the most for themselves, are in a position to make contributions again as self-supporting citizens, remove themselves from the category of social and economic liability. Their effectiveness follows from completion of the program. The success of many other men can be ranked just below graduates—again on the criteria of length of stay in the program, days worked, money earned and dues paid to the state, days out of jail, hospitals, agencies—and most important, days sober in company with other men trying to achieve the same goal. These lengthy memberships, though they may end in relapse, constitute attempts to live without alcohol in a new kind of environment.

CONVERSION OF RELAPSE TO THERAPEUTIC ADVANTAGE

In a certain sense, The Compass Club has taken some clients who have been "failures" from the viewpoint of other treatment programs and made "successes" of them. It has done so, apparently, by capitalizing on the very defects of the offender's qualities—his tendency to relapse, to become a "repeater." This characteristic, most noxious to treatment, correctional and welfare personnel, is turned to therapeutic advantage in the club's program.

For "the program" evokes the very behavior which is a source of annoyance and a sign of failure to all other agencies. The staff seeks, by all the means at their disposal, to induce dependency on the club, on themselves, on the membership. In so doing, they seek to make possible those conditions whereby members are willing to transfer dependence on alcohol either to a group of people or to a set of social norms, "the program." All staff measures point to getting members to "stick close to the program," to put the club before job, family, any other social obligations. And, as men near the completion of the program, counselors continually exhort them on the necessity of maintaining some "follow-up." Embracing Alcoholics Anonymous, "staying close" to the Alumni Club, visiting The Compass Club at every opportunity after graduation—the staff encourages one and all of these. At the same time, for men who "relapse," staff arranges hospitalization for them, encourages them to think of readmission into the club for another try.

A result is that the club has established its own "revolving door." The consequences of its "revolving door" however are quite the reverse from those other agencies where "repeaters" are considered to be failures. Not so, by any means in Shelter House; more often, they show real improvements. This is quite the opposite of what the "revolving door" means in other agencies.

For example, probably one-third of all "repeaters" in the state jail system account for about two-thirds of all drunkenness arrests. At the club, one-third of all men admitted to the program comprise almost 60% of all admissions; and, as time goes by, the number will probably increase. The differences in "repeating" at the club are two-fold.

First, "repeaters," irrespective of ultimate reasons for separation, remain in the club longer than do first admissions (median stay for first admissions is only 25 days, for repeaters at first admission it is 40 days, on second admission 35 days, on third admission 75 days). Secondly, the percentage of "according to plan" discharges among repeaters is exactly twice that of first admissions. Thus, dependency and recidivism at the club make distinct contributions to organizational effectiveness.

From this organizational paradox, two important conclusions seem to follow. Certain types of offenders are more apt to perform the club member's role more successfully than others. The club is more successful in inducing independent responses in some, but not all of its members. The differences between these types of members, in part, arise out of their previous adaptation to the network of triple dependency. Among those members who relied more in the past on treatments for alcoholism, there is not only the tendency to seek help, but more importantly, the tendency to accept it in the form the club makes available. These men seem to have suffered more inner shame and punishment for their drinking, and have always sought a way out, irrespective of the frequency of relapse. By contrast the bulk of men who drop out of the program early (more than 40% of the "without notice" group leave the program within the first seven days) continue to cling to a picture of independence in the face of the adversities which attend alcoholism. These men have experienced greater external punishment for drinking, on the average having many more arrests and fewer past treatments for alcoholism. They have drunk, on the average, more heavily for a few more years than the successful graduate group; they have a high frequency of relapse which impels them to seek help. But the form in which the help arises soon antagonizes them. Then they decide they cannot abide even the club's simple routine and want to try it "on their own." In some cases, these men have strong urges for sobriety, yet grave doubts of ever accomplishing it. They respond to sudden changes by rapid relapse; many rebel against the dependent relationship with staff by arguing that since they have jobs now they have "straightened out." Talk about drinking problems finally annoys them and they leave, most of the time by getting drunk.

In its permissive attitude towards relapse, The Compass Club invites readmission. It draws its readmission, mainly from a group who appear to have gained some profit from their original experience at the club and who seek to extend it. While this group seems better fitted to gain from the club's program at the outset, because of the innumerable difficulties which beset the average chronic drunkenness offender, even they experience relapse. And, it will be noted, so do "successful graduates." But since relapse and readmission do not appear to connote any sign of failure either on the part of staff or of members, the opportunities for making the second admission more productive seem to increase. In any case, it would seem that experience with "relapse" and with "repeaters" in the club often leads to results quite opposite from what these terms ordinarily connote in other treatment settings.

DRUG ADDICTION AND SYNANON

Rita Volkman Johnson and Donald R. Cressey

Drug addicts, when they enter a conventional treatment center, often do so only to "take a rest" and to reduce the size of their habit. They "take" the staff and their supplies, but not their values, conning staff and leaving only to revert to drug use. Thus, most conventional treatment centers have high rates of recidivism.

Addicts can, however, change through application of the principles of differential association. Through association, role-models who have adopted conventional values can socialize others to these definitions.

From Rita Volkman and Donald R. Cressey, "Differential Association and the Rehabilitation of Drug Addicts," *American Journal of Sociology,* 69 (September 1963), pp. 129–42. Copyright © 1963 by The University of Chicago Press. Reprinted by permission.

If status is awarded in accordance with conformity to these norms, conventional norms and values come in time to displace the deviant norms and values.

Synanon exemplifies, albeit unintentionally, these sociological principles. High intense rates of contact are provided in an antidrug group composed of former drug users. Persons in Synanon rise in rank as they go through the prescribed stages based on their resocialization and the learning of new roles in an antidrug community. Results to date confirm the soundness of this approach. Because of the confrontation methods used, however, the caution provided for the Marshall Program as to the type of person for whom the program could be detrimental also would apply here.

In 1955 Cressey listed five principles for applying Edwin Sutherland's theory of differential association to the rehabilitation of criminals.[1] While this article is now frequently cited in the sociological literature dealing with group therapy, "therapeutic communities," and "total institutions," we know of no program of rehabilitation that has been explicitly based on the principles. The major point of Cressey's article, which referred to criminals, not addicts, is similar to the following recommendation by the Chief of the United States Narcotics Division: "The community should restore the former addict to his proper place in society and help him avoid associations that would influence him to return to the use of drugs."[2]

Cressey gives five rules (to be reviewed below) for implementing this directive to "restore," "help," and "influence" the addict. These rules, derived from the sociological and social-psychological literature on social movements, crime prevention, group therapy, communications, personality change, and social change, were designed to show that sociology has distinctive, non-psychiatric theory that can be used effectively by practitioners seeking to prevent crime and change criminals. Sutherland also had this as a principal objective when he formulated his theory of differential association.[3]

Assuming, as we do, that Cressey's principles are consistent with Sutherland's theory and that his theory, in turn, is consistent with more general sociological theory, a test of the principles would be a test of

1. Donald R. Cressey, "Changing Criminals: The Application of the Theory of Differential Association," *American Journal of Sociology,* LXI (September, 1955), pp. 116–20 (see also Cressey, "Contradictory Theories in Correctional Group Therapy Programs," *Federal Probation,* XVIII [June, 1954], pp. 20–26).
2. Harry J. Anslinger, "Drug Addiction," *Encyclopaedia Britannica,* VII (1960), pp. 677–79.
3. Edwin H. Sutherland and Donald R. Cressey, *Principles of Criminology* (6th ed.; Philadelphia: J. B. Lippincott Co., 1960), pp. 74–80.

the more general formulations. Ideally, such a test would involve careful study of the results of a program rationally designed to utilize the principles to change criminals. To our knowledge, such a test has not been made.[4] As a "next best" test, we may study rehabilitation programs that use the principles, however unwittingly. Such a program has been in operation since 1958. Insofar as it is remarkably similar to any program that could have been designed to implement the principles, the results over the years can be viewed as at least a crude test of the principles. Since the principles are interrelated, the parts of any program implementing them must necessarily overlap.

"Synanon," an organization of former drug addicts, was founded in May, 1958, by a member of Alcoholics Anonymous with the assistance of an alcoholic and a drug addict. In December, 1958, Volkman (a non-addict) heard about the two dozen ex-addicts living together in an abandoned store, and she obtained permission of the Synanon Board of Directors[5] to visit the group daily and to live in during the weekends. In July, 1959, she moved into the girls' dormitory of the group's new, larger quarters and continued to reside at Synanon House until June, 1960. Cressey (also a non-addict) visited the House at Volkman's invitation in the spring of 1960; for one year, beginning in July, 1960, he visited

Table 1. Age and Sex*

Age (in Years)	Males		Females		Total	
	No.	Per Cent	No.	Per Cent	No.	Per Cent
18–20	0	0	1	7	1	2
21–30	17	44	11	79	28	54
31–40	18	48	2	14	20	38
41–50	1	3	0	0	1	2
51–60	2	5	0	0	2	4
Total	38	100	14	100	52	100

*Median ages: males, 31.0; females, 27.5.

the organization on the average of at least once a week. He deliberately refrained from trying to influence policy or program, and his theory about the effects of group relationships on rehabilitation were unknown to the group. Most of the interview material and statistical data reported below were collected by Volkman during her 1959–60 period of residence and were used in the thesis for her Master's degree, prepared

4. See, however, Joseph A. Cook and Gilbert Geis, "Forum Anonymous: The Techniques of Alcoholics Anonymous Applied to Prison Therapy," *Journal of Social Therapy*, III (First Quarter, 1957), pp. 9–13.
5. The Board at first was composed of the three original members. It is now made up of the founder (an ex-alcoholic but a non-addict) and seven long-term residents who have remained off drugs and who have demonstrated their strict loyalty to the group and its principles.

under the direction of C. Wayne Gordon.[6] As both a full-fledged member of Synanon and as a participant observer, Volkman attended about three hundred group sessions, a few of which were recorded. She was accorded the same work responsibilities, rights, and privileges as any other member, and she was considered one of Synanon's first "graduates."

THE SUBJECTS

Background data were available on only the first fifty-two persons entering Synanon after July, 1958. These records were prepared by a resident who in July, 1959, took it upon himself to interview and compile the information. We have no way of determining whether these fifty-two persons are representative of all addicts. However, we believe they are similar to the 215 persons who have resided at Synanon for at least one month.

Age and sex distributions are shown in Table 1: 44 per cent of the fifty-two were Protestant, 35 per cent Catholic, 8 per cent Jewish.[7]

Table 2. Educational Attainment

	No.	Per Cent
Part grade school	1	2
Completed grade school	3	6
Part high school	24	46
Completed high school	11	21
Part college	13	25
Completed college	0	0
Total	52	100

Racially, 27 per cent were Negro, and there were no Orientals; 19 per cent of the Caucasians were of Mexican origin and 13 per cent were of Italian origin. Educational attainment is shown in Table 2. Although the data on early family life are poor because the resident simply asked "What was your family like?" it may be noted that only five of the fifty-two indicated satisfaction with the home. Words and phrases such as "tension," "arguing," "bickering," "violence," "lack of warmth," "went back and forth," and "nagged" were common.[8]

The sporadic and tenuous occupational ties held by the group are

6. Rita Volkman, "A Descriptive Case Study of Synanon as a Primary Group Organization" (unpublished Master's thesis, Department of Education, University of California, Los Angeles, 1961).
7. In May, 1961, 20 per cent of the residents were Jewish.
8. Cf. Research Center for Human Relations, New York University, *Family Background as an Etiological Factor in Personality Predisposition to Heroin Addiction* (New York: the Author, 1956).

indicated in Table 3. This table supports the notion that addicts cannot maintain steady jobs because their addiction interferes with the work routine; it suggests also that these members had few lasting peer group contacts or ties, at least so far as work associations go. In view of their poor employment records, it might be asked how the addicts supported their addictions, which cost from $30 to $50 a day and sometimes ran to $100 a day. Only four of the men reported that they obtained their incomes by legitimate work alone; thirty (79 per cent) were engaged in illegitimate activities, with theft, burglary, armed robbery, shoplifting, and pimping leading the list. One man and seven women were supplied with either drugs or money by their mates or families, and five of these females supplemented this source by prostitution or other illegitimate work. Five of the fourteen women had no income except that from

Table 3. Length and Continuity of Employment

No. of Years on One Job	Unsteady (Discontinuous or Sporadic)	Steady (Continuous)	Total
Under 1	36*	4	40
2–3	3	2	5
4–5	1	3	4
6 or over	2	1	3
Total	42	10	52

* Of this category 67 per cent defined their work as "for short periods only."

illegitimate activities, and none of the women supported themselves by legitimate work only.

Institutional histories and military service histories are consistent with the work and educational histories, indicating that the fifty-two members were not somehow inadvertently selected as "easy" rehabilitation cases. The fifty-two had been in and out of prisons, jails, and hospitals all over the United States. Table 4 shows that ten men and one woman had been confined seven or more times; the mean number of confinements for males was 5.5 and for females 3.9. The table seems to indicate that whatever value confinement in institutions might have had for this group, it clearly did not prevent further confinements.

In sum, the pre-Synanon experiences of the fifty-two residents seem to indicate non-identification with pro-legal activities and norms. Neither the home, the armed services, the occupational world, schools, prisons, nor hospitals served as links with the larger and more socially acceptable community. This, then, is the kind of "raw material" with which Synanon has been working.[9]

9. Of the fifty-two members 60 per cent first heard about Synanon from addicts on the street or in jails, prisons, or hospitals; about a fourth heard about it on television or read about it in a magazine; and the remainder were told of it by members or past members.

Table 4. Confinements in Institutions

No. of Confinements	Male	No. Female	Total*
1–3	9	6	15
4–6	12	7	19
7–9	8	0	8
10–12	0	1	1
13–15	2	0	2
Total confinements	166	59	225

*Three males indicated "numerous arrests," and four supplied no information. These seven were not included in the tally.

THE PROGRAM

Admission. Not every addict who knocks on the door of Synanon is given admission. Nevertheless, the only admission criterion we have been able to find is *expressed willingness* to submit one's self to a group that hates drug addiction. Use of this criterion has unwittingly implemented one of Cressey's principles:

If criminals are to be changed, they must be assimilated into groups which emphasize values conducive to law-abiding behavior and, concurrently, alienated from groups emphasizing values conducive to criminality. Since our experience has been that the majority of criminals experience great difficulty in securing intimate contacts in ordinary groups, special groups whose major common goal is the reformation of criminals must be created.

This process of assimilation and alienation begins the moment an addict arrives at Synanon, and it continues throughout his stay. The following are two leaders' comments on admission interviews; they are consistent with our own observations of about twenty such interviews.

1. When a new guy comes in we want to find out whether a person has one inkling of seriousness. Everybody who comes here is what we call a psychopathic liar. We don't take them all, either. We work off the top spontaneously, in terms of feeling. We use a sort of intuitive faculty. You know he's lying, but you figure, "Well, maybe if you get a halfway positive feeling that he'll stay. . . ." We ask him things like "What do you want from us?" "Don't you think you're an idiot or insane?" "Doesn't it sound insane for you to be running around the alleys stealing money from others so's you can go and stick something up your arm?" "Does this sound sane to you?" "Have you got family and friends outside?" We might tell him to go do his business now and come back when he's ready to do business with us. We tell him, "We don't need you." "You need *us*." And if we figure he's only halfway with us, we'll chop off his hair.

It's all in the *attitude*. It's got to be positive. We don't want their money. But we may just tell him to bring back some dough next week. If he pleads and begs—the money's not important. If he shows he really cares. If his attitude is good. It's all in the attitude.

2. Mostly, if people don't have a family outside, with no business to take care of, they're ready to stay. They ain't going to have much time to think about themselves otherwise. . . . Now, when he's got problems, when he's got things outside, if he's got mickey mouse objections, like when you ask him "How do you feel about staying here for a year?" and he's got to bargain with you, like he needs to stay with his wife or his sick mother—then we tell him to get lost. If he can't listen to a few harsh words thrown at him, he's not ready. Sometimes we yell at him, "You're a goddamned liar!" If he's serious he'll take it. He'll do anything if he's serious.

But each guy's different. If he sounds sincere, we're not so hard. If he's sick of running the rat race out there, or afraid of going to the penitentiary, he's ready to do anything. Then we let him right in. . . .

This admission process seems to have two principal functions. First, it forces the newcomer to admit, at least on a verbal level, that he is willing to try to conform to the norms of the group, whose members will not tolerate any liking for drugs or drug addicts. From the minute he enters the door, his expressed desire to join the group is tested by giving him difficult orders—to have his hair cut off, to give up all his money, to sever all family ties, to come back in ten days or even thirty days. He is given expert help and explicit but simple criteria for separating the "good guys" from the "bad guys"—the latter shoot dope. Second, the admission process weeds out men and women who simply want to lie down for a few days to rest, to obtain free room and board, or to stay out of the hands of the police. In the terms used by Lindesmith, and also in the terms used at Synanon, the person must want to give up drug *addiction*, not just the drug *habit*.[10] This means that he must at least *say* that he wants to quit using drugs once and for all, in order to realize his potentials as an adult; he must not indicate that he merely wants a convenient place in which to go through withdrawal distress so that he can be rid of his habit for a short time because he has lost his connection, or for some other reason. He must be willing to give up all ambitions, desires, and social interactions that might prevent the group from assimilating him completely.

If he says he just wants to kick, he's no good. Out with him. Now we know nine out of ten lie, but we don't care. We'd rather have him make an attempt and *lie* and then get him in here for thirty days or so—then he might stick. It takes months to decide to stay.

10. Alfred R. Lindesmith, *Opiate Addiction* (Bloomington: Principia Press, 1947), pp. 44–66.

Most fish [newcomers] don't take us seriously. We know what they want, out in front. A dope fiend wants dope, nothing else. All the rest is garbage. We've even taken that ugly thing called money. This shows that they're serious. Now this guy today was sincere. We told him we didn't want money. We could see he would at least give the place a try. We have to find out if he's sincere. Is he willing to have us cut off his curly locks? I imagine cutting his hair off makes him take us seriously. . . .

Although it is impossible to say whether Synanon's selective admission process inadvertently admits those addicts who are most amenable to change, no addict has been refused admission on the ground that his case is "hopeless" or "difficult" or that he is "unreachable." On the contrary, before coming to Synanon, twenty-nine of the fifty-two addicts had been on drugs for at least ten years. Two of these were addicted for over forty years, and had been in and out of institutions during that period. The average length of time on drugs for the fifty-two was eleven years, and 56 per cent reported less than one month as the longest period of time voluntarily free of drugs after addiction and prior to Synanon.

Indoctrination.   In the admission process, and throughout his residence, the addict discovers over and over again that the group to which he is submitting is antidrug, anticrime, and antialcohol. At least a dozen times a day he hears someone tell him that he can remain at Synanon only as long as he "stays clean," that is, stays away from crime, alcohol, and drugs. This emphasis is an unwitting implementation of Cressey's second principle:

The more relevant the common purpose of the group to the reformation of criminals, the greater will be its influence on the criminal members' attitudes and values. Just as a labor union exerts strong influence over its members' attitudes toward management but less influence on their attitudes toward say, Negroes, so a group organized for recreation or welfare purposes will have less success in influencing criminalistic attitudes and values than will one whose explicit purpose is to change criminals.

Indoctrination makes clear the notion that Synanon exists in order to keep addicts off drugs, not for purposes of recreation, vocational education, etc. Within a week after admission, each newcomer participates in an indoctrination session by a spontaneous group made up of four or five older members. Ordinarily, at least one member of the Board of Directors is present, and he acts as leader. The following are excerpts from one such session with a woman addict. The rules indicate the extreme extent to which it is necessary for the individual to subvert his personal desires and ambitions to the antidrug, anticrime group.

Remember, we told you not to go outside by yourself. Whenever anybody leaves this building they have to check in and out at the desk. For a while, stay in the living room. Don't take showers alone or even go to the bath room alone, see. While you're kicking, somebody will be with you all the time. And stay away from newcomers. You got nothing to talk to them about, except street talk, and before you know it you'll be splitting [leaving] to take a fix together. Stay out of the streets, mentally and physically, or get lost now.

No phone calls or letters for a while—if you get one, you'll read it in front of us. We'll be monitoring all your phone calls for a while. You see, you got no ties, no business out there any more. You don't need them. You never could handle them before, so don't start thinking you can do it now. All you knew how to do was shoot dope and go to prison.

You could never take care of your daughter before. You didn't know how to be a mother. It's garbage. All a dope fiend knows how to do is shoot dope. Forget it.

There are two obvious illustrations of the antidrug and anticrime nature of the group's subculture. First, there is a strong taboo against what is called "street talk." Discussion of how it feels to take a fix, who one's connection was, where one took his shot, the crimes one has committed, or who one associated with is severely censured. One's best friend and confidant at Synanon might well be the person that administers a tongue lashing for street talk, and the person who calls your undesirable behavior to the attention of the entire group during a general meeting.

Second, a member must never, in any circumstances, identify with the "code of the streets," which says that a criminal is supposed to keep quiet about the criminal activities of his peers. Even calling an ordinary citizen "square" is likely to stimulate a spontaneous lecture, in heated and colorful terms, on the notion that the people who are *really* square are those that go around as bums sticking needles in their arms. A person who, as a criminal, learned to hate stool pigeons and finks with a passion must now turn even his closest friend over to the authorities, the older members of Synanon, if the friend shows any signs of nonconformity. If he should find that a member is considering "sneaking off to a fix somewhere," has kept pills, drugs, or an "outfit" with him when he joined the organization, or even has violated rules such as that prohibiting walking alone on the beach, he must by Synanon's code relinquish his emotional ties with the violator and expose the matter to another member or even to the total membership at a general meeting. If he does not do so, more pressure is put upon him than upon the violator, for he is expected to have "known better." Thus, for perhaps the first time in his life he will be censured for *not* "squealing" rather than for "squealing."[11] He must identify with the law and not with the criminal intent or act.

The sanctions enforcing this norm are severe, for its violation theatens the very existence of the group. "Guilt by association" is the rule. In several instances, during a general meeting the entire group spontaneously voted to "throw out" both a member who had used drugs and a member who had known of this use but had not informed the group. Banishment from the group is considered the worst possible punishment, for it is stressed over and over again that life in the streets "in your condition" can only mean imprisonment or death.

That the group's purpose is keeping addicts off drugs is given emphasis in formal and informal sessions—called "haircuts" or "pull ups"—as well as in spontaneous denunciations, and in denunciations at general meetings. The "synanon," discussed below, also serves this purpose. A "haircut" is a deliberately contrived device for minimizing the importance of the individual and maximizing the importance of the group, and for defining the group's basic purpose—keeping addicts off drugs and crime. The following is the response of a leader to the questions, "What's a haircut? What's its purpose?"

> When you are pointing out what a guy is doing. We do this through mechanisms of exaggeration. We blow up an incident so he can really get a look at it. The Coordinators [a coordinator resembles an officer of the day] and the Board members and sometimes an old timer may sit in on it. We do this when we see a person's attitude becoming negative in some area.
>
> For a *real* haircut, I'll give you myself. I was in a tender trap. My girl split. She called me on the job three days in a row. I made a date with her. We kept the date and I stayed out all night with her. Now, she was loaded [using drugs]. I neglected—or I refused—to call the house. By doing this I ranked everybody. You know doing something like that was no good. They were all concerned. They sent three or four autos looking for me because I didn't come back from work. You see, I was in Stage II.
>
> X found me and he made me feel real lousy, because I knew he worked and was concerned. Here he was out looking for me and he had to get up in the morning.
>
> Well, I called the house the next morning and came back. I got called in for a haircut.
>
> I sat down with three Board members in the office. They stopped everything to give the haircut. That impressed me. Both Y and Z, they pointed out my absurd and ridiculous behavior by saying things like this—though I did not get loaded, I associated with a broad I was emotionally involved

11. See Lewis Yablonsky, "The Anti-Criminal Society: Synanon," *Federal Probation,* XXVI (September, 1962), pp. 50–57; and Lewis Yablonsky, *The Violent Gang* (New York: Macmillan Co., 1962), pp. 252–63.

with who was using junk. I jeopardized my *own* existence by doing this. So they told me, "Well, you fool, you might as well have shot dope by associating with a using addict." I was given an ultimatum. If I called her again or got in touch with her I would be thrown out.

("Why?")

Because continued correspondence with a using dope fiend is a crime against *me*—it hurts *me*. It was also pointed out how rank I was to people who are concerned with me. I didn't seem to care about people who were trying to help me. I'm inconsiderate to folks who've wiped my nose, fed me, clothed me. I'm like a child, I guess. I bite the hand that feeds me.

To top that off, I had to call a general meeting and I told everybody in the building what a jerk I was and I was sorry for acting like a little punk. I just sort of tore myself down. Told everyone what a phony I had been. And then the ridiculing questions began. Everybody started in. Like, "Where do you get off doing that to us?" That kind of stuff. When I was getting the treatment they asked me what I'd do—whether I would continue the relationship, whether I'd cut it off, or if I really wanted to stay at Synanon and do something about myself and my problem. But I made the decision before I even went in that I'd stay and cut the broad loose. I had enough time under my belt to know enough to make that decision before I even came back to the house. . . .

Group cohesion. The daily program at Synanon is consistent with Cressey's third principle, and appears to be an unwitting attempt to implement that principle:

The more cohesive the group, the greater the member's readiness to influence others and the more relevant the problem of conformity to group norms. The criminals who are to be reformed and the persons expected to effect the change must, then, have a strong sense of belonging to one group: between them there must be a genuine "we" feeling. The reformers, consequently, should not be identifiable as correctional workers, probation or parole officers, or social workers.

Cohesion is maximized by a "family" analogy and by the fact that all but some "third-stage" members live and work together. The daily program has been deliberately designed to throw members into continuous mutual activity. In addition to the free, unrestricted interaction in small groups called "synanons," the members meet as a group at least twice each day. After breakfast, someone is called upon to read the "Synanon Philosophy," which is a kind of declaration of principles, the day's work schedule is discussed, bits of gossip are publicly shared, the group or individual members are spontaneously praised or scolded by older members. Following a morning of work activities, members meet in the dining room after lunch to discuss some concept or quotation that has been written on a blackboard. Stress is on participation and expression; quotations are selected by Board members to provoke controversy and examination of the meaning, or lack of meaning, of words. Discussion sometimes continues informally during the afternoon work period and in "synanons," which are held after dinner (see below). In addition, lectures and classes, conducted by any member or outside speaker who will take on the responsibility, are held several times a week for all members who feel a need for them. Topics have included "semantics," "group dynamics," "meaning of truth," and "Oedipus complex."

There are weekend recreational activities, and holidays, wedding anniversaries, and birthdays are celebrated. Each member is urged: "Be yourself," "Speak the truth," "Be honest," and this kind of action in an atmosphere that is informal and open quickly gives participants a strong sense of "belonging." Since many of the members have been homeless drifters, it is not surprising to hear frequent repetition of some comment to the effect that "This is the first home I ever had."

Also of direct relevance to the third principle is the *voluntary* character of Synanon. Any member can walk out at any time; at night the doors are locked against persons who might want to enter, but not against persons who might want to leave. Many do leave.

Holding addicts in the house once they have been allowed to enter is a strong appeal to ideas such as "We have all been in the shape you are now in," or "Mike was on heroin for twenty years and *he's* off." It is significant, in this connection, that addicts who "kick" (go through withdrawal distress) at Synanon universally report that the sickness is not as severe as it is in involuntary organizations, such as jails and mental hospitals. One important variable here, we believe, is the practice of not giving "kicking dope fiends" special quarters. A newcomer kicks on a davenport in the center of the large living room, not in a special isolation room or quarantine room. Life goes on around him. Although a member will be assigned to watch him, he soon learns that his sickness is not important to men and women who have themselves kicked the habit. In the living room, one or two couples might be dancing, five or six people may be arguing, a man may be practicing the guitar, and a girl may be ironing. The kicking addict learns his lesson: These others have made it. This subtle device is supplemented by explicit comments from various members as they walk by or as they drop in to chat with him. We have heard the following comments, and many similar ones, made to new addicts lying sick from withdrawal. It should be noted that none of the comments could reasonably have been made by a rehabilitation official or a professional therapist.

It's OK boy. We've all been through it before.
For once you're with people like us. You've got everything to gain here and nothing to lose.

You think you're tough. Listen, we've got guys in here who could run circles around you, so quit your bull——.

You're one of us now, so keep your eyes open, your mouth shut and try to listen for a while. Maybe you'll learn a few things.

Hang tough, baby. We won't let you die.

Status ascription.   Cressey's fourth principle is:

Both reformers and those to be reformed must achieve status within the group by exhibition of "pro-reform" or anti-criminal values and behavior patterns. As a novitiate . . . he is a therapeutic parasite and not actually a member until he accepts the group's own system for assigning status.

This is the crucial point in Cressey's formula, and it is on this point that Synanon seems most effective. The house has an explicit program for distributing status symbols to members in return for staying off the drug and, later, for actually displaying antidrug attitudes. The resident, no longer restricted to the status of "inmate" or "patient" as in a prison or hospital, can achieve any staff position in the status hierarchy.

The Synanon experience is organized into a career of roles that represent stages of graded competence, at whose end are roles that might later be used in the broader community. Figure 1 shows the status system in terms of occupational roles, each box signifying a stratum. Such cliques as exist at Synanon tend to be among persons of the same stratum. Significantly, obtaining jobs of increased responsibility and status is almost completely dependent upon one's attitudes toward crime and the use of drugs. To obtain a job such as Senior Coordinator, for example, the member must have demonstrated that he can remain free of drugs, crime, and alcohol for at least three to six months. Equally important, he must show that he can function without drugs in situations where he might have used drugs before he came to Synanon. Since he is believed to have avoided positions of responsibility by taking drugs, he must gradually take on positions of responsibility without the use of drugs. Thus, he cannot go up the status ladder unless his "attitudes" are right, no matter what degree of skill he might have as a workman. Evaluation is rather casual, but it is evaluation nevertheless—he will not be given a decent job in the organization unless he relinquishes the role of the "con artist" and answers questions honestly, expresses emotions freely, co-operates in group activities, and demonstrates leadership. In a letter to a public official in May, 1960, the founder explained the system as follows:

Continued residence [at Synanon], which we feel to be necessary to work out the problem of interpersonal relationships which underlie the addiction symptom is based on adherence by the individual to standards of behavior, thinking, and feeling acceptable to our culture. There is much work to be done here, as we have no paid help, and each person must assume his share

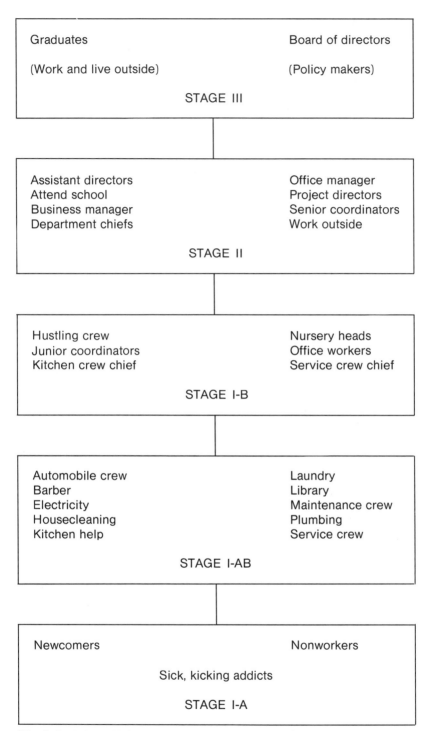

Fig. 1. Division of labor and stratification system, Synanon, June, 1962.

of the burden. Increased levels of responsibility are sought and the experience of self-satisfaction comes with seeking and assuming these higher levels and seems to be an extremely important part of emotional growth.[12]

An analogy with a family and the development of a child also is used. Officially, every member is expected to go through three "stages of growth," indicated by Roman numerals in Figure 1. Stage I has two phases, "infancy" and "adolescence." In the "infancy" phase (I-A) the member behaves like an infant and is treated as one; as he kicks the habit "cold turkey" (without the aid of drugs) in the living room, he is dependent on the others, and he is supervised and watched at all times. When he is physically and mentally able, he performs menial tasks such as dishwashing and sweeping in a kind of "preadolescent" stage (I-AB) and then takes on more responsible positions (I-B). In this "adolescence" phase he takes on responsibility for maintenance work, participates actively in group meetings, demonstrates a concern for "emotional growth," mingles with newcomers and visitors, and accepts responsibilities for dealing with them. In work activities, for example, he might drive the group's delivery truck alone, watch over a sick addict, supervise the dishwashing or cleanup crews, or meet strangers at the door.

Stage II is called the "young adult stage." Here, the member is in a position to choose between making Synanon a "career," attending school, or going to work at least part time. If he works for Synanon, his position is complex and involves enforcing policy over a wide range of members. In Stage III, "adult," he moves up to a policy-making position in the Board of Directors or moves out of Synanon but returns with his friends and family for occasional visits. He can apparently resist the urge to resort to drugs in times of crisis without the direct help of Synanon members. One man described this stage by saying, "They go out, get jobs, lose jobs, get married, get divorced, get married again, just like everyone else." However, the group does maintain a degree of control. Graduates are never supposed to cut off their ties with their Synanon "family," and they are expected to return frequently to display themselves as "a dope fiend made good."

From Table 5 it is apparent that seniority in the form of length of residence (equivalent to the number of "clean" days) is an important determinant of status. As time of residence increases, responsibilities to the group, in the forms of work and leadership, tend to increase. In June, 1962, twenty-seven of the 105 members of Synanon were in Stage III. It should be noted that while stage is associated with length of residence, advancement through the stages is not automatic. The longer one lives at Synanon, the "cleaner" he is, the more diffuse the roles he performs, and the higher his status.

12. See Volkman, *op. cit.,* pp. 90–96.

Table 5. Length of Residence and "Stage" of Members, June, 1962

Length of Residence (in Months)	Stages I	II	III	No.	Per Cent
1–3	20	0	0	20	19
4–6	15	0	0	15	14
7–9	7	3	0	10	9
10–12	2	0	0	2	2
13–15	3	4	0	7	7
16–18	3	0	2	5	5
19–21	4	1	0	5	5
22–24	0	4	1	5	5
25 and over	0	12	24	36	34
Total	54	24	27	105	100

It is also important to note that high status does not depend entirely upon one's conduct within the house. Before he graduates to Stage III a member must in some way be accorded an increase in status by the legitimate outside community. This is further insurance that status will be conferred for activities that are antidrug in character. In early 1960, the members began to take an active part in legitimate community activities, mostly in the form of lectures and discussion groups. Since Synanon's inception, more than 350 service groups, church groups, political groups, school and college classes, etc., have been addressed by speakers from Synanon. Such speeches and discussions gain community support for the organization, but they further function to give members a feeling of being important enough to be honored by an invitation to speak before community groups. Similarly, members are proud of those individuals who have "made good" in the outside community by becoming board members of the P.T.A., Sunday-school teachers, college students, and members of civic and service organizations. Over thirty-five Synanon members are now working full or part time in the community, holding a wide range of unskilled (janitor, parking attendant), skilled (truck driver, carpenter, electrician), white-collar (secretary, photographer), and executive (purchasing agent) posts.

Further, the legitimate status of the *group* has increasingly risen during the last two years. Since the summer of 1960, an average of 100–150 guests have attended open-house meetings, and the guests have included distinguished persons from all walks of legitimate life. Well-known psychiatrists, correctional workers, businessmen, newspapermen, and politicians have publicly praised the work of the group. There have been requests for Synanon houses and for Synanon groups from several communities, and Synanon projects are now being conducted at Terminal Island Federal Prison and the Nevada State Prison. Recently, the group has been featured in films, on television and radio shows, and in national magazines. At least two books and a movie are being written about it. Over five hundred citizens have formed an organization called "Sponsors of Synanon." Even strong attacks from some members of the local community and complicated legal battles about zoning ordinances have served principally to unite the group and maximize the *esprit de corps*.

The "synanon."   Synanon got its name from an addict who was trying to say "seminar." The term "Synanon" is used to refer to the entire organization, but when it is spelled with a lower-case *s* it refers only to the meetings occurring in the evenings among small groups of six to ten members. Each evening, all members are assigned to such groups, and membership in the groups is rotated so that one does not regularly interact with the same six or ten persons. The announced aim of these meetings is to "trigger feelings" and to allow what some members refer to as "a catharsis." The sessions are not "group therapy" in the usual sense, for no trained therapist is present. Moreover, the emphasis is on enforcing anticriminal and antidrug norms, as well as upon emotional adjustment.[13] These sessions, like the entire program, constitute a system for implementing Cressey's fifth principle, although they were not designed to do so.

The most effective mechanism for exerting group pressure on members will be found in groups so organized that criminals are induced to join with noncriminals for the purpose of changing other criminals. A group in which criminal A joins with some noncriminals to change criminal B is probably most effective in changing criminal A, not B; in order to change criminal B, criminal A must necessarily share the values of the anticriminal members.

In the house, the behavior of all members is visible to all others. What a member is seen to do at the breakfast table, for example, might well be scrutinized and discussed at his synanon that evening. The synanon sessions differ from everyday honesty by virtue of the fact that in these discussions one is expected to *insist on* the truth as well as to tell the truth. Any weapon, such as ridicule, cross-examination, or hostile attack, is both permissible and expected. The sessions seem to provide an atmosphere of truth-seeking that is reflected in the rest of the social life within the household so that a simple question like "How are you?" is likely to be answered by a five-minute discourse in which the respondent searches for the truth. The following discussion is from a tape recording of a synanon session held in June, 1961. It should be noted that an "innocent" question about appearance, asked by an older mem-

---

13. See Cressey, "Contradictory Theories in Correctional Group Therapy Programs," *op. cit.*

ber who has become a non-criminal and a non-addict, led to an opportunity to emphasize the importance of loyalty to the antidrug, anti-crime group.

What are you doing about losing weight?
Why? Is that your business?
I asked you a question.
I don't intend to answer it. It's not your business.
Why do you want to lose weight?
I don't intend to answer it.
Why?
Because it's an irrelevant and meaningless question. You know I had a baby only three weeks ago, and you've been attacking me about my weight. It's none of your business.
Why did you call your doctor?
Why? Because I'm on a diet.
What did he prescribe for you?
I don't know. I didn't ask him.
What did you ask for?
I didn't. I don't know what he gave me.
Come on now. What kind of pills are they?
I don't know. I'm not a chemist. Look, the doctor knows I'm an addict. He knows I live at Synanon. He knows a whole lot about me.
Yeah, well, I heard you also talking to him on the phone, and you sounded just like any other addict trying to cop a doctor out of pills.
You're a goddamned liar!
Yeah, well X was sitting right there. Look, does the doctor know and does the Board know?
I spoke to Y [Board member]. It's all been verified.
What did Y say?
I was talking to . . .
What did Y say?
Well, will you wait just a minute?
What did Y say?
Well, let her talk.
I don't want to hear no stories.
I'm not telling stories.
What did Y say?
That it was harmless. The doctor said he'd give me nothing that would affect me. There's nothing in it. He knows it all. I told Y.
Oh, you're all like a pack of wolves. You don't need to yell and scream at her.
Look, I heard her on the phone and the way she talked she was trying to manipulate the doctor.
Do you resent the fact that she's still acting like a dope fiend and she still sounds like she's conning the doctor out of something? She's a dope fiend. Maybe she can't talk to a doctor any differently.

Look, I called the doctor today. He said I should call him if I need him. He gave me vitamins and lots of other things.

Now wait a minute. You called to find out if you could get some more pills.

Besides, it's the attitude they heard over the phone. That's the main thing.

Yeah, well they probably projected it onto me.

Then how come you don't like anyone listening to your phone calls?

Are you feeling guilty?

Who said?

Me. That's who. You even got sore when you found out X and me heard you on the phone, didn't you? You didn't like that at all, did you?

Is that so?

(Silence.)

I don't think her old man wants her back.

Well, who would? An old fat slob like that.

Sure, that's probably why she's thinking of leaving all the time and ordering pills.

Sure.

(Silence.)

My appearance is none of your business.

Everything here is our business.

Look, when a woman has a baby you can't understand she can't go back to normal weight in a day.

Now *you* look. We're really not interested in your weight problem now. Not really. We just want to know why you've got to have pills to solve the problem. We're going to talk about that if we want to. That's what we're here for.

Look, something's bugging you. We all know that. I even noticed it in your attitude toward me.

Yeah, I don't care about those pills. I want to know how you're feeling. What's behind all this? Something's wrong. What is it?

(Silence.)

Have you asked your old man if you could come home yet?

(Softly.) Yes.

What did he say?

(Softly.) He asked me how I felt. Wanted to know why I felt I was ready to come home. . . .

(Silence.)

(Softly.) I did it out of anger. I wasn't very happy. *(Pause.)* A day before I tried [telephoning him] and he wasn't there. *(Pause.)* Just this funny feeling about my husband being there and me here. My other kid's there and this one's here. *(Pause.)* A mixed-up family.

Why do you want to stay then? Do you want to be here?

No. I don't want to be here. That's exactly why I'm staying. I need to stay till I'm ready.

Look, you've got to cut them loose for a while. You may not be ready for the rest of your life. You may not ever be able to be with those people.

(Tears.)

I know. . . .

After the synanon sessions, the house is always noisy and lively. We have seen members sulk, cry, shout, and threaten to leave the group as a result of conversation in the synanon. The following comments, every one of which represents the expression of a pro-reform attitude by the speaker, were heard after one session. It is our hypothesis that such expressions are the important ones, for they indicate that the speaker has become a reformer and, thus, is reinforcing his own pro-reform attitudes every time he tries to comfort or reform another.

> Were they hard on you?
> I really let him have it tonight.
> I couldn't get to her. She's so damned blocked she couldn't even hear what I was trying to tell her.
> Hang tough, man; it gets easier.
> One of these days he'll drop those defenses of his and start getting honest.
> Don't leave. We all love you and want you to get well.

At Synanon, disassociating with former friends, avoiding street talk, and becoming disloyal to criminals are emphasized at the same time that loyalty to non-criminals, telling the truth to authority figures, and legitimate work are stressed. We have no direct evidence that haircuts, synanons, and both formal and spontaneous denunciations of street talk and the code of the streets have important rehabilitative effects on the actor, as well as (or, perhaps even "rather than") on the victim. It seems rather apparent, however, that an individual's own behavior must be dramatically influenced when he acts in the role of a moral policeman and "takes apart" another member. It is significant that older members of Synanon like to point out that the "real Synanon" began on "the night of the big cop out" (confession). In its earliest days, Synanon had neither the group cohesiveness nor the degree of control it now has. Some participants remained as addicts while proclaiming their loyalty to the principle of antiaddiction, and other participants knew of this condition. One evening in a general meeting a man spontaneously stood up and confessed ("copped out") that he had sneaked out for a shot. One by one, with no prompting, the others present rose to confess either their own violations or their knowledge of the violations of their friends. From that moment, the Board of Directors believe, the organization became a truly antidrug group; there has been no problem of drug use since.

THE RESULTS

Of the fifty-two residents described earlier, four are "graduates" of Synanon, are living in the community, and are not using alcohol or drugs. Twenty-three (44.2 per cent) are still in residence and are not using alcohol or drugs. Two of these are on the Board of Directors and eleven are working part or full time. The remaining twenty-five left Synanon against the advice of the Board and the older members.

Information regarding the longest period of voluntary abstinence from drugs after the onset of addiction but prior to entering Synanon was obtained on forty-eight of the fifty-two persons. Eleven reported that they were "never" clean, six said they were continuously clean for less than one week, ten were continuously clean for less than one month. Thirty-nine (81 per cent) said they had been continuously clean for less than six months, and only two had been clean for as long as a one-year period. Twenty-seven (52 per cent) of the fifty-two residents have now abstained for at least six months; twelve of these have been clean for at least two years and two have been off drugs continually for over three years.

Between May, 1958 (when Synanon started), and May, 1961, 263 persons were admitted or readmitted to Synanon. Of these, 190 (72 per cent) left Synanon against the advice of the Board of Directors and the older members. Significantly, 59 per cent of all dropouts occurred within the first month of residence, 90 per cent within the first three months. Synanon is not adverse to giving a person a second chance, or even a third or four chance: of the 190 persons dropping out, eighty-three (44 per cent) were persons who had been readmitted. The dropout behavior of persons who were readmitted was, in general, similar to first admissions; 64 per cent of their dropouts occurred within the first month, 93 per cent within the first three months after readmission.

Of all the Synanon enrolees up to August, 1962, 108 out of 372 (29 per cent) are known to be off drugs. More significantly, of the 215 persons who have remained at Synanon for at least one month, 103 (48 per cent) are still off drugs; of the 143 who have remained for at least three months, 95 (66 per cent) are still non-users; of the 87 who have remained at least seven months, 75 (86 per cent) are non-users. These statistics seem to us to be most relevant, for they indicate that once an addict actually becomes a member of the antidrug community (as indicated by three to six months of participation), the probability that he will leave and revert to the use of drugs is low.

CONCLUSIONS

Synanon's leaders do not claim to "cure" drug addicts. They are prone to measure success by pointing to the fact that the organization now includes the membership of forty-five persons who were heroin addicts for at least ten years. Two of these were addicted for more than thirty years and spent those thirty years going in and out of prisons, jails, the U.S. Public Service Hospital, and similar institutions. The leaders have rather inadvertently used a theory of rehabilitation that implies that it is as ridiculous to try to "cure" a man of drug addiction as it is to try to "cure" him of sexual intercourse. A man can be helped to stay away from drugs, however, and this seems to be the contribution Synanon is making. In this regard, its "success" rate is higher than that of those institutions officially designated by society as places for the confinement and "reform" of drug addicts. Such a comparison is not fair, however, both because it is not known whether the subjects in Synanon are comparable to those confined in institutions, and because many official institutions do not concentrate on trying to keep addicts off drugs, being content to withdraw the drug, build up the addicts physically, strengthen vocational skills, and eliminate gaps in education backgrounds.[14]

We cannot be certain that it is the group relationships at Synanon, rather than something else, that is keeping addicts away from crime and drugs. However, both the times at which dropouts occur and the increasing antidrug attitudes displayed with increasing length of residence tend to substantiate Sutherland's theory of differential association and Cressey's notion that modifying social relationships is an effective supplement to the clinical handling of convicted criminals. Drug addiction is, in fact, a severe test of Sutherland's sociological theory and Cressey's sociological principles, for addicts have the double problem of criminality and the drug habit. The statistics on dropouts suggest that the group relations method of rehabilitation does not begin to have its effects until newcomers are truly integrated into the antidrug, anticrime group that is Synanon.

QUESTIONS FOR DISCUSSION

1. Considering Cloward's explanation of delinquency in terms of anomie and differential association, how would the program of the Puerto Rican Forum or Carmichael and Hamilton's proposals be expected to affect delinquent subcultures in Puerto Rican and black communities?

2. The success of the Marshall Program, half-way houses such as the one described by Rubington, and Synanon have been primarily interpreted in terms of differential association theory. Do interpretations vis-à-vis anomie theory also underlie elements of their success? Why or why not?

3. Do you see the concepts of differential association or anomie as useful in interpreting other types of social problems besides crime and delinquency? If so, what solutions would be suggested for these problems in terms of the deviant behavior perspective?

4. Compare the programs described in this section with rehabilitation programs to deal with the same problems that would follow from the social pathology

14. Cf. Harrison M. Trice, "Alcholism: Group Factors in Etiology and Therapy," *Human Organization,* XV (Summer, 1956), pp. 33–40 (see also Donald R. Cressey, "The Nature and Effectiveness of Correctional Techniques," *Law and Contemporary Problems,* XXIII [Fall, 1958], pp. 754–71).

perspective. What are the basic differences and/or similarities? Which would you expect to be more effective?

5. How might the effective elements in the programs described in this chapter be utilized for rehabilitation in other settings, such as prisons and mental hospitals, where inmates are not volunteers or specially selected?

6. What kinds of factors are neglected by programs based on the theories of anomie and differential association? How might these limitations be overcome?

7. Summarize what you think are the major strengths and weaknesses of the deviant behavior perspective and the solutions it suggests.

SELECTED REFERENCES

Empey, Lamar T., and Steven G. Lubeck, *The Silverlake Experiment: Testing Delinquency Theory and Community Intervention,* Chicago: Aldine-Atherton, 1971.

Empey and Lubeck describe a rigorous attempt to solve delinquency by applying the principles of the deviant behavior perspective.

Maxwell, Milton, "Alcoholics Anonymous: 'An Interpretation," in David J. Pittman (ed.), *Alcoholism,* New York: Harper & Row, 1967.

In this article, the effectiveness of Alcoholics Anonymous is interpreted from the deviant behavior perspective.

McCorkle, Lloyd W., Albert Elias, and F. Lovell Bixby, *The Highfields Story: An Experimental Treatment Project for Youthful Offenders,* New York: Henry Holt, 1958.

A program to help juvenile delinquents by means of "guided group interaction," applying Sutherland's principle of differential association, is described.

Sagarin, Edward, *Odd Man In: Societies of Deviants in America,* Chicago: Quadrangle Books, 1969.

Sagarin's collection shows attempts to destigmatize and resocialize alcoholics, midgets and dwarfs, homosexuals, gamblers, drug addicts, convicts and ex-convicts, mental patients, and transvestites through application of the principles of anomie and differential association.

Trice, Harrison M., "Sociological Factors in Association with A. A.," *Journal of Criminal Law, Criminology, and Police Science,* 48 (November/December 1957), pp. 378–86.

This article examines a lacuna in differential association theory: why do certain individuals select and accept affiliation with certain groups and their norms, while others do not? This question is researched with respect to social-psychological differences between alcoholics who do and do not affiliate with Alcoholics Anonymous. Treatment activity is suggested that would predispose more alcoholics toward Alcoholics Anonymous.

6 LABELING

However they are viewed, social problems seem to be embedded in culture and in social organization. Their pervasiveness and durability have raised the question of whether they are the consequences of certain forms of social structures or simply inevitable, taken-for-granted features of social life that persist in social structures.

The first position implies that changes in culture and social organization would solve many of these problems. The difficulty with this position, taken simply, is that through historical as well as cross-cultural study it is possible to show that similar problems exist under divergent socio-cultural conditions and that dissimilar problems occur under similar socio-cultural conditions. For example, industrial pollution occurs in both the United States and in the Soviet Union, a case of the same problem occurring under different social conditions.

The second position cannot deal with the fact that changes in social problems do take place. It is a nihilistic, anti-intellectual attitude, which in the end claims that the study of social problems is neither serious nor important. Nonetheless, both attitudes beg the question: why are there social problems?

Many writers point out that the definition of a social problem includes a subjective as well as an objective aspect. Thus many patterned responses to discrepant states of culture and social organization have yielded high rates of deviant behavior without these situations becoming defined as social problems. White-collar crime in the business world is one example, and cheating on exams is another. Also, the value conflict perspective has demonstrated that different groups contest each other over whether certain objective situations should be defined as problems. Nonetheless, there seem to be a number of situations over which there is no disagreement among most of the population. At this point, then, we can turn the subject on its head and make the definition of social problems sociologically problematic in its own right. We do this when we look at social problems from yet a fifth perspective, when we ask the question: who says this is a social problem?

243

CENTRAL FEATURES OF THE LABELING PERSPECTIVE

This perspective asks a novel battery of questions. What conditions are necessary in order for a given situation to become designated a social problem? What is the natural history of the designation of a social problem? Who says what situation is a social problem? To whom does he say so, how often, in what channels of communication, why, with what credibility and effectiveness, and with what results?

These questions all reveal the key feature of the labeling perspective on social problems. Social problems are just another aspect of the social reality that men create. This reality rests rather heavily and sometimes shakily on the process of social definition whereby men search for, create, and sustain meanings, and then live by them. W. I. Thomas' theorem captures the core of the perspective: "If men define situations as real, they are real in their consequences." Social problems, then, are regarded as social constructs that men create and then act upon. Social problems are what people say they are. Some people, however, have more power in defining social problems than do others. Thus labeling asks the student to study those who have the say-so on social problems.

The place.   In the case of certain pervasive and long-standing social problems, such as school segregation, a basic policy for solving the problem on a broad scale exists. The policy has been formulated as law, and school and community officials have a mandate to act in accordance with this government policy. Certainly, there has been a good deal of resistance, both organized and unorganized, but the major definition of this social problem has been established—codified in law, in numerous public statements, and in action.

To a very great extent, this same situation exists for many of the country's "recognized" social problems. There are, however, many social problems that are not recognized as such on any large scale. Such social problems become recognized after significant persons examine a particular social situation, describe it as a social problem to a wider public, and demand that something be done about it. Western history, particularly since the Industrial Revolution, has seen a number of reformers who have devoted their time and energies to calling attention to such social problems. Reformers, primarily emanating from the middle class, have succeeded in getting large numbers of persons to view situations that were not previously defined as social problems as being such and warranting some kind of remedial action. When they obtain agreement on their definition of the situation, they have "labeled" it a social problem and a wider public has ratified the label.

William Lloyd Garrison and Harriet Beecher Stowe, for example, labeled slavery a social problem. Elizabeth Cady Stanton and Lucrezia Mott defined the prohibition of woman suffrage as a social problem. Senator Joseph R. McCarthy designated communism in government a problem. Michael Harrington refocused attention on poverty with his book *The Other America,* and Betty Friedan triggered the women's movement with *The Feminine Mystique.* Recently, Seymour Hersh defined murder in uniform as a social problem with his book on the My-Lai massacre. And, of course, Ralph Nader has pinpointed the lack of quality control in industry to be a social problem.

Within the university, historians and sociologists have given attention to the process whereby given situations come to be labeled as social problems. For example, *The Discovery of the Asylum* by David Rothman shows how criminals and the mentally ill came to be redefined in America as persons who required a special status, a secluded place, and a rigorous regimen. Gerald Platt in his book *The Child-Savers* describes how middle-class women created the notion of the juvenile delinquent, and then a special institution, the juvenile court, for treating delinquents. Finally, Joseph R. Gusfield in his *Symbolic Crusade* described how middle-class women filled the ranks of the W.C.T.U., defining conditions as problems and fighting first for the abolition of slavery, working-class education, and temperance, then later for abstinence.

The attitude. In attitude, middle-class reformers are typically *crusading, morally outraged, proselytizing, quantifying,* and *object-centered.* Once convinced that a situation is a social problem worthy of their efforts, they embark on a campaign. They seek followers wherever possible and communicate their own personal sense of outrage. They provide a list of the number of infractions and some count of the negative consequences. They focus all of their attention on the social problem as the object and seek to enlist others in reformist actions. Central to their success is their ability to label a situation in such a way that followers not only see it their way but also are persuaded regarding the collective action that must be taken to remedy the situation.

To understand this social process, the student of labeling proceeds with somewhat different attitudes. He *looks for facts* (more than followers) and *seeks understanding* (more than action). All sociologists of social problems, regardless of orientation, collect data and try to fit them to theories in this way. If the student of social problems is also *qualitative* and *subject-centered,* however, then his work is likely to fall into the young tradition of the labeling perspective. In this tradition, students of social problems look at the problem from the participant's point of view (whether that participant is an agent of social control or a social deviant). In proceeding inductively, they recognize the fact that official records must be examined less as data on the problem itself than as evidence of the labeling process. Students of labeling have tended to pay more attention to qualitative data than to quantitative data. For them, a "social problem" comes into being only when a situation is subjectively viewed as a problem. Their main task is to understand how such a view comes about.

The content.　The content of the reformer's perspective on social problems does not coincide with that of the sociologist of labeling. To a very great extent, the reformer's thought is concerned with the core values of his culture and the extent to which the problem situations he so designates threaten those important values.

Sociologists of labeling, by contrast, align their views on social problems with a larger body of sociological theory. Symbolic interactionism, phenomenology, ethnomethodology, and structural-functionalism,[1] all have made their contributions to the labeling perspective. Though not every sociologist who has written in this tradition would necessarily accept the title of labeling theorist, nonetheless there appears to be a basic set of ideas to which they more or less subscribe. This framework is as follows:

a. Interaction, the basic social process, is possible because people communicate with one another by means of shared symbols.

b. It is through such symbolic definitions and their communication that people are able to adjust their mutual lines of action with one another.

c. There is always an emergent quality to interaction, however, and situations do not always coincide with the prevailing definitions.

d. Actions produce reactions based on the perceived definitions.

e. Undefined, poorly defined, or negatively defined situations are usually viewed as disturbing and disruptive.

f. Some of these situations are labeled as social problems if significant persons succeed in obtaining social ratification for such a definition.

THE FORMULA

When social problems are so christened, a reformer has two options. If he restricts himself to labeling, as a muckraker, he considers his task finished once he has called attention to the problems and authorities

---

1. The deviant behavior perspective, by contrast, rests almost exclusively on structural-functional theory.

take some corrective action. If he goes beyond labeling, then he must pursue organization. Organization takes three forms: the single purpose or single constituency unit (W.C.T.U. and N.A.A.C.P.), the multipurpose unit (Nader's Raiders), and the consulting unit (Saul Alinsky's Industrial Areas Foundation). These units indicate the degree and extent to which social reform has been bureaucratized and professionalized at the present time. Nonetheless, the success of their efforts turns ultimately on labeling, the strategy basic to their problem-solving formula.

Sociologists working in the young tradition of labeling have a somewhat different vocabulary, doctrine, and recipe.

The vocabulary. Some of the key terms in the lexicon of labeling include: *accommodation, construction of social reality, control agent, criminalization, defining agent, definition, deviant career, decriminalization, identity, interactive process, label, labeled, labeler, life chances, moral career, moral enterprise, moral entrepreneur, neutralization, normal crimes, normalization, official agency, official records, organizational processing, reconstitution, retrospective interpretation, sanction, self-fulfilling prophecy, self-image, secondary deviation, situated meaning, social reaction, societal reaction, stigma, stigmatization, symbolic crusade, symbolic interaction, typification,* and *typing.*

The beliefs and doctrines. Reformers generally seek to change institutions, clients, or practices by instituting the new and eliminating the old. In so doing, they function as critics of culture and of human nature. They call attention to institutions that serve the wrong clients or to institutions that ought to serve no clients in the institution's present condition. They seek to usher some clients out of old institutions and into new ones. Finally, they find certain practices such as drinking, smoking, taking drugs, polluting the environment, cheating the public, mistreating blacks and other ethnics, and making war, injurious. Generally, the reformer believes that problems arise from the frailty of human nature; he sees people seeking power only to abuse it, or being simply greedy or immoral.

Sociologists of labeling, on the other hand, have a somewhat more analytic and sequential scheme for accounting for the rise and development of social problems. This accounting scheme is as follows:

a. Established institutions and agencies of social control deal with the standard social problems of the society.

b. Interaction and consensus, the reciprocal bases of social order, undergo change both within and between these institutions and agencies.

c. A shift in the status and power of actual and potential defining agents often occurs.

d. New agents and definitions infiltrate these institutions and agencies.

e. New labels are devised for the extant social problems.

f. With the ratifications of the label and the realignment of control agents, the social problem situation is socially reconstituted.

The interpretive scheme of the labeling perspective differs from that of the reformer. The reformer, using a common-sense notion, attributes the development of social problems to the strengths and weaknesses of people and their institutions. The labeling perspective, on the other hand, sees changes in culture and social structure as underlying the emergence of social problems under the conditions noted above.

The recipe.   Reformers adapt their campaigns to their changing fortunes, an outcome of their efforts to define situations as problems and then influence a subsequent course of action. Reformers sometimes succeed and sometimes fail in defining a social problem effectively. In neither instance, however, have they usually operated with a systematic and generalized recipe.

Labeling theorists, on the other hand, are able to sketch out a general recipe which must be followed through all of its steps if a successful campaign is to be mounted against a particular social problem. That recipe, complete with assumptions and sequences, is as follows:

a. Social problems reside in their definitions.

b. Social control responses define, create, and sustain social problems.

c. Social control follows from social definition.

d. These definitions are successfully applied and enforced only by persons with the power to do so.

e. Once a social problem has been socially ratified, there are only two ways to solve the problem: either change the definition from a problem to a nonproblem or decrease the power of those able to apply the definition.

Thus, solutions to social problems developed from the labeling perspective rely heavily upon law and education. Since law is the formal apparatus of social control, it would seem that if a change in legal definition takes place, then the social problem situation can be redefined. In this sense, the law is a two-way street. It is capable both of defining situations as social problems and of redefining these and other situations as not being problems. Three of the four readings in this section argue for a change in legal definition as a way of helping to solve the problem with which they are concerned.

In addition, education of both the general public and agents of social control is an implicit or explicit part of any proposal to alter a social problem in accordance with the labeling perspective, because it is through the process of education that new social definitions are acquired. The use of education also leads to another possibility. If, for example, agents of social control became convinced that marijuana smoking actually did no harm, and if they also became convinced that enforcement of the law did immeasurably more harm than the actual smoking, they might no longer enforce the law even though it still remained on the books.

If the process of education fails, then raising the costs of applying the old label is still another possibility. Raising or lowering costs are contingent on moral, economic, and political pressure, any one of which, if successful, exemplifies a change in the power of the control agent to apply the problem definition.

THE HISTORY OF THE LABELING PERSPECTIVE

The process of social differentiation by marking persons and situations as "problems" is universal. It has occurred in all times and in all places and has not escaped the notice of either classical or contemporary sociologists. Durkheim in his work on the elementary forms of religion showed how tribes divided up their world of "good" and "evil" by means of totemic animals, these properties to be later generalized and applied to members of the tribe who departed from social rules.[2] There have also been many early gropings in American sociology toward a full-fledged labeling perspective. Frank Tannenbaum, for example, spoke of the "dramatization of evil" and indicated that if the community labeled a young boy as a delinquent, they would in fact get a delinquent.[3]

Although many of these insights are more broadly covered by the approach of symbolic interactionism, the very first systematic and specific statement of the postulates of the labeling perspective appeared in 1951 in Edwin M. Lemert's *Social Pathology*.[4] Lemert spoke of sociopathic behavior and nowhere said a word about labeling. Nonetheless, his set of postulates form the basis of the labeling perspective. Lemert argued that departures from social norms, ultimately rooted in a conflict of definitions, produce societal reactions ranging from mild to severe disapproval. Only behaviors or situations that are effectively dis-

2. Emile Durkheim, *The Elementary Forms of the Religious Life,* translated from the French by Joseph Swain, New York: Collier Books, 1961.
3. Frank Tannenbaum, *Crime and the Community,* New York: Columbia University Press, 1938.
4. Edwin M. Lemert, *Social Pathology,* New York: McGraw-Hill, 1951.

approved constitute issues and are so labeled. This disapproval, a process of definition and control, produces a deviant by constituting the person's status, role, and self-conception; and disapproval produces a social problem by reconstituting the situation and thereby altering its received public conception.

Factors that ultimately affect these processes include the frequency, duration, and social visibility of situations and events. Additional factors include the tolerance level of defining agents toward the act or situation, exposure to sanctions, and the nature and strength of these sanctions.

Lemert's work has led a number of others to place great emphasis on the fact that agents of social control and reformers control subsequent events through the kinds of definitions they place upon them. For these are the agents who decide what will be officially recognized as social problems. Howard S. Becker popularized this emphasis in his book *Outsiders,* published in 1963.[5] This book made it even clearer how selective definition and selective enforcement are the rule rather than the exception. Thus, a number of sociologists have since made important contributions to the labeling perspective by indicating how diverse agents of social control, through their power to define both situations and persons as social problems, order and control the population of events with which they have to deal.

SUMMARY AND CONCLUSION

The labeling perspective begins by making the definition of social problems a sociological problem. It does this by asking the question: "Who says so?" Once the question is put this way, the answer is straightforward and easy to come by, at least in theory. Standard social problems are dealt with in the course of regular social routine by recourse to regulatory institutions and social agencies. "Problems" outside these routines may escape recognition or definition as such. Indeed, many of the routines inside such institutions and agencies are similarly not accorded status as problems. Consequently, for a new definition to come into being, a significant person is required, one with a new point of view, one with less commitment to, or vested interests in, the status quo. The labeling perspective, in a combination of detached and committed views, has tried to set forth the natural history of such matters, and also to specify the conditions under which social problems can become reconceptualized. From this perspective, it is only through such reconceptualization and de-labeling that a social problem is solved.

5. Howard S. Becker, *Outsiders: Studies in the Sociology of Deviance,* New York: The Free Press, 1963.

MARIHUANA RECONSIDERED

Lester Grinspoon

In "Marihuana Reconsidered," Lester Grinspoon argues that repressive law with regard to psychoactive substances has almost always failed to curb their use and has, in fact, produced major problems of its own. For example, marihuana smoking itself does not have any clearly deleterious effects for society or for the individual, but the criminal definition attached to it does. It results in stigma and the limitations accruing from a criminal label for the marihuana user who gets caught. Moreover, the political and legal structure which arbitrarily criminalizes such a widespread activity loses its credibility.

The answer, Grinspoon argues, is to change that definition and legalize marihuana use. In this way, the user would be protected from the criminal label. Laws could be established to ensure that marihuana is used safely (e.g. the prohibition of driving while intoxicated) and that the quality of the marihuana sold is regulated. Thus the integrity of the law would be maintained.

The history of punitive-repressive measures to discourage the use of drugs is one which offers little support to those who believe that the best approach to the "problem" of the widespread use of marihuana is Draconian legislation. The spread of tobacco smoking during the sixteenth and seventeenth centuries was the most dramatic "epidemic" of drug use in recorded history. The "foule weed" was adopted by cultures so different—literate and nonliterate, for example—that cultural and social determinants must have played a trivial role, if any at all, in its spread. In almost all instances of tobacco use, prohibitions against it failed, whether they were justified on grounds of impairment to health, religion, good taste, or by the threat of inducement to criminal activity. The history of the use of tobacco would seem to indicate that social controls are impotent when a society is confronted by an attractive psychoactive substance, "even if that substance serves no primary physiological need or traditional interpersonal function."[1] In their initial re-

From Lester Grinspoon, *Marihuana Reconsidered,* Cambridge, Mass.: Harvard University Press, pp. 344–46, 347–48, 349, 350, 351, 351–52, 354–59, 361–71, 431–32. Copyright © 1971 by the President and Fellows of Harvard College. Reprinted by permission of the publishers.

1. R. H. Blum and associates, "Drugs, Behavior, and Crime," *Society and Drugs: Social and Cultural Observations* (San Francisco, 1969), I, pp. 277–91.

sponse to the introduction of tobacco into most societies during the sixteenth and seventeenth centuries, the authorities were in fact much
more intolerant in their attempts to curb its use than are modern authorities. This is especially surprising when one considers that it is modern
evidence which has demonstrated clearly the health dangers arising
from tobacco use. Another very similar example is provided by the
seventeenth-century spread of coffee drinking in the Arab Near East,
in spite of the most extreme penalties, including death.[2]

The impotence of lawmaking in suppressing the use of psychoactive
substances is illustrated again by fairly recent North African history.
When from 1956–1960 the cultivation of *Cannabis sativa* was prohibited
in Tunisia and Algeria, vineyards replaced hemp fields, and alcohol consumption took the place of cannabis with no consequent improvement
in public health. B. W. Sigg believes this demonstrates that where large
segments of the population are in the habit of using nonaddictive eupho-
riants, repressive control is futile.[3]

One can go further and consider the possibility that repressive measures may actually be counterproductive, even more harmful to the individual and to his society than the "evil" originally intended to be suppressed. Thus, opium smoking is on the decline around the world, but
in the sections of Asia where it has been outlawed, heroin has become
the far more dangerous substitute.[4] In India, where the government has
been acting slowly by implementing laws to control cultivation and distribution, but not by legally banning cannabis use entirely, a slow reduction in use has been reported. However, this reduction has been accompanied by a rising frequency in the use of alcohol.[5]

At the end of the nineteenth century in Ireland, there was an attempt
to suppress the use of hard liquor through temperance campaigns, heavy
taxation, and (attempted) strict enforcement of the tax laws. The campaign was a success in that the Irish greatly reduced their intake of
hard liquor; instead, they switched to the substitute ethyl ether, which
provided a short-lived intoxication involving a "hot all the way down"
sensation, followed by thunderous flatus, and, within ten minutes, a
high, which could be repeated and which left no hangover. The use of
ether became so widespread that in one area of Ulster an eighth of the
population were labeled "etheromaniacs." The subsequent alarm over
the ether "epidemic" became so great that the various pressure groups

2. Ibid., pp. 100–101.
3. Ibid., p. 74, citing B. W. Sigg, *Le Cannabisme chronique: Fruit du sous developpement
et du capitalisme* (Marrakesch, 1960; Algiers, 1963).
4. Ibid., p. 55, citing *Narcotic Addiction,* ed. J. A. O'Donnell and J. C. Ball (New York,
1966).
5. R. N. Chopra and G. S. Chopra, "The Present Position of Hemp Drug Addiction in
India." *Indian Med. Res. Mem.,* 31 (1939), pp. 1–119.

which had promoted the campaign reversed their field, and the Irishman happily returned to other psychoactive substances, notably back to his whiskey.[6]

In Japan, after World War II, amphetamines became freely and legally available. Their use began to skyrocket to the point where it was estimated that five million Japanese were habitual users. In response to this medicosocio emergency, a highly punitive law was enacted in 1953 against both users and sellers. But whereas the amphetamine problem was considered solved by 1955, the number of narcotic addicts had begun to rise steadily. The increase in the use of narcotics became so alarming that in 1963 a new law, intended to be as severe as the 1953 antiamphetamine legislation, was passed. It solved the heroin problem, but the number of barbiturate users now began to rise, and in fact is still rising. In addition there is now a sharp increase in the practice of solvent inhalation ("glue-sniffing"). At the present time marihuana is used to a very slight extent in Japan.[7]

Prohibition of alcohol in this country failed because violations were so frequent, blatant, and widespread through all socioeconomic groups. The public increasingly doubted that alcohol was so undesirable, and the cost of and fallout from enforcement became intolerable.

The ostensible reason for the general alarm about the use of marihuana is the belief that it leads to drug abuse, which means that it harms the individual who takes the drug and that he is more likely to inflict injury on society in general. However, regardless of the legal status of its use, if a drug, when taken in its usual doses, is not biologically detrimental, then from a functional (and a common sense) point of view its use cannot constitute "drug abuse."

• • •

While there can be no question that the use of psychoactive drugs may be harmful to the social fabric, the harm resulting from the use of marihuana is of a far lower order of magnitude than the harm caused by abuse of narcotics, alcohol, and other drugs. Marihuana itself is not criminogenic; it does not lead to sexual debauchery; it is not addicting; there is no evidence that it leads to the use of narcotics. It does not, under ordinary circumstances, lead to psychoses, and there is no convincing evidence that it causes personality deterioration. Even with respect to automobile driving, although the use of any psychoactive

6. Blum et al., *Society and Drugs,* pp. 35–36, citing K. H. Connell, "Ether Drinking in Ulster," *Quart. J. Stud. Alcohol,* 26 (1965), pp. 629–53.
7. L. E. Hollister, "Criminal Laws and the Control of Drugs of Abuse: An Historical View of the Law (Or, It's the Lawyer's Fault)," *J. Clin. Pharmacol. J. New Drugs* (1969), pp. 345–48.

drug must perforce be detrimental to this skill, there exists evidence that marihuana is less so than alcohol. Marihuana use, even over a considerable period of time, does not lead to malnutrition or to any known organic illness. There is no evidence that mortality rates are any higher among users than nonusers; in fact, relative to other psychoactive drugs, it is remarkably safe.

There is, however, a real relationship between crime and cannabis in this country: the criminogenic character of the present laws against the possession, sale, or even the giving away of marihuana; and this constitutes a great irony. The unique nature of this criminogenic effect in the United States is that antimarihuana laws have intensified—and to some extent created—the basic but complex sociological and legal problems they were ostensibly designed to avoid or eliminate. The laws which prohibit the possession, sale, and giving away of cannabis passed by the individual states and the federal government since the mid-1930's have created an entirely new species of "criminal," very often an individual who is truly unable to see himself, in any real sense, as engaged in any criminal activity, and whose typical attitude toward the antimarihuana legislation is a combination of scorn, indifference, and frustration. It is not at all unreasonable to suppose that a government (or, more particularly, a special law-enforcement agency of that government) which strikes marihuana users as downright ludicrous in its extremely punitive approach to prohibition of marihuana will also seem ludicrous in other important respects. We certainly have reason to question how marihuana users will (and do) interpret the pronouncements of various governmental drug-abuse-control agencies concerning other drugs that may well be vastly more dangerous to the individual and to society in terms of both short- and long-term effects.

"When only the poor sought paradise by way of pot, nobody cared about the enhancement and enrichment of perception. They just flung 'em in jail."[8] Increasingly, however, the middle class is experiencing at first hand the unsettling effects (to say perhaps the least) of prohibitions against the use of marihuana. Sometimes it is their own children who are apprehended, sometimes they themselves. It is worth noting that prior to the initial 1937 antimarihuana legislation, and "despite its increasing popularity in the thirties . . . most middle-class Americans still had no contact with marihuana and knew little, if anything, about it."[9] In fact, in the same year that the Federal Bureau of Narcotics was established (1930), only sixteen states had laws prohibiting or limiting any aspect of marihuana-related activity, and the statutes in these states

8. F. Mount. "The Wild Grass Chase," *National Review,* Jan. 30, 1968, p. 83.
9. "Editor's Foreword: The Marihuana Myths," in *The Marihuana Papers,* ed. D. Solomon (Indianapolis, 1966), p. xv.

prescribed what were generally light penalties, and they were laxly—if at all—enforced. But according to one hypothesis:

> The anxiety-producing stresses of the depression had made the country panic-prone. Deprived of the facts and primed on hysteria-provoking, apocryphal horror stories given to the press by the Federal Bureau of Narcotics, Americans were sold a mythological bill of goods. They were told that marihuana was a "killer drug" that triggered crimes of violence and acts of sexual excess; a toxic agent capable of driving normal persons into fits of madness and depraved behavior; a destroyer of the will; a satanically destructive drug which, employing lures of euphoria and heightened sensuality, visited physical degeneration and chronic psychosis upon the habitual user.[10]

• • •

The critical question with regard to damage to the social fabric is whether the present highly repressive and overly punitive approach is not more damaging and more costly than any dangers or cost inherent in the widespread use of marihuana.

• • •

A conservative estimate is that one-third of the California population between the ages of 16 and 29 have committed the very serious crime (as determined by the legal sanctions, at any rate) of using marihuana and thereby exposed themselves to the possibility of arrest, a felony conviction, and imprisonment. And both the percentage and the age-range are rising each year. As J. Kaplan points out, it is most unhealthy for a society to turn a large percentage of its young people into felons or even define them as such.[11] The young, occasional user of marihuana may have a good deal of trouble adjusting to the official local and federal police view of him as a criminal liable to the most severe punishments, whether fines, imprisonment, or both, of the states or federal government. It is far from unreasonable to suppose that he will feel genuine resentment toward what he feels increasingly forced to view as the "other side" of the law, and that he will see the police less as protectors of rights and property and more as intruders and spies. It is conceivable that this attitude shift might lead to further, more dangerous criminal activity—for if one is already branded a criminal and lives under the threat of a heavy jail sentence and/or fines, what essential difference can it possibly make (or so one might think) if one commits

10. Ibid.
11. J. Kaplan, "What Legislators Should Consider," in *Drugs and Youth*, ed. Wittenborn et. al., p. 254.

another crime for which the sentence is less (although the actual social cost, and the cost to the new criminal, may well be greater)? Many young marihuana users employ this particular argument.

. . . At the very least it must be supposed that current antimarihuana laws have a deleterious effect on the attitude of the young toward the law, and particularly on their respect for it. They are supported in their feeling of alienation by what they can only see as hypocrisy all around them—a judgment that seems to come easily for young people, and which these particular laws in fact help to institutionalize for them. They earnestly believe, and many doctors would agree, that marihuana is, at the very least, less harmful than the alcohol, tobacco, tranquilizers, barbiturates, weight reducing drugs, and so on, which older people, the same who criminalize the young, consume compulsively if not habitually, and for which they are in no way punished or made to feel the weight of social disapproval. To them the prohibition on the use of marihuana represents the imposition by one group in a position of political power of its own standards and norms of morality on another group, one without any effective political power—at least for the present. . . .

That the number of people who are experimenting with and using marihuana is increasing at a dramatic rate cannot be denied. Marihuana-arrest statistics cannot be taken at face value because (1) they reflect not just the prevalence of drug use but also such factors as the interest and diligence of enforcement agencies in apprehending users, and (2) they are, for almost all states, either incomplete, not differentiated from narcotics arrests in general, or do not cover a long enough period of time to have any validity. But this statement does not apply to California, where the statistics on marihuana arrests have been distinguished from all others, and the records are accurate back to at least 1962. However, it is also true that any marihuana-arrest statistics, so long as they are not gross misrepresentations, are especially important in at least one other respect: although they are an imperfect barometer of prevalence, they do indicate at least a part of the cost of enforcing laws which make criminals of those who use marihuana. Thus in 1962 there were approximately 3,500 adult arrests in California for violation(s) of the (state) antimarihuana laws; in 1963 there were 4,500; in 1964, 6,500; in 1965, 8,500; in 1966, 14,000; in 1967, 24,000.[12] These figures indicate an increase of almost 700 percent in 6 years.

But the total cost, as Kaplan points out, is not simply in terms of the criminalization of thousands of people; it must also be estimated in terms of the financial costs which usually must be paid from restricted or limited resources that must also maintain law enforcement policies

12. Ibid., p. 256.

and programs, judicial activities, and correctional and rehabilitative programs. California spent an estimated 75 million dollars in processing marihuana violations in 1968.[13]

• • •

Roughly three-quarters of those arrested for marihuana violations have had only minor or no difficulty with the law previously. Of those arrested for possession of marihuana in California, about one-third are incarcerated for some period of time.[14] It is an unfortunate fact that most of the jails and prisons in this country are chronically overcrowded and understaffed. To send a person whose behavior presents no essential threat to the fabric of society to such a place is absurd. Worse, it throws someone whose only "crime" may be that he has smoked marihuana into the closest contact with a number of much more serious (from the point of view of the threat of direct social harm) offenders, and increases the likelihood that he will engage in other, perhaps non-drug-related criminal activities, after he is released: the criminogenic nature of the penalties provided by the antimarihuana laws also includes the effects on users of imprisonment. But even those who are not imprisoned have their futures seriously scarred inasmuch as their arrest records follow them through life and jeopardize their chances of getting jobs, gaining entrance to schools, or being accepted as members in many organizations.

Judge J. J. Saunders of California, in an address to a young audience in 1967, stated that he was "heartsick . . . over the number of young people who come into my court charged with narcotics violations. Many of them, I felt, really didn't know the consequences. These consequences . . . can be severe, and the time spent in prison is the least of it. When the convict is released from prison, he becomes a second-class citizen economically. . . . Persons convicted of a felony in narcotics cases will not be licensed by the state in a wide variety of fields, ranging from accounting and medicine to engineering and funeral directing. You can't even be a barber, . . . and most school districts will not hire teachers with a conviction on their records and the government will not give them clearance to work in the defense industry."[15]

Yale University Dean G. May was recently quoted in a national magazine article as saying:

13. Ibid.
14. N. L. Chayet, "Legal Aspects of Drug Abuse," in *Drugs and Youth,* ed. Wittenborn et al., p. 241.
15. J. Glenn, "Narcotics Conviction Can Hurt Job Chances Students Warned," *Los Angeles Times,* Nov. 29, 1967; also in E. R. Bloomquist, *Marijuana,* Beverly Hills, California, 1968, p. 133.

> No amount of discussion . . . can detract from the hard facts that at the present time possession, use or distribution of illegal drugs, including marijuana, makes anyone involved with narcotics, even in a single experiment carried out in the privacy of one's home, liable to arrest, conviction, fine, and imprisonment. Regardless . . . of the disposition, . . . the arrested . . . is immediately faced with . . . bail money and legal fees, which often exceed $1,000. The long range expense to the student may be even greater . . . a conviction for narcotics law violation may preclude consideration for graduate or professional school acceptance, disqualify for graduate fellowships, jeopardize employment opportunities upon graduation, and be a source of personal disadvantage for the convicted student for the rest of his life.[16]

Even though the Federal Bureau of Narcotics has publicly stated for a number of years that it is not concerned with the prosecution of the student or occasional user, but only the dealer or heavy user, the state laws are usually vigorously implemented, and many young people are convicted under them with a great zeal on the part of the authorities.[17]

> There [i.e. in the cases over which the state has jurisdiction], the rigidity of the laws has sometimes resulted in the imposition of penalties that were out of proportion to the seriousness of the crime. This has resulted in senseless prison time being imposed on casual users or juvenile offenders, a punishment that has been both cruel and ineffective. In some instances misguided jurists have sent users to jail to "cure" a nonexistent "addiction." Jails being what they are, these individuals, registered as criminals with all that this label implies, have been forced in some instances into a criminal existence by those very forces sworn to prevent crime.[18]

One can imagine what being arrested for possessing marihuana does to a young person who believes he has been apprehended for doing something which many, if not most, of the other young people he knows do—something which he believes to be quite harmless. If in this most important formative and suggestible period of his life he is already leaning toward social disenchantment, this kind of experience, one would suspect, will very likely push him a long way toward bitter social alienation.

So dramatically is the use of marihuana increasing that one of the most important variables in assessing the results of any poll is the date when it was conducted. The results of a poll conducted in Massachusetts in March 1970 indicated that of those interviewed, about one-half of the college students, one-fourth of the employed persons, and one-fifth of the high school students admitted to having smoked marihuana at least

---

16. L. Shearer, "Why Students Take Pot," *Parade*, June 4, 1967, p. 10, quoting Dean George May.
17. J. E. Ingersoll, interview, *U.S. News and World Report*, May 25, 1970, p. 42.
18. Bloomquist, op. cit., p. 134.

once during the preceding year. When these same young people were asked to express an opinion on the extent of marihuana use, their estimates were even higher than their own personal admissions. Their impression was that among youth in general more than half have experimented with marihuana.[19] It must be expected that at the present rate the use of marihuana will become so widespread and accepted that the present marihuana laws will be labeling a sizable fraction of the population as criminals. This means that some of them will go to jail or prison, or, at the very least, be fined or given a suspended sentence or be placed on probation. In any event, the threat to many people of the possibility of having a criminal record is increasing with the great increase in marihuana use, even if the enforcement of the state laws is (in the future) somewhat relaxed. But even that majority of users who are never arrested are adversely affected by the fact that they are labeled as participating in a criminal activity, and thereby—in many instances—made to feel like criminals. This can only enhance their sense of alienation and bitterness. What is more, one is beginning to perceive among young people today a growing sense of camaraderie concerning their shared status as "criminals." (Along with the public flouting of the antimarihuana laws at smoke-ins and even, recently, by individuals on the main streets of places like Cambridge, Massachusetts, the planting of marihuana has become something of a fad among youth, who in most cases make little or no effort to conceal their gardens even to the point where it has become fashionable to plant cannabis in quite conspicuous places: not only open window boxes and front-yard gardens, but even in "the center strip of Park Avenue in New York City, the lawn in front of a police station in ultra-respectable Westchester County, the United Nations building, and, twice recently, in front of the state capitol in Austin, Texas.")[20]

Many of the young feel that they are all "criminals" together, fighting against the existence of unjust, hypocritical, and irrational laws, and their use of marihuana is carried like a banner. I have talked with some very solid young people who, when told that one risk of marihuana-use concerning which they could be quite certain was the legal one, rejoined with considerable affect that *that* was precisely why they had no intention of stopping. It seems that these laws lend themselves to use by young people as a catalyst both for the enhancement of cohesiveness of a subculture and for alienation from the larger society. Furthermore, the criminalizing of such a large segment of this critical generation promotes in them a sense of distrust which at times may appear to be some-

19. "Fifty Percent of College Students Have Smoked Marihuana," *Boston Globe,* poll conducted by Becker Research Corporation, March 13, 1970.
20. J. Fort, "Pot: A Rational Approach," *Playboy,* Oct. 1969, p. 222.

what paranoid. The hard fact is that the enforcement of these laws involves the use of informers and entrapments. Anyone who is familiar with informing or entrapment or has read of the experiences of Professor Leslie Fiedler will appreciate the basis of this distrust.[21] In fact, it is possible . . . that the paranoid thinking which some people experience while marihuana-intoxicated may have as much to do with the total setting, which in a very real sense cannot be trustworthy, as it has to do with any psychopharmacological property of the drug. In any event, an environment which leads to a paranoidlike stance is decidedly not healthy, and criminalization contributes to this kind of stance.

There are those who are mindful of these and other costs and are particularly sensitive to the short- and long-term effects of the criminalization of a large segment of young people who already have considerable doubt and ambivalence about making a commitment to the values and life-styles that have served their elders; these people wish to change the existing marihuana laws. But they believe that legalizing marihuana use would be too precipitous, and that to whatever extent the present laws act as a deterrent, this would be lost. Instead, they think of reducing the penalties for use or possession, or only for the actual possession, to below the criminal level. M. P. Rosenthal, for example, is willing to accept the risk that some of the deterrent effect of the present laws may be lost in changing the punishment for possession from a felony or a misdemeanor to a civil violation.[22] Under this proposed alternative, people who sell marihuana, however, would still be treated as criminals. One caveat to this proposal is that, among the unorganized distributors particularly, there are and will be many whom one is trying to protect from criminalization; however, the proposal's proponents accept this one price which must be paid if the law is to have any leverage on distribution. But the price might be higher than the proponents of this approach suppose. In a survey of 204 marihuana users, E. Goode found that 44 percent had sold the drug at least once.[23] This type of approach, which makes the real target the dealer rather than the user, is modeled on heroin addiction, where the drug peddler is seen as profiting while he spreads and intensifies human degradation and misery. It assumes that there is a clear-cut distinction between user and seller. But nowadays, at least where marihuana is concerned, the user and seller are largely indistinguishable; almost half of users sell to some extent and almost all sellers use. To think of the marihuana dealer as "preying" on and profiting from a hapless, helpless victim—the pot

21. L. Fiedler, *Being Busted* (New York, 1970).
22. Rosenthal, "Marihuana: Some Alternatives," in *Drugs and Youth,* ed. Wittenborn et al., pp. 260–79.
23. E. Goode, "The Marijuana Market," *Columbia Forum,* 7 (1969), p. 6.

smoker—is again to use opiate addiction as a paradigm and to entertain a view which is ludicrously inapplicable.

• • •

The use of marihuana is a highly personal form of behavior, and as its use does not encourage crime, sexual debauchery, or other antisocial activity, why should its use and distribution be interfered with by the state in more than a regulatory fashion? Perhaps the most unfortunate aspect of the antimarihuana legislation is that it defines a crime which is a crime without any victim. Although marihuana smoking is not usually thought of as a private activity, the small, congenial groups which gather to "turn on" might be considered individuals engaged together in a hobby such as, say, wood-carving, insofar as any detrimental or harmful consequences to society-at-large are concerned. When a bank or grocery store is held up, the police do not have to engage in spy-like activities prior to their knowledge of the crime: the owner or manager will contact them immediately. This is not the situation at all in the case of cannabis use. There is no victim, and in most cases, with the exception of certain hyperzealous antimarihuana crusaders, no one will call the police to report that marihuana smoking is occurring in the vicinity. The attempt to enforce the antimarihuana legislation entails activities on the part of the police that are very similar to those employed by any police state. As an example, Fort relates how the Chicago police have adopted the practice—a holdover from the days of the "Syndicate"—of using search warrants, obtained in a way that any American court would find intolerable, in order to enter apartments where they believe marihuana is being used and make arrests:

> The police have obtained from the courts the right to use what are called "blank warrants"—warrants in which the witness who alleges he has seen the crime is permitted to sign a false name. This is supposed to be necessary to protect informers. . . .
>
> As the *Sun-Times* noted: . . . "The police do not have to disclose the name of the informer or the time when the drugs were bought. There is also a device known as constructive possession: The police can arrest anybody found in the vicinity of prohibited drugs, whether he's an innocent visitor or the real culprit. The frame-up is easy. Plant the drugs, get the search warrant, grab everybody in sight. It could happen to you and you'd never have the right to face your accuser." William Braden, a *Sun-Times* reporter, also uncovered one informer, a heroin addict, who admitted signing dozens of such warrants without the names of the accused on them. The narcotics squad could then type in the name of any individual whose apartment they wanted to raid and it would be perfectly "legal" in form—but a terrifying distance in spirit from the actual meaning of the Constitution. Such raids, of

course, violate the Sixth Amendment—guaranteeing the right "to be confronted with the witnesses" against you—as well as the Fourth (no "unreasonable searches"); and they occur everywhere in the nation.[24]

The 1968 "Omnibus" crime bill gave authorization to not only federal but also local police officials to tap the telephones of suspected marihuana users. It is clear that since the use of cannabis has spread throughout the country without any clear relationship or limitation to a particular socioeconomic class, there is scarcely a person outside the Federal Bureau of Narcotics or the White House who is not, in theory, as liable as the known junkie to have his phone tapped for the compiling of evidence that would put him in jail for the rest of his life. This suggests the possibility that police may use the threat of a marihuana "bust," for example, to insure that "undesirable types"—by which is usually meant persons who dress in the "hippie" garb—leave the city limits. And it is not very far-fetched to suppose that the police in some cities would hardly hesitate if they thought they could pin a marihuana rap on members of an organization like the Black Panthers.

Consider a case that is cited by Fort from the point of view, not so much of the chicanery of the law enforcement officials and the absurdity of the lower court, as of fundamental morality—the question of common decency and good faith among men which "peace officers" are supposed to defend:

> John Sinclair, a poet, leader of the Ann Arbor hippie community and manager of a rock group called MC-5, became friendly, around October 1966, with Vahan Kapagian and Jane Mumford, who presented themselves to him as members of the hippie-artist-mystic subculture that exists in all of our large cities. Over a period of two months, they worked to secure his confidence and friendship and several times asked him to get them some marijuana. Finally, on December 22, Sinclair, apparently feeling that he could now trust them, gave two marijuana cigarettes to Miss Mumford—one for her and one for Kapagian. He [Sinclair] was immediately arrested; his "friends" were police undercover agents.
>
> Sinclair has been convicted of both "possessing" and "dispensing" marijuana and faces a minimum of 20 years under each statute, and a maximum of life for the sale. If his appeal is not upheld, the very smallest sentence he could receive is 40 years. As his lawyers pointed out in his appeal, "The minimum sentence to which [Sinclair] is subject to imprisonment is 20 times greater than the minimum to which a person may be imprisoned [in Michigan] for such crimes as rape, robbery, arson, kidnapping or second-degree murder. It is more than 20 times greater than the minimum sentence of imprisonment for any other offense in Michigan law, except first-degree murder."[25]

24. Fort, op. cit., pp. 22, 225.
25. Ibid., p. 225.

Suppose, for the moment, that the use of marihuana does promote the development of what has been called the "amotivational syndrome," and that the widespread existence of this will change the life style of our society. Even under these circumstances, whether such a change would constitute a "harm" is basically a value judgment about what kind of a society is both possible and ideal. The fact which we must face up to is that it is already clear the younger generation is bringing about a significant change in societal morality. Aside from the question as to whether legislation of morality which appreciably diminishes personal rights is constitutionally proper, there is the serious question as to the effectiveness of such legislation.

Criminal law often prohibits forms of behavior which are pleasurable to some and about which there is considerable doubt as to social harmfulness. Among these forms are the so-called moral offenses, including such behavior as homosexual conduct. This type of legislation comes into existence more out of exaggerated moral concerns and sense of responsibility than from any empirically demonstrated danger to the society. Judging by the paucity of data indicating danger to society and the high pitch of moral concern about its use, the offense represented by the use of this drug appears to be more in the nature of a moral one. And just as it is unlikely that society would disintegrate with the removal of criminal sanctions against homosexuality, so it is unlikely that the striking-out of penalties for the use of marihuana would lead to a similar fate.

Justice Brandeis, as though reaffirming John Stuart Mill, wrote in a dissenting opinion of the Supreme Court:

> The makers of our Constitution undertook to secure conditions favorable to the pursuit of happiness. They recognized the significance of man's spiritual nature, of his feelings, and of his intellect. They knew that only a part of the pain, pleasure, and satisfactions of life are to be found in material things. They sought to protect Americans in their beliefs, their thoughts, their emotions and their sensations. They conferred, as against the government, the right to be let alone—the most comprehensive of rights and the right most valued by civilized man. To protect that right, every unjustifiable intrusion by the government upon the privacy of the individual, whatever the means employed, must be deemed a violation of the 4th Amendment.[26]

In commenting on the "pursuit of happiness" alluded to by Justice Brandeis, A. D. Brook says:

> [It] . . . seems to be the most basic right of the individual in our society, a right which certainly lies within the penumbra of all other rights. It is the right for which all other rights are designed. It is the right to do with one's

26. Justice Brandeis, Dissenting Opinion, Olmstead et al. v. United States, 277 U.S. 438, 471 (1927).

entire life what one wishes, including the right to seek pleasure in whatever form that pleasure presents itself, provided, of course, that such a pursuit is not overbalanced by harm done to others. Arguably, it is also the right to achieve euphoria, the right to get "high," the right to experience new sensations, the right to expand and change one's consciousness, even the right to be silly, and finally, even the right to withdraw, the right to "cop out." It is submitted that these are rights that have "redeeming social value," and that the freedom to engage in behavior leading in any of these directions outweighs the exaggerated, and in some cases, fanciful harms that have been attributed to marijuana use.[27]

New social norms are increasingly and dramatically colliding with older statutory proscriptions. The legal institution cannot remain insensitive to these changes without incurring damage to itself. But, of course, courts lack the flexibility and prerogatives to provide solutions to social problems; ultimately it is the legislatures which can experiment, improvise, change direction, and even reverse field when necessary. In fact, just because a court has so few alternatives, it exercises great caution: a court may strike down a statute as unconstitutional, but in doing so it may leave a major social problem without an adequate solution.

As it becomes increasingly accepted that enforcement of the existing marihuana laws is more costly and dangerous than is use of the drug itself, at least as it is used at present in the United States, enforcement will become increasingly difficult. There is every indication that a great number of people are ignoring these laws now and that even more will be doing so in the future. It is not simply that more people are using marihuana, but larger numbers of people who are older are also smoking it. The number of people breaking these laws even now is so great that if a substantial fraction of them were arrested, the courts would be overwhelmed with the volume. One can predict that it will not be long before it will be a rare jury that does not have among its members at least one who uses marihuana, is convinced of its relative harmlessness, and will find it difficult to be a party to the conviction of someone else who uses the drug. In the absence of any statutory changes, what may happen is that law enforcement officials faced with increasing numbers of violators and shrinking numbers of convictions will arrive at a point where they decide that any efforts to enforce the laws as written are futile and that the only realistic approach to the widespread use of marihuana will be systematically to ignore it.

Something of this nature recently happened in the Netherlands, where

---

27. A. D. Brooks, "Marihuana and the Constitution: Individual Liberties and Puritan Virtues," in *Drugs and Youth,* ed. Wittenborn et al., p. 297.

the government has been moving toward the position that at least in the case of marihuana it is more sensible for a society to live with it than to fight its use. Officially marihuana remains outside the law, but even high law enforcement officials acknowledge that this is so because the Netherlands (like the United States) is party to the Single Convention governing traffic in drugs. Compared to the furtiveness and police action associated with drug usage in the United States, the Dutch laissez-faire attitude toward marihuana is striking, and nowhere is it more obvious than in two psychedelically lit, government-subsidized youth clubs, *Paradiso* and *Fantasio,* in downtown Amsterdam. In each of these clubs as many as 1,000 young people 16 years old and over can be found on any night, many of them smoking marihuana while pushers openly ply their trade, offering potential customers free samples. The police are fully aware of the activities and transactions that go on inside but make no effort to interfere. The clubs' managers and staff are alert to the use and sales of harder drugs and eject those so involved. As the man responsible for police affairs says of the present attitude, "It is forbidden to sell drugs but it is difficult to stop . . . young people had no place to go. Now we have less trouble in the streets."[28] However, the Dutch New Left activists are concerned about the effects that this attitude of the officials and the existence of the clubs may have on their efforts to impress upon young people the need to remake Dutch society. As one of them put it, "One bad effect . . . is that the clubs reduce political pressure. People think that if they've won the fight to have the clubs and drugs, then everything must be all right."[29] As for the extent of marihuana consumption, according to H. Cohen, a researcher at the University of Amsterdam, the dealers in the city handle a supply sufficient for about 10,000 regular users. "The increase in use . . . has not been great since 1960. Numerically, it is not a serious problem."[30]

In view of the present public attitudes toward smoking marihuana in the United States, it seems unlikely that legislatures are going to legalize the use of marihuana in the near future. I think it is likely, then, that this same type of widespread ignoring of the antimarihuana laws will very shortly come to pass. But the laissez-faire approach is no solution. It is mere transitory accommodation with a number of liabilities. First, one must expect that while such an accommodation may become widespread, it will nonetheless remain capricious. Second, since the present laws will presumably still exist, the user, while he may not be pursued,

28. D. S. Greenberg, "Hash in Holland: The Dutch Find It Easier to Let Traffic Flourish," *Science,* 165 (1969), p. 476.
29. Ibid.
30. Ibid., p. 478.

will still be labeled a criminal; and third, such an approach provides no way of imposing any degree of quality control upon distribution.

A more rational approach to the problem of the smoking of marihuana in the United States would include legalization of the use of marihuana, regulation of its distribution, and the development of sound educational programs about it.[31]

By "legalization" is meant the freedom for people above a certain age, say 18, to use marihuana (*bhang*) of a predetermined potency. The penalties associated with its use, as with alcohol, would deal with those circumstances wherein the user endangers the lives or well-being of others, as, for example, in operating a motor vehicle while intoxicated. Such legalization would immediately put an end to the costs and harmfulness of the present legal approach. It has to be assumed that the legalization of the use of marihuana would result in more widespread use. However, since at the present time the use is increasing explosively, it is at least conceivable that the prevalence of its use will reach roughly the same level sometime in the not too distant future with or without legalization. Furthermore, there is even a possibility that for some groups legalization will mean less use; those young people whose use is largely determined by a need to oppose hypocrisy and the establishment may feel less compelled to smoke pot when it is freely available. And very young people, those for whom its use may be the most harmful, may be more willing to forego its use now with the understanding that they will be able to use it when they reach age 18, just as most of them do not surreptitiously and illegally drive automobiles at a younger age perhaps largely because they know that when they reach 16 they will, with certain restrictions, be able to drive legally. This will by no means bring an end to the use of marihuana among high school and junior high school students, but it is more likely to have a dampening than an accelerating effect on use in this age group.

In this proposed approach the distribution of marihuana is regulated much as that of alcohol is now. The use of cannabis products is generally less dangerous than the use of either tobacco or alcohol, and the use of marihuana, as it is commonly smoked in this country, is the least harmful of all. The regulations controlling the distribution of cannabis would limit it to marihuana (*bhang*), of, say, 1.5-percent tetrahydrocannabinol

---

31. Although the United States became a party to the Single Convention on the control of narcotic drugs in 1961, it is doubtful that this constitutes a serious obstacle to the legalization of the use of marihuana. In the first place the treaty applies to hashish and not to the leaf preparations of cannabis; secondly, the provisions contain the qualification that their application is subject to a signatory's "constitutional limitations," so that a nation reserves for itself the decision of whether or not the Single Convention violates its internal laws (see "United Nations Single Convention Can't Stop Legalized Marijuana!", *Marijuana Review*, 1 [1969], p. 11).

potency. This would do much to insure the continued use of the milder form through smoking, rather than through the ingestion of more powerful forms such as hashish (*charas*). Just as, with the easy availability of liquors of limited potencies, people do not generally seek out pure ethanol, so it is expected that with the unfettered availability of marihuana, few would seek out hashish. Another important advantage of regulation is that the consumer could be certain not only that he is getting unadulterated marihuana, but also that it is of a potency familiar to him. Thus, there would be no danger of marihuana laced with other drugs. The risk of attaining more of a high through autotitration than the user desires or is prepared for would be minimized if the available product were of a more or less uniform, predictable potency. The risk of the kinds of reactions that have been described earlier, resulting from large amounts of ingested hashish, would be all but impossible under these circumstances.

If this type of approach is to have any effectiveness in stemming the push toward the use of "hallucinogens," amphetamines, and narcotics, it must be accompanied by honest educational programs. To date, such approaches have tended to lump marihuana with the "hallucinogens" or, even more inappropriately, with the true medical narcotics. The law as it presently stands reinforces this when it provides stiffer penalties for the use of marihuana than it does for LSD. Young people who have "learned" for themselves that marihuana is not very harmful then regrettably tend to treat with skepticism information from the same sources about the dangers of other drugs and are more likely to experiment with them. The present laws put the drug educator in a difficult position. He can discuss honestly the dangers of LSD, amphetamines, and heroin. But when he talks about marihuana, and particularly when he is asked about its dangers relative to those of alcohol, he can either be less than candid and risk losing credibility with regard to the other drugs, or he can acknowledge that except for the risk of getting caught, there is little reason on the whole to believe that marihuana as it is used now in the United States is more dangerous than alcohol. If he admits this lack of negative evidence regarding marihuana, he risks being accused by the community (or the school authorities) of encouraging the use of marihuana and thereby criminal behavior. If he tells the students candidly of the relative dangers of marihuana, LSD, amphetamines, and heroin, and he tells them what the penalties are for the use of these, he risks being interpreted as mocking the law. When the use of marihuana is legalized, it will be possible for the drug educator to have more credibility among the young people than he now can have.

However, if he is to be credible for an audience which seems particularly sensitive to breaches of integrity, he must be scrupulously objective about the material he presents. A case in point is an advertisement sponsored by the National Institute of Mental Health which appeared in several campus newspapers in November 1969. It showed the picture of a man and bore the title "Happy Twenty-First Birthday, Johnny." The ad read, "Most people take him for about 35."[32] Then came a few paragraphs of a reasonable description of the dangers of using amphetamines, followed by an invitation to write for free drug booklets to the National Institute of Mental Health. On January 6, 1970, two months later, the *Harvard Crimson,* one of the papers which had published the ad, also published a letter from the man who had posed for the picture, thanking the paper for belatedly recognizing his twenty-first birthday: "I was touched and proud to find your paper commemorating my twenty-first birthday. . . . I guess it just slipped by nine years ago when it happened, and I was a Junior [at Harvard]. But that's all right, I know how busy you are up there, getting out a paper every day, and all."[33] Not only was he in fact thirty years old, he was made up to look even older in the photograph. Needless to say, the student readers treated the incident with derision, and one wonders how seriously they will now consider the reasonably objective information offered in the advertisement. For that matter, one doubts the credibility—as a source of drug information—that they will grant to the National Institute of Mental Health. As mentioned earlier, there is some evidence that students will respond rationally to credible sources of objective evidence concerning the dangers of various drugs. And there is every reason to believe that deceitfulness in drug education will in the long run be counterproductive.

Most people in the United States, at least today, believe that to legalize the use of marihuana would be to invite national tragedy. Among them are those whose attitudes toward the use of this intoxicant are so emotionally overdetermined that they would remain unpersuaded by any amount of evidence of its relative harmlessness or by the most compelling arguments for the sagacity of legalization. Others, who are willing to consider the possibility, believe—as they have heard countless times—that not enough is known about the drug to make such a change which seems to them precipitous and premature. It is quite true that among the hundreds and hundreds of papers dealing with cannabis, there is relatively little methodologically sound research. Yet out of this vast collection of largely unsystematic recordings emerges a very strong impression that no amount of research is likely to prove that cannabis is as dangerous as alcohol and tobacco. The very serious dangers of tobacco, particularly to the pulmonary and cardiovascular systems, are

32. *Harvard Crimson,* Jan. 6. 1970, pp. 1, 4.
33. Ibid.

becoming increasingly well known. Alcohol, on the other hand, is generally considered to be a serious danger for "only a minority" of people
in this country, namely the alcoholics, who are conservatively estimated
to number about 5 to 6 million. Another minority group, the alcohol
abstainers, are actually considered by most people to be somewhat
deviant. We read in the newspapers of how upper-middle-class parents
support and even encourage alcohol use among their teenage children,
of how a session of Congress began with cocktails, and, more recently
of the exchange between Apollo astronauts and a television comedian,
well known for his use of alcohol, during which he gleefully exclaimed
that he was higher than they. So-called social drinking is as American
as apple pie—this despite the clearly demonstrated dangers of even this
kind of drinking.[34] It is a curious fact that the only socially accepted
and used drugs known to cause tissue damage (alcohol and tobacco) are
the ones whose use Western society sanctions. It is reasonably well
established that cannabis causes no tissue damage. There is no evidence
that it leads to any cellular damage to any organ. It does not lead to
psychoses *de novo,* and the evidence that it promotes personality deterioration is quite unconvincing, particularly in the forms and dosage
used in the United States today. Although it is clear that much more
must and will be learned about the derivatives of this fascinating psychoactive plant, it is not so clear what specifically needs yet to be
learned before we are ready to embark on a more reasoned approach
to the social use of marihuana. Given the fact that large segments of any
population will use psychoactive drugs and given the psychoactive drugs
presently available, marihuana is among the least dangerous. A fortiori,
we must consider the enormous harm, both obvious and subtle, short-
range and long-term, inflicted on the people, particularly the young,
who constitute or will soon constitute the formative and critical members of our society by the present punitive, repressive approach to the
use of marihuana. And we must consider the damage inflicted on legal
and other institutions when young people react to what they see as a
confirmation of their view that those institutions are hypocritical and
inequitable. Indeed, the greatest potential for social harm lies in the
scarring of so many young people and the reactive, institutional damages that are direct products of present marihuana laws. If we are to
avoid having this harm reach the proportions of a real national disaster
within the next decade, we must move to make the social use of marihuana legal.

34. M. Hayman, "The Myth of Social Drinking," *Amer. J. Psychiat.,* 124 (1967), pp. 585–94.

ABORTION REFORM

Edwin M. Schur

A cultural ideal has been that pregnancy, planned or unplanned, should be consummated in the birth of a child, wanted or unwanted. In most states the law supports this view. Nonetheless, women do seek and obtain abortions. The laws against abortion, then, do not eliminate the demand for the service but rather establish an illicit market. The cost, psychological strain, and physical danger to the woman, the corruption of the legal system, and the gross inequality in the risks associated with abortion for different class levels all result, directly or indirectly, from the legal proscription against abortion.

Legalizing abortion makes the service openly available and professionally controlled. Profits are taken out of human misery, the integrity of the law is maintained, and the label of criminality is removed. Perhaps most important of all, inequality in the distribution of risks is eliminated.

No comprehensive understanding of abortion is possible unless the practice is placed within a broad social and cultural context. As Alice S. Rossi has wisely noted, we must go beyond a narrow medical-psychiatric view of abortion to consider its relation to such matters as norms governing sexual relations, patterns of reproductive motivation, life goals and approved social roles of women, rights of privacy, and demographic trends.[1] I would like to approach the question of abortion from a somewhat different (though I believe complementary) tack—emphasizing some of the dominant features of abortion under current American policy as an immediately experienced social situation. In other words, the focus of my essay will be on the human drama of abortion-seeking and abortion-obtaining, as it is variously defined and experienced by the key participants in this process—primarily the woman herself, medical practitioners, illegal operatives, and law enforcement officials.

Because of the empahsis they have placed on the role of informal norms, sanctions, and processes in determining and shaping human

From Edwin M. Schur, "A Sociologist's View," from *Abortion in a Changing World,* Vol. I, edited by Robert E. Hall, New York: Columbia University Press, 1970, pp. 197–205. Reprinted by permission.

1. See Alice S. Rossi, Social change and abortion law reform, Paper presented to American Orthopsychiatric Association, Chicago, March 21, 1968 (mimeographed).

behavior, sociologists often have tended to pay insufficient attention to the more formal mechanisms of social control such as the law. Recently, however, there has been, among sociologists analyzing deviant behavior and social problems, a renewal of interest in studying the formal, as well as informal, processes of social definition by which society labels certain kinds of behavior as deviant or even criminal, together with the more direct processes of interaction between official agencies of control and individuals engaging in deviating behavior. This emphasis on "societal reactions" is most appropriate in viewing the abortion problem, for it is quite evidently true that it is our society which has somewhat arbitrarily and, many of us would submit, inadvisably, characterized the woman's behavior as an involvement in "crime." It is also true that the reactions to the woman's plight, exhibited by various officials (which category in this instance might well include medical practitioners and hospital administrators, as well as police and other law enforcers), significantly affect her behavior and her self-image. And the fact that present abortion laws do not effectively curb abortion does not mean that they are completely without social effect. On the contrary, they significantly color the entire abortion situation, producing a variety of consequences for abortion-seeking women, for the medical profession, and for law enforcers, many of which may be viewed as being highly dysfunctional from the standpoints both of individual and social well-being and of the integrity of (and respect for) the American legal system.

In a book published several years ago,[2] I discussed abortion as constituting an example of "crimes without victims"—situations in which an attempt is made to proscribe by criminal law the willing exchange in private, between adults, of widely demanded (though socially disapproved) goods or services. This characterization of abortion has been hotly contested, especially by some adherents to the Roman Catholic church's official position, who insist that in fact the fetus is a "victim" in the abortion situation. Others might well argue that the woman seeking the abortion is in many ways victimized by the illegal abortionist. These points are indeed debatable ones. But I did not intend, in using the term "crimes without victims" to focus merely on the fact that the alleged "offense" involves no interpersonal harm or, certainly, less interpersonal harm than the carrying to term of an unwanted child. More central to my analysis, really, was a stress on the consensual, transactional, aspect of the supposed "crime." This consensual element critically determines the unenforceability of our current laws: since women have no wish to bring formal complaints against the operators who complied with their requests for termination of pregnancy, the

---

2. Schur, Edwin M., *Crimes Without Victims,* Englewood Cliffs, N.J., Prentice-Hall, 1965.

obtaining of adequate evidence on which to base prosecution is extremely difficult, and effective enforcement cannot occur. The ramifications of this strange situation, in which our society allows patently unenforceable laws to stay on the books, include significant effects on both attitudes and behavior among all of the major participants in the abortion situation.

Let us consider first the position of the abortion-seeking woman. It is quite true that our present abortion laws, and many of the proposed reform provisions as well, are an affront to woman's dignity and an abridgment of her freedom. "Do we," Garrett Hardin has properly asked, "promote human dignity by requiring women to beg?"[3] But just as the feminist's concern to increase "career" opportunities for women has been largely a middle-class oriented concern, so too perhaps has been some of the irritation we express about women having to plead for abortions. A much more serious consequence of our present law (which, admittedly, could, in a very general sense, be subsumed under the pleading point if one wished to do so) has been the creation of significant socioeconomic differentials in access to abortion facilities, differentials which add up to a glaring discrimination against lower-class women.

After all, if her initial pleading is not successful, the middle- or upper-class woman may still be able to obtain a competent, reasonably safe, illegal operation. Her dignity has indeed been affronted, but her pregnancy has been terminated, and she may not be all that much worse off for the experience, physically or psychologically. Her lower-class counterpart is not so lucky. Not only is she much less likely to be able to obtain a so-called "therapeutic" abortion,[4] even if she has some idea that this might be a possible solution to her problem; but also we know that the quality of the criminal abortion a woman receives is directly related to the price she can pay. This in turn means that both the physical and psychological dangers attending an illegal operation are much greater in her case than in that of the knowledgeable woman of means. Although we do not have adequate national data on the socioeconomic distribution of deaths from abortion, it is noteworthy that in New York City one of every two maternal deaths among nonwhites and Puerto Ricans has been attributed to abortion, whereas among whites the figure is one out of four.[5] And we can be confident, I believe, that the incidence of postabortal medical complications short of death are much higher among lower-class women than among those of higher socioeco-

3. Hardin, Garrett, Abortion and human dignity. Lecture presented at University of California, Berkeley, April 29, 1964.
4. See Edwin M. Gold et al., *Amer. J. Public Health,* 55:964–72 (1965); also Robert E. Hall, *Amer. J. Obst. Gynecol., 91:*519 (1965).
5. Gold et al., *Amer. J. Public Health, 55:*965 (1965).

nomic status. An important factor here involves recourse to attempts at self-induced abortion. We can assume that even some well-educated middle-class women attempt to induce abortion themselves before exploring other means or, in some cases, when early efforts to locate an abortionist fail. The likelihood is strong that such attempts are extremely common among lower-class women, and of course these attempts are highly dangerous.

Apart from the danger of serious medical complications or even death, the abortion-seeking experience of the lower-class woman is bound to be especially unpleasant. She is more likely to encounter untrained and unscrupulous abortionists, and to be exploited by them. For her, the search for an adequate abortion is almost certain to be a long and dismal one—a search that frequently ends in failure. A sociological study of abortion-seeking recently found that even among relatively sophisticated middle-class women, the process of following the path from initial sources of information to success in obtaining a satisfactory illegal abortion, is a long and complicated one[6]—although some of the recently established consultation services may be changing this. The lower-class woman is doubly hampered in this regard. She suffers from the lack of close contact with knowledgeable sources of information (at least about the better abortionists), and her financial resources are inadequate for the purpose of obtaining a safe and competent operation.

There is reason to believe, also, that our present laws greatly heighten any guilt feelings and other adverse psychological effects associated with abortion. We know from comparative research that in countries with less restrictive policies women obtaining abortions display little adverse psychological reaction. And there is some evidence that even in this country, at least for those women obtaining abortion from trained medical practitioners, serious psychological difficulties are infrequent. Here again, the more sordid conditions confronted by lower-class women may take a special toll. One recent study found that a highly organized illegal abortion clinic attempted to present a "front" and "rhetoric" of respectability and professionalism, which might help to ease the psychological distress of its "patients."[7] But for the woman unable to foot the bill, even this kind of gloss on what may be the harsh realities is not present.

We have very little reliable information concerning the specific effects on women of our society's having formally designated abortion a "crime." It seems likely, however, that this very designation itself

---

6. Lee, Nancy Howell, "Acquaintance Networks in the Social Structure of Abortion," unpublished Ph.D. dissertation, Harvard University, 1967.
7. Ball, Donald W., *Social Problems, 14*:293–301 (1967).

influences the social psychological atmosphere surrounding many abortions. That she is being forced into "criminal" activity may even affect some women who have few conscious qualms about seeking an abortion and who can do so expeditiously and efficiently. For almost any woman under our system, then, the abortion situation has some very undesirable aspects. While it is true that feelings of deprivation are often relative, so that the middle-class woman's need to plead her case may be as upsetting to her as the lower-class woman's situation is to her, the enormous disparity in the objective conditions of abortion for the different social classes perpetrated by our present policies is an outrage.

The situation of the medical practitioner is also, as we well know, significantly influenced by existing abortion laws. Doctors are, of course, under pressure from all sides—from abortion-seeking women on the one hand and (at least potentially) from law-enforcement officials on the other, from diverse segments of the public, and from abortion reform organizations. Under the present statutes in most American jurisdictions it is rarely possible to follow the dictates of the law and at the same time do what is professionally considered in the best interest of the patient. Common solutions to this dilemma include various types of evasion and subterfuge. As many observers have noted, the hospital abortion board system has the significant function of allowing individual doctors to evade an imputation of direct personal responsibility for rejection of abortion requests. This system was also instrumental in producing the striking decline in hospital abortions during recent years, which Lawrence Lader described as "resulting from one of the greatest cases of jitters ever to afflict the medical profession."[8] Another type of evasion is seen when the doctor refers his patient to a known abortionist, thus minimizing his own risk while possibly increasing hers. Sometimes doctors evade the issue by an outright refusal to help in any way. In the study of abortion-seeking mentioned earlier it was found that the main object of most of the abortion-seekers' "complaints of rudeness, insults, or lack of sympathy" was the physician, and usually "the woman's own physician as opposed to a strange doctor."[9]

With respect to the granting of hospital abortions, subterfuge may be the rule rather than the exception. It has been suggested that given modern medical advances the very term "therapeutic abortion" is really a kind of semantic ruse, and that what is needed instead is "humane abortion," "to preserve the mental health of the mother, to reduce marital stress, and to make it possible for children to be born into families in which they are wanted."[10] We know that doctors often

8. Lader, Lawrence, *Abortion,* p. 24, Indianapolis, Bobbs-Merrill, 1966.
9. Lee, "Acquaintance Networks," p. 97.
10. Hardin, Garrett, "Semantic Aspects of Abortion," *ETC., 24,* September 1967.

enter into collusive agreements with patients to recommend hospital abortion even where the circumstances are not such as to satisfy the legal requirements. And particularly in cases where interruption of pregnancy is said to be psychiatrically indicated, the recommendation usually requires the psychiatrist to interpret the woman's situation in a way that goes considerably beyond conventional psychiatric diagnosis. One reform-oriented psychiatrist has stated that "being caught in an unprepared-for pregnancy is *prima facie* evidence of immaturity or neurotic conflict; therefore, emotional fitness for parenthood should be questioned."[11] Now I have no doubt that the author of this statement believes this to be true, and probably some other psychiatrists do as well. But what is more significant is that psychiatrists are placed by the current law in the position of having to make diagnoses of psychopathology even where they don't really believe the woman is mentally ill. It should be enough to say that the woman's best interests indicate termination of pregnancy, but of course to date this has not been the sole criterion applied to assessing requests for abortion.

(Let me add, with reference to the argument that the woman *alone* should make the decision with respect to abortion, that even if there were no criminal laws whatsoever in this area, a certain minimal and nonbureaucratized medical screening of cases would presumably still be called for. One assumes there are some cases in which abortion is medically contraindicated, and one also assumes that no doctor should undertake a surgical intervention without first making a determination of its medical advisability.)

There are, to be sure, legitimate practitioners who do not evade the issues but rather do all they can to help their patients obtain "legal" or at least safe abortions, and many otherwise legitimate practitioners (who are not in the abortion "business") perform occasional non-hospital-accredited abortions for long-time patients or in other circumstances they consider sufficiently compelling. Also playing an important role in the abortion situation, however, are the strictly illegal operators (some untrained medically), for whom the current legal policies have produced the basis of a thriving business. With legal supply severely restricted, the demand for their scarce services is so great that the professional abortionist finds himself in a situation similar to that of an unchallenged monopolist in the business world.[12] And as Rongy stated many years ago, restrictive legislation set in motion an endless circle:

11. Aarons, Z. Alexander, *Amer. J. Psychiat.*, *124*:56 (1967).
12. See Herbert L. Packer, *American Scholar*, *33*:551–57 (1964); also Thomas C. Schelling, "Economic Analysis and Organized Crime," in President's Commission on Law Enforcement and Administration of Justice, *Task Force Report: Organized Crime*, pp. 114–26, Washington, U.S. Government Printing Office, 1967.

The ready willingness of women to visit an abortionist brought him immense profits. A fraction of these profits made it possible to cause an abortion with a greater degree of safety to the woman and a smaller chance of exposure of either the woman or the doctor. This led to a further appeal to women who wished to bring an abrupt termination to their pregnancies. And so the chain was complete.[13]

The unenforceability of abortion laws suggested by this statement poses serious problems from the law enforcer's standpoint. Not only are the police well aware that these laws simply cannot be enforced on any systematic basis, but like the public at large they hold ambivalent attitudes toward such statutes and they are aware that the abortionist is meeting a community need. Elimination of abortionist is an unrealistic goal in any case; the most that can be attempted is an occasional exposé of an abortion "ring" or "mill" to satisfy the periodic demand for a "crackdown." A pernicious side effect of laws of this nature is the invitation to police corruption. While some abortionists may have sufficient mobility and organization to escape detection, it seems likely that any abortionist who operates for any length of time "undetected" is in fact paying for protection. As the task force on police of the President's Crime Commission has pointed out, "A considerable number of the most serious and persistent kinds of unethical conduct are connected with failure to enforce laws that are not in accord with community norms."[14] Clearly the integrity of the legal system is threatened by the persistence of such unenforceable laws and by the ethical misconduct (or in some other instances, repressive enforcement techniques) they invite.

Though almost totally ineffective as a deterrent, our present abortion policies do, then, have social effects. Obviously, complete removal of all criminal laws restricting abortion would be the most straightforward way of ameliorating this situation. At the same time, I am not entirely pessimistic regarding the potential for substantial improvement under the recent and more moderate reform proposals, provided that these are interpreted very broadly, by courts and by medical practitioners, particularly as to the meaning given to the woman's mental health. But whatever type of change we see in the near future, it is at least becoming widely recognized that our present restrictive laws have helped to produce a human drama the prevailing conditions of which represent an affront to the dignity of virtually *all* the major participants, as well as producing much social harm and individual unhappiness.

13. Rongy, Abraham, *Abortion: Legal or Illegal?* p. 117, New York, Vanguard Press, 1933.
14. President's Commission on Law Enforcement and Administration of Justice. *Task Force Report: The Police,* pp. 211–12, Washington: U.S. Government Printing Office, 1967.

A DIFFERENT PERSPECTIVE ON SCHIZOPHRENIA

R. D. Laing

Schizophrenia is a label generally applied under conditions where be-haviors are strange and bizarre to the person so labeled as well as to others in contact with him. It is usually assumed that the behavior results from genetic, psychic, or environmental causes. The label "schizophre-nia" goes on to define this behavior as an "illness," which in turn needs to be treated and its development arrested.

In R. D. Laing's view, this traditional conception and labeling aborts the personal growth that can emerge from an unusual experience. "Treatment" creates an artificial, imprisoning, and stigmatizing situa-tion. A patient becomes a nonagent involuntarily subject to the controls of others.

If the label were set aside, the person could be provided with a setting where he could freely pursue his own line of action, ultimately fitting experience and behavior, and the inner and the outer worlds, in ways that make sense to him. Ultimately, this could lead to a sense of rebirth for the person, rather than the sense of degradation which emanates from the traditional perspective.

• • •

In the last decade, a radical shift of outlook has been occurring in psy-chiatry. This has entailed the questioning of old assumptions, based on the attempts of nineteenth-century psychiatrists to bring the frame of clinical medicine to bear on their observations. Thus the subject matter of psychiatry was thought of as mental illness; one thought of mental physiology and mental pathology, one looked for signs and symptoms, made one's diagnosis, assessed prognosis and prescribed treatment. According to one's philosophical bias, one looked for the etiology of these mental illnesses in the mind, in the body, in the environment, or in inherited propensities.

The term "schizophrenia" was coined by a Swiss psychiatrist, Bleuler, who worked within this frame of reference. In using the term schizo-phrenia, I am not referring to any condition that I suppose to be mental rather than physical, or to an illness, like pneumonia, *but to a label that some people pin on other people under certain social circumstances.**

From R. D. Laing, *The Politics of Experience,* New York: Pantheon Books, 1967, pp. 70–76, 82–90. Copyright © 1967 by R. D. Laing.

*Our italics, M. S. W. and E. R.

The "cause" of "schizophrenia" is to be found by the examination, not of the prospective diagnosee alone, but of the whole social context in which the psychiatric ceremonial is being conducted.[1]

Once demystified, it is clear, at least, that some people come to behave and to experience themselves and others in ways that are strange and incomprehensible to most people, including themselves. If this behavior and experience fall into certain broad categories, they are liable to be diagnosed as subject to a condition called schizophrenia. By present calculation almost one in every 100 children born will fall into this category at some time or other before the age of forty-five, and in the United Kingdom at the moment there are roughly 60,000 men and women in mental hospitals, and many more outside hospitals, who are termed schizophrenic.

A child born today in the United Kingdom stands a ten times greater chance of being admitted to a mental hospital than to a university, and about one fifth of mental hospital admissions are diagnosed schizophrenic. This can be taken as an indication that we are driving our children mad more effectively than we are genuinely educating them. Perhaps it is our way of educating them that is driving them mad.

Most but not all psychiatrists still think that people they call schizophrenic suffer from an inherited predisposition to act in predominantly incomprehensible ways, that some as yet undetermined genetic factor (possibly a genetic morphism) transacts with a more or less ordinary environment to induce biochemical-endocrinological changes which in turn generate what we observe as the behavioral signs of a subtle underlying organic process.

But it is wrong to impute a hypothetical disease of unknown etiology and undiscovered pathology to someone unless *he* can prove otherwise.[2]

> The schizophrenic is someone who has queer experiences and/or is acting in a queer way, from the point of view usually of his relatives and of ourselves. . . .
>
> That the diagnosed patient is suffering from a pathological process is either a fact, or an hypothesis, an assumption, or a judgement.
>
> To regard it as fact is unequivocally false. To regard it as an hypothesis is legitimate. It is unnecessary either to make the assumption or to pass judgement.
>
> The psychiatrist, adopting his clinical stance in the presence of the pre-diagnosed person, whom he is already looking at and listening to as a patient, has tended to come to believe that he is in the presence of the "fact"

1. See H. Garfinkel, "Conditions of Successful Degradation Ceremonies," *American Journal of Sociology,* Volume LXI (March 1956), pages 420–4; also R. D. Laing, "Ritualization in Abnormal Behavior" in *Ritualization of Behavior in Animals and Man* (Royal Society, Philosophical Transactions, Series B [in press]).

2. See T. Szasz, *The Myth of Mental Illness* (New York: Harper & Row, 1961; London: Secker & Warburg, 1962).

of schizophrenia. He acts as if its existence were an established fact. He then has to discover its cause or multiple etiological factors, to assess its prognosis, and to treat its course. The heart of the illness then resides outside the agency of the person. That is, the illness is taken to be a process that the person is subject to or undergoes, whether genetic, constitutional, endogenous, exogenous, organic or psychological, or some mixture of them all.[3]

Many psychiatrists are now becoming much more cautious about adopting this starting point. But what might take its place?

In understanding the new viewpoint on schizophrenia, we might remind ourselves of the six blind men and the elephant: one touched its body and said it was a wall, another touched an ear and said it was a fan, another a leg and thought it was a pillar, and so on. The problem is sampling, and *the error is incautious extrapolation.* *

The old way of sampling the behavior of schizophrenics was by the method of clinical examination. The following is an example of the type of examination conducted at the turn of the century. The account is given by the German psychiatrist Emil Kraepelin in his own words.

> Gentlemen, the cases that I have to place before you today are peculiar. First of all, you see a servant-girl, aged twenty-four, upon whose features and frame traces of great emaciation can be plainly seen. In spite of this, the patient is in continual movement, going a few steps forward, then back again; she plaits her hair, only to unloose it the next minute. *On attempting to stop her movement,* we meet with unexpectedly strong resistance; *if I place myself in front of her with my arms spread out* in order to stop her, if she cannot push me on one side, she suddenly turns and slips through under my arms, so as to continue her way. *If one takes firm hold* of her, she distorts her usually rigid, expressionless features with deplorable weeping, that only ceases so soon as one lets her have her own way. We notice besides that she holds a crushed piece of bread spasmodically clasped in the fingers of the left hand, which she absolutely *will not allow to be forced from her.* The patient does not trouble in the least about her surroundings so long as you leave her alone. *If you prick her in the forehead with a needle,* she scarcely winces or turns away, and leaves the needle quietly sticking there without letting it disturb her restless, beast-of-prey-like wandering backwards and forwards. *To questions* she answers almost nothing, at the most shaking her head. But from time to time she wails: "O dear God! O dear God! O dear mother! O dear mother!", always repeating uniformly the same phrases.[4]

3. R. D. Laing and A. Esterson, *Sanity, Madness and the Family,* Volume I, *Families of Schizophrenics* (London: Tavistock Publications, 1964; New York: Basic Books, 1965), page 4.
4. E. Kraepelin, *Lectures on Clinical Psychiatry,* edited by T. Johnstone (London: Baillière, Tindall and Cox, 1906), pages 30–31.

*Our italics, M. S. W. and E. R.

Here are a man and a young girl. If we see the situation purely in terms of Kraepelin's point of view, it all immediately falls into place. He is sane, she is insane; he is rational, she is irrational. This entails looking at the patient's actions out of the context of the situation as she experienced it. But if we take Kraepelin's actions (in italics) — he tries to stop her movements, stands in front of her with arms outspread, tries to force a piece of bread out of her hand, sticks a needle in her forehead, and so on — out of the context of the situation as experienced and defined by him, how extraordinary *they* are!

A feature of the interplay between psychiatrist and patient is that if the patient's part is taken out of context, as is done in the clinical description, it might seem very odd. The psychiatrist's part, however, is taken as the very touchstone for our common-sense view of normality. The psychiatrist, as *ipso facto* sane, shows that the patient is out of contact with him. The fact that he is out of contact with the patient shows that there is something wrong with the patient, but not with the psychiatrist.

But if one ceases to identify with the clinical posture and looks at the psychiatrist-patient couple without such presuppositions, then it is difficult to sustain this naïve view of the situation.

Psychiatrists have paid very little attention to the *experience* of the patient. Even in psychoanalysis there is an abiding tendency to suppose that the schizophrenic's experiences are somehow unreal or invalid; one can make sense out of them only by interpreting them; without truth-giving interpretations the patient is enmeshed in a world of delusions and self-deception. Kaplan, an American psychologist, in an introduction to an excellent collection of self-reports on the experience of being psychotic, says very justly:

> With all virtue on his side, he (the psychiatrist or psychoanalyst) reaches through the subterfuges and distortions of the patient and exposes them to the light of reason and insight. In this encounter between the psychiatrist and patient, the efforts of the former are linked with science and medicine, with understanding and care. What the patient experiences is tied to illness and irreality, to perverseness and distortion. The process of psychotherapy consists in large part of the patient's abandoning his false subjective perspectives for the therapist's objective ones. But the essence of this conception is that the psychiatrist understands what is going on, and the patient does not.[5]

H. S. Sullivan used to say to young psychiatrists when they came to work with him, "I want you to remember that in the present state of our society, the patient is right, and you are wrong." This is an outrageous

5. Bert Kaplan (ed.), *The Inner World of Mental Illness* (New York and London: Harper & Row, 1964), page vii.

simplification. I mention it to loosen any fixed ideas that are no less outrageous, that the psychiatrist is right, and the patient wrong. I think, however, that schizophrenics have more to teach psychiatrists about the inner world than psychiatrists their patients.

A different picture begins to develop if the interaction between patients themselves is studied without presuppositions. One of the best accounts here is by the American sociologist Erving Goffman.

Goffman spent a year as an assistant physical therapist in a large mental hospital of some 7,000 beds, near Washington. His lowly staff ṣtatus enabled him to fraternize with the patients in a way that upper echelons of the staff were unable to do. One of his conclusions is:

> There is an old saw that no clearcut line can be drawn between normal people and mental patients; rather there is a continuum with the well-adjusted citizen at one end and the full-fledged psychotic at the other. I must argue that after a period of acclimatization in a mental hospital, the notion of a continuum seems very presumptuous. A community is a community. Just as it is bizarre to those not in it, so it is natural, even if unwanted, to those who live it from within. The system of dealings that patients have with one another does not fall at one end of anything, but rather provides one example of human association, to be avoided, no doubt, but also to be filed by the student in a circular cabinet along with all the other examples of association that he can collect.[6]

A large part of his study is devoted to a detailed documentation of how it comes about that a person, in being put in the role of patient, tends to become defined as a nonagent, as a nonresponsible object, to be treated accordingly, and even comes to regard himself in this light.

Goffman shows also that by shifting one's focus from seeing the person out of context, to seeing him in his context, behavior that might seem quite unintelligible, at best explained as some intrapsychic regression or organic deterioration, can make quite ordinary human sense. He does not just describe such behavior "in" mental hospital patients, he describes it within the context of personal interaction and the system in which it takes place.

> . . . there is a vicious circle process at work. Persons who are lodged on "bad" wards find that very little equipment of any kind is given them—clothes may be taken away from them each night, recreational materials may be withheld, and only heavy wooden chairs and benches provided for furniture. Acts of hostility against the institution have to rely on limited, ill-designed devices, such as banging a chair against the floor or striking a sheet of newspaper sharply so as to make an annoying explosive sound. And the more inadequate this equipment is to convey rejection of the hospital,

6. E. Goffman, *Asylums. Essays on the Social Situation of Mental Patients and Other Inmates* (New York: Doubleday Anchor Books, 1961), page 303.

the more the act appears as a psychotic symptom, and the more likely it is that management feels justified in assigning the patient to a bad ward. When a patient finds himself in seclusion, naked and without visible means of expression, he may have to rely on tearing up his mattress, if he can, or writing with faeces on the wall—actions management takes to be in keeping with the kind of person who warrants seclusion.[7]

• • •

"Schizophrenia" is a diagnosis, a label applied by some people to others. This does not prove that the labeled person is subject to an essentially pathological process, of unknown nature and origin, going on *in* his or her body. It does not mean that the process is, primarily or secondarily, a *psycho*pathological one, going on *in* the *psyche* of the person. But it does establish as a social fact that the person labeled is one of Them. . . .

There is no such "condition" as "schizophrenia," but the label is a social fact and the social fact a *political event*.[8] This political event, occurring in the civic order of society, imposes definitions and consequences on the labeled person. It is a social prescription that rationalizes a set of social actions whereby the labeled person is annexed by others, who are legally sanctioned, medically empowered and morally obliged, to become responsible for the person labeled. The person labeled is inaugurated not only into a role, but into a career of patient, by the concerted action of a coalition (a "conspiracy") of family, G. P., mental health officer, psychiatrists, nurses, psychiatric social workers, and often fellow patients. The "committed" person labeled as patient, and specifically as "schizophrenic," is degraded from full existential and legal status as human agent and responsible person to someone no longer in possession of his own definition of himself, unable to retain his own possessions, precluded from the exercise of his discretion as to whom he meets, what he does. His time is no longer his own and the space he occupies is no longer of his choosing. After being subjected to a degradation ceremonial[9] known as psychiatric examination, he is bereft of his civil liberties in being imprisoned in a total institution[10] known as a "mental" hospital. More completely, more radically than anywhere else in our society, he is invalidated as a human being. In the mental

7. E. Goffman, op. cit., page 306.
8. T. Scheff, "Social Conditions for Rationality: How Urban and Rural Courts Deal with the Mentally Ill," *Amer. Behav. Scient.,* March, 1964. Also, T. Scheff, "The Societal Reaction to Deviants: Ascriptive Elements in the Psychiatric Screening of Mental Patients in a Midwestern State," *Social Problems,* No. 4, Spring, 1964.
9. H. Garfinkel, "Conditions of Successful Degradation Ceremonies," *American Journal of Sociology,* Volume LXI, March, 1956.
10. E. Goffman, *Asylums. Essays on the Social Situation of Mental Patients and Other Inmates* (New York: Doubleday Anchor Books, 1961).

hospital he must remain, until the label is rescinded or qualified by such terms as "remitted" or "readjusted." Once a "schizophrenic," there is a tendency to be regarded as always a "schizophrenic."

Now, why and how does this happen? And what functions does this procedure serve for the maintenance of the civic order? These questions are only just beginning to be asked, much less answered. Questions and answers have so far been focused on the family as a social subsystem. Socially, this work must now move to further understanding, not only of the internal disturbed and disturbing patterns of communication within families, of the double-binding procedures, the pseudo-mutuality, of what I have called the mystifications and the untenable positions, but also to the meaning of all this within the larger context of the civic order of society—that is, of the *political* order, of the ways persons exercise control and power over one another.

Some people labeled schizophrenic (not all, and not necessarily) manifest behavior in words, gestures, actions (linguistically, paralinguistically and kinetically) that is unusual. Sometimes (not always and not necessarily) this unusual behavior (manifested to us, the others, as I have said, by sight and sound) expresses, wittingly or unwittingly, unusual experiences that the person is undergoing. Sometimes (not always and not necessarily) these unusual experiences expressed by unusual behavior appear to be part of a potentially orderly, natural sequence of experiences.

This sequence is very seldom allowed to occur because we are so busy "treating" the patient, whether by chemotherapy, shock therapy, *milieu* therapy, group therapy, psychotherapy, family therapy—sometimes now, in the very best, most advanced places, by the lot.

What we see sometimes in *some* people whom we label and "treat" as schizophrenics are the behavioral expressions of an experiential drama. But we see this drama in a distorted form that our therapeutic efforts tend to distort further. The outcome of this unfortunate dialectic is a *forme frustre* of a potentially *natural* process, that we do not allow to happen.

In characterizing this sequence in general terms, I shall write *entirely* about a sequence of experience. I shall therefore have to use the language of experience. So many people feel they have to translate "subjective" events into "objective" terms in order to be scientific. To be genuinely scientific means to have valid knowledge of a chosen domain of reality. So in the following I shall use the language of experience to describe the events of experience. Also, I shall not so much be describing a series of different discrete events as describing a unitary sequence, from different points of view, and using a variety of idioms to do so. I suggest that this natural process, which our labeling and well-intentioned therapeutic efforts distort and arrest, is as follows.

We start again from the split of our experience into what seems to be two worlds, inner and outer.

The normal state of affairs is that we know little of either and are alienated from both, but that we know perhaps a little more of the outer than the inner. However, the very fact that it is necessary to speak of outer and inner at all implies that an historically conditioned split has occurred, so that the inner is already as bereft of substance as the outer is bereft of meaning.

We need not be unaware of the "inner" world. We do not realize its existence most of the time. But many people enter it—unfortunately without guides, confusing outer with inner realities, and inner with outer —and generally lose their capacity to function competently in ordinary relations.

This need not be so. The process of entering into *the other* world from this world, and returning to *this* world from the other world, is as natural as death and giving birth or being born. But in our present world, which is both so terrified and so unconscious of the other world, it is not surprising that when "reality," the fabric of this world, bursts, and a person enters the other world, he is completely lost and terrified and meets only incomprehension in others.

Some people wittingly, some people unwittingly, enter or are thrown into more or less total inner space and time. We are socially conditioned to regard total immersion in outer space and time as normal and healthy. Immersion in inner space and time tends to be regarded as anti-social withdrawal, a deviation, invalid, pathological *per se,* in some sense discreditable.

Sometimes, having gone through the looking glass, through the eye of the needle, the territory is recognized as one's lost home, but most people now in inner space and time are, to begin with, in unfamiliar territory and are frightened and confused. They are lost. They have forgotten that they have been there before. They clutch at chimeras. They try to retain their bearings by compounding their confusion, by projection (putting the inner on to the outer), and introjection (importing outer categories into their inner). They do not know what is happening, and no one is likely to enlighten them.

We defend ourselves violently even from the full range of our egoically limited experience. How much more are we likely to react with terror, confusion and "defenses" against ego-loss experience. There is nothing intrinsically pathological in the experience of ego-loss, but it may be very difficult to find a living context for the journey one may be embarked upon.

The person who has entered this inner realm (if only he is allowed to experience this) will find himself going, or being conducted—one cannot clearly distinguish active from passive here—on a journey.

This journey is experienced as going further "in," as going back through one's personal life, in and back and through and beyond into the experience of all mankind, of the primal man, of Adam and perhaps even further into the beings of animals, vegetables and minerals.

In this journey there are many occasions to lose one's way, for confusion, partial failure, even final shipwreck; many terrors, spirits, demons to be encountered, that may or may not be overcome.

We do not regard it as pathologically deviant to explore a jungle or to climb Mount Everest. We feel that Columbus was entitled to be mistaken in his construction of what he discovered when he came to the New World. We are far more out of touch with even the nearest approaches of the infinite reaches of inner space than we now are with the reaches of outer space. We respect the voyager, the explorer, the climber, the space man. It makes far more sense to me as a valid project —indeed, as a desperately and urgently required project for our time— to explore the inner space and time of consciousness. Perhaps this is one of the few things that still make sense in our historical context. We are so out of touch with this realm that many people can now argue seriously that it does not exist. Small wonder that it is perilous indeed to explore such a lost realm. The situation I am suggesting is precisely as though we all had almost total lack of any knowledge whatever of what we call the outer world. What would happen if some of us then started to see, hear, touch, smell, taste things? We would hardly be more confused than the person who first has vague intimations of, and then moves into, inner space and time. This is where the person labeled catatonic has often gone. He is not at all here: he is all there. He is frequently very mistaken about what he is experiencing, and he probably does not want to experience it. He may indeed be lost. There are very few of us who know the territory in which he is lost, who know how to reach him and how to find the way back.

No age in the history of humanity has perhaps so lost touch with this natural *healing* process that implicates *some* of the people whom we label schizophrenic. No age has so devalued it, no age has imposed such prohibitions and deterrences against it, as our own. Instead of the mental hospital, a sort of reservicing factory for human breakdowns, we need a place where people who have traveled further and, consequently, may be more lost than psychiatrists and other sane people, can find their way *further* into inner space and time, and back again. Instead of the *degradation* ceremonial of psychiatric examination, diagnosis and prognostication, we need, for those who are ready for it (in psychiatric terminology, often those who are about to go into a schizophrenic breakdown), an *initiation* ceremonial, through which the person will be guided with full social encouragement and sanction into inner space and time, by people who have been there and back again. Psychiatrically, this would appear as ex-patients helping future patients to go mad.

What is entailed then is:

i. a voyage from outer to inner,
ii. from life to a kind of death,
iii. from going forward to going back,
iv. from temporal movement to temporal standstill,
v. from mundane time to eonic time,
vi. from the ego to the self,
vii. from outside (post-birth) back into the womb of all things (pre-birth),

and then subsequently a return voyage from

1. inner to outer,
2. from death to life,
3. from the movement back to a movement once more forward,
4. from immortality back to mortality,
5. from eternity back to time,
6. from self to a new ego,
7. from a cosmic fetalization to an existential rebirth.

I shall leave it to those who wish to translate the above elements of this perfectly natural and necessary process into the jargon of psychopathology and clinical psychiatry. This process may be one that all of us need, in one form or another. This process could have a central function in a truly sane society.

I have listed very briefly little more than the headings for an extended study and understanding of a natural sequence of experiential stepping stones that, in some instances, is submerged, concealed, distorted and arrested by the label "schizophrenia" with its connotations of pathology and consequences of an illness-to-be-cured.

Perhaps we will learn to accord to so-called schizophrenics who have come back to us, perhaps after years, no less respect than the often no less lost explorers of the Renaissance. If the human race survives, future men will, I suspect, look back on our enlightened epoch as a veritable Age of Darkness. They will presumably be able to savor the irony of this situation with more amusement than we can extract from it. The laugh's on us. They will see that what we call "schizophrenia" was one of the forms in which, often through quite ordinary people, the light began to break through the cracks in our all-too-closed minds.

Schizophrenia used to be a new name for dementia praecox—a slow, insidious illness that was supposed to overtake young people in particular and to be liable to go on to a terminal dementia.

Perhaps we can still retain the now old name, and read into it its etymological meaning: *Schiz*—"broken"; *Phrenos*—"soul" or "heart." The schizophrenic in this sense is one who is brokenhearted, and even broken hearts have been known to mend, if we have the heart to let them.

But "schizophrenia," in this existential sense, has little to do with the clinical examination, diagnosis, prognosis and prescriptions for therapy of "schizophrenia."

NEUTRALIZING THE HOMOSEXUAL LABEL

Martin S. Weinberg and Colin J. Williams

In outlining a program for "Neutralizing the Homosexual Label," Martin Weinberg and Colin Williams propose that aspects of social organization which implicitly or explicitly support the moral meanings of homosexuality as sinful, immoral, dangerous, or perverted must be a primary target for change. Their concerns emanate from the consequences of these moral meanings. For homosexuals these include prejudice, discrimination, harassment, hostility, exploitation, self-punishment, and ghettoization. For heterosexuals the consequences include the support of a system that sees as its right the adjudication of what is moral or immoral with regard to the private behavior of consenting adults, the right to punish those citizens whose "life styles" breach its arbitrarily delimited dictates, and a system that degrades the political and legal ideals of our society. The declared need is to reject the view that homosexuality is a social problem and to recognize that traditional societal reactions toward homosexuality are the social problem. The authors make specific recommendations for implementing this goal.

It is evident that the actual and perceived reaction of the heterosexual world causes problems for the homosexual's self-image and social functioning. Although by no means uniform, the social response to homosexuals generally varies mostly in its degree of negativeness, from a detached tolerance to a sometimes violent rejection. Our cross-cultural

The above section presents some practical considerations that are included as an epilogue to a forthcoming book by Weinberg and Williams tentatively titled *Homosexual Adaptations: A Study in Three Western Societies*. This book examines major tenets of labeling theory cross-culturally with a sample of approximately 2500 male homosexuals.

comparisons showed that in the Netherlands and Denmark among other things the homosexual was able to live a less secretive life than the homosexual in America.

On the basis of our fieldwork and knowledge of the homosexual's situation it is clear to us that such differences can be accounted for in terms of the differences in the response toward homosexuals in the societies that we studied. The more tolerant and liberal attitudes of the European societies appear to make for considerable differences. It would seem obvious, therefore, that a major strategy in alleviating some of the homosexual's problems in the United States is to alter responses toward him in this society.

This is no simple task in a society traditionally erotophobic as well as anti-homosexual. One way of handling this question is to analyze the components of social response in order to evaluate which and whose are most susceptible to change in the desired direction. An important distinction, proved useful in the study of minority groups, is that between prejudice and discrimination, between a stereotyped *attitude* and the *behavior* associated with it. The relationship between attitudes and behavior has received much discussion in the literature; however, one thing that appears to be true is that the

> . . . evidence indicates that specific attitudes shape themselves to behavior. People who actually work with Negroes, especially as equals, develop attitudes favorable towards working with Negroes. . . . Thus the mass of modern evidence runs counter to the "attitudes first" fallacy, which holds that prejudice is a lurking state of mind that spills over into overt behavior.[1]

An even more important suggestion from the cited work is that *both* attitudes and behavior are affected by the social situation in which they exist. For example, attitudes and behavior are different in an integrated than in a segregated situation. The implications from such research, therefore, seem clear: to change attitudes, change the social situation so that behavior can be affected in the desired direction. Thus, in helping the homosexual, it may be less useful to directly try and change attitudes toward him than to change the social situation which discriminates against him; at least, the latter must be attempted as well as the former.[2]

---

1. Earl Raab and Seymour Martin Lipset, "The Prejudiced Society," in Earl Raab (ed.), *American Race Relations Today,* New York: Anchor Books, 1962, p. 41. This also seems the case for *general* attitudes, *ibid.* For other commentaries on the relationship between attitudes and behavior, see Frank R. Westie and Melvin De Fleur, "Verbal Attitudes and Overt Acts: An Experiment on the Salience of Attitudes," *American Sociological Review,* 23 (December 1958), pp. 667–73; Irving Deutscher, "Words and Deeds: Social Science and Social Policy," *Social Problems,* 13 (Winter 1966), pp. 235–54; Howard J. Ehrlich, "Attitudes, Behavior, and Intervening Variables," *American Sociologist,* 4 (February 1969), pp. 29–34.
2. This is by no means a novel suggestion. Many commentators, e.g. the Task Force on Homosexuality, decry discrimination. Their reasoning, however, is based upon *moral* con-

Those aspects of social organization that support the moral meanings of homosexuality as sinful, immoral, dangerous, perverted, revolting or sick, and which maintain discriminatory behavior toward homosexuals must be, therefore, a primary target for change. The following institutional areas have been seen by most commentators—homosexual and heterosexual—as beginning arenas for change.

The Law and its Enforcement. Changing the law is important, not only because of its contribution to discrimination but also because of its indirect effect in evaluating homosexuality. We have already detailed the discriminatory effects of the law. In most states consenting homosexual behavior between adults is a criminal offense despite the absence of evidence that such behavior is harmful to the persons involved or to society in general. The effect of this legislation on the homosexual is, however, to surround a major part of his self-identification with, if not feelings of guilt and shame, at least, unease. The major consequence of the legal milieu is the encouragement of covertness, and although as we have seen, the effects of duplicity are variegated, nowhere did we find them affecting the homosexual's adjustment in any *positive* way. Such phenomena as sex in public restrooms, the anonymity of homosexual relationships, the ghettoization of the homosexual community, all are partly rooted in the criminalization of this form of sexual expression.

As well as its effect upon the homosexual, anti-sexual laws, as many commentators have noted, also extract a price from the heterosexual majority. This can be seen in the arguments put forward by the proponents of homosexual law reform;[3] for example, the intrusion upon the liberty of citizens by interfering with what the Wolfenden Committee called the "realm of private morality and immorality" which, they bluntly state, is "not the law's business." Associated with this is what some lawyers have seen as a constitutional issue, that the sodomy laws exceed the legitimate police powers of the state and that they attempt to sustain a morality that has a religious basis.[4]

The sodomy laws, themselves virtually unenforceable, are perhaps not as important as the laws under which most homosexuals are actually

---

siderations, i.e. that it is immoral to discriminate against minorities. Morality aside, our view is based upon more *practical* considerations—how to change people regardless of the goal of that change. This is not to say, however, that we do not share the moral concern of these other commentators.
3. See, for example, *Report of the Committee on Homosexual Offenses and Prostitution,* London: HMSO, 1957 (The Wolfenden Report); Edwin M. Schur, *Crimes Without Victims,* Englewood Cliffs, N.J.: Prentice-Hall, 1965; Gilbert M. Cantor, "The Need for Homosexual Law Reform," in Ralph W. Weltge (ed.), *The Same Sex,* Philadelphia: The Pilgrim Press, 1969, pp. 83–94; Sanford H. Kadish, "The Crisis of Overcriminalization," *Annals of the American Academy of Political and Social Science* (November 1967), pp. 157–70.
4. Cantor, *op. cit.*

prosecuted.[5] As we have seen, the police usually resort to a variety of other laws concerning soliciting, lewd conduct, etc., against homosexuals. In order to obtain evidence, the police have relied upon such devices as entrapment by decoys, peepholes and one-way mirrors in public restrooms which, to say the least, degrades the ideals of the law and law enforcement and makes for police corruption. In addition, the attempted legal control of homosexuals seems a waste of the time and resources of law enforcement agencies. Our remarks, of course, do not apply to those sexual acts (homosexual or heterosexual) which involve force, fraud, intimidation or which involve minors (when such a group is reasonably defined). As to solicitation, the New York stipulation of a citizen complaint is a step in the right direction, although we see no reason why homosexual solicitation should be a matter for the criminal law.

Finally, as well as the effect that the law has on the homosexual's personal identity, its consequences seem even more serious with regard to his public identity. Not only being convicted of a homosexual offense but merely being arrested is usually enough for one to receive the official and often the public label of "homosexual." Many employers, both public and private, ask on application forms whether the applicant has ever been arrested. If the answer is "yes," the employer can check court records to find the specific offense. In those cases where the arrests do not lead to conviction, arrest records should be expunged. Otherwise, the employment chances of many persons are unjustly limited, and given the prejudice against homosexuals, such records make it even more difficult for them to get a job.[6]

In conclusion, therefore, it appears that laws directed at homosexuals are inefficient, immoral, and open to abuse. Furthermore, we would suggest that fears of the negative consequences of repealing such laws are not supported by either logic or data and that the burden of proof as to such consequences should be on the shoulders of those who insist upon such laws.[7] As we have seen from our study of two societies which do not criminalize consenting adult homosexuality, such a demonstration would be difficult to obtain.

5. Nonetheless, it still seems difficult to get them repealed. In October, 1971, the California legislature defeated a bill (the "Brown Bill") that would have legalized all forms of sexual behavior between consenting adults in private.

6. The Mattachine Society of New York's legislative program for 1971 proposes that it be a misdemeanor for an employer to ask a job applicant if he has ever been arrested. They also propose the same for anyone divulging information about persons acquitted of any crime. They recommend sealing records to this end. Another proposal makes bonding companies which refuse to bond a homosexual, guilty of a misdemeanor. *Mattachine Times,* November/December, 1970, p. 15.

7. Some of the arguments for retaining laws against homosexuality are considered by the Wolfenden Committee, *op. cit.,* pp. 21 ff., and Schur, *op. cit.,* pp. 107 ff.

The Federal Government.   Homosexuals at present are banned from federal employment. The basis for such exclusion is a Senate report in the 1950's at the height of the Communist scare which claimed that homosexuals were unsuitable for government employment.[8] Their unsuitability was supposedly due to their lack of emotional stability, their attempts to seduce "normal" persons, their "corrosive" influence on other employees, their attempts to hire other homosexuals for government jobs, and their possible risks to security. Although the report has no legal power, its conclusions became part of Civil Service policy, which resulted in the removal of suspected homosexuals from government employment and the exclusion of any other homosexuals from federal employment.[9]

Such exclusion of homosexuals from federal employment on such dubious grounds clearly represents discrimination. Furthermore, although there may be truth in some of the allegations—e.g. security risks —what is often overlooked is that the same logic regarding vulnerability to blackmail could be applied to others, such as heterosexuals involved extramaritally, and that the government's attitude itself contributes to the potential for this problem, e.g. by firing homosexuals if their homosexuality is discovered.[10]

Non-Federal Government and Private Employment.   Other employers may not have formal statements of exclusion for homosexuals, although, as often is the case for blacks, informal procedures are sometimes used to discriminate against them. In many states the teaching profession is closed to homosexuals, and in the medical, dental, and legal professions arrests for homosexual acts (regardless of conviction) can lead to a person being denied, or having withdrawn, his professional license. Again the situation is one of arbitrary exclusion and dismissal from employment, usually with no recourse to a hearing. With private employers the situation is no better. Even in such a relatively liberal city as New York it has been observed that:

> It is currently the practice of many companies located in New York to refuse jobs to homosexuals, supposedly to "protect company morale" when,

8. U.S. Senate. Committee on Expenditures in the Executive Departments, Subcommittee on Investigations. Interim Report: "Employment of Homosexuals and Other Sex Perverts in Government." Senate Document No. 241. December, 1950.
9. See, for example, a letter written by John W. Macy, Jr., former chairman of the Civil Service Commission to the Mattachine Society of Washington, February 25, 1966, reprinted in Lewis I. Maddocks, "The Law and the Church vs. the Homosexual," in Ralph W. Weltge (ed.), *op. cit.*, p. 101. For a review of some of the government's current policies and practices over this question, see, Frank Kameny, "My Sex Life is None of My Government's Goddamned Business," *Vector* (October 1970), pp. 10–12.
10. For a convincing argument against federal employment policies, see, William Parker, *Homosexuals and Employment*, San Francisco, 1970, pp. 13–19. Also note that the N.I.M.H. Task Force on Homosexuality proposes similar recommendations.

in reality, the applicant is rejected for being homosexual per se in spite of his qualifications and mode of behavior.

Employers use several devices to discover whether an applicant is homosexual: special arrangements with employment agencies in which the agencies use a code to indicate whether, to their knowledge, the job seeker is homosexual; a request on the application form for the release of draft records, which disclose any references to homosexual behavior; a request for information regarding the draft classification of applicants who have not served in the military, and the marital status of all persons seeking employment; and employers sometimes contact private agencies whose sole purpose is to gather information on applicants in order to determine anything which might not be in what the firm considers its best interests.[11]

With such a threat to their work lives, most homosexuals, therefore, feel forced into evasion and lying when it comes to choosing or maintaining themselves in an occupation. As we have seen [in our study] the more prestigious the occupation, the more the felt need for secrecy. In such fertile soil as this, blackmailers reap a rich harvest. Other than perhaps disclosure to family members, the threat to employment is probably the most serious consequence of being publicly labeled as homosexual.

The Military. Another source of institutionalized discrimination against homosexuals occurs in the armed forces. In line with federal employment policies, homosexuals are excluded from the military and for many of the same stated reasons—unsuitability, being a threat to good order and discipline, and being a security risk.[12] Questions about homosexual behavior until recently were asked at induction.[13] If a homosexual admitted his sexual orientation, he could not serve, and furthermore, his homosexuality became a matter of official record which could become known to others. If he did not admit to being homosexual, he was forced into duplicity and ran the risk of being discovered while in the military and separated with a less than honorable discharge. This kind of possibility exists for all homosexuals in the military. A bad discharge makes homosexuals ineligible for veterans benefits. It also means that their future employment can be threatened since discharge papers are often asked for by prospective employers. Discrimination in this situation is clear, not only in the manner in which homosexuals are processed

11. *Mattachine Times,* January, 1971, p. 1.
12. For an account of military policy and the way homosexuals are treated in the armed forces, see Colin J. Williams and Martin S. Weinberg, *Homosexuals and the Military: A Study of Less than Honorable Discharge,* New York: Harper & Row, 1971.
13. The question, "Have you ever had or have you now, homosexual tendencies?" which for the last 20 years every draftee has had to answer during his pre-induction physical exam (under penalty of perjury) has recently been eliminated. The law still provides for automatic exemption, however, for the homosexual who declares himself and can prove it.

by the military, but also in the fact that prior military record plays little part in the separation of homosexuals from the military. In the vast majority of cases, separation is with a less than honorable discharge.[14]

Religion. As we stated at the beginning of . . . [our] book, religious dogma has played a large part in initiating and sustaining negative definitions of homosexuality in the Western world. Today, religion in general has less influence on people's lives in this country, although, of course, many of our customs and moralities are based upon unrecognized religious codes.

It is our opinion that, while not directly of primary importance, religion is important enough to be considered. This is because those persons who are most negative toward homosexuals are often religious, and because religious institutions are still important enough to become catalysts for positive change. One target for change should be the clergy. By changing religious perspectives it is possible, if clergy make an effort, to have this change filter down to the laity. Clergy should, then, help to dissipate the conception of "homosexual as sinner."

As well as ministering to their own congregations, churches can affect the attitudes of others through such pronouncements. The Unitarian's National Assembly in 1970 rejected the "sickness theory" of homosexuality and endorsed homosexual civil rights. In practicing what they preach, they called for a special effort on the part of their members to assist homosexuals and accept homosexuals in their ministry. The United Presbyterians and Lutherans in national assembly also have endorsed homosexual law reform yet still define homosexuality as a sin (the former denomination also seeing it as a sickness). While it is difficult to determine the influence of such pronouncements, at the very least they deny a religious basis for such intolerance and can be of some consolation to the religious homosexual.

The preceding institutional areas seem to us to be major targets for change because of their support of a moral meaning of homosexuality that leads to grave injustices for a large minority. In the long run, however, it is the attitude of rejection, fear and contempt, and the latent hostility in everyday encounters that must be changed as well as these institutions. It is these feelings—the informal elements of social reaction—that our results suggest must be changed, although obviously it is difficult to do so even when their structural supports have been eliminated. Their resistance to change may be due to various factors about which we can only speculate: viz., the psychological function that prejudice has for some persons, the sociological role of minority groups for

14. Colin J. Williams and Martin S. Weinberg, "The Military: Its Processing of Accused Homosexuals," *American Behavioral Scientist,* 14 (November/December 1970), pp. 203–17.

majority groups, the erotophobia of American society, and so forth. But whatever the basis for prejudice, attempts should be made to combat anti-homosexual attitudes directly. The following suggestions are offered in this regard.

Sex Education.   Sex education courses usually restrict themselves to heterosexual behavior and reproduction. It would seem that the introduction of information on homosexuality in the context of a valid and *non-moralistic* framework, and as a not uncommon form of sexual expression, would affect attitudes in a positive way. While research in other areas of prejudice suggests that the impact of education is limited,[15] it may help to dispel falsehoods about a phenomenon too often presented as sick, alien and bizarre.

Such sex education courses should include the education of adults. It should be compulsory for professionals and others who have much to do with homosexuals. These include the police, physicians, and especially psychiatrists who have played a major role in perpetuating negative views of homosexuality.

The Mass Media.   The Task Force on Homosexuality noted the need to study the effects of the portrayal of homosexuality in literature, drama, films, etc., on the public. At present, the media seem to sustain prevailing stereotypes of the homosexual. The stereotype of the male homosexual as effeminate, flighty, and amusing often appears on television. Motion pictures, directed at a more selective audience, have only just begun to treat homosexuality in a more objective manner. Before the late 1960's, motion pictures, to quote one reviewer, used homosexuality "as a sensational third act revelation, after which the character discovered to be homosexual must obligingly commit suicide."[16] Whereas television has emphasized the effeminate aspect of the homosexual stereotype, movies have focused on homosexuals' sickness and guilt.

How a more balanced picture of homosexuals can be gained through the media is difficult to determine. The greater openness that charac-

---

15. For example, Stember reviewed a number of studies of the relationship between education and ethnic and racial prejudice and concluded that,

> Its chief effect is to reduce traditional provincialism—to counteract the notion that members of minorities are strange creatures with exotic ways, and to diminish fear of casual personal contact. But the limits of acceptance are sharply drawn; while legal equality is supported, full social participation is not.

Charles H. Stember, *Education and Attitude Change,* New York: Institute of Human Relations Press, 1961, p. 171.

16. Gene D. Phillips, "Homosexuality in the Movies," *Sexual Behavior,* 1 (May 1971), p. 21.

terizes movies today may make for more representative films. For example, a character's homosexuality might be presented in such a way that it is secondary to his other attributes. A Western movie might explore the role of homosexuality in a society devoid of females. With regard to T.V., the presence of homosexuals on talk shows might counterbalance the stereotypes provided in the comedy shows. The activities of ethnic minority groups against the dissemination of stereotypes in the media have provided a model that homosexual militants have copied; what their success will be remains to be seen.

In general, however, research on the effects of mass media does not provide great hope for changing attitudes.[17] Such research has shown that people avoid perspectives contrary to their own, either by simply not exposing themselves to such messages or by evading their implications through misinterpretation of their content. Such changes as we have suggested, however, could be of use in supporting the attitudes of those favorable to a more human treatment of the homosexual, making it more difficult for those who hold unfavorable attitudes to express them.[18]

Other Public Support.   Research in changing attitudes has considered the *source* of attitudes to be an important variable in attitude change.[19] Thus, for example, the more credible, attractive, and powerful the source, the more persuasive its effects. It would appear that if persons who are credible, attractive and powerful present more favorable attitudes towards homosexuals, then other people's attitudes can be modified.

In terms of credibility, professional persons such as physicians, psychiatrists and social scientists could be effective. As we have suggested, greater sex education in medical schools could provide physicians with up-to-date knowledge on homosexuality. Psychiatrists seem to be increasingly moving away from the "sickness" model of homosexuality. Social scientists, too, are moving away from seeing homosexuality as intrinsically a "social problem" to viewing the social reaction toward homosexuals as the major problem. If indeed the professions are moving toward a view of homosexuality as a non-pathological variant of sexual

17. See, for example, Arthur R. Cohen, *Attitude Change and Social Influence,* New York: Basic Books, 1964.
18. We have given less attention to the written media here than perhaps is warranted. We do agree, however, with the Wolfenden Committee's proposal that the press report homosexual offenses or homosexual conduct in such a way as to avoid the public labeling of those involved. *Committee on Homosexual Offenses and Prostitution, op. cit.,* p. 78.
19. For a summary of source variables and their effects, see William J. McGuire, "The Nature of Attitudes and Attitude Change," in Gardner Lindzey and Elliot Aronson (eds.), *The Handbook of Social Psychology,* Reading, Mass.: Addison-Wesley, 1969, esp. pp. 177–200.

expression, efforts must be made to get their memberships to communicate these views to the general public.[20]

As to "attractive" sources, the situation is more subjective—people differ widely in the persons to whom they are attracted. Attractiveness has been seen to involve similarity (seeing the source as similar to oneself), familiarity (amount of contact), and liking, the underlying motivation for the subject being to "enhance his self-esteem through his identification with the source."[21] Sources that might be tapped to provide favorable attitudes toward homosexuals could include persons from the entertainment world or the sports world. Consider, for example, a professional football player admitting to being homosexual, and its effect on homosexual stereotypes, or an entertainer plugging homosexual civil rights in a commercial spot as many do for ethnic minorities.

Finally, the power of the source is important, perhaps the most important element, in changing attitudes. For example, if the power and influence of the government were to be used to encourage favorable attitudes toward homosexuals, it could be tremendously effective. Politicians in Great Britain have championed the rights of homosexuals despite widespread lack of public support. Perhaps currently an important gesture would be for the President to acknowledge and support the recommendations of the Task Force Report on Homosexuality.

So far we have suggested that the heterosexual majority might help improve the situation of the homosexual minority by removing discrimination and trying to change anti-homosexual attitudes. A third strategy should be to give *positive* support to homosexuals to live their lives without any problems. Not only should opportunities toward the integration of homosexuals into the wider society be provided, but support should also be given to specifically homosexual institutions. What comes to mind is the type of governmental support given to homosexuals in the Netherlands, on the one hand, and the type of organization achieved by C.O.C. [the major homophile organization in the Netherlands], on the other. This, we feel, would be facilitated by a reconceptualization of homosexuals as a minority group, and by the acceptance of minority life styles as part of the wider society.[22] Until such tolerance is translated

---

20. Unfortunately, "experts" and "professionals" in the area of sexual behavior are often self appointed. This is problematic when their popularity is high but their knowledge is low. A case in point is the collage of misinformation and stereotyped thinking about homosexuality found in the best seller of David Reuben, *Everything You Always Wanted to Know About Sex (But Were Afraid to Ask),* New York: McKay Company, 1969.

21. McGuire, *op. cit.,* p. 187.

22. See the essays by Kameny and Hacker in Edward Sagarin (ed.), *The Other Minorities,* Waltham, Mass.: Ginn & Co., 1971. Similar proposals are made by Grey and West. Anthony Grey and Donald J. West, "Homosexuals: New Law But No New Deal," *New Society* (March 27, 1969).

into a wider acceptance, the costs of rejection, too, must be mitigated by providing special aid for homosexuals and their particular problems; e.g. a Minorities Board such as exists in the Netherlands and which deals with the particular problems of *all* Dutch minorities.

By way of summary, we conclude that changing social reactions toward homosexuals is no easy task. As far as people's attitudes are concerned, it is best to work toward changing them indirectly through changing those institutions that sustain negative views of homosexuality by their discriminatory behavior. Prime targets for change have been outlined. Nonetheless, attempts to change attitudes directly should be attempted wherever possible, and various strategies have been suggested to this end.

Whatever the fate of such suggestions, in the long run the social situation of the homosexual will probably benefit most from general changes occurring in the wider society. One of these is the increasing acceptance of minority groups and different life styles by the younger generation. This generation, which grew up during the fight for racial equality and discussions over the dress and life style of the hippie movement, despite the increasing conservatism of growing older, will, we feel, bring about a significant increment in acceptance when it comes to occupy positions of power and influence in society. The homosexual will no doubt benefit. . . . [In the manuscript from which this was excerpted, the discussion now turns to more of a "value conflict" perspective and how in the long run the destiny of the homosexual will probably lie in his own efforts.]

QUESTIONS FOR DISCUSSION

1. What are your positions regarding the legalization of marihuana and abortion? Is it, in your opinion, "unconstitutional" for either or both to be illegal? What issues underlie the question of their constitutionality?

2. Based on the Grinspoon and Schur arguments regarding marihuana and abortion, does the legalization of opiates make sense to you? Explain your position.

3. With what aspects of Laing's position regarding schizophrenia do you agree and disagree? What concrete steps for dealing with "schizophrenics" might follow from Laing's argument?

4. How do you feel about Weinberg and Williams' position regarding neutralization of the homosexual label? Are these suggestions relevant to other problems? For example, do you think these suggestions could be combined with those from the Marshall Program to help in the rehabilitation of persons who serve time in correctional institutions?

5. Compare the labeling perspective with the value conflict perspective in the way problems are conceptualized and solutions suggested. How are they complementary? How are they in conflict?

6. Do you think redefinition of situations and behaviors as not being problems as suggested by the labeling perspective is a useful solution, or is it simply denying problems which people should be actively working to correct? Explain your position.

7. Do you think the labeling perspective is useful for suggesting solutions to social problems in general or only for very specific types of problems? Explain your position.

8. Summarize what you think are the major strengths and weaknesses of the labeling perspective and the solutions it suggests.

SELECTED REFERENCES

Freidson, Eliot, "Disability as Social Deviance," in Marvin B. Sussman (ed.), *Sociology and Rehabilitation,* Washington, D. C.: American Sociological Association, 1966, pp. 71–99.

With physical disability as a case in point, Freidson delineates the role of labeling by official agencies. The labeling framework of the agency is described as producing the size of the "problem population" and consequently the greater or lesser sense of urgency regarding the problem and its solution. The nature of its treatment is also described as following from the agency's labeling framework.

Green, Richard, "Homosexuality as a Mental Illness," *International Journal of Psychiatry,* 10 (March 1972), pp. 77–128.

An examination of homosexuality from biological, psychological, and sociological standpoints raises thoughtful questions regarding its being labeled as abnormal. The article is followed by retorts from half a dozen professionals known for their work in the area of homosexuality.

Ryan, William, *Blaming the Victim,* New York: Pantheon Books, 1971.

Ryan examines the dynamics and consequences of teachers' labeling students according to academic potential and motivation.

Szasz, Thomas S., "The Ethics of Addiction," *International Journal of Psychiatry,* 10 (March 1972), pp. 51–76.

Szasz's article and the replies to it by three experts in the field of drug addiction focus on what underlies the labels applied to drug use. The "politics" of drug prohibition is examined.

III THE PROSPECTS

7 THE MOSAIC OF SOLUTIONS

When violated expectations are constituted as a social problem, laymen, sociologists, and professional problem-solvers begin thinking about them, using a perspective and often devising solutions which their perspective suggests to them. Sometimes solutions are quite deliberately formulated from a perspective, as when sociologists plan a program for the rehabilitation of juvenile delinquents. Sometimes, however, solutions evolve quite naturally in response to persistent social troubles. Thus, for example, leaders of the women's liberation movement were not conscious that they were analyzing their situation from the value conflict perspective. Nonetheless, we can analyze their protest in terms of this perspective. The point is that whenever an attempt is made to solve a social problem, a perspective is at work either explicitly or implicitly.

This book provides a framework for analyzing social problems and their solutions by setting forth a grammar of solutions and presenting twenty proposed solutions whose syntaxes are clarified through perspectival analysis. In what follows, we summarize and conclude with a synopsis of the perspectives, their major themes, their interrelationships, and the conditions of their future uses.

A REVIEW

Social pathology. Ultimately, persons create problems for the society at large. Suffering broad hereditary taint or massive moral defect as a result of poorly regulated impulses, such persons perform acts which disrupt society and call attention to the enormous gap between their own conduct and the moral norms and expectations of the established social order. Such actions provoke moral indignation. A campaign is mounted to correct such persons or to restrain them. Later, this perspective pinpoints the pathology in the society. Through overregulation of people, brought on mainly through institutional hypertrophy, society dehumanizes people and their relationships. If change is to come about, all persons must re-educate themselves as human beings who seek a humane social existence.

301

Social disorganization.   Because of culture conflict, normlessness, or breakdown of rules, situations do not meet expectations. For the most part, these failures in expectations come about because of rapid social change that throws the social system into a state of disequilibrium. It is possible to reduce problems by slowing down the rate of change and developing a clear, consistent, and effective set of rules, thus bringing all parts of the system into adjustment.

Value conflict.   Groups have different interests and values. Awareness of the difference comes about when the groups come into abrasive contact with regard to rights, goods, or opportunities. The issue is highlighted, and polarization and organization are sought. A struggle ensues and both sides suffer damages. The struggle subsides as the more powerful side, or the one that has made more enduring coalitions with other groups, wins.

Deviant behavior.   A social problem may center on persons engaged in a pattern of rule violation, e.g. theft. Rule breakers adopt illicit means for gaining valued ends, usually with the support of persons similarly situated. Once the tolerance limits of victims, potential victims, and moral enterpreneurs have been reached, strong social controls are marshalled against the deviant persons. Change then comes about by placing the rule breaker in primary group contact with similarly situated persons who uphold conventional norms, and by opening up legitimate routes to socially approved goals.

Labeling.   Key persons in agencies of social control, interest groups, or social classes judge a certain situation to be a social problem. Seeking to control problems, such judges succeed in popularizing their definition. This definition, however, often creates even greater problems. Solutions lie in the redefinition of the situation. The result is that situations, previously defined as problems, are now judged to be acceptable and the people involved in them are no longer subject to sanction or stigma.

THEMES

The papers included in this volume reveal the following themes in the solutions for social problems which each of the perspectives prescribes.

Social pathology.   In the early years of American sociology, social pathologists were both optimistic and reformist. They assumed natural law and the notion of social and moral progress. Taking all of this for granted, their concern was to help those who seemed to have fallen by the wayside of the mainstream of progress. Social and moral progress was thought to rest ultimately on allowing the best to rise in the struggle for social existence. Consequently, those who lost out in the struggle did so ultimately because of a lack of moral fiber. Such persons needed to be retailored to fit the moral order.

An examination of latter day social pathologists reveals an inversion of this stance. The solution remains constant, namely, education in the broadest sense. Now, however, the social order itself is seen as immoral and inhuman. To avoid crisis, people must do something drastic to realize themselves as human beings. Only in this fashion can a more humane order result. Consequently, it is possible to say that the major theme of current social pathology solutions is the development of *humanism*.

Social disorganization.   As a consequence of science, a set of rules for discovering reality and an enormous growth of technology in almost every sphere of life was made possible. William F. Ogburn noted that men changed material culture quicker than nonmaterial culture (the sphere of rules, symbols, beliefs, myths, etc.). Thus, social and technical organization exist in a dynamic equilibrium. Since technology advances more rapidly than social organization, cultural lag follows. The metaphor of the machine extends to the definition and solution of the problem. To solve social problems, this perspective suggests restoring balance between social and technical elements, between these parts of society. It therefore seems reasonable to suggest that the major theme of any solution derivable from this perspective is *mechanics*.

Value conflict.   Divergent interests and values make conflicts inevitable. Ultimately, conflicts are resolved in favor of the person or the group that amasses and applies the most power. The value conflict perspective recognizes that power is a resource centered on organization. The principal unit of power in society is, moreover, not the person but the group. Thus, as persons become aware of their common interests and values, they may band together and engage in political struggle as a way of solving social problems. Thus, the theme of value conflict solutions is *solidarity*.

Deviant behavior.   Many social problems revolve around behavioral deviations—patterns of seeking to gain what everyone wants in ways that few people find acceptable. The deviant behavior perspective suggests that causes and solutions will be found in social structure and social process. As a result, this perspective stresses a redistribution of life chances, of social and cultural opportunities. Only if persons formerly well established in deviant roles have a chance to make more frequent contact with legitimate role-models and a chance to behave in legitimate ways, will their old ways disappear. There is a kind of egalitarianism involved in this perspective in its concern for the redistribution of opportunities for learning conformist behavior and achieving cultural goals. Also, because of the terms in which the solution is formulated, we believe it fair to characterize the central theme of the deviant behavior solution as *opportunity*.

Labeling.   Groups in a plural society constantly negotiate and renegotiate social reality. Determining what behaviors and situations are problems is part of this process. The same behaviors and situations in a different segment of the society, or in a different society, may be disregarded or defined as acceptable. Much, then, depends upon who is the "judge" of social problems. Oftentimes, as the labeling perspective points out, judges change, and as they change so may the definition of the situation. Similarly, the license to control may pass from one agency to another, as when criminal conduct is redefined as a symptom of mental illness. In yet other circumstances, the license to control may be taken away entirely, in which case it is possible to say that the behaviors and situations have been secularized, to be treated as matters of fact in the social settings of their occurrence. Over and over this theme recurs in the solutions the labeling perspective prescribes for social problems. As a result, its central theme may be called *redefinition*.

Each of these shorthand phrases is intended to capture the central idea repeated as different writers suggest solutions to assorted social problems from each of these perspectives.

THE INTERRELATIONSHIP OF PERSPECTIVES

Although the student may have received the idea that the same perspective is necessarily employed in a problem's analysis and proposals for its solution, this is not the case. It does not have to follow, for example, that because a problem has been analyzed from the social disorganization perspective, the solution to the problem must also employ that perspective. The solution may be derived from another perspective. Some examples of possible combinations follow.

Poverty.   Here we can combine social pathology with value conflict. In the early form of social pathology, poor people were so by reason of their own indolence, improvidence, and intemperateness. The modern version finds poverty a dehumanizing and immoral feature of a sick society. The solution according to value conflict is to band together with others in the same situation, form a coalition, and protest against the inequities of the situation. Bayard Rustin provides an excellent example of such a combination of perspectives in his paper on poverty and the need for coalition.[1]

Drug use. Here we can illustrate a combination of the deviant behavior and labeling perspectives. Use of illegal drugs may be analyzed in terms of differential association and learning of definitions favorable to such a breach of criminal law. The same analyst may go on, however, to propose that drug use not be defined as a social problem unless it clearly victimizes the user or others.

Prison conditions. It is possible to combine the analysis of social pathology with the solution of social disorganization. Thus, a case could be made from the early form of the pathology perspective that the bulk of inmates are markedly deviant persons by reason of socialization failure and the like; or from the contemporary form of this perspective, that prison conditions are inhumane. In any case, many aspects of social life inside prisons today constitute a grave social problem. According to many penologists, these problems could be markedly reduced if a new set of rules were both established and clarified so as to restore equilibrium.

The problem of academia. A final example combines social disorganization and value conflict. Students may resent the social disorganization of their university (e.g. rules regarding requirements continually changing, "cultural lag," apparent conflicts in rules, a sense of normlessness regarding the rules) and employ value conflict techniques to pressure the university into more effective organization.

A social problem also can engender consideration from all five perspectives. This constitutes yet another form of interrelation of perspectives. Application of the five perspectives to the problem of welfare illustrates the point. Currently, some 14 million Americans are on welfare. This is a social problem of considerable magnitude. A host of values are threatened. Traditional incentives to work, individual and civil rights, freedom, justice, and charity are among the values involved. Welfare is a serious social problem with great economic, moral, and political overtones. In view of all this, different groups have formulated the problem from a number of different points of view and have suggested solutions in keeping with these several viewpoints. Below is an outline of proposals for welfare reform *actually advanced by citizens or government agencies.*

1. Bayard Rustin, "Minority Groups: Development of the Individual," in William Ewald, Jr., *Environment and Policy: The Next Fifty Years,* Bloomington, Indiana: Indiana University Press, 1968, Chap. 1.

Social pathology.   According to the early pathology perspective, until the poor are educated to the moral values of those who help them, no escape from poverty seems possible. Most recently, proposals have come forth which imply that the progeny of the poor will also continue into adult poverty. To prevent this outcome, some have suggested that poor families be paid not to reproduce or that mothers on welfare be sterilized.

Social disorganization.   New York City's Department of Social Welfare is a good example of how system overload leads to social disorganization. The department, a $2 billion welfare bureaucracy of 27,000 employees, had a backlog of unprocessed forms costing upward of $20 million a year, long delays in catching clients who cash duplicate checks (after claiming the originals were lost), and high rates of worker inefficiency. To reduce system overload, a new executive director instituted quota systems to improve worker efficiency, overtime to reduce the paper backlog, and a computer system to speed up identification of duplicate check cashers.[2]

Value conflict.   For most Americans, to be on welfare is a status loss. Consequently, many Americans do not apply for welfare assistance even when they are entitled to it. When they do apply, because of the stigma of welfare, they assume they have few rights whatsoever. To remedy this situation, George Wiley, a Ph.D. in chemistry, organized welfare mothers into an organization called the National Welfare Rights Organization. N.W.R.O. has become a militant group that publicizes to all citizens the conditions under which they are entitled to welfare assistance, and vigorously defends the rights of all members of the organization.

Deviant behavior.   Several states, among them Delaware, Massachusetts, and New York, have required that welfare recipients come to state employment offices to pick up their checks. Before obtaining these checks, however, they must signify their willingness to accept any employment. Should work be found for them, they must take the job. Otherwise, they will become ineligible for welfare assistance. These proposals seek to strengthen the notion that a welfare client is a deviant role and to make work opportunities available.

Labeling.   Some years ago, the Mayor of Newburgh, New York, instituted a drive against what he considered an alarming increase in the number of poor people who were on the welfare rolls.[3] First, he implied

2. "Welfare Fraud: The Backlash," *Newsweek* (January 31, 1971), pp. 58–59.
3. Edgar May, *The Wasted Americans,* New York: Signet Books, 1964.

the bulk of welfare recipients were lazy, shiftless, and members of what have been called the disreputable poor. Second, he raised a cry about the possibility of extensive welfare chiseling. Third, he required that the names of all persons receiving welfare assistance be posted in a number of public places. Attacking, strengthening, and then publicizing the stigmatized welfare label, he actually succeeded for a time in reducing the number of persons on Newburgh's welfare rolls.

The foregoing sets of examples suggest that perspectives can be interrelated in at least three ways: by combination, by comparison, and by iatrogenesis. In combination, one perspective defines, while a second solves. This relationship synthesizes possibilities and opens up a number of differing ways of conceiving problems and devising solutions. Combination is important if only that it can unfreeze some routine solutions which do not so much resolve the problem as standardize its occurrence. In comparison, many perspectives are applied as a way of coping with a social problem, as in the welfare illustration. This allows for attacking different aspects of the problem, and for comparative analysis of various recipes and their outcomes. The policy-studies movement may very likely produce an applied science of social intervention; if so, comparative analysis will most likely be one of its important methods of research. In iatrogenesis, a problem defined and solved in accordance with one perspective, results in a host of other problems defined by other perspectives. One of the best examples of iatrogenesis in American history is the Volstead Act, the Eighteenth Amendment to the Constitution. In prohibiting the manufacture and sale of alcoholic beverages, the action of Congress caused more rather than less people to drink. In turn, prohibition created a demand for alcoholic beverages which gangsters supplied, fostered the development of organized crime and political and police corruption, and led to the death or blindness of many people who drank methyl alcohol rather than ethyl alcohol. The solution to the problem of drinking, drunkenness, and alcoholism was couched in terms of value conflict: vocal members of a declining middle class composed of rural-oriented white Anglo-Saxon Protestants uniting against the custom of public drinking which numerous immigrants had brought to this country. Their solution produced problems in terms of the perspectives of social disorganization and deviant behavior.

In reading proposed solutions to social problems, the reader should examine the possibilities of combining perspectives when studying a given social problem, raise the question in his mind of whether a comparative study is at all feasible, and, perhaps most important, look at the possibilities that the proposed solution might create more problems than it solves.

THE FUTURE

In conclusion, this book acquaints students with sociological frame-works currently used to understand social problems and their possible solutions. In each of the five perspectives it has illustrated what their approach could be to particular problems and the form of the solution for which they may call. The book has tried to set forth the premises underlying their metaphors and arguments, and has called attention to what is entailed in seeking solutions according to the recipes implied by these perspectives. The book can be characterized as a sociological essay on the assumptions of sociological perspectives on social problems.

Whether testing theories, applying social knowledge to problems, or criticizing society for failure to fulfill its promises, awareness of these assumptions is helpful. Of course, this book is but an introduction to a complex field. The sociology of solutions will very likely engage the attention of sociologists even more in the years to come. In these last paragraphs, however, we would like to make some guesses on the future conditions under which the various perspectives will be used.

Order and conflict have been two basic and interlocking themes in sociological work. Indeed, these movements of sociological thought parallel the changing fortunes of society. As society moves closer to crisis, conflict theory becomes more popular. Perspectives making implicit or explicit assumptions of such conflict will more often come into play in thinking about social problems and their solutions. For example, in periods of heightened conflict, problems of deviance become problems of politics.[4] Groups band together to alter accepted definitions of their identity. Changes in these definitions ultimately demand changes in the distribution of power of those who make the definitions by which the society lives.

Under conditions of decreased social conflict, however, order theory becomes more popular. Perspectives that make explicit or implicit assumptions built around a model of social order will more often become influential for analyzing social problems and formulating remedial action.

There is a distinction, however, between the conditions under which a given style of thought comes into being and gains popularity and the conditions under which it is put to use. Consequently, we offer this paradox in conclusion. Conflict perspectives may be adopted by more people, sociologists and nonsociologists alike, yet be applied less fully.

---

4. For a useful discussion of this shift, see Irving Louis Horowitz and Martin Liebowitz, "Social Deviance and Political Marginality: Toward a Redefinition of the Relation between Sociology and Politics," *Social Problems,* 15 (Winter 1968), pp. 280–96.

By contrast, order perspectives may be adopted by fewer people, yet be applied more fully. The reasoning behind this notion is simple.

Conflict ideas are close to the ideas of everyday life. Moreover, conflict draws segments of people together and crystallizes their sentiments. At the same time, conflict does not provide a basis for cohesive and harmonious relations in a complex, urban-industrial society. Thus, when it comes to establishing routines to cope with social problems on a continuing basis, the conceptions of resocialization and the construction of effective social guidelines are more likely to be given attention.

QUESTIONS FOR DISCUSSION

1. Now that you are familiar with all five perspectives, which one(s) do you prefer for analyzing and proposing solutions for social problems? Does the usefulness of each perspective vary with the particular social problem you are trying to analyze and solve? Can you analyze a social problem that concerns you and formulate a coherent policy to deal with it along the lines suggested by one of these perspectives?

2. Consider some social problem currently discussed in the mass media or among your acquaintances. In terms of the five perspectives, which is reflected in the way the problem and its solution are conceived by each of the following: you, your parents, experts on the subject, newsmen, legislators, the people directly involved in the problem situation, churches, people of different ages, people of different class statuses? What might account for differences in the perspectives of these different groups?

3. To what extent do the five perspectives overlap? Can one perspective be seen as more or less subsuming any of the others?

4. Using some social problem that interests you (except welfare, which the authors have already treated in the text), discuss how the problem can be analyzed and solutions formulated from each of the five perspectives. What are the major differences between the five analyses and solutions? Which perspective seems most fruitful to you? Or would an eclectic approach using elements from the different proposals be preferable? Analyze the problem combining analyses from various perspectives with proposed solutions from other perspectives.

SELECTED REFERENCES

Colfax, J. David and Jack L. Roach (eds.), *Radical Sociology,* New York: Basic Books, 1971.

These papers maintain that solutions to major social problems will not come about until there is a radical transformation of society. Sociologists may make a major contribution to these solutions if they will first radicalize themselves. The change requires abandonment of scientific objectivity.

Etzioni, Amitai, *The Active Society: A Theory of Societal and Political Processes,* New York: The Free Press, 1968.

Etzioni develops a complex view on how a society can define and solve its own problems.

Freeman, Howard E. and Clarence C. Sherwood, *Social Research and Social Policy,* Englewood Cliffs, N.J.: Prentice-Hall, 1970.

Freeman and Sherwood provide a brief statement of how to link problem-solving policy with systematic research on the consequences of such intervention.

Lazarsfeld, Paul F., William H. Sewell, and Harold L. Wilensky (eds.), *The Uses of Sociology,* New York: Basic Books, 1967.

This collection assesses potential and actual applications of sociological knowledge to the solution of social problems and problems associated with such applications.

Lynd, Robert S., *Knowledge for What?* Princeton: Princeton University Press, 1939.

* Lynd says social scientists can maintain their ethics and their objectivity if and only if they produce knowledge that helps in solving social problems.

Reynolds, Larry T. and Janice M. Reynolds (eds.), *The Sociology of Sociology: Analysis and Criticism of the Thought, Research, and Ethical Folkways of Sociology and Its Practitioners,* New York: David McKay, 1970.

This book presents a collection of papers by sociologists which demonstrate that the definition and solution of social problems by sociologists is actually a "social problem" within the field itself.